Early Italian Painting to 1400

Early Italian Painting to 1400

ROBERT OERTEL

Frederick A. Praeger, Publishers
New York · Washington

Books that matter
Published in the United States of America in 1968
by Frederick A. Praeger, Inc., Publishers
111 Fourth Avenue, New York, N. Y. 10003
© 1966 in Stuttgart, Germany, by W. Kohlhammer GmbH,
Stuttgart Berlin Köln Mainz
All rights reserved
Library of Congress Catalog Card Number: 68-13133
Printed in West Germany by W. Kohlhammer GmbH, Stuttgart

Contents

Foreword

Works of art need a receptive eye if they are to come to life. This is true of our own time and even more so of works of the distant past. There is no direct approach to the art of the past. Familiarity with what is being done today is necessary for an understanding of ancient art – and it can only be understood in its historical context. Art history is subject to the same paradox as all attempts to arrive at historical truth: we cannot comprehend the past except by reference to our own experience, and yet if we are not aware that the reality of the past is at variance with our present experience, the truth will elude us. Thus if we hope to understand the works of an early master we must try to grasp the significance of their strange and unfamiliar elements.

The rediscovery of early Italian painting was preceded by a long preparatory phase that extended back as far as the end of the eighteenth century, and indeed some useful work in this field had already been done in the seventeenth century. For a good part of our knowledge of medieval works of art we are indebted to the antiquarian interests of the Baroque era. Furthermore, many old paintings and mosaics, now lost, were preserved in Baroque engravings and drawings. These copies have become indispensable to present-day research. It was only towards the end of the eighteenth century, however, that this antiquarian interest was converted into an authentic historical approach. This was when Italian scholars first started to engage in systematic research into the records, including those of the Middle Ages, for the purposes of art history. The first collections of Italian Primitives were founded at that time, but the predominant interest was still antiquarian: collectors wanted 'antiques', not works of art.

It was left to the Romantics to open the way to a more thorough understanding of the works of the early Italian masters. In about 1800, French, English, and German art lovers, as well as the Italians, began to take an interest in this period. Large collections were formed, and wall- and panel-paintings became known through books and other publications. Many works of art were dispersed in the process of secularization and found their way in to museums and private collections. Those interested in the arts at last became aware of pre-Raphaelite painting, as it was then characteristically called.

At first the surge of admiration for the Renaissance in the latter part of the nineteenth century obscured this interest in the art of the earlier Primitive period, which was regarded merely as the 'preliminary stage of the Renaissance'. That is how Henry Thode described it in 1885 in his book on St Francis of Assisi. It is only in our own century, thanks particularly to Friedrich Rintelen, that we have again realized the greatness of Giotto as an artist, and the influence of his powerful mind is still growing. Giotto therefore stands at the centre of the present work. Its theme in broad terms is the prelude to Giotto, the extent of his historical significance (which has only recently been recognized), and his wide stylistic influence.

A substantial part of the book is concerned with these very recent discoveries. Rintelen's monograph of 1912 on Giotto is a lasting record of an approach to Giotto, the first of its kind that is still in accord with our present-day interpretation. But precisely because Rintelen fastened so accurately on the topical values of Giotto's art, he missed the artist's true historical significance, the full course of his development, and the wide range of his influence. Both aspects of Giotto, the historical and the artistic, must be taken into account if we are to form a true picture of him today.

Italian painting before Giotto, especially the rich and characteristic panel-painting of the twelfth and thirteenth centuries, has to a large extent been rediscovered only in recent decades, and the process has not yet come to an end. New works of that period, which have hitherto escaped notice or have been concealed beneath later paintings, are constantly coming to light. And similarly many wall-paintings, some of unique importance, have only recently been discovered. It is part of our task to draw attention to the more important of these discoveries, and to indicate the most recent scientific conclusions. The notes are devoted mainly to this purpose.

Since the first appearance of this book in 1953 the range of discoveries has further increased, and the discussion of what is known has extended and become more penetrating. Relevant new findings have been taken into account in the text as far as possible, but many had to be assigned to the notes.

In the illustrations, a number of well-known masterpieces inevitably had to be reproduced. We have attempted, however, to include as many illustrations as possible of newly-discovered material or recently restored works. The author is indebted to scholars and friends for their valuable suggestions and contributions, which are acknowledged in the relevant notes to the text.

Introduction

In our search for the beginnings of Italian painting, a study of the main lines of historical development provides an apparently simple answer. The period around 1300 is the obvious turning-point. Like Dante in the history of Italian language and poetry, Giotto, in painting, stood at the threshold of centuries of new development. With the appearance of these two Florentines, Italy assumed her distinctive national role in Western civilization. The intellectual awakening at the beginning of the fourteenth century did not come about through political activity, nor was it primarily due to economic and social advances. It was the achievement of two artistic geniuses. The development of city states – the first independent Italian accomplishment in the field of political organization – could do no more than prepare the ground, and was in itself only an expression of particular interests, often in bitter rivalry with each other. From the resulting restraints Dante found release only through a tragic quarrel with his native city; Giotto disregarded those restraints from the very beginning.

A new era in the history of art had begun. Seen from the High Renaissance, the Trecento is an 'early' period, Giotto its beginning, and everything before him prehistory. The new movement, which started around 1300, spread beyond national boundaries even in Giotto's own time. Dante's influence remained confined to the regions where the Italian language was known, but the language of painting created by Giotto was understood north of the Alps too, where it left early traces.[1] Italian artists, above all the painters of Roman and Sienese origin active in Avignon, became the inspiration of Europe. There was no lack of native creative talent in the north, where the fourteenth century was also a period of change and spiritual revival. However, without the impulse initiated by Giotto and his contemporaries neither the refined courtly art of the Burgundian miniature painters, nor Master Bertram's powerful simple style, nor the exuberant flowering of Bohemian painting at the time of Charles IV and his son Wenceslas, would have been possible. Even the van Eyck brothers owed essential elements of their style to the revival of Italian painting initiated under Giotto. Italy had already assumed a European role. The turning-point around 1300 is as important in the development of the whole of Western art as it is in the history of Italian art.

And again it was Italy, only a century later, that was the first European country to cross from the Middle Ages into the modern age. This process, the start of the Renaissance, took place with almost unbelievable swiftness and vigour. Historians have attempted to set back the decisive moment, and to detect the roots of the Renaissance in the fourteenth and even in the thirteenth century; they have also tried to do the reverse by stressing the continuing survival of medieval trends well into the Renaissance. But a glance at the countries north of the Alps suffices to put all these qualifications and reservations in their right perspective.

The transition was more clearly and decisively marked in Italy in the first half of the fifteenth century than in any other country. It manifested itself chiefly in art, as had been the case in the earlier transition around 1300. The post-medieval concept of life based on natural science found its first vivid expression in the visual arts, and above all in painting. The technique of central perspective, initiated in Florence about 1420, was a product of the same analysis of space based on mathematical laws which later made possible the advance of natural science and the discoveries of Copernicus, Kepler and Galileo. Never before or since has there been such close contact between art and science. Artists finally succeeded in ridding themselves of the social and intellectual trammels of the Middle Ages. The first phase in the history of Italian art thus came to an end. But is it really possible to determine the origins so unequivocally? Perhaps our first brief survey has oversimplified the problem.

The belief that the intellectual and artistic awakening of 1300 marked the beginning of Italian history in the full sense of the word rests on a long and significant tradition: it was a conviction current among the people of the epoch itself. Parallel with the great achievements in art a consciousness of history developed. A sense of history already runs through Dante's great poem. Although the poet himself still clung to the ancient traditions and although his numerous historical figures were only symbols and examples for his complex theological argument, the *Divine Comedy* had an influence on the historical awareness of succeeding generations that can hardly be overestimated. Dante's commentators contributed as much to the Italians' sense of history as the official chroniclers of the Trecento.

Towards the end of the century we find Italians beginning to write their own art history. At that time Filippo Villani introduced a number of biographies of painters into his work on famous Florentines. Giotto and his predecessor, Cimabue, were hailed as the men who had revived the 'almost extinct' art of painting.[2] These two, and Giotto's more important pupils, were discussed with brevity and accuracy. At about the same time Cennino Cennini wrote *Il libro dell'Arte*, a manual for painters describing the techniques of the workshops of the late Giotto school.[3] He writes, 'Giotto translated art from Greek into Latin, and made it modern,' a surprisingly perceptive statement in a textbook written in the spirit of the Middle Ages. 'Greek', meaning the Byzantine style, stands for the past which Giotto had superseded. It is also significant that this second-generation pupil of the great master considered the 'modern' style – in which he no doubt included his own achievement – to be Latin rather than Italian. In this sentence Cennino formulated the basic thesis of Florentine art historians. Lorenzo Ghiberti, in his *Commentarii* of about 1450, took the same line: he too looked on Giotto as the founder of the new art, the conqueror of the *maniera greca*. He draws a sharp distinction between three periods – classical, medieval and modern. To him, however, the Middle Ages were only a period of decay, a historical vacuum. This division into periods was the humanists' conception of history transposed into the history of art.[4] Realizing as we do today that Giotto was rooted in the Middle Ages as firmly as his contemporary Dante, we find it remarkable that Ghiberti emphasizes the modernity of Giotto's rather than his own age.

Giorgio Vasari, the sixteenth-century biographer of artists, used the word *rinascita* in this context for the first time; but he meant the rebirth of art in Giotto's time, and not the period that we today regard as the Renaissance. Vasari saw Giotto as the true initiator of the modern age. He used the idea of the 'darkness' of the Middle Ages, the rudeness and barbarism of the Gothic era, to intensify its contrast with the brilliance both of antiquity and of the re-born modern age. Thus Ghiberti's basic approach remained valid for Vasari. Nevertheless, Vasari realized that the Middle Ages had been a constructive and creative period, although this did not moderate his condemnation of them. Furthermore, with his greater knowledge, he was able to analyze the 'modern' period, beginning about 1300, with more discrimination than his predecessor. His work, first published in 1550, followed by a second, much enlarged edition in 1568, determined ideas about Italian art until well into the nineteenth century.[5] This lasting influence of Vasari was due partly to his impressive and elaborate theory of the evolution of art, especially in its application to the change that took place between the thirteenth and fourteenth centuries, and partly to his postulation of the basic division into periods. For many years to come, the sharp dividing line drawn by Vasari was to distort the image of all earlier periods.

This view established so early by Renaissance art historians was still accepted in its essentials at the time of Jakob Burckhardt. We now realize that it was a grossly over-simplified view of history. We see the Middle Ages as a separate and distinct period of immense cultural productivity, and in the course of the last fifty years European nations have been rediscovering 'their' respective medieval art. But the change in our approach to art history has also made us see apparently familiar facts in a new perspective. Giotto no longer stands at the beginning. His work was indeed the first decisive step on the way to the Renaissance, the foundation for everything that followed, but it was also the climax, the consummation of many diverse trends originating in the distant past. He did not just supersede the Byzantine artistic tradition; indeed he was indebted to it for essential elements of his style. Furthermore, Gothic culture was at its culmination in Europe in about 1300, and we realize now that it was also an essential element in the formation of Giotto's style. There was a third element which Renaissance art history, in its creative self-assurance and its admiration for rediscovered classical art, neglected: medieval painting in Italy itself. It was neither Gothic, nor Byzantine, nor simply Romanesque in the sense in which the word is applied to the art north of the Alps. But can it be called 'Italian' in the same way that Giotto's art was an expression of the Italian spirit; and if so, how far back does Italian medieval painting reach?

We know of hundreds of panel-paintings, mainly from Tuscany, but also from Latium and Umbria, that were done in the thirteenth and even in the twelfth century. The origins of this craftsmanlike, but highly developed and prolific, art are lost in obscurity. The increasing discoveries of panel-paintings from still earlier times suggest that since the early Christian era the tradition of panel-painting – like the art of icons in the East – had never completely disappeared in Italy.[6] Wall-paintings were produced in Italy throughout the centuries, and especially in Rome where there seems to have been no interruption at all.[7] To trace these roots we have to look even further into the past, until we arrive at the origins of Christian art, the catacomb paintings. But these cannot possibly be called Italian. So we must search for a new point of departure.

From the time it ceased to be the centre of the Roman empire, Italy merged into a new supra-national community. During the early and later parts of the Middle Ages the unity of Europe was a palpable reality. Church and empire knew no national frontiers. The universality of religion and the common mode of daily life remained undisturbed even when the differences between the two dominant powers intensified, and when particular interests pursued their own ends. The great universal principles of the system were not seriously challenged until the end of the thirteenth century. Thomas Aquinas, the greatest philosopher of the Middle Ages, lived and taught in Paris and Cologne just as he did in his native Italy. The intellectual upper class was not the only group that felt itself related to the whole of Europe. The religious revival led by St Francis of Assisi, a genuinely popular movement, spread within a few years of the saint's death (1226) to all Western countries. At that time Italian national awareness was still at an embryonic stage.[8] St Francis himself, in addition to Italian, spoke Provençal, the Romance offshoot that prepared the way in Italy for the 'vulgar' tongue. As a written language Italian barely existed before the beginning of the thirteenth century; at least there are no traces of literary works. If language is taken as the criterion (it is the only one we have), Italy was last among the Western nations to awaken to an awareness of itself. Whenever 'national' standpoints were taken in the course of medieval controversies, they were merely tactical expedients, to be discarded when no longer required. Since the decline of antiquity Italy had indeed been only a 'geographical expression'. When the records of German emperors mention the 'Kingdom of Italy', they refer to the regions that once formed the territory of Lombardy: Lombardy and Tuscany, with the duchies of Spoleto and Benevento in looser association. Sandwiched in between the north and the south was the *Patrimonium Petri,* the papal state, with political interests entirely of its own. Rome itself was a territorial power not to be underrated in comparison to the emperor and the pope, and its citizens in the Middle Ages did not like to be called Italians. The Byzantines, the Saracens, and the Normans ruled in the south. The Hohenstaufens' attempt to unite the peninsula from the south collapsed in the face of opposition from the papacy; a new foreign rule – that of Anjou – replaced the old one. Nevertheless Frederick II, with his ambition to turn the country into a single state, had implanted the idea of Italian unity. Even Dante still hoped for its realization. And so, well after the attempt had failed, the Hohenstaufen dream contributed to the emergence of an Italian spirit of unity.

It must be admitted, however, that until the end of the thirteenth century the Italians were not conscious of sharing a common culture, and it may be asked again whether we can talk about 'Italian' culture and art before that time. A similar question applies with equal justification to the cultures of Germany and France. Today we hesitate to answer in the affirmative with the same alacrity as we did a short while ago. Perhaps we should consider the medieval elements common to all these nations more relevant to our assessment of history than the peculiar national characteristics that separated them. Perhaps, too, we are reading something into those times which did not materialize until much later.

A clear-cut solution will never be possible, but it will be useful to bear this question in mind. It is true that pictorial art offers a field in which an awakening nation, still unaware of itself, can find the first possibilities of self-expression. We must not forget, however, that art in the Middle Ages had a function different from that in later times. At the beginning its exponents were members of the clergy; from the twelfth century onwards they were mainly craftsmen. Their mode of work differed greatly from our conception of creative activity. The idea of individuality was unknown; artistic creation was to a large extent only reproductive. Choice of subject and formal presentation were dictated by rules to an extent which we can no longer conceive, and the margin left for the artist's individual expression was negligible. In fact, artistic expression was entirely governed by theological formulas evolved over the centuries, which transcended the life of any individual and also all national and regional peculiarities.

The intellectual content of art was common to the whole Western world. Artists could wander from country to country and find the same familiar assignments everywhere. Frequently, when no local talent was available, they were summoned from far afield. The painter Johannes, an Italian, was summoned by Otto III to decorate the cathedral at Aachen, and builders were brought to Germany from Lombardy and even from Greece. Johannes, himself raised for his services to the rank of bishop by the emperor[9], died at the court of the bishop of Liège. Not long after, in the first half of the eleventh century, the Lombard painter Nivardus was summoned by Abbot Gauzlin of Fleury to his monastery on the Loire.[10] These examples, known to us by chance, show the danger of looking upon medieval works of art as products of local traditions. The freedom of movement of the artists was as unlimited as that of their patrons, whose close contact with each other extended beyond all frontiers. Portable works of art, illuminated manuscripts and prototypes for wall-paintings found their way to the most distant regions of the Western world. Particularly in the early part of the Middle Ages, art history presents a picture of constant interchange between all parts of Christendom.

1 The early Middle Ages

Pilgrims who visited the capital of Christendom in the Middle Ages found the great basilicas decorated with extensive picture cycles. The early Christian mosaics in Santa Maria Maggiore showing scenes from the Old Testament are still extant. Rows of glittering pictures cover the long walls of the nave.[1] San Paolo fuori le mura must have been an even more impressive sight. Two rows of pictures, one above the other – frescoes, not mosaics – extended along both sides of the nave. On each wall there were about forty separate scenes, from the Old Testament on the right, and from the lives of the Apostles on the left. According to tradition there was a similar arrangement of pictures in the old St Peter's. On the walls of the nave, in double rows, scenes from the life of Christ faced scenes from the Old Testament. In the vestibule there was a fresco cycle of the life of St Peter.[2] The impact this profusion of pictures must have made on the innocent eyes of medieval pilgrims is hardly conceivable today.

Painters and patrons from all over Europe found in Rome the 'correct' representation, authenticated by church authority and tradition; but they were naturally also affected by the style of these works, and especially by the paintings of the early Christian era, in which something of the spirit of classical painting survived. The spectator had constantly before his eyes well-designed figures in animated, expressive movement, remnants of the highly-developed ability to convey a sense of space through techniques of light and shade, foreshortening and perspective. The awareness of classical art and its skills, although it now had to be reacquired, was thus never completely lost.

This is the reason for the exceptional position of Italian, and especially Roman, art in the Middle Ages. Even the Byzantine influence that continually swept across Italy lost its force in Rome. The early Christian narrative cycles, in particular the series of pictures from the Old and New Testaments, had many imitators in Rome itself, in Latium, and even further afield, right up to the transition of 1300.[3] Even the elaborate decoration of the nave of San Francesco at Assisi reveals the iconographic influence of the Roman frescoes, which despite some later overpainting go back to the fifth century.[4] Giotto himself was deeply indebted to these Roman models, and evidently made a thorough study of Roman wall-paintings from pagan times.

Only a fraction of the former wealth of Rome has survived, but it is enough to enable us to see the outline of more than a millennium of ecclesiastical monumental painting. The complex of Santa Maria Antiqua, which stood at the foot of the Palatine near the Forum Romanum, was rediscovered under more recent buildings after a long period of oblivion. At this site alone there are wall-paintings from the sixth, seventh, and eighth centuries, some painted on top of others, which reveal the multitude of intellectual and artistic trends in Italy during that turbulent era.[5] Art has never been so international and full of conflicting trends as it was in Rome at that time. The great breach between the realism of the classical style and the new pictorial language of Christian art, intent on representing spiritual values, was not yet defined. However, in the oldest surviving painting from Santa Maria Antiqua, a fragmentary Madonna, we can see that the new transcendental style had already gained ground in the sixth century[6]. But there is also evidence in Santa Maria Antiqua to show that the classical tradition had not exhausted its influence completely. Above the Madonna, on the famous Palimpsest Wall, there is a head of an angel from an Annunciation, which is part of a layer of paintings done about the second quarter of the seventh century.[7] This fragment, painted in a gentle, atmospheric style, comes as a surprise after the severity of the sixth-century manner. If we had not known the sequence of the layers we should never have taken this illusionistic style for the later of the two.

The paintings of Santa Maria foris portas in Castelseprio, the most important frescoes discovered in Italy in recent decades, also show traces of the classical tradition that survived in the seventh century.[8] This small church north of Milan and not far from Tradate is all that remains of an early medieval settlement. The frescoes, in half life-size, showing scenes from the life of Mary and the childhood of Jesus, are painted in a lively sketchy technique *(pl. 1)*. These figures convey a gentle animation and a sense of movement and mental alertness, which distinguish them sharply from the figures in the 'transcendental' style, which are usually presented in a severely frontal view and without any reference to space or time. The bold manner is reminiscent of the most daring improvisations of late classical illusionistic painting and much of the detail, especially the landscape and architectural motifs, is derived from classical art. But we do not know if they were in fact direct survivals of classicism, nor where the painters came from who created works in this late classical tradition on Lombard soil. Perhaps they were Hellenistic Syrians or Alexandrians,

driven from their native lands by the tide of Islam, or Byzantines who had
fled from the iconoclasts. Or perhaps they were simply local masters trained
on late classical or Eastern models. Since the discovery of the frescoes all these
possibilities have been considered, and dates have been suggested varying from
the beginning of the seventh to the second quarter of the tenth century. It has
rightly been pointed out that characteristics which come remarkably close to
the Byzantine manner, such as the treatment of draperies with sharp metallic
edges and white highlights, appear side by side with late classical illusionistic
elements. But in comparison with works of the tenth century the Castelseprio frescoes are fresher and more original in style. It would therefore seem
possible – and there is external supporting evidence – to place them in the
seventh or the first half of the eighth century, despite the inadequate proof
and the absence of comparable works of that period.[9]

The sharp difference of opinion about the Castelseprio frescoes is an example
of the complex development of early medieval painting and the co-existence
of a great variety of styles. The other great post–war discovery, the frescoes
in the church of the Carolingian monastery of St Johann zu Münster (Müstair) in Graubünden, a much larger find than Castelseprio, also poses several
problems for research. A small part of this work came to light a few decades
ago, and since 1947 the whole decoration has been found underneath the
whitewash in a remarkably intact state.[10] The monastery, founded by Charle-
magne, is situated on one of the mountain passes used by the Franks as routes
into upper Italy. Though the style of painting is undoubtedly Carolingian of
the first quarter of the ninth century, it has little in common with Carolingian art north of the Alps as we know it. There are some associations with
the St Gall and north Italian manuscript illuminations, but they are confined
to the figure types and to particular formal elements.[11] We know of no
other place in the north, or in Italy, where a popular narrative style of equal
power and monumentality existed at that time. The illusionistic effect of the
details is diminished by the clarity of the composition and the architectural
severity of the painted framework. The walls on each side of the room have
five rows of pictures, one above the other, each divided into eight separate
scenes: the top row, which continues across the entrance wall, tells the story
of David and Absalom; the life of Christ is shown in the four lower rows.
On the east side there are three apses covered with narrative and symbolic
representations, and the west wall has a huge Last Judgment, the earliest known
to us.

It is natural to think of Italy as the most likely place for the creation of
this typical combination of late classical and Byzantine components. The

technique and style are crude and careless, but the work displays such complete assurance that it could only have been executed by a group of craftsmen accustomed to monumental assignments. Everything points to an established tradition, which hardly existed at that time in the north. Indeed it would seem only natural to assign the work for this remote Alpine monastery, on the route towards the south, to Italian painters, presumably from Milan.[12] This then may be the answer to the problem presented by the monument of Carolingian painting in the Alps; and if no other purpose has been served we are at least reminded that the borders between the separate artistic regions in the early centuries of the Middle Ages were fluid and easily crossed.

Careful restoration has recently disclosed yet another work of monumental painting, though in a very fragmentary state. It is the decoration of the nave of San Salvatore in Brescia, which was probably done only a little later than the paintings at Müstair.[13] A rough reconstruction of the richly articulated decorative scheme is possible, although only isolated fragments of the figurative scenes are preserved. They are harsher and more vigorous in style than the Müstair paintings, but the difference is not so great as to rule out dating them in the Carolingian period.[14] The drawings preserved underneath the paint, the so-called *sinopie,* are of special interest and will be referred to again.[15]

Until the startling discoveries of recent decades, the only larger ninth-century fresco cycle known to us was that of San Vincenzo al Volturno, not far from Monte Cassino.[16] These paintings can be dated with relative accuracy: the figure of the abbot Epiphanius, the donor in the Crucifixion scene, places them between 826 and 843 *(pl. 2)*. The lively expressive figures are painted with exceptional freedom. There is apparently no stereotype design, nor any intention to follow a traditional formula. The style appears to have been derived from several sources, and yet it is original and progressive rather than eclectic. There are associations with the north, but these are of such a general character that it is hardly possible to classify the paintings as plainly Carolingian.[17] All that can be said with certainty is that the northern influences were transmitted by way of Monte Cassino, within whose domain the abbey of San Vincenzo lies.

Monte Cassino, the parent monastery of the Benedictine Order, was – as we shall see later – the centre of brisk artistic activity in the eleventh century. We can perhaps assume that this was already so in the Carolingian period, for we have some documentary evidence to this effect; but there are no other examples of monumental art, apart from the San Vincenzo paintings, to indicate whether at that time the artistic projects of the abbots were products of a school at Monte Cassino. Art-historical attemps to establish correlations in this early period remain dubious owing to the scarcity of surviving works.

Yet new discoveries in southern Italy have greatly increased our over-all knowledge of early medieval painting. Since 1942 wall-paintings were discovered in a small oratory in the Basilica dei SS. Martiri in Cimitile, near Nola.[18] Though in an incomplete state of preservation, they are of considerable stylistic and iconographic interest. In addition to the apse decoration, there are narrative scenes from the life of Christ, his Passion and Resurrection. The formal language is powerful but popular, almost coarse, and on stylistic grounds the works can be dated around 900. This date is corroborated by architectural evidence and can be supported by historical argument.[19]

The fragments of figure compositions, discovered in 1947 in Santa Sofia in Benevento, are probably even older than the Cimitile frescoes, and their linear style is more animated. This dynamic manner is reminiscent of San Vincenzo al Volturno, but it is probable that the Benevento discoveries date from the middle of the ninth century – possibly after the earthquake in 847, which made it necessary to restore the church.[20]

In Rome, a number of ninth-century mosaics and paintings indicate that there too a specific medieval style, dominated largely by linear elements, was in the process of formation. A typical example is the wall-painting of the *Ascension,* painted about 850, in the Lower Church of San Clemente.[21] The attendant apostles, concisely and confidently drawn, are gathered in dramatically expressive groups *(pl. 3b)*. Closer observation reveals the surprising fact that the two lively, well-articulated groups of apostles are almost completely symmetrical. The development of this style is seen again in a series of narrative scenes from Santa Maria Egiziaca (temple of Fortuna Virilis), probably done around 880 *(pl. 3a)*.[22] These compositions are as expressive as northern works of the late Carolingian period, but have a greater clarity and superior pictorial structure. The Italian talent for monumental composition is becoming apparent here, but there is still no sign of a specifically local tradition. In Rome, as elsewhere in Europe, the tenth century brought a decline in creative force. Its revival towards the end of the century, which eventually also led to considerable achievements here, seems to have originated in other centres.

2 The eleventh and twelfth centuries

The earliest and most important example of the revival of monumental painting in Italy is found in the north, not far from Como. It is the decoration of the apse of the former parish church of San Vincenzo in Galliano near Cantù.[1] The date of the work can be determined with some accuracy by reference to the consecration of the church in 1007; it is therefore a Lombard counterpart of the paintings at Oberzell on the island of Reichenau which were done possibly a decade or two earlier. The donor of San Vincenzo, Ariberto da Intimiano, was made archbishop of Milan by Emperor Henry II in 1018, and in all probability the painters whose work has survived in Galliano were brought by Ariberto from Milan.[2] As happens so often with medieval art, we can here deduce something about the style of a flourishing and influential school from an isolated work, fortuitously preserved in an out-of-the-way place. Only in such a context can the paintings in this rural church, of little importance at the time of its founding, be explained. The low, broad apse is transformed by the paintings into an imposing monumental structure. The figures on the vaults, although preserved only in fragments, are among the most impressive heritages of the Middle Ages. In addition there are narrative scenes of amazing liveliness and unusually rich and original ornamentation. No doubt the painters at work here commanded all the knowledge available at the time.

The main figure, Christ in Benediction, looms in enormous supernatural size. The prophets, Jeremiah and Ezekiel, bow to the ground and prepare the way for him with their fervent gestures *(pl. 4)*. Next to them, holding scrolls with the inscriptions *Peticio* and *Postulatio,* stand the two archangels who intercede on behalf of mankind. At their sides choirs of saints offer their crowns of martyrdom.[3] The colours glow with a cold fire. Jeremiah wears a bluish-grey robe with green shadows and white highlights, and a strident brick-red cloak. The flesh is done in ochre with green and red shadows. Sparkling white lights

flicker over the surfaces disrupting their own cohesion but awakening instead
a lively plastic life. This, as well as the facial types, clearly reveals Byzantine
influences, but the painters may also have resorted directly to late classical
frescoes and mosaics. However, the decorative highlights, often applied in
sharp linear strokes, are also reminiscent of the paintings at Oberzell. The scenes
of the St Vincent legend which fill the lower zone of the apse show an even
closer affinity to the Reichenau style. The representation of the architecture
is plainly 'Ottonian', and the free treatment of the surfaces is equally unlike
the Byzantine manner. This technique recalls the contemporary Reichenau
miniatures, the *Book of Pericopes* of Henry II, and the Bamberg *Apocalypse*.
The gradations in size according to spiritual importance of the central figures
in the main painting in the apse is another feature in common with these
works. The enormous mandorla surrounding Christ is also a sign of northern
influence, but the motif of the standing Christ is particularly Roman.[4] Byzantine art was familiar only with half-length and enthroned representations of
the Pantocrator, and in countries north of the Alps the Salvator Mundi is also
generally shown seated in the chair of the apocalyptic judge.[5] However, this
is the only closer connection between Galliano and Roman painting. The
decoration of the apse of San Bastianello on the Palatine, done at about the
same time, *c.* 1000, also has an upright figure of Christ, but artistically it is
provincial and not comparable with the grandiose creation at Galliano.[6] The
schematic arrangement of the figures in several horizontal rows is much inferior to the free grouping and careful relationships in scale that distinguish
the Galliano work. Even in their use of ornamental motifs taken directly from
classical models, the painters of Galliano are superior to their Roman contemporaries. The anterior border of the arch of the apse, painted in an illusionistic manner with glass goblets, fish, crabs, turtles and other marine creatures,
is unique in medieval art. Features such as the elaborate decorative meander
frieze and other ornamentation have striking parallels in the Oberzell paintings.
The association between Galliano and the artistic centre of south-west Germany does not seem to have been of an accidental or sporadic nature.

It is certain that the style of the Galliano work is not to be attributed to a
local painter or any single important artist. We are confronted here with a
major work of Lombard painting in the Ottonian peroid, a work that stands
at the junction of all the main stylistic trends of the time. There even seems
to be a connection with Carolingian painting, for example with the paintings
in St Johann at Müstair: the bold technique and ease of the monumental style
are clearly the product of a kindred temperament. By comparison, the paintings at Oberzell are somewhat abstract and more in the classical spirit. There the

pictorial element is kept in balance by line and ornament, whereas in Galliano everything is dominated by the original pictorial force.

It would be natural to suppose that Milan was the centre of this Lombard art. It was the capital of the country, many of its great early churches presumably still stood, at least in part, and its metropolitan church, Sant'Ambrogio, was closely associated with the donor of San Vincenzo in Galliano. Some examples of eleventh-century monumental painting are still extant in Milan itself.[7] True, none of them is directly comparable with the San Vincenzo apse, but records of the art of those early times have come down to us so haphazardly that this does not necessarily invalidate our supposition. Nevertheless, wherever the actual centre may have been, the surviving remnants of Lombard painting justify the esteem shown in the reports about the two contemporary painters, Johannes and Nivardus.[8]

There is hardly any other area of art history as dependent on the accidents of preservation as medieval monumental painting. The urge to create new modes of expression itself often led to the destruction of older works; and consequently there are fewest surviving remnants in just those places where artistic life was most prolific and tradition most ancient. In wall-paintings fresh layers were constantly being superimposed on earlier ones. Indeed, most of the early works now known to us were discovered, after much painstaking labour, beneath later layers of paint or whitewash. We can hope to find wall-paintings in an untouched state of preservation only in places outside the main stream of development, or where the creative forces were exhausted at an early stage. It is rare, however, to come across complete and undamaged medieval monuments in their original colour. As a rule they are found only in small, remote rural churches, and only very exceptionally in larger buildings. These miracles of preservation give us a picture of the period when the walls of all the churches and chapels of the land were covered with monumental paintings. In all the leading art centres, pictorial decoration of churches was the rule rather than the exception. It was only where means and resources were lacking that pictorial representation was confined to the choir, but even then some decorative scheme was always sought for the other parts of the edifice. Whenever possible the nave was covered with figurative representations in the manner of the great Roman basilicas. This practice came to an end only with the appearance of the Gothic style, which replaced painted walls with areas of coloured glass.

The finest example of an early medieval ecclesiastical building, fully decorated with paintings and almost completely intact, is found in Italy. It is the basilica of Sant'Angelo in Formis near Capua[9], situated in the vicinity of the Monte Cassino monastery, whose abbot, Desiderius (1058–86), is mentioned as donor in an inscription above the portal.[10] Desiderius' name is associated with the thriving artistic life at Monte Cassino in the second half of the eleventh century, vividly recorded by the chroniclers.[11] He engaged skilled craftsmen in all fields, especially mosaicists from Byzantium and builders from Amalfi and Lombardy. A distinct and lively narrative style of manuscript illumination also developed, valuable examples of which have been preserved.[12] The mosaics of the Byzantine masters have all perished, but the impressive achievements of monumental painting under Desiderius, or a little later, can still be seen in Sant'Angelo in Formis. Scenes from the New Testament extend in three rows, one above the other, along the high walls of the nave from the west entrance to the main apse *(pls I, 5)*. In the apse is the seated Christ, awesome and sublime, between symbols of the evangelists; beneath him stand the three archangels, St Benedict, and the donor in an abbot's gown offering a model of the church.[13]

The entrance wall opposite is almost completely covered with a Last Judgment, in its traditional place in the West.[14] The narrative painting continues along the aisles with scenes from the Old Testament. The basilica and its decorative scheme and choice of scenes are Western, but their stylistic and iconographic elements are predominantly Byzantine.[15] Nevertheless, it is doubtful whether this is the work of Byzantine or local artists. The vigour of the narrative, the compact grouping of the figures, the simple rectangular division of the surfaces, appear to be Italian, and strongly inclined towards the Romanesque. Everything is designed for dramatic effect. The figure of Christ, and his large halo inscribed with a cross, dominates all the scenes. The blind man who bows humbly before him appears again in the same picture, with sight restored, washing his healed eyes at the well *(pl. 6b)*. The adulteress approaches him hesitantly, while the Pharisees whisper suspiciously and venomously behind her back *(pl. 6a)*. The Lord shows his condemnation of her accusers by his stern expression and the mild gesture he makes towards the terrified woman who turns to him in contrition and yet with a glint of hope in her face. Although this art is still primitive in conception and technique, it has profound humanity and great narrative power. The stocky figures painted with coarse brush-strokes in a traditional colour scheme are surprisingly expressive. The faces are all variations of a single type – narrow forehead, large eyes, and boldly-marked red cheeks. And yet how much life and animation this simple formula produces! The palette, too, is quite limited: bright blue, yellow and a darker shade of ochre, rich reddish-brown, earthy green, much chalk-white lavishly applied, and a mixture of the primary colours with white – that is all. These meagre resources are handled with masterly crafts-manship but without subtlety. Even the sharpest contrasts are reduced by the harsh blue of the sky in every scene. Firm reddish-brown outlines enclose the areas that have been hastily coloured in. The style is lively and bold, the stories are told in a popular way, and the forms have a kind of rustic strength. Although the stylistic origins of the painting are unmistakably Byzantine, new and distinctive elements are clearly emerging.

There is, however, one figure in Sant'Angelo in Formis which diverges from this popular, provincial character type. There is nothing primitive in the half-length figure of the archangel Michael in the tympanum of the main portal in the west vestibule *(pl. 7)*. This figure is severe and elegant, remote and delicate; the closely-applied brush-strokes are full of verve. The celestial radiance of this angel and his touch of Hellenistic grace give an impression of unequalled nobility. The face is designed in large clear planes with fascinating asymmetry. The seemingly accidental difference between the two sides of the face is a characteristic and deliberate device of monumental Byzantine art which appears here in its clearest mature form. The handling of the colours is delicate, sensitive and lively. The cloak is painted with blue and red strokes producing the effect of a purple ground. The same technique is used with even greater subtlety in the modelling of the flesh, and it is discernible again in the medallion picture of *Maria orans,* supported by two angels, in the upper part of the arch.[16] The scenes from the life of the hermits in the four vaults of the vestibule are done in a similar but somewhat weaker manner.

The key to the striking stylistic differences between the paintings in the vestibule and those inside the church probably lies in the history of the construction of the building. The existing vestibule, with its five pointed-arch arcades, is not original, but a later restoration, probably of the late twelfth century. Observations made when the upper lunette fresco above the main portal was removed indicate that the paintings were done some time after the restoration.[17] The austere and polished style of the two portal lunettes does not preclude a date around 1200 or early in the thirteenth century, but it is impossible to say whether the paintings are the work of a Byzantine artist or of an Italian trained on Eastern models.[18]

In the interior of the basilica, the disparity in style and time becomes very obvious. There, too, in the main apse, are the figures of the three archangels, among them St Michael, the patron saint of Sant'Angelo *(pl. I)*. There is no doubt that Byzantine models determined the type and posture of the figures, the sumptuousness of the draperies, the splendid sweep of the wings, and

I   Sant'Angelo in Formis · The main apse

indeed all the basic pictorial and plastic forms. But here the technique is extremely simplified. The linear expression is frozen into a set formula of almost mask-like concentration; the colours are reduced to a small number of strongly contrasting tones. The Byzantine influence, which at first glance seems to dominate the work, has in fact been only partly assimilated. For the first time a new style, the powerful 'vulgar' style of Italian painting, asserts itself.[19]

It is customary in eleventh-century Italian art to talk about a Benedictine style, the roots of which are to be found in the Monte Cassino school, and which is supposed to have greatly influenced painting in Rome.[20] This may be true of manuscript illumination, which reached its peak in Monte Cassino at the time of Desiderius, for manuscripts of Monte Cassino did indeed serve as models for the wall-painters of Rome; but they are actually an eclectic mixture of local and Byzantine elements.[21] The monumental art of Monte Cassino, as seen in Sant'Angelo in Formis and in a small group of related monuments, had no real effect on art in Rome.[22]

The wall-paintings in the Lower Church of San Clemente in Rome, probably done around 1100, mostly have a Western medieval, rather than a Byzantine, character.[23] With their elegant, animated figures and their delicate harmony of colour, they form a transition between the free style of Ottonian art and the stricter order of the Romanesque. Their affinity with northern art is unmistakable, yet the sense of form is clearly and typically Italian, even Roman. It is apparent in the lucid unfolding of the narrative, the confident balancing of the composition, and finally in certain plastic elements which are introduced without disrupting the flat Romanesque pattern. The recurring compact groups, without parallel in northern art at that time, are especially noteworthy.

An example is the vivid scene showing the mother embracing her rescued son in the burial chapel of St Clement at the bottom of the Black Sea *(pl. 8)*. The water around the chapel is swarming with marine creatures. From the left, a procession approaches from the Chersonese city-gate, and the sea recedes as it does every year on the feast of the saint. The child is well and healthy after a whole year in the flooded sanctuary. The mother bends passionately over him; in the next scene she presses him thankfully to her bosom. With naive confidence, the artist suspends the laws of nature in order to conform to the letter of the pious legend; but the realistic elements – the chapel surrounded by water, and the crowd streaming from the city's gate – are not neglected. However, the convincing unity of the picture is not due to the

27

visible relationships of the scenes, but lies rather in the even rhythm of form and colour and the smooth, though severe, flow of line.

The style of San Clemente with its slender figures, bright colours, and cool elegant linear manner, had a lasting effect in Rome and Latium. The decoration of the choir and transept in Sant'Elia near Nepi, north of Rome, not far from Città Castellana, is probably the closest to it in time.[24] An inscription on the apse painting, presumably done in the first quarter of the twelfth century, names the Roman painters Johannes, Stephanus and Nicolaus, as the authors of the work. A boldly drawn figure of Christ draped in a cloak of yellow ochre – the substitute for gold – towers in the vault of the apse against a blue background. Attending Christ are Peter and Paul, a flock of lambs on a gold ground, angels, and female martyrs in splendid robes. At the sides of the apse, on the east walls of the transept, the twenty-four elders of the Apocalypse march in solemn order, arranged in two horizontal rows *(pl. 9)*. Scenes from the Apocalypse and the legend of the founding of the church cover the walls of the transept. It is the best preserved and artistically most important monumental cycle of the Middle Ages to survive in the vicinity of Rome.

The paintings in the choir of San Pietro in Tuscania must have been done at about the same time.[25] Even in their fragmentary state they have a powerful impact due mainly to the truly gigantic Christ clad in white, who seems about to sunder the expanse of the main apse. The figure rises almost to the apex of the apse and bends with its curvature. Angels in vigorous movement hover all around *(pl. II),* and the apostles below gaze upwards in frenzied excitement. It is an *Ascension* of striking elemental force and ahead of its time. The powerful style uses bright highlights and vivid colours as the sole means of dominating the huge expanse, and can be regarded as a slightly belated stylistic parallel to Sant'Angelo in Formis. There seems, however, to be no derivative connection between the two works, and the distinct Byzantine components of Sant'Angelo are completely absent here. Some of the details are more reminiscent of the style of the early eleventh century which we observed in San Vincenzo at Galliano.

The six scenes from the life of St Peter, preserved on the right wall of the presbytery in the same church, are quite different *(pl. 10a)*. They are in the San Clemente style, but advanced to a slightly more elegant and formalistic stage. Evidently painted shortly after the apse decoration, they demonstrate the variety of artistic trends that co-existed in Rome at the time.

There is no space here to describe the less important monuments of Rome's twelfth-century wall-painting.[26] The next large cycle known is from the end of this period. After long neglect the decoration of San Giovanni a Porta

Latina, probably done under Pope Celestine III (1191–8) or slightly later, has been successfully restored to a relatively complete condition *(pl. 10b)*.[27] Unfortunately the apse decoration has been lost. But the nave and tribune, now restored to their original state, give a general idea of the Romanesque decorative scheme, consisting of Old and New Testament scenes on the walls of the nave, a *Last Judgment* on the entrance wall, and apocalyptic scenes in the tribune. The apse probably contained a full-length figure of Christ.

A similar cycle, partly disfigured by restoration but recognizable in outline, is found in the abbey church of San Pietro near Ferentillo.[28] Painted in about 1200, it is close to San Giovanni a Porta Latina in theme and style. Both cycles have a vivid, popular, narrative style, a common basis in older Roman tradition, and a notable freedom from Byzantine influence.

The same features appear in the fine apse decoration of San Silvestro in Tivoli, with its abundance of figures. It is commonly dated too early, and was probably done about 1200, or even later.[29] At first glance this style seems to be a mannered late development of the San Clemente stylistic trends, which in fact persisted in Rome into the thirteenth century. But the richer palette and accumulation of calligraphic features of the Tivoli apse point unequivocally to a relatively late date.

The close connection with panel-painting can be plainly seen in the precious triptych preserved in the cathedral at Tivoli.[30] The centre panel shows Christ Enthroned in golden robes. The wings *(pl. 12)* contain the Virgin and St John the Evangelist, painted in a graceful classical style. At the bottom of the wing panels are representations of the Death of the Virgin and the Ascension of St John(?). This triptych is the principal work to survive out of what seems to have been a large group of similar works. Four such complete triptychs with the same representations have been preserved in the vicinity of Rome (one of them, however, dating from the beginning of the fourteenth century). Of other triptychs, only centre panels, with Christ Enthroned, have survived.[31] Most of these panels date from the first half of the thirteenth century *(pl. 13)*, and it is unlikely that the Tivoli triptych was done much earlier than 1200. Without doubt it is derived in type and style from earlier models now lost, which may account in part for the general archaic impression it makes. The fine eclecticism of its style stands out, but already the thirteenth-century sense of the organic is unmistakably present.[32]

With regard to northern art, this early appearance of panel-painting in Italy may seem surprising. Portable pictures on wooden panels are very rare north of the Alps in the Romanesque period: there are about two dozen in Germany and none has been found in France. In Italy, however, there are hundreds of

29

such pictures from the thirteenth and even the twelfth century. Only in Catalonia have a comparable number of paintings on wood panels survived, in the form of retables and antependia.[33] This uneven distribution cannot just be attributed to the accidents of preservation. It is more likely that in Italy many of the commissions were at an early stage entrusted to panel painters, whereas north of the Alps they continued to be reserved for goldsmiths and sculptors. Some features of the painted altarpieces indicate that they were originally considered as substitutes for goldsmiths' work.[34] Other devotional pictures, following the model of Byzantine icons, were also painted on wood in Italy.

Recent research has shown that this tradition goes back to the early Middle Ages. Two of the icons venerated in the churches of Rome are probably of seventh-century origin: the Madonnas in the Pantheon and in Santa Maria Nuova near the Forum.[35] The large panel of the *Enthroned Madonna and Two Angels* in Santa Maria in Trastevere is only slightly later. Since the removal of subsequent overpainting it has been recognized as a work of the eighth century.[36] All three are painted in the encaustic technique inherited from the late classical period. The last of them, showing the Madonna enthroned and a pope as donor kneeling at her feet, in Western fashion, was certainly done in Rome and not imported from Byzantium.

Even Christ on the Cross, the traditional subject for sculpture in the north, became a favourite theme for panel-painting in Italy. The painted crucifix panels cut to the shape of the cross, which have survived in surprisingly large numbers, are among the most characteristic creations of Italian medieval art[37] and have no precedents in Byzantine art.[38] They were placed behind or above the altar, or more frequently on the screen, or the bar that was used instead of a screen to separate the laity from the choir.[39] Their function thus corresponded to that of the sculptured Triumphal Cross familiar in Romanesque art of the north.

The earliest surviving example of this type is a work of Tuscan painting, the *Crucifix* by Master Guillielmus, dated 1138, in the cathedral of Sarzana.[40] The rich iconographic formula of the early crucifixes, combining the main figure with subsidiary scenes and figures, is here fully and clearly developed. Stylistically it is pure Romanesque without any sign of Byzantine influence. From the maturity of the style and technique it is plain that this is no experimental beginning, but an isolated remnant, preserved by chance, of a well-established tradition. Another dated Crucifix of the twelfth century has survived in Umbria, the work of Master Albertus (dated 1187) in the cathedral of Spoleto *(pl. 28)*.[41] It is obviously also one of a long line of such works, since lost. Its marked Byzantine style is reminiscent of the paintings in the vestibule of Sant'Angelo in Formis.[42] There is no recognizable connection with either the Roman or Tuscan schools – evidence of the strong and varied artistic life of different Italian districts at that time.

Whereas in Umbria art remained tentative and provincial, in Tuscany it developed constantly under the patronage of the cities, where political and economic power was concentrated. The stylistic features of the *Sarzana Crucifix* point to the school of Lucca, the earliest authenticated works of which belong to the second half of the twelfth century.

Before turning to developments in Tuscany, we must glance at painting in northern Italy since the end of the eleventh century. Lombardy was a centre of the Romanesque style. The monumental churches and imposing palaces of its fortified cities testify to the greatness of that era, although the pictorial decoration is unfortunately almost entirely lost. The only large-scale wall-paintings preserved in Lombardy are, however, of the transitional stage between the Ottonian and early Romanesque styles, and not of the High Romanesque.

We have long been familiar with the almost intact pictorial cycle of apocalyptic representations in the remote church of San Pietro al Monte, in the rocky wilderness near Civate, not far from Lecco on Lake Como.[43] In addition, recent discoveries have disclosed a series of fragmentary paintings in San Calocero, a church in Civate itself.[44] Whereas in San Calocero the narrative sequence is interrupted by the later addition of a vault, in San Pietro al Monte the architecture, stucco decoration and painting are almost intact. San Pietro is a single-aisle church built on a slope rising towards the west, with the entrance at the east end. The vestibule has three vaulted aisles richly decorated with paintings, and on the wall facing the nave there is a single representation of the *Angels Fighting the Apocalyptic Dragon (pls 14a, II)*. Cool and abstract colours – green, brick-red, yellow ochre, blue, and white – cover the surface in a rhythmic flow. Even the haloes glow with variegated colour. All the faces are of the same type, generally shown in three-quarter profile. The type of the features and the drawing of hands and drapery is unmistakably Byzantine, but the Western medieval sense of form is equally marked. All the shapes are smooth and round as pebbles. Although the struggle with the demon is presented dramatically, these angels, all holding their lances in the same way and making the same gestures, are representatives of one and the same spirit. The constant repetition of a standard formula here reveals an artistic power whose source we are only beginning to understand. The secret may lie in the fact that such works are not the accomplishment of some anonymous individual artist but express the cumulative effort of a long tradition. These powerful forms have acquired a timeless and impersonal validity *(pls 15a, 15b)*.

The paintings of San Pietro al Monte and the well-preserved stucco decoration were probably done in about 1100.[45] The San Galliano paintings of the beginning of the eleventh century are freer and bolder by comparison, but more archaic in style. The Romanesque formula is only just taking shape, and the artistic potentialities still seem uncertain. In Civate on the other hand, although there too the style is at its early formative stage, the commitment to the Romanesque is more firmly established than in Galliano. The free manipulation of the figures, so marked in San Galliano, has disappeared. Only rarely does a figure stand out by its size, like the figure of Christ, now unfortunately destroyed, in the scene of the *Angels Fighting the Apocalyptic Dragon*. Everywhere else there is a striking uniformity of scale as well as of type and gesture. These are Romanesque, and not Ottonian traits. The visionary mood that pervades the apse paintings of San Galliano has given way to a formal solemnity.

By comparison, the newly discovered frescoes of San Calocero in Civate are still fairly free and animated, although they were probably done not much earlier than the San Pietro al Monte cycle, possibly dating to the end of the eleventh century.

Among the scant remains of Lombard wall-painting of the High Romanesque period, the decoration of the crypt of San Giovanni Domnarum in Pavia (*c.* 1200) is the only monument of considerable size and importance.[46] It consists of half-length life-size figures of saints, and a badly damaged Christ at the apex of the vault. The painting is bold and technically fluent. The well-modelled faces are of an unmistakably Byzantine stamp.

These paintings in Pavia were done at a time when Lombard architecture was at the peak of its development and had achieved a distinct High Romanesque style of its own. Sculpture, which was still closely associated with architecture, kept pace with this development. However, this style was not so prevalent that it penetrated all fields of artistic creativeness to an equal extent.

Painting looked to the established culture of Byzantium, a frequent source of inspiration throughout the Middle Ages. This was a natural propensity,

II Civate San Pietro al Monte
Angels Fighting the Apocalyptic Dragon (detail)

particularly in northern Italy, where Venice, with her ancient trade connections, formed the gateway to the East. The Fourth Crusade brought about the conquest of Constantinople and the establishment of the Latin Empire of the East in 1204. Venice furnished the ships that carried the Crusaders to the Bosphorus, and did not fail to gather her reward. Her political supremacy in the eastern Mediterranean originated from this time. The façade and vestibule of St Mark's were decorated with booty from the East: columns, marble panels, and reliefs; the celebrated bronze horses were also part of the loot. The mosaic work in St Mark's that had been in progress for a whole century received a new impetus. Large numbers of painted icons and illuminated Greek manuscripts undoubtedly also reached the West in Venetian ships. It is also possible that Byzantine artists emigrated to Venice and the Adriatic seaboard.

The decoration of the crypt in the cathedral of Aquileia dating from the first half of the thirteenth century is one of the works in which the emerging Italo-Byzantine style found its purest expression.[47] It is a truly medieval ensemble, well-preserved and remarkably consistent *(pl. 16a)*.[48] All the walls and vaults, and even the columns, are covered with paintings. Ochre, white, reddish-browns, brick-red, and cool, dull green are the dominant colours in its present state. The bright blue of the ground and of many parts of the draperies, added in tempera, has now largely disappeared. The semicircular wall surfaces show the *Crucifixion,* the *Descent from the Cross* and *Lamentation,* and the *Death of the Virgin.* In the vaults are eighteen scenes from the legend of St Hermagoras, the patron saint of Aquileia *(pl. 17)*. The very charming decoration around the base is done like a curtain on which animated figures are sketched lightly with a brush – as, for example, the Crusader in pursuit of a mounted Asian archer *(pl. 16b)*. The freshness and naturalness of these improvisations contrast strongly with the gravity of the main scheme.

Byzantine monumental painting of the type that has come down to us in the Nerez frescoes in Macedonia (dated 1164) provided the model for this stylistic phase.[49] In Aquileia everything is slightly harder and more brittle, and the sharp angularity of the forms is emphasized by the hard white highlights. The abrupt awkward movements and some clumsiness in the composition, especially in the legendary scenes for which no Byzantine models existed, are reminiscent of Romanesque practice. The inscriptions are in Latin. There is therefore no reason to suppose that this is the work of artists from Byzantium. Instead we may speak of a provincial Byzantine art on Italian soil, whose exponents were presumably local artists.

35

3 Early Tuscan panel-painting

The powerful influence of Byzantine art, which was to have a lasting effect in the Venetian region, also left a deep mark on Tuscan painting in the early decades of the Duecento. In Tuscany, as in Lombardy, the art of the second half of the twelfth century was dominated by a native and apparently well-established Romanesque sense of form. Architecture was in the forefront, but the skill of the painters was also evident, and was demonstrated in the panel-paintings which then began to appear in Tuscany in far greater numbers than in any other part of Italy. But whereas architecture obstinately adhered to the recognized Romanesque canons, painting experienced a sharp stylistic crisis and change of direction. Works of a distinct Byzantine character follow-ed masterpieces in the Romanesque style without noticeable transition. This happened in Lucca and in Pisa, the two cities where, judging from the evidence of surviving monuments, Tuscan pictorial tradition originated.

The oldest Pisan Crucifix *(pl. 22),* undoubtedly of the twelfth century, is a well-conceived and richly composed structure like the *Sarzana Crucifix* al-ready mentioned, and it too is probably the product of a long process of development.[1] Ten narrative scenes surround the principal figure. Fastened to the cross with four nails, and appearing to stand rather than hang, Christ looks down at the faithful with wide open eyes. This is the Triumphant Christ, victor over sin and death, familiar to us in northern Romanesque works. At the side of the Triumphant Christ the Pisan artists depicted Him suffering in the agony of death, in order to leave no doubt about the meaning of the main figure. On each side of the approximately life-size Christ are three narra-tive scenes, ranging from the *Arrest on the Mount of Olives* to the *Appearance of the Risen Christ to the Apostles,* and including the scene of the *Crucifixion* in the traditional form showing Christ with closed eyes at the moment of death. The *Last Supper* and the *Washing of the Feet (pl. 24a)* are shown on the panels at the ends of the horizontal beam of the cross. The *Pentecost* is at the foot, and the *Ascension* at the top. The style is bold and powerful, equally removed from the tentative versatility of the Ottonian manner and the elegance of the Byzantine. All the forms are reduced to their basic essentials; in the same way as in Romanesque architecture everything can be referred to the square, the semicircle, the cube, the column and the arch. All the objects and spaces are firmly defined. The choice of colour is governed by the principle of contrast and sharp division of the surfaces. There are no transitional shades, and no features that unify the whole design. The artistic unity is achieved by an abstract pattern of simple forms and strong bright colours. It is a most accomplished pictorial parallel to the proud Romanesque buildings which distinguish the town of Pisa even today.

Like this architecture, which is the purest realization of the Italian Romanesque concept of form, Pisan painting boldly exhibited its own distinctive style, its independence of foreign models. However, a second Crucifix, painted in Pisa a generation or two later, in the first decades of the thirteenth century, reveals an entirely different artistic aspiration *(pl. 23)*.[2] Its style is no longer plain and primitive, but reaches a higher level of expression, imbued with noble pathos, and controlled by a strict artistic discipline. In its intellectual content, too, it is far removed from the older crucifixes. This is *Christus patiens,* our redeemer who suffered for our sins, not the triumphant victor over death. Indeed, the theme of the main figure is really Death on the Cross. The side scenes *(pl. 24b)* depict only the events from the Crucifixion onwards, beginning with the Descent from the Cross. The panels on the horizontal beams are devoted to St John and the women, the witnesses to the sacrifice. In the crowning panel, however, the Saviour does appear triumphant, accompanied by angels and cherubim. Whereas the earlier painter naively surrounds the symbolic figure of Christ the King with scenes from the Passion and the Resurrection, in the later work the symbolism is in harmony with the events that are illustrated. The Death on the Cross, the critical event in the story of the Passion, is raised to a supra-historical level. The countenance of the dying Christ, inclined to one side with eyes shut and features ennobled through pain and submission, expresses the full significance of this well-conceived and singularly accomplished work *(pl. 25)*. The style is almost pure Byzantine. The uninterrupted flow of line, the passionate and yet perfectly competent style, is reminiscent of the head of the angel above the portal of Sant'Angelo in Formis, although this is presumably the work of a Tuscan master and not of an immigrant artist from Greece. The *Christus patiens* type, which in the course of the thirteenth century superseded the Triumphant Christ in Italy and north of the Alps, is ultimately also of Byzantine derivation.[3]

Neighbouring Lucca underwent a similar development. The oldest Crucifix preserved there is a work of high quality, genuinely Romanesque in its combination of severe forms and rich ornamentation.[4] But in Lucca too, the encroachment of Byzantine influences early in the Duecento overshadowed the beginnings of an indigenous style. The *Crucifix* of about 1210–20, signed by Berlinghiero, is not only simpler in structure than the earlier types, but stylistically on a different plane *(pl. 29)*.[5] The mature Byzantine style has become, to a certain extent, Italianized. Berlinghiero's work is far superior to the older Crucifixes in the modelling, formal integration, and economy of artistic means. It is no longer a conglomeration of isolated forms placed side by side, but a formal and pictorial unity. The large number of side scenes has been suppressed and the figures of the mourners brought into an organic relationship with the central figure.

Byzantine art clearly did for Italian painting what the Gothic did for the Late Romanesque of the north; it helped to overcome the tendency to isolated forms, and pointed the way out of the maze of ornamental detail and motifs towards a compact unity of representation. The willingness throughout Italy at that time to assimilate an artistic style from the East must not be thought of in terms of 'foreign infiltration', but as an awareness of the need for a superior model to inspire Romanesque painting with new life, and to save it from formalistic stagnation.[6]

For a while, however, it looked as though the traditional local style had been abandoned only to be replaced by a new kind of formalism. A son of Berlinghiero, Buonaventura Berlinghieri, painted an altarpiece in 1235 which is still in the Franciscan church in Pescia, not far from Lucca *(pl. 31)*.[7] The figure of St Francis which fills the centre of the panel recalls a Byzantine icon. The saint is strange and forbidding, a sombre ascetic with set features, which reflect nothing of the humane *Poverello* familiar in history, and the proportions transcend any human scale. It does not bring to mind the poet of nature, the joyous bridegroom of poverty, who revived religious life in western Europe. The position of the hands with stigmata and book corresponds to the Byzantine picture of Christ in Benediction, and the small scale of the legendary scenes on the sides intensifies the isolation and unworldly sublimity of the main figure.

It is questionable whether the faithful of the thirteenth century saw their saint as the remote and godlike creature represented in the Pescia panel – a conception that is contradicted by the oldest representation of St Francis in the rocky monastery of Sacro Speco near Subiaco.[8] This is not a portrait in the modern sense, but it gives us a milder and more intimate interpretation than the Pescia panel. Even more contradictory to the severe Byzantine conception of the saint are the tender scenes surrounding the main figure in the Pescia panel itself. These six scenes, among them the *Stigmatization* and the *Sermon to the Birds*, later to become such well-known themes, are the earliest surviving pictorial versions of the St Francis legend *(pls 30a, 30b)*. The fresh naivety of the narrative scenes as well as the style are truly Romanesque, with only a thin veneer of Byzantine elegance and severity.

The St Francis retable at Pescia was not an isolated piece, nor the oldest of its type in spite of the early date. A work of very similar design, known only from an old illustration, bears the date 1228.[9] It was in that year that the saint was canonized, only two years after his death, and this type of representation was already established. About half a dozen other St Francis panels, some only slightly later than the Pescia altarpiece, are still extant.[10] They all show the saint as a towering figure, surrounded by subsidiary scenes. Outwardly this type of altarpiece was not new: the basic pattern of the oldest altar paintings showed Christ or Mary as the central figure, with smaller narrative pictures on each side. But these were all on wide horizontal panels.[11] The St Francis pictures are the first to be done on tall vertical panels; hitherto this had been customary only in tabernacles with movable wings and in simple devotional pictures without side pieces. This emphasis on the vertical was an essential element of the new style, and soon appeared in representations of other saints.[12] The innovation was no sooner introduced than it settled into an established type repeated hundreds of times – which illustrates the close relationship that existed at that time between the creative forces and the stabilizing influences of tradition.

In its basic pattern this variant is still reminiscent of the earlier Crucifixes with narrative side scenes, but the type of the Crucifix itself was simplified. Berlinghiero already omitted the side scenes, and showed only Mary and St John on the central panel beside the main figure of Christ. Giunta Pisano, the leading master of the Pisan school in the second quarter of the Duecento,[13] went one step further in his Crucifix for the burial church of St Francis at Assisi. It was donated in 1236 by Elias of Cortona, the second successor to St Francis as head of the Franciscan Order, and the founder of the church. Presumably it served as the triumphal cross in the present Lower Church; it was later kept in the Upper Church, and has only recently been lost.[14]

There are three other Crucifixes signed by Giunta Pisano.[15] The oldest of these, in Santa Maria degli Angeli near Assisi, already shows the new features clearly *(pls 26, 27)*. It was probably done at about the same time as the San Francesco Crucifix, around 1236. Christ alone is pictured on the central panel,

39

and the half-length figures of Mary and St John are placed in the side panels of the cross-piece. The body of Christ is strongly modelled; its axis is noticeably curved to the side, and the head bent in a kind of counterpoise to the line of the body. The eyes are closed. In a separate panel at the top is a half-length figure of the living Christ in Benediction holding a book. This is the final simplification of the Ascension scenes that used to crown the earlier Crucifixes. The harmony of the parts and the concentration on the essentials of the subject are significant achievements. Although there were Byzantine precedents for the figure of Christ in this form and with this expression, it was through Giunta Pisano that it became the standard type of Italian Duecento Crucifixes. Giunta himself made no further alterations. He only perfected the proportions and expression. Even as late as the end of the century a master like Cimabue could add nothing to this solution. Only the young Giotto succeeded in giving it a new technical excellence and a radically transformed intellectual content. Even he, however, did not touch the outward form of the composition of the Crucifix, with its parts harmoniously arranged in relation to the central figure, which persisted into the fourteenth century.[16]

4 Florence and Siena in the Duecento

The middle of the Duecento saw the beginning of a new phase in the history of Tuscan painting. The schools of Pisa and Lucca lost their pre-eminence. In Lucca the tradition of the Berlinghiero workshop survived for a number of decades, and such refined and mature works as the *Madonna* from the former Lenbach Collection (now in private possession in West Germany, *pl. 32*), were still being produced there as late as 1260.[1] However, more important than the continuance of the Lucca style locally was the influence it had on Florence and Siena. The *St Zenobius Altarpiece* (1240–50), once in the crypt of Florence Cathedral, is the work of a Florentine master clearly under the influence of the Berlinghieri school.[2] Even at this early stage of technical dependence on outside sources, specific Florentine features are apparent: the feeling for structure and clarity of form, and the dramatic tension produced by the controlled rhythm of the composition *(pl. 34a)*.

In Siena too, independent creative forces emerged soon after the middle of the century. Coppo di Marcovaldo, the first Florentine painter known to us by name, was active in both cities. The earliest work attributable to him with certainty is the *Madonna del Carmine* of about 1250–60 in Santa Maria Maggiore in Florence *(pls 33, 34b)*.[3] It is derived from the Byzantine type of the Nikopoia; the Madonna sits on the throne in a frontal position, holding the Child on her lap with both hands. The Madonna and Child are done in low relief, while the rest is painted. This, and the broad frame studded with sculptured rosettes, may be a recollection of the origins of religious panel-painting. There is an obvious attempt to simulate the effect of goldsmiths' work.[4]

According to the records, Coppo fought for Florence in the battle of Montaperti in 1260, and was taken prisoner by the Sienese. A year later he completed the large *Madonna* in Santa Maria dei Servi in Siena. An inscription, recently uncovered, bears his name and the date 1261.[5] The arrangement of the Child placed on one side with the Madonna turning towards him is based on the *Hodegetria* type, which takes its name from a once celebrated miraculous image in Constantinople. The Madonna was, however, originally a standing figure; the seated figure never acquired any great importance in Byzantine art.[6] In the West, on the other hand, this motif was also used for enthroned Madonnas. Coppo's *Madonna* is one of the earliest examples in Tuscan art, but unfortunately this important picture has lost an essential part of its original character: the faces of the Madonna and Child were 'modernized' at the beginning of the Trecento – that is to say, they were overpainted in the style of the Duccio school. Luckily we still have another large *Madonna* by Coppo, in Santa Maria dei Servi at Orvieto *(pl. 35)*. Though not authenticated by an inscription, its attribution to Coppo is hardly disputed now.[7] Mary is seated on a throne with a high lyreshaped back, and holds the Child in her right arm. The deep blue and red draperies interwoven with gold, and the dark tint of the flesh, produce an effect of harmony and solemn grandeur. The forms are precise and have a metallic hardness; the drawing and modelling have a true Florentine sharpness, and reveal the native Florentine sense of plastic and sculptural values. This style, then, manifests itself at an early stage, when the *maniera greca* was at the height of its development.

The Sienese counterpart of Coppo di Marcovaldo was Guido da Siena, who has long been regarded as the real founder of Tuscan painting in his native town.[8] It seems that the two artists influenced one another. Coppo's *Madonna* of 1261 could have been done in competition with Guido; and yet Guido and his workshop drew inspiration from Coppo. Guido's large *Madonna,* now in the Palazzo Pubblico in Siena *(pl. 36),* gives the impression of an attempt to surpass the work of the Florentine artist whose influence is apparent in Mary's robe and other features.[9] It is even larger than Coppo's work and more spacious in composition. A Gothic clover-leaf arch spans the figures. All the outward characteristics point to a late date, possibly around 1280, and this is confirmed by the style of painting. The inscription on the picture, however, is strangely inconsistent and has until now been the cause of constant controversy. Next to the painter's name, 'Guido de Senis', is the surprisingly early date 1221. It was this date that led earlier art historians to regard Guido da Siena as a master of exceptional significance. In the rivalry between the two leading schools, Florence and Siena, this date was used to assert Siena's claim to priority and to demolish Vasari's 'Florentine' interpretation, according to which the whole history of modern art begins with Cimabue.

Despite the inscription, however, present-day opinion, based on an incomparably wider knowledge of monuments, definitely excludes the early dating of the *Palazzo Pubblico Madonna*.[10] Around 1220 Sienese painting was still at a stage of provincial dependence. The Madonna of Santa Maria in Tressa, near Siena, of about this time, is a work of late Romanesque style under the influence of the Lucca school.[11] Guido's art, on the other hand, reveals a thorough knowledge of the Byzantine conception of form and an early inclination to the Gothic.

We have another large work by Guido, an altar dossal, originally with seven half-length figures, of which only five now remain *(pl. 37a)*.[12] The inscription, though incomplete, secures a date in the eighth decade of the Duecento. Whereas the head of the *Palazzo Pubblico Madonna,* like that of Coppo's *Servi Madonna,* was over-painted about 1300, the heads in this dossal are well preserved *(pl. 37b)*. They clearly show that Guido was a contemporary of Coppo's – though their artistic temperaments were quite different. Both artists diverge equally from the Byzantine model, and have the same concern for physical form, perfection of detail, and pictorial substance. But whereas Coppo's style is angular and sharp, crystalline and sculpturally hard, Guido's is rounded and elegant, smooth in its transitions, and fluid in its lines. The small panel of the *Annunciation,* now at Princeton *(pl. 38)*, is a good example. It is one of a series of twelve scenes from the life of Christ, since dispersed among many collections.[13] Guido's style is patently affected by the melancholy of the Byzantine models, which to Coppo were only a source of formal ideas to be expressed essentially in plastic terms. In these two painters, the first recognizable artistic personalities, Florence and Siena confronted each other as distinctly opposite worlds.

Like the sense of plastic form and spatial clarity, the frequent dryness and brittleness is also Florentine. Nowhere else was the sober, middle-class, workman-like character of the new panel-painting so marked as in Florence. The Magdalene Master, so-called after the altarpiece showing the Saint surrounded by scenes from her life, reveals himself at every point as a bourgeois craftsman to whom the hieratic severity and full-blown culture of Eastern art must have been alien and incomprehensible.[14] In his pictures the Byzantine influence is reduced to an empty manner – the *maniera greca* in the later, pejorative sense of the expression. The best work of this bourgeois art was done in the service of popular piety, in the form of homely and unpretentious devotional pictures. Panels such as those of the Master of Bagnano are still admired for their technical soundness.[15] Some of the pictures, especially those that have escaped the hands of hasty restorers, have survived the seven centuries since they were painted with hardly any deterioration. Their bright colours still have the same freshness as when they left the workshops of the Florentine painters.

In the prolific activity of the second half of the Duecento a master emerged in Florence, in the last quarter of the century, who was once again to inspire the traditional Eastern forms with genuine passion and elevate them to monumental greatness: Cimabue.[16] In his large *Madonna* for Santa Trinita, now in the Uffizi *(pls 39, 40, 42a)*, he shows the mother of God as a powerful presence outside time and space and yet brought close to us by the compelling, fervent gaze of her wide-open eyes. Twice life-size, she sits on a throne surrounded by a circle of angels in perfect symmetry. The Madonna and Child, closely united by the blue-gold and red-gold of their draperies, are the centre of the chromatic composition. Lighter but muted tones are reserved for the angels. The distribution of colours on the two sides, like the figures of the angels, forms a mirror image. The symmetry is broken only in the lower zone, where one of the Prophets is shown in a vermilion robe, as if to imply that this group has no part in the order of the divine region. The structure of the throne is quite clear in spite of the archaic perspective; the bright ochre-brown wood, slightly shaded in parts, has the weightless look of a coloured design. The gold ground behind the Prophets also adds to the weightless appearance of the massive throne. This work combines Florentine clarity and abstract medieval grandeur. And so, in this one instance, a few years before the appearance of Giotto, the heavy bourgeois spirit of the Florentine painters attained the elevated heights of true sacred art, which was to disappear at the end of the Duecento.

Almost contemporaneous with Cimabue's Madonna is another even larger Madonna, the *Rucellai Madonna,* named after the Rucellai chapel in Santa Maria Novella in Florence *(pls 41, 43)*.[17] The commission was given to the Sienese painter Duccio in 1285, and the detailed contract still exists.[18] Duccio was at least ten years younger than Cimabue,[19] and this picture, his earliest authenticated work, speaks the language of a new generation. Its measurements, four and a half meters high and three meters wide, are larger than anything known until then, but the surface is not filled as densely as Cimabue's, and the composition is lighter and more atmospheric. The throne is delicate and well-designed. Its many perpendiculars lead the eye upwards. The angels, gentle figures clad in filmy draperies, seem to float in front of the gold ground. Kneeling, they worship the Virgin and her divine Son, and lightly support the throne by the touch of their fingers. Duccio, like all the Sienese, was evidently much more deeply affected by the spirit of the *maniera greca* than Cimabue. Byzantine nobility and melancholy are reflected in the countenance of Mary, and even more strongly in the faces of the angels. But this was not the only source of Duccio's style. The delicate and graceful touches

III CIMABUE *Madonna with Angels* · Assisi, San Francesco, Lower Church

that he found in Byzantine works were also present, though in a different form, in the new art of the West. The faint verticality in Duccio's composition, the sense of space apparent in the oblique view of the throne, and finally the ornamental form of the throne itself, show that the young Sienese master was by no means unaffected by the Gothic movement, which was becoming increasingly influential in Italy. The cathedral, which was being built in those decades, demonstrates that, especially in Siena, this influence was received with enthusiasm. The new style eventually triumphed during Duccio's own lifetime. Simone Martini, one of Duccio's pupils, identified himself, with fewer reservations than any of his Italian contemporaries, with the Gothic sense of form. In the fourteenth century, Siena became a Gothic city, and has outwardly remained so to this day.

In the *Rucellai Madonna* the new influence is still only barely perceptible. But by comparison Cimabue's composition, although done at about the same time or perhaps slightly later, seems much more archaic. Despite its clear structure there is something sombre and oppressive in the form and expression and the archaic overcrowded surface – an effect which is intensified by the severe symmetry. Duccio, on the other hand, knew how to combine greater freedom in the detail with a concentration on the essentials. Although his Madonna is the dominant figure, she does not overwhelm the other parts of the composition. Colour plays an important role in the design; the deep blue of the Virgin's cloak provides a tranquil centre for the free interplay of the delicate colours of the surrounding angels. The tonal values of the two halves of the picture are the same, but the colours themselves differ. In his handling of colour, Cimabue adheres to a stricter symmetry; every single colour of the angels' draperies is faithfully reproduced on the opposite side. The draperies of his Madonna and Child are interwoven with shining gold so that they become integrated in the uniform ornamentation of the whole picture. Cimabue has not yet emerged from the Middle Ages, whereas Duccio's picture has a palpable unity and obeys a law and licence of its own; it is thus a step towards the new order that was to prevail in Italian painting. The sole decoration of the Duccio Madonna's deep-blue mantle is the characteristic gold zigzag line of the hem, which is, as it were, a symbol of the new freedom, as well as a personal signature recurring repeatedly in Duccio's work. The ornamentation and gold are confined to those parts that require decoration according to the post-medieval convention – the throne, and the precious brocade covering its back.

In all probability Duccio painted the *Rucellai Madonna* in Florence, for the great size of the panel makes it unlikely that it was transported over a long distance. In spite of this, it is a major work of Sienese painting, and represents its principles of design in exemplary fashion, as for instance in the free choice of colours and their light, detached delicacy. The draperies of the angels are in pale blue and lilac beside soft carmine and translucent sea-green – colours that are also typical of Duccio's later work. The careless gay colour and the opacity of the average Florentine productions are primitive compared with such refinement. The major Florentine painters, Coppo and Cimabue, were inclined to work in monochrome, which is best suited to the expression of plastic values, and, as far as possible, the colours were disposed decoratively, often in a pedantic and calculated order. The symmetrical colour arrangement of the angels in the *Santa Trinita Madonna* is found in all those Florentine Madonna paintings of the Duecento that have an angel in each upper corner: in these cases the colours of both the upper and lower parts of the draperies of the angels on the right and left always correspond. In Sienese painting this correspondence is just as consistently avoided. The marked difference between the two schools is indicated in such apparently trivial matters. It is also clear that, apart from technical rules, the painters' workshops of the time transmitted a number of aesthetic principles – the first traces of an artistic discipline – which were adhered to strictly.

But more important than these still essentially medieval workshop practices was the emergence of well-defined artistic personalities, who overreached the traditional rules. We come back to the most significant of these masters, Cimabue. He was probably born between 1240 and 1250, and the first documentary reference to him is as a witness to an ecclesiastical administrative act in Rome in 1272.[20] We do not know the nature of the commission that brought him to Rome, but as he was in company with high-ranking clerics he could not have been a mere beginner at that time. What can be assumed with certainty is that the artistic impressions he gathered in Rome were of the utmost importance in the formation of his style. Unfortunately he is not referred to again in the records until the beginning of the new century. In 1302 he was working, together with other masters, on the apse mosaics of Pisa Cathedral. In this large work only one figure, St John the Evangelist, is attributable to him.[21] The date of his death is not known.

The Crucifix in San Domenico in Arezzo is the only panel-painting before the *Santa Trinita Madonna* that can be assigned to Cimabue with certainty. Probably painted around 1270, it is of the type originated by Giunta Pisano, and is done in the austere sculptural and expressive manner characteristic of Coppo di Marcovaldo.[22] The *Santa Trinita Madonna*, however, already reveals the mature, unmistakably personal style of Cimabue. Modern research is inclined to date it later than the *Rucellai Madonna,* that is to say, around 1285–90, but there is no conclusive evidence.[23] On the other hand, the close link between Cimabue's Madonna panel and his frescoes at Assisi is beyond dispute. Recent opinion supports this, and maintains that the frescoes were begun much earlier than was previously supposed, dating them towards the end of the 1270s. We shall come back to this presently.

Cimabue's contribution to the decoration in the Florence Baptistry is still uncertain. Quite possibly he collaborated in the scenes of Joseph's life. Several scenes from *Genesis* also show traces of his style, in spite of all the disfigurement due to intervening restoration.[24]

The large Crucifix which Cimabue made for Santa Croce, the Franciscan church in Florence, probably belongs in the last years of the century *(pls 44, 45).*[25] As the name implies, the church was dedicated to the Holy Cross and the memory of the Crucifix with cherub wings that appeared to St Francis at his stigmatization. Probably Cimabue's work was set up as a triumphal cross on the screen, which would explain its exceptional size, 4.48 by 3.90 meters. The over life-size figure of Christ appears even larger than the actual dimensions might suggest because of its slenderness and the wide sideways curve of the body. The triangle formed by the arms and the ascending line of the legs intersects the rectangular shapes of the frame and binds them together. Christ suffers, yet He is remote and weightless. The painting is a network of fine overlapping brush-strokes, and though by no means naturalistic, it radiates vehement life and creative power; the form is richer and more refined than that of the Madonna panel. The doubts occasionally expressed in regard to Cimabue's personal authorship of the Crucifix are certainly unjustified.[26] This work exemplifies his late style. The high pathos of the Assisi frescoes has disappeared, but the stature of the monumental forms achieved there remains, and their expressive power has here attained a final intensity.

5 Assisi and Rome

The significance of Cimabue's paintings at Assisi, briefly mentioned in the last chapter, can be fully understood only when they are considered in their proper context.[1] In the grandiose structure that developed during the thirteenth century over the burial place of St Francis, architecture and painting form an organic whole. No other medieval building contains such an abundance of paintings as the double church of San Francesco at Assisi, which in fact consists of two churches built one above the other: the sombre tomb-like Lower Church with its low vaults and massive walls, and above it the bright and spacious Upper Church with extensive walls and vaults providing ample space for painting. The Gothic forms which give the Upper Church its character are well suited to express the Italian balanced sense of space. The single-aisled nave, consisting of four almost square bays, has the appearance of a compact hall *(pl. 47a)* in which height and width form a harmonious relationship.[2] On the sides of the windows there are large clear spaces. Below them the wall provides a continuous series of picture surfaces which were filled with twenty-eight scenes from the St Francis legend – that great work executed by Giotto and his pupils in the last years of the Duecento. Beyond these rows of pictures, the transept and the polygonal choir are as compact and well-proportioned as the nave *(pl. 46)*.[3]

This grandiose and lavishly decorated building, in strange contrast to the rule of poverty, the essence of Franciscan teaching, was begun as early as 1228 at the instigation of Elias of Cortona, then minister-general of the Order. He completed the Lower Church and probably also planned the Upper Church, though on quite a different and more modest scale than the eventually executed structure. The idea of a double church with a single aisle and cruciform ground plan doubtlessly originated with Elias. The Upper Church, as it stands

today, involved a radical alteration in the plan, presumably made soon after after
1247. This change, which gave the building its Gothic character, was inspired by the fashionable Ile-de-France architecture and not, as supposed until recently, by the cathedral of Angers.[4]

The Upper Church was consecrated in 1253. It seems, however, to have been in a rough state of construction at the time,[5] since the papal approval for collecting alms for the completion and maintenance of San Francesco was renewed in that year for a further period of twenty-five years. In 1266 the approval was confirmed and extended for an additional three years. After that the records are silent for more than two decades. Only when Nicholas IV, minister-general of the Franciscan Order from 1274–9, ascended the papal throne do we find again a reference to the providing of funds for the building. During his short reign (1288–92), the pope issued as many as eight bulls to promote the construction, and presumably also the decoration, of San Francesco.[6] It can be assumed, however, that building had not stopped in the interim period. The splendid portal on the south side of the Lower Church was probably built soon after 1279.[7] There are also grounds for supposing that at about this time Cimabue decorated the choir of the Upper Church.

The entire pictorial decoration of the choir, the crossing, the south transept, and part of the north transept are by Cimabue and his workshop. The pictures on the vault above the crossing, the four evangelists, heralds of salvation, are the focus of the whole conception. They are large seated figures represented in the Byzantine manner as scribes and philosophers. Beside each evangelist is a picture of a walled city, symbolizing a portion of the Christian world. Three of the cities are imaginary places, but the fourth, 'Ytalia', allotted to St Mark, is a faithful medieval rendering of Rome. Many of its well-known buildings and monuments are crowded within the walls without regard to their actual position in the city. One of them, only recently identified by its crown of pinnacles and its stepped gables,[8] is the Capitol, the seat of the senate – indicated by the minute coats-of-arms barely visible to the naked eye. Besides the letters SPQR these escutcheons contain the emblem of the Orsini family – and not, as was previously supposed, that of the Savelli.[9] This could not have been chosen at random, but is Cimabue's covert way of paying homage to the great Roman family. No details are known of his connection with the Orsini, but it is very likely that he was closely associated with these influential patrons during his stay in Rome. As the coats-of-arms do not appear on an ecclesiastical building but on the Capitol, they must refer to the Orsini in their capacity as senators. In these decades members of the Orsini family repeatedly served as senators, and therefore no definite chronological conclusions can be drawn from the appearance of their emblems in Cimabue's picture. It is tempting, however, to associate it with the precise moment in history when Nicholas III, an Orsini pope, himself assumed the office of senator for a period of two years (1279–80), when the senatorial term of Charles of Anjou ended and was not renewed. Two other members of the Orsini family served as senators together with the pope. Moreover, in 1279 one of these, Matteo Rosso Orsini, was in addition appointed cardinal protector of the Franciscan Order. Despite the absence of conclusive evidence it is extremely likely that Cimabue referred to this historical constellation in his picture of Rome. It is as though he dated his work with a symbolic allusion, and thus provided a chronological clue for the experts.[10]

This dating, if accepted, demarcates the period during which the entire decoration of the Upper Church was carried out. Cimabue's portion was evidently the first to be completed as it was natural to start from the choir and the transept. These pictures, whose general character and style of figures shows them to be older than those in the nave, form the point of departure for the whole decorative scheme.

The only place where the decoration is quite different is the upper zone of the north transept where work must have been under way before Cimabue was appointed. The decorative elements of the borders and friezes are pure Gothic, and in the pictures there are noteworthy attempts at rendering perspective in the representations of Gothic architecture. Cimabue, on the other hand, tried by means of his decoration wherever possible to restyle the architectural features of the buildings and give them a classical character, which is particularly marked in the nave. The pictures in the north transept are dedicated to the glory of Christ and the apostles. They were painted by an artist of great ability, whose origins remain a complete mystery. Even his technique is quite different from that of Cimabue: the *a secco* painting was applied on a highly finished drawing in linear style, which is all that now survives. This technique suggests that the artist was trained in the north, but the bold elegance of the linear style indicates that he was probably an Italian, possibly a Sienese. Apparently he still continued his work for some time while Cimabue and his assistants were painting beside him and radically changing the decorative scheme he had begun. The lower zone of the north transept was, however, eventually assigned to Cimabue. It contains a large Crucifixion and scenes from the lives of the apostles.

In the choir Cimabue painted many scenes from the life and glorification of the Virgin, and in the south transept apocalyptic themes, choirs of angels, and another Crucifixion. Unfortunately this powerful pictorial sequence is now only faintly visible: the iconographic content of the scenes can be deciphered only with great difficulty and the former magnificence of the compositions is lost. Cimabue used a *fresco secco* technique on a monochrome base of warm ochre colours. In many extensive areas the underpainting is the sole surviving remnant. In so far as this second layer is preserved, it is discoloured by the chemical changes that frequently occur in wall-paintings of that time. The lead-white that was added to most colours, especially the flesh tints, has turned black through oxidation. As a result the pictures now have the appearance of photographic negatives.[11] Apart from the ochre tone present everywhere, only an occasional muted brick-red has escaped this change. Larger areas that have retained their original colour can be found only in the middle zone of the south transept among the choirs of angels, where bright, heavily impasted white, vivid green, and deep red are still visible. The brilliance and unabated intensity of these colours match the effects produced by contemporary panel-paintings. It is no longer possible to visualize the radiance these colours must have had when they covered all the walls, vaults and ribs of the building. In addition there was the glitter of the gilded haloes and gold highlights of the draperies and the large gold areas of the vaults above the crossing, where the evangelists were shown enthroned. Only a vigorous generation charged with primitive sensuous emotion could express its faith and its vision of the heavenly world to come in such realistic terms.

The formal structure of the paintings is exceptionally clear and essentially monumental. Voluminous, yet powerfully modelled figures with expressive heads and richly designed draperies are arranged in horizontal rows behind and above one another. The scenes of the Death of Mary, her Assumption, and her Glorification in the midst of the heavenly host, are typical examples.[12] Other compositions, for instance *Mary on her Death-bed surrounded by the Apostles,* display an astonishing spatial content. Although there is as yet no consistent organization of space in perspective, the figures, conceived in separate blocks, convey together a sense of three-dimensional space. Here Cimabue reveals himself as the direct precursor of Giotto, who also creates an effect of depth by means of his figures. The severe emphasis on basic horizontal and vertical planes also recurs in Giotto's work. The modelling of the figures and the tectonic construction of the paintings are Florentine traits, and reappear, though on a different stylistic principle, in Masaccio.

In spite of all this Cimabue was no formalist. The agitated, furrowed faces already noticed in the prophets of the Florentine Madonna panel appear everywhere in Assisi. The angels are grave and powerful, with low foreheads, large sharply-cut eyes, and strongly modelled jaws.[13] It is a thoroughly virile art that brings to mind the great Florentines of later days: Masaccio, Donatello, and Michelangelo. Cimabue's figures have the same *terribilità,* a profound and almost alarming solemnity.

This elemental and, as it were, inarticulate disquiet, the mood common to all these figures, is intensified to a deep pathos whenever the subject matter of the picture itself demands enhanced emotion. The Crucifixion scene in the south transept is swept by a gust of passion *(pl. 49).* A real storm has risen and tugs at the loin-cloth of the almost twice life-size Christ. The dense, wildly excited crowd of spectators resembles a corn-field swaying in the wind. The centurion, distinguished by a halo, points with a gesture of unforgettable expressiveness to the dead Son of God. The twelve angels hover around the cross in postures of utter despair *(pl. 50).* Only in the group of mourners on the left, where grief is deepest, is all outward show of sorrow avoided. St John takes Mary's right hand in his, and in a movement of classical nobility they turn gently towards each other. The other women identify themselves with this silent group. Only the passionate Mary Magdalene impulsively stretches her hands towards Christ, but stands motionless, as though taking a vow. At her feet St Francis, a humble monk, kneels beside the cross and bows over the dripping blood of the Redeemer.

Another equally large Crucifixion covers the corresponding wall in the north transept. The composition is roughly the same, but the dramatic impact of this version, evidently done later, is much weaker than its older counter-part. Cimabue seems to have entrusted its execution to his workshop.[14]

But the *Madonna with Angels and St Francis* in the transept of the Lower Church is another work by Cimabue's own hand, and probably the last he did in Assisi *(pl. III).* Though faded and gravely impaired by numerous restorations, this fragment is still one of the most impressive in the church. In the obscurity of the low oppressive room, the forms reveal themselves as the consummation of Cimabue's achievement in the field of monumental painting. The drapery and the human forms become united and round as in classical sculpture, and the movements are free and fluid. This has often been remarked upon; but it hardly justifies the assumption that Cimabue renewed his contact with classical works. It is more likely that his plastic sense, the sculptor's inclination for the austere beauty of simple forms, that had long been an essential characteristic of Cimabue, here reached its full expression.

The very scale of the frescoes done by Cimabue and his workshop suggests that the master's activities in Assisi extended over a number of years. On historical grounds, the early part in the choir and the crossing of the Upper

Church can, as already seen, very probably be dated to the end of the 1270s. The last portion, stylistically represented by the *Enthroned Madonna* in the Lower Church, seems to have been done shortly after 1280. There is at least one piece of evidence to confirm this hypothesis: the frescoes, dated 1284, painted by the Florentine, Corso di Buono, in the choir of San Giovanni Evangelista in Montelupo *(pl. 42b)* half-way between Florence and Pisa, for which Cimabue's fully developed style at Assisi must have served as model.[15] The type and style of the figures are similar, and the predominant reddish and brown colours correspond to the basic tones of Cimabue's palette, although their range is more limited. The historical argument for the dating of Cimabue's work at Assisi thus obtains direct and independent support from this stylistic relationship.[16]

While Cimabue was painting his Madonna in the Lower Church, the work in the nave of the Upper Church was probably also in progress. The narrative sequence of the pictures starts from the crossing: scenes from the Old Testament, beginning with the Creation, are on the north wall, and the life of Christ is on the south wall. Each series is arranged in two horizontal rows. The order of execution followed the sequence of the narrative, so that the scenes near the crossing were done first, and those on the entrance wall last. Only the lower zone, intended for the St Francis legend, was left empty for the time being. The vaults were also decorated according to a uniform plan: the first and third, counting from the crossing, were reserved for non-figurative ornamentation. Bounded by wide colourful borders, these large deep-blue surfaces span the room like celestial canopies. The precious ultramarine, originally strewn with golden stars, is repeated in the vaults of the choir and the transepts. All the parts of the cruciform room were thus united under a starry sky.[17] The figurative scenes with their gold ground, alternating rhythmically between the ornamented vaults, do not disrupt but rather contribute to the harmony of the scheme. The four Fathers of the Church in the first vault nearest the portal correspond to the four Evangelists in the vault above the crossing. They too are shown as full-figure scribes, each accompanied by a clerk.[18] The centre of the ceiling is reserved for Christ attended by Mary, John the Baptist, and St Francis interceding on behalf of humanity. Thus the traditional Intercession scene of Byzantine iconography is here enlarged to include the saint in whose honour the building was erected. The figures are huge half-length representations in medallion form, each accompanied by two angels. Contrary to Byzantine portrayals of Christ, whose Benediction is often a gesture of stern authority, the figure of Christ radiates gentleness and an abiding sublimity. This is the Roman Church interpretation, and differs significantly from the Byzantine conception. The artistic precedents for these paintings are also to be found in Rome. The style of this vault, the Vault of the Saints, is similar to that of Jacopo Torriti, and even more to that of his pupil Rusuti. Both masters are known from signed mosaic works preserved in churches in Rome.

The scenes on the walls of the nave are also inspired by Roman tradition. The scheme itself – the placing of Old Testament scenes opposite scenes from the New Testament – was a Roman practice; many of the scenes, especially those from the Old Testament, derive their iconography from Roman traditions established in early Christian times.[19] Even the style of the painting is largely influenced by early models. Another and still more powerful feature is the classical spirit and classical feeling for form, which becomes increasingly more pronounced as the work progresses from the crossing to the entrance wall. The nave of San Francesco must, therefore, be the work of Roman painters, or artists trained in Rome. The *Creation (pl. 52)*, in the top row of the north wall nearest to the crossing, has long been attributed to Filippo Rusuti, an attribution unexpectedly confirmed by the drawing of the head of the Creator *(pl. 53)* that came to light when the picture was lifted from the wall.[20] It is a brush under-drawing in red and ochre for the finished painting, which was presumably done in *fresco secco*. In comparison with the sensitive style of the preliminary sketch, the final work *(pl. 52)* appears dry and conventional. It is impossible to tell whether this is due to the complicated technical process, or whether Rusuti left the completion to an assistant.[21]

In the frescoes of the nave, especially in the scenes from the life of Christ, we can see, in addition to the Roman element, the influence of Cimabue's style. Furthermore, an attempt has been made to identify the manner of the young Duccio in the fragmentary Crucifixion scene.[22] But the nature of the relationship between Duccio and Cimabue is a matter that requires further clarification.[23]

The encounter between Florentine and Roman masters in the large joint project of Assisi was of major importance for the evolution of the new Italian painting. In order to understand the complex and quite dramatic phenomenon that occurred in the last decades of the Duecento, we must turn once again to Rome, to examine briefly the development there from about the middle of the century.

Medieval art in Rome presents a rich but by no means uniform picture. At the outset it could be said that since the decline of antiquity 'Roman art' no longer existed, but only art in Rome. The Eternal City was too big and too universal to establish a local school of distinct character such as existed in Florence and Siena. In the Middle Ages there were artists and works of a Roman character, but there was hardly any Roman concept of form, nor were there any typical or consistent features of a Roman style. Unlike Tuscany, where the smaller centres made their contribution and jointly formed a unified 'artistic landscape' with a distinctive style, Latium, the district around Rome, was a sphere of Roman influence with no creative energy of its own. Thus, the paintings in the Sylvester Chapel near SS. Quattro Coronati in Rome do not show any specific Roman features except perhaps a certain dryness, and a technical routine easily resorted to when creative powers cannot keep pace with the influx of numerous commissions. Rome had always been fertile soil for academicism characterized by a massive and spacious style; and in so far as this can be said of any medieval work of art, it applies to the sequence of the legendary scenes in the Sylvester Chapel. Their style is typical of the middle of the Duecento, and the date of execution is evidently closely related to the consecration of the chapel in 1246.[24] With dramatic vividness, the paintings tell the story of Constantine's dream of the appearance of the two apostles, and of St Sylvester, who receives the papal tiara from the emperor *(pl. 18)*. The basic Byzantine style is still evident everywhere, but is transformed, as in Tuscan painting of the same period, into something popular and Romanesque. The chromatic effect is determined by the richly applied chalk white, the contrasting brownish-red outlines and the predominant dull earthy tones. The barrel vaulting of the long room was apparently originally blue, covered with a pattern of stars, like the spectacular sky vaulting that appeared later at Assisi and eventually became a feature of most Trecento churches.

In the abbey of Grottaferrata in the Alban hills there are remains of paintings probably done soon after 1272.[25] The Romanesque formula and the bold emphasis on the outlines are no longer evident here. Moses, shrinking away from the snake, is modelled in large compact forms *(pl. 19a)*. His head, Byzantine in character, is naturalistic, and individual features such as the eyes are not exaggerated or enlarged in the medieval manner. The gestures are expressive, fluid and natural. Once again, the classic features of Byzantine art demonstrate their liberating and stabilizing power. It was only the acceptance of the neo-Hellenistic concept that provided Italy with the conditions for the growth of an independent realistic pictorial style.

From here it was a barely perceptible step to the art of Pietro Cavallini, and yet this was one of the decisive turning-points in the history of Western art. Cavallini's apostles in the *Last Judgment* in Santa Cecilia in Rome are seated in a row on wooden chairs, each completely isolated, and without any gesture to draw them together *(pl. 19c)*. They hold their respective attributes in different ways, and nearly all of them are looking in different directions. The regular arrangement of the figures was a Byzantine practice, and can also be seen in the *Last Judgment* in the Demetrios Cathedral at Vladimir;[26] but there a certain uniformity is preserved through the manner in which each apostle holds an open book in front of him, and their postures and the arrangement of their draperies are also roughly the same. Cavallini, however, varied the postures and draperies of the figures, and although the type of head is the same – straight, narrow nose, eyes closely set, small mouth – there is a rich variety of hair style, demeanour, and age. They look like seated marble statues, each individually designed, and accidentally placed next to one another. All they have in common is a sculptural compactness and the solid material from which they are made. The draperies, modelled with rich gradations from light to dark, are of the same tough, heavy material. The luminous, though not very intense, colours are subdued by the strong, almost tangible sculptural effect. What mattered to Cavallini was form, the individual figure, its volume and weight. Space exists only to the extent that it is created by the figures. The only thing that unites these painted statues to some degree is light: the apostles seated on the left are uniformly lit from the left, and those seated on the right are lit from the right.

The fire and noble spirituality of the *Vladimir Apostles,* which are here taken as typical of Byzantine art, have almost completely disappeared: Cavallini's apostles retain only the primitive power and sober solemnity. The heads of the younger apostles appear more animated than those of the older bearded figures. The new and individual spirit of Cavallini's painting is expressed most clearly in the figure of Christ in the *Last Judgment (pl. 19b)*, radiating infinite compassion. The large countenance has the exalted calm of the classical images of the gods. The gestures are simple (only the right hand stretched out to the blessed is completely preserved), and have acquired a new and profound meaning. Although the Byzantine model is closely followed in the facial types and attitudes – probably with the intention of faithful imitation – the completely different Western conception asserts itself plainly. Its roots lie in the local Roman tradition, in the paintings of the great basilicas of early Christian times.

Hitherto the gigantic pictorial sequences in San Paolo and Old St Peter's had influenced medieval art chiefly through their representational content. They served as a kind of monumental iconographic manual. Now they were once again to become a fruitful artistic source, for which we are fortunate to have documentary proof. Ghiberti records that Cavallini executed an extensive commission in San Paolo fuori le mura. His task was to restore the pictorial decoration of the basilica, originally done in the fifth century, and in his work he was careful to reproduce the iconography of the existing scenes. Though evidently damaged, most of the scenes were recognizable in their broad outlines. Cavallini overpainted them with new pictures (which is what the Middle Ages understood by restoration). Some of the early Christian compositions were retained in their original form, and remained until they were destroyed, together with Cavallini's work, in the fire of 1823. However, we still have a complete set of copies of these works commissioned by Cardinal Francesco Barberini in the seventeenth century,[27] which convey the content of the scenes, and also give an idea of their style. Fragmentary inscriptions, reproduced by the Baroque copyists, enable us to date Cavallini's activities in the nave of San Paolo between 1277 and 1290,[28] the years in which he evolved the style seen in Santa Cecilia. The copies clearly show that Cavallini's paintings in San Paolo differed from the fifth-century originals in the more slender proportion of his figures and the greater variety of architectural motifs, in part Gothic, that he introduced. Yet inevitably, the grand style and the figures of the early Christian compositions, full of classical recollections, exerted a profound influence on Cavallini's work. His later independent productions can only be understood in the light of the knowledge of early Christian art that he acquired during his work in San Paolo.

This applies both to the Santa Cecilia frescoes and to the mosaic cycle in Santa Maria in Trastevere, where Cavallini added six scenes from the life of Mary to the existing twelfth-century apse mosaics. The scenes were probably completed in 1291, but this date has not been authenticated.[29] Their classical mood, especially when compared with contemporary Roman mosaics, has always been noticed. It is particularly strong in the first scene, the *Birth of the Virgin (pl. 20a)*, which has the clarity of a classical relief. The activity of the midwives is tempered by tender human warmth and sympathy. The freedom of movement and the grouping reveal a mastery of composition – the result of long years of close contact with classical Christian art. The solemn monumental effect of the *Presentation in the Temple (pl. 20b)* depends on the rhythmic skill with which the figures and the architectural forms of the background are brought into harmony. Other scenes, especially the *Nativity of Christ* and the *Death of the Virgin,* still adhere closely to Byzantine iconography. Common to the entire series, however, is the sculptural conception of the figures, the clear distribution of light and shade in the scenes, which are nearly all lit from a single direction, and finally the economy of the means used to suggest space, far superior to the formal Romanesque manner. The two architectural pieces placed side by side to form the interior setting for the *Birth of the Virgin*, are symbolic rather than representational. The same applies to the building in front of which the Three Kings pay homage to Mary, although it shows a surprising understanding of perspective. Indeed many of the elements that were soon to be assimilated and given harmonious expression by a greater artist, Giotto, are already to be found in the work of Cavallini.

It seems that directly after the completion of these mosaics Cavallini began the decoration of Santa Cecilia, i. e., at the beginning of the 1290s.[30] In addition to the *Last Judgment*, remnants of scenes from the Old Testament are preserved on the south wall of the nave, and a fragment of an Annunciation scene on the north wall. As was customary, scenes from the New Testament were placed opposite scenes from the Old Testament. Between the windows there were also large figures of prophets standing beneath painted baldachins in pure Gothic form.[31] The new style from north of the Alps was thus familiar to Cavallini, and here too we can trace the sources of his acquaintanceship. In San Paolo, Cavallini had already worked side by side with Arnolfo di Cambio, the Florentine sculptor-architect, whose tabernacle in San Paolo, still extant, bears the date 1285. The association was renewed in Santa Cecilia. Cavallini's painted Gothic baldachins with their moulded gables correspond to Arnolfo's tabernacle, which stands in the choir and is dated 1293.

Later, Cavallini came into even closer contact with the Gothic, in Naples, where Gothic architecture of great monumentality developed under the rule of the Anjou family. The convent church of Santa Maria Donnaregina, one of their principal enterprises, was decorated with frescoes by pupils of Cavallini, presumably under his direction. Stylistically this large and important work, abounding in narrative detail, belongs to a much later stage of development than his surviving works in Rome. The new concept of painting developed by Giotto already shows its influence here, though it is not yet fully assimilated. The records mention Cavallini in Naples in 1308, but the paintings in Donnaregina were probably produced only around 1320.[32]

To conclude our account of this creative period, which prepared the way for the frescoes at Assisi and the advent of Giotto, we must turn again to Rome. There are two works to be considered: the mosaic apse decorations

IV GIOTTO, *Esau and Isaac*
Assisi, San Francesco

in the Lateran Basilica and in Santa Maria Maggiore.[33] Both these works, among the most magnificent mosaics of all time, were commissioned by Nicholas IV, the same pope who was so active in promoting the continuation of the work in San Francesco. They were done by Jacopo Torriti, and can be dated between 1288 and 1292 by reference to Pope Nicholas' reign. Torriti's style is still closer to the Byzantine tradition than Cavallini's. However, in Torriti's work, especially in the scenes from the life of Mary in the apse of Santa Maria Maggiore, we find the same classical Roman clarity and freshness already noticed in the Vault of the Saints in Assisi. As principal motif for the Santa Maria Maggiore mosaics, Torriti took the *Coronation of the Virgin* (*pl. 21a*), a Western type of composition developed in France.[34] Thus a Gothic element was introduced into the work, which is otherwise based on early Christian and Byzantine tradition. The Gothic influence also becomes noticeable in the style of the figures in the work of Filippo Rusuti, a pupil of Torriti, who decorated the façade of Santa Maria Maggiore with mosaics before 1308.[35]

The transept of Santa Maria Maggiore was also decorated with wall-paintings under the patronage of Nicholas IV, and impressive remnants are still preserved. Large-scale spiral scroll-work and a huge painted console framing fill the upper zone and support a frieze with medallions containing over life-size busts of prophets.[36] The figures are rock-like, as though chiselled in stone, and their expressions are equally hard (*pl. 21b*). The wide-open eyes have a piercing, almost menacing, look. The detail of the faces, ears, hair, beards, is defined in a severe, brittle style, and the drapery folds are sharp as crystal.

These busts of prophets were done by a painter of the Cavallini school, and although they have been attributed to the young Giotto, it hardly seems likely that they are the work of a young man.[37] In the two Isaac scenes at Assisi and in the Crucifix of Santa Maria Novella, where Giotto's style can be detected for the first time with some certainty, everything is livelier, richer, and more varied. But here, even in the characteristic details which identify a painter, there is little to suggest that the prophets are by the hand of Giotto. Nevertheless there appears to be a close connection between the paintings in Santa Maria Maggiore and certain parts of the nave decoration at Assisi. The anonymous Roman painter, whom we may call the Master of the Prophet Busts, was perhaps one of the artists whom Giotto entrusted with the execution of the Vault of the Doctors and the St Francis legend. But this anticipates a train of thought that must be developed in the following chapter on the Assisi frescoes.

6 Giotto: the early years

The great picture cycle in the nave of San Francesco at Assisi is the last of the large pictorial series that were derived from models in the basilicas of San Paolo and Old St Peter's in Rome. The mere fact of its survival in its present state of preservation makes this cycle unique today, but even at the time when it was painted the work was in a sense unique: it placed the iconographic scheme of Old and New Testament scenes in their traditional positions opposite one another, but in addition there was the decoration of the vaults, which had no parallel in the Roman basilicas with their open rafters; and furthermore the single-aisled church provided space for a third row of pictures in the lower zone, which in other churches was interrupted by columns or arcades. This was a suitable place to illustrate the life of St Francis, the patron saint of the church. Extending along the walls of the nave there are twenty-eight scenes from the St Francis legend, beginning and ending at the crossing *(pls 47a, 47b, 56–59, V, VI)*. The pictures are smaller in scale than the Biblical representations in the zone above, but still almost life-size. They confront the spectator directly and fascinate the most casual visitor with their intensity and forthright popular style. But even more powerful than the miraculous and moving events of the story are the lofty monumentality and austere grandeur of gesture and composition. Everything is told with simple directness. Bright and lively colours are used wherever suitable, for it needed vivid tones to prevent the deep blue of the background, now for the most part lost, from becoming the dominant note. One iconographic element, however, restrained this zeal for colour: the grey and brown cowls of the Franciscans who are prominent figures in almost all the scenes. Consequently the chromatic effect is mainly sober and earthy. The solemn splendour which Cimabue's paintings in the choir must have had is absent, partly because it is inappropriate to the subject, but also for artistic reasons. The scenes are illuminated with abstract clarity, not by a mysterious unnatural light.[1]

The narrative purports to be a faithful historical record, and to tell not a legendary tale but the simple truth. The life of St Francis is told as part of the history of Christendom, for nothing less than this is the subject of the enormous decorative scheme of the nave of the Upper Church. There can be no doubt that iconographically it was conceived from the start according to a uniform plan, although it is apparent at first glance that this uniformity is not reflected in the artistic character of the work. The St Francis legend is stylistically more advanced than the decoration in the upper zones of the nave, and has all the appearance of having been done by a younger generation. The Old Testament scenes nearest the crossing seem, in comparison, particularly archaic. Discrepancies of this kind were unavoidable in an undertaking of such vast size. Several groups of artists of different schools seem to have worked here successively.[2] Intermittent interruptions in activity must also have occurred, possibly because of shortage of means, but perhaps also because the artists summoned from Rome had other commitments there.[3] Only the final scenes of the upper zone, those nearest the entrance wall, reveal a stricter discipline. The collective method of production was abandoned here and replaced by the superior artistic ability of a single individual. This individual, who created a new conception of artistic responsibility, and at the time a new style, could only have been Giotto.

So far historians have not been able to agree on the nature and scale of Giotto's intervention. The only fact that is almost beyond dispute is that he was active in Assisi. No definitive documentary evidence exists, but one contemporary source, the *Chronicle* of Riccobaldo da Ferrara, mentions explicitly that Giotto worked in the Franciscan church at Assisi.[5] Attempts have been made to connect this reference with the Giottesque paintings in the Lower Church. However, these were all workshop productions, and for the most part executed later than Riccobaldo's record. The chronicler's information must therefore refer to the Upper Church only, and for a long time the St Francis legend alone was associated with Giotto. Some historians accepted his authorship without reservation, while others disputed it hotly.

This dispute reflected two basically different approaches to the whole problem of Giotto. The one, disposed to follow tradition and the evidence of the records, accepted the St Francis cycle as an early work of Giotto, done around 1300. The other, adopting a severely critical attitude, emphasized the wide stylistic disparity between the St Francis scenes and the grand austere style of the mature master, and regarded these paintings as the work of a follower of Giotto, or even of a local Umbrian school.[6] Unfortunately this valid criticism led to a misinterpretation of historical events, in which admiration for Giotto's mature art prevented a proper understanding of his early development. For a long time these two irreconcilable views existed side by side. The dispute about the St Francis cycle seemed to have been reduced to the level of a professional controversy in which the arguments had been exhausted. In the absence of proof, prejudice prevailed, and the few historians who from an early stage had taken a less doctrinaire and more synoptic view of the problem were ignored.[7]

The Giotto exhibition in 1937 at last initiated a re-appraisal. The impetus did not come from the Assisi frescoes, but from a panel painting, the *Crucifix* in Santa Maria Novella *(pls 60, 61)*.[8] This is a major work of Giotto's, but although known for a long time, it had attracted little attention until then. It had always hung on the entrance wall of the church, but rather high up and inadequately lit, so that it shared the fate of all the early works of the master: the narrow conception of his style was blind to anything that did not conform to the accepted ideal. Even a relatively early documentary authentication, going back as far as 1312, was disregarded, not through ignorance or carelessness, but simply because the information did not seem to tally with the current conception of Giotto. One may, therefore, speak of a real rediscovery, which finally put this great Crucifix in its rightful place in the history of Florentine painting and in Giotto's own development. On the basis of analogous works, and of what appear to be replicas, a date in the last decade of the Duecento has been established.[9]

This is the style of Giotto at the age of about twenty-five, when his youthful powers were at their height.[10] The massive figure hangs heavily on the cross, its chest stretched, the abdomen pressed forward, the broad hips somewhat uncertainly foreshortened. It is far removed from the slender formalized figure drooping weightlessly that we encountered in Cimabue's mature work, the Crucifix from Santa Croce. There is pathos and deep emotion in Cimabue's figure, but it was Giotto who first depicted with unflinching realism the humanity of Christ and the agony of the martyred body. However, its new, harsh realism is not the main substance of this impressive work. The noble features of the deeply bowed head are relaxed and ennobled after the long struggle. The hands with their slender, shapely fingers, open like wings. The tension of the skin, the contour of the muscles and the bones beneath are modelled with great delicacy and deep interest in the realities of suffering and death. The type of the crucified figure, with bent knees and feet pierced by a single nail, is Gothic, and here makes its first appearance in Italian painting.[11] Mary and St John on the side panels are not racked with pain, as in Cimabue's Crucifix, but contemplate Christ with noble composure. Giotto's leaning towards realism is kept in check by his firm emotional control and his unerring and confident sense of style.

This work, which has come back into our purview unexpectedly, also throws an unexpected new light on the monumental cycle at Assisi. The confusion of styles in the St Francis sequence now begins to take on some order, and a pattern of consistent development emerges. Furthermore, Giotto's own part can be more clearly defined. Unless all the indications are misleading, his constructive mind and personal style can already be discerned in the Old Testament scenes in the upper zone of the north wall.

It has always been observed that the two Isaac scenes, *Jacob's Deception* and *Esau and Isaac (pls 54, 55, IV)*, are far superior in artistic quality to the other scenes. Their clear spatial structure, narrative power and rich warm colour have always attracted attention. For a long time they were thought to be the work of a 'great unknown', the so-called Isaac Master.[12] Had such a master indeed existed, he, and not Giotto, would have been the founder of modern painting; here for the first time are present all the basic elements that constitute the new conception of a 'picture' as formulated by Giotto: the clearly defined pictorial stage, the box-like architecture – the interior and exterior of which are shown with equal clarity – the composition subjugated to the strict rule of the verticals and horizontals, the disposition of the picture surface with reference to the edges of the frame, and finally the sculptural compactness of the figures, full of a new vitality. Only by satisfying these formal requirements could the calm and moving drama, which makes the two Isaac scenes so memorable, be brought to life. The blind, groping Isaac in the second picture, which is the better preserved of the two, has no precedent in iconographic tradition. His sightless eyes face the frank gaze of Esau, who approaches without yet suspecting that he has been cheated of his father's blessing. The young woman accompanying him looks on apprehensively.[13] In the first scene the approach to Isaac is more guarded: Jacob, his hands and neck covered with the hide of the slaughtered kid, stands at the foot of the bed, with the side nearest his father in shadow. Isaac has grasped his son's hand, but Jacob remains still as a statue. Between the two stands Rebecca, the instigator of the plot, whose son is obedient only to her will. The halo which distinguishes Jacob from Esau signifies that he has received the blessing. The story is told with the greatest economy of means, but the monumentality of the forms gives weight even to this spare narrative, and the total effect is of a tense and accomplished drama.

Further examination of the Isaac scenes strengthens the conviction that the style, the personal touch, cannot be attributed to anyone but Giotto. The *Santa Maria Novella Crucifix* provides a useful comparison. The head of Christ, in spite of its entirely different expression, is closely related to Esau's head *(pls 55, 61)*; one need only visualize it upright and with eyes open. The forms have the same generous structure, and although there may be differences in

67

detail, the nose, mouth, chin, and cheeks are modelled with the same delicacy and economy. The half-length figures of Mary and St John on the side panels of the Crucifix support the comparison. Their restrained, silent sorrow has the same emotional quality as the wordless and almost gestureless drama of the Isaac scenes.

From these observations we can establish the extent of Giotto's participation in the decoration of the nave at Assisi. He seems to have appeared there for the first time when he executed the two Isaac scenes at the beginning of the 1290s. Still relatively young, and presumably determined to prove his ability, he painted them with his own hand, and his artistic individuality clearly sets him apart from the crowd of anonymous painters, particularly if one compares the wall-paintings with the Crucifix, which was probably done shortly after the Isaac scenes. Giotto, therefore, returned once more to Florence before continuing his work at Assisi. And at an earlier date he must have been in Rome. Familiarity with Cavallini's style, with the iconography of the early Christian paintings in San Paolo and with Christian and pre-Christian classical art, are all essential to the Isaac scenes. Giotto must have spent some time in close contact with Cavallini.[14] It can be assumed that from early times he travelled freely, and was almost as much at home in Rome as in Florence.

The two Isaac scenes are in the bay next but one to the entrance wall in the Upper Church. It would appear that the painting of the upper zone proceeded steadily in that direction, which was the practical way of working. It is therefore not surprising that Giottesque ideas, later to be taken up again in the Arena Chapel, also appear in the last bays and on the entrance wall.[15] Comparison with the *Santa Maria Novella Crucifix* suggests that part of these scenes are also in Giotto's personal style, particularly the *Lamentation of Christ,* and the two Joseph scenes on the opposite wall.[16]

Shortly afterwards Giotto seems to have been given a leading position at Assisi. This, as Vasari reports, might well have been at the time when Giovanni da Muro held the office of minister-general of the Order, between 1296 and 1304.[17] An entirely new kind of relationship between spatial depth and pictorial surface is apparent in the Doctors' Vault. The richly articulated thrones and desks of the Church Fathers, decorated in Roman style, and the niche-like cabinets of their assistants, are placed in the vault in careful, though still empirical, perspective. The marked foreshortening makes the centre of the church floor below the vault the only natural and proper viewpoint. The stress on the horizontals at the base of the thrones gives the vaulting above the ribs a unified dome-like shape. Neither Cimabue, in the vault above the

crossing, nor the Master of the Saints' Vault attempted anything comparable.
This new sense of space in itself is indicative of Giotto. The central viewpoint,
the planned arrangements of the profusion of detail are Giotto's, and so is
the accuracy with which the details, the elaborate marble and wooden structures, are rendered. The types of the figures, clearly revealing Roman training,
are accommodated to this development. They still have an echo of the style
of the Isaac scenes, but now everything has become harder and colder. The
same is true of the style of the draperies and of the colours, in which sharp
chalky tones now predominate.

This hardness and austerity closely associates the Doctors' Vault with the
St Francis legend. Apart from the theme and scale – the vault representations
are much larger – there are few differences between the two that extend
beyond the usual variations in execution occurring in any particular workshop.
It would seem that the same group of workmen did the St Francis legend
directly after the vault,[18] and the connections just demonstrated make it
plausible that Giotto was the leading figure in this operation. It appears,
however, that from then on he entrusted the execution of his designs largely
to assistants. Although the compositions as a whole, or at least most of the
scenes from the *Giving of the Cloak* to the nineteenth scene, the *Stigmatization*,
bear the mark of his genius, some of the detail does not. His style evidently
went through a hardening phase at this time, possibly as a result of renewed
contact with Roman painting. But the connection with the two Isaac scenes
is still plain. The bearded heads of the Church Fathers are reminiscent of the
patriarchial head of Isaac, though lacking its profound inspiration. The youthful St Francis in some of the scenes recalls the sons of Isaac, but the fire, the
youthful energy and alertness, are missing. The sculptural severity of the
forms is reduced to schematic roundness and smoothness. The archaic element
is predominant, and this also applies to the figures, which are possibly by
Giotto's own hand. The group of the pope with members of the Curia in
the *Confirmation of the Rule of the Order (pl. 57)* is a characteristic example.
The standard pattern is broken in only a few places, as for instance in the
expressive heads of the outraged father and his companions in the scene of
St Francis Renouncing his Family (pls 58, V). But these are exceptions. Despite
the magnetism of the St Francis legend as a whole, and the skill of many of
its compositions, the individual parts remain strangely hard and cold, and the
warmth and forcefulness of the narrative are not reflected in the painting itself. The intimate mood of the legend, which from the start was at odds with
the characteristic effort to achieve monumentality, has been entirely lost in
the execution of the pictures.

It would thus seem likely that the famous cycle is Giotto's work only in the very limited sense that it is an interpretation of his designs by inadequate assistants. This would explain why the work has been the subject of such dispute and inconsistent assessments among art historians.

The solution to the problem lies in the distinction between design and execution, a distinction that is essential for a just assessment of the artistic value of the St Francis cycle. Modern concepts of 'originality' and 'authorship' must be discarded. The cooperative system of work that we observed in the upper zone and vaults of San Francesco should put us on our guard against applying present-day criteria to Giotto's methods and creations. Even techniques of artistic production have a history of their own, and are as much an expression of a general intellectual attitude as a style in the familiar narrower sense. Giotto's contribution to this field was no less epoch-making than his achievement in stylistic creation. To understand this side of his historical importance it is necessary to look again at the technical conditions affecting his work.

The duality of design and execution is technically as old as the art of painting itself. In all the archaic periods, in Egypt, in Greece, and in medieval Europe, it was customary to draw directly on the picture medium itself, wall or panel, and then cover the drawing with layers of paint. The drawing, which also served as the design, was the concern of the master. As a rule the execution of the painting – depending on the scale and importance of the commission – was the task of his assistants. The painters in the rocky monasteries on Mount Athos, trained in the Byzantine tradition, still followed this practice in the nineteenth century.[19] In this kind of artistic approach the drawing is merely an expedient, a preliminary stage in the execution of the work.

From the technical evidence in their paintings, it can be inferred that Giotto and his contemporaries were the first post-classical artists to abandon this archaic practice. They treated the design of monumental painting as an independent operation to be executed with care and accuracy. The model for this was the mosaic technique, in which it was essential to begin with a full-scale drawing of the composition on the wall surface. The drawing was done with a brush on the rough initial layer of mortar, which was then covered in sections with finer mortar into which coloured stones and pieces of glass

V GIOTTO, *St Francis Renouncing His Family*
Assisi, San Francesco

were pressed. In the same way the designs for wall-paintings were now sketched in full size on the wall, as a rule in charcoal. When the first drawing was completed, it was repeated with the brush, usually in a reddish tone. The term *sinopia* (red earth), which has recently come into common use, derives from this.[20] Such monumental drawings are found underneath almost all Trecento frescoes, and come to light wherever the top layer has peeled off or been removed.[21] The most striking example of this is in the Campo Santo in Pisa, which was heavily damaged in the Second World War. The frescoes had to be detached; as a result, the full-scale drawings – of amazing quantity and quality – became visible *(pl. 100b)*.[22] The execution of the painting would then continue, as in mosaic, on fresh plaster applied in sections from day to day, the so-called *giornata* (day's work). Design and painting were thus no longer merged, but formed two basically separate operations, distinguished further in the materials of the two layers of plaster, coarse and fine, applied one on top of the other.[23] This technique provided the conditions for the development of the classical *buon fresco* of the Renaissance with its glossy surface and durable colours.

Technically, the painters of the Middle Ages had been facing an insoluble dilemma. As the system of *giornata* was unknown, work on the fresh, fast-drying plaster had to be carried out with great speed. A compromise was to combine two modes of operation. Only the design and the first layer were done in fresco. After the ground had dried the painting was done in distemper, casein, or tempera. This produced only a superficial binding of the colours. There was thus a choice between a durable but hasty execution under constant pressure, the fresco, and a more careful but less permanent method.

It was here that the innovation introduced towards the end of the thirteenth century became a valuable aid and was evidently already put to systematic use by Giotto in the St Francis legend at Assisi. The division of the picture surface into smaller sections enabled all the parts to be executed carefully, almost entirely in fresco. Giotto used the tempera technique only for specific colours, such as blue,[24] and for ornaments and the like. His technique is on the whole much closer to that of the Middle Ages than to the fully developed fresco technique of the Renaissance. He was certainly not acquainted with mechanical devices for transferring the design to the top layer, that is to say, with the traced drawing and the cartoon. The freshly applied sections of plaster always covered the drawing just at the places where it was to be painted. Giotto, and all the other Trecento artists, relied, in the execution of each particular 'day's work', on memory and on their highly developed formal training. This is why Giotto's newly created style quickly lapsed into a formula.

It was doubtless Giotto's intention from the start to create manageable formulas, because only in this way could he train his numerous assistants in a uniform style. At the time of the execution of the St Francis legend the training of his assistants, that is to say, the formation of the Giotto workshop, was just beginning – and this is the explanation of the frequent discrepancy between the master's intentions and the inadequacy and schematism of the execution.

Naturally the painting had to be briefly sketched again with the brush on the top layer as well, and this was done free-hand, usually in fine, confident lines. Although the design on the rough mortar of the wall had, through Giotto's innovation, become of major importance, it served only to determine the general disposition and arrangement of the picture. The monumental drawing, completely subjected to the requirements of the given space, harmonized the painting and the architecture in the most natural way. It was only in the course of the fifteenth century that such full-sized designs on the wall surface were replaced by small-scale drawings in paper, which were then transferred to the wall through the medium of cartoons. The process of design was detached from the actual painting, and removed to the abstract sphere of the 'atelier', and with this the original unity of wall-paintings and architecture, which gave such painting its natural monumentality, was irrevocably lost.

Giotto's part in this development can be fairly accurately seen in the paintings in the nave of San Francesco. He was not the first to divide the wall surfaces into separate sections. This had always been done when the height of the area to be painted exceeded the reach of the painter standing on the scaffolding. We can see that the apse of Sant'Angelo in Formis *(pl. I)* is divided into two horizontal zones, each approximately the height of a man. The huge figure of Christ must have been drawn, in broad outline at least, on the surface beneath the painted layer.[25] The large Old Testament scenes at Assisi were done in exactly the same way: there is a distinct dividing line passing through the middle of the figure of Abraham in the *Sacrifice of Isaac.* Twice life-size, this figure had to be painted in two sections.[26] In the two Isaac scenes these sections are already considerably smaller. The divisions, coinciding as a rule with the contours of the figures, though cutting across them occasionally, are frequently visible. Each picture thus consists of several *giornate,* and must have been first designed on the wall in its entirety. The next stage in the development can be observed in the Lamentation scene. Once more the sections become smaller in size and the seams between them finer and more precise. The painter evidently tried to conceal the seams between the separate *giornate.* Cavallini's work is at about the same stage in this

74

technique, which may possibly have been originated by him. He was, after all, well acquainted with the mosaic technique, which served as model for the *giornata* system.[27]

In the St Francis legend the seams between the plaster sections are handled with remarkable skill, unsurpassed in later times. Nevertheless the divisions are visible in many places even to the naked eye, particularly in the *Sermon to the Birds (pl. 56)*. By detailed examination it has lately become possible to determine with great accuracy the number of *giornate,* their outlines and sequence.[28] Nothing of the underlying monumental drawing can now be seen in any of these pictures, but the brush sketches on the fine plaster have become visible in several places.[29] These were painted in light ochre colours and not in the usual reddish brown.[30] Their style is noticeably bolder and more sweeping than the meticulous manner of painting above.

In the frescoes in the Arena Chapel in Padua, Giotto's major work, the system evolved at Assisi became an established practice. Each picture surface consists of twelve to fifteen *giornate.* In some scenes, for example the *Crucifixion,* the divisions are plainly visible. Nevertheless, here too the seams are carefully handled so that the surface appears completely uniform.[31] In later years Giotto adopted an entirely different technique. In the Peruzzi Chapel in Florence the division into *giornate* is abandoned, and the painting is done almost exclusively *a secco,* i. e., on dry plaster.[32] It is not known whether this was an isolated experiment or a fundamental departure from the method developed at Assisi and Padua. On the other hand it is certain that Giotto's pupils and followers generally adhered to the *giornata* division. This postulates the existence of a *sinopia,* which was also used by Simone Martini, whose monumental drawings, of the highest quality, have been found in Assisi and Avignon *(pls 82c, 82d)*. In both cases these drawings are patently the decisive phases in the process of design.[33]

We have gone into these technical details because Giotto's art cannot be understood without them. However, it is not technique that controls artistic development, but rather the contrary: a new kind of artistic approach always produces new techniques. Especially in the Middle Ages, the greatest artists were always also the most accomplished craftsmen. With Giotto in particular, the significance of the technical development and its dependence on the great stylistic change that was taking place appear clearly.

Giotto was a plain craftsman, who in time rose to become a director of great enterprises. He started with panel-painting, which flourished in thirteenth-century Tuscany. On the other hand there was no substantial tradition of monumental painting in Florence in the last quarter of the Duecento.[34]

For the mosaic decoration of the Baptistry, artists trained in the Byzantine style were called in, possibly from Venice. Cimabue seems to have first entered the field of great monumental art in Rome, and this is also true of Giotto. There Giotto found masters experienced in wall-painting and mosaics, and he soon rose from the position of trainee and assistant to that of a recognized leader. The monumentality of his mature style was no longer dependent on external circumstances. His Padua frescoes are surprisingly small in their overall measurements: the figures are barely half life-size. It is by virtue of their intellectual artistic principle, the *disegno,* that they became the model for the great Italian fresco art of the following centuries.

Disegno, drawing, is the central concept of Florentine art theory, familiar to us through numerous contemporary writings throughout the whole period of the Renaissance. It means design, aim, idea, that which constitutes the intellectual core of a work of art; and the word is still commonly used in Italian today in this wider sense. The Florentine theorists also understood the term in this way, but at the same time they remained conscious of its narrower meaning. *Disegno,* in these two senses, the concrete and the ideal, was the distinctive feature of Florentine art at all times. A figure by Donatello, a façade by Brunelleschi or Alberti, is characterized by *disegno,* meaning that in this lies its highest artistic merit. However, nowhere is the power of *disegno* so striking as in a Giotto composition.

It may seem idle to consider Giotto as a draughtsman seeing that not a single drawing by his hand has been preserved. All we have are a few copies of frescoes of the Giotto school at Assisi and of Giotto's large mosaic in Rome, the *Navicella,* and nearly all these Trecento drawings are recognizable at a glance as copies.[35] They are what we should call reproductions. Work that is nowadays done by means of duplicating techniques was then done by hand. The most common type of drawing in the Middle Ages was the *exemplum,* the sample drawing, which was used to convey the idea of a picture or a particular motif. Besides these, there were freer experimental sketches by the miniaturists in the margins of pages in books or on blank sheets. However, these were usually playful attempts and scribbles; only rarely do they look like serious designs.[36]

It was not until the Trecento, and at first only as an exception, that a new type of drawing appeared: drawings submitted to the patron before the start of work. They also served as the basis of the contract signed with the painter. Such drawings were prepared especially in cases where the required subject had no iconographic precedent or traditional model. As a rule, in the type of compositions that followed the traditional Christian iconography, the painter dispensed with the preliminary drawing. It was not until the fifteenth century that artists started to leave us large numbers of original drawings, sketches, designs, and studies of models.[37]

Our lack of real drawings from the Middle Ages is not accidental. It would be strange if they had all been lost. The truth is that they simply did not exist: drawing as we know it is a creation of the Renaissance. The Trecento was a transitional period, and the real advance to modern drawing practice came only in the fifteenth century.

And yet Giotto was a great draughtsman. Each of his pictures, and each single figure, demonstrates this. His medium was the monumental drawing. To Giotto and his contemporaries the design, meaning the pictorial idea both in its iconographic and its artistic sense, was still bound to the actual size and conditions of the wall and the room. To Giotto it would have seemed quite futile to anticipate in a small-scale drawing the arrangement of a composition and the distribution of the masses. He had no need of such an abstraction, which would merely have added to his difficulties. In this respect his methods were still medieval and archaic. The only new element, of profound importance for the future, was his systematic separation of the operations of design and execution. Both could now be carried out without haste. Design was given more weight, and the painstaking execution, already apparent in the St Francis cycle and characteristic of all Trecento painting, became possible because of it. This was much more than a technical achievement. It facilitated composition, and made a new level of accuracy and refinement of representation accessible to monumental wall painters. Developed by Giotto into a complete system of work it opened rich possibilities, and without it the realistic delineation, first signalized in the Doctors' Vault, could not have been achieved.

In the light of this, the St Francis legend can now also be considered a creation of Giotto's. By the standards of his time it was fully a work of the master. The improved procedures and the new systematic organization of the workshop enabled him to realize his artistic intentions despite the individual differences of the assistants he had to engage. Giotto's composition, scenic structure, and the tone of his narrative were essentially preserved. Only the depth of meaning and crystalline transparency of the slightly later Padua frescoes could not yet be achieved. The crowd of assistants was too varied, the Giotto school still at its formative stage. Nevertheless, the establishment of a common style among his collaborators had progressed so far that any attempt to separate the St Francis legend into the work of 'masters' and 'hands' is bound to fail.[38]

Only the first and the last three scenes are so different from the rest that they can be attributed with some certainty to another recognizable painter, the St Cecilia Master.[39] He probably took his compositions from designs by Giotto, but modified them, elongating the proportions and introducing new details.[40]

The remaining scenes exhibit to some extent the same principles of composition that appear soon afterwards in Padua, such as the use of architectural elements to augment figure groups, as in *St Francis Renouncing his Family* *(pl. V)*, and the use of landscape to dramatize events, as in the *Miracle of the Spring*, where the great bright slope of rock carries the saint's prayer upwards in a manner that is unmistakably Giottesque. The landscapes in the *Flight into Egypt* and the *Lamentation,* in Padua, are similarly used to heighten the action. Other compositions, especially the crowd scenes towards the end of the cycle, appear to go further in attempting such effects than anything Giotto produced in Padua, but these can be regarded as bold experiments in an unknown field and were not pursued further by the mature master. The whole course of his development, now more clearly apparent than in the past, was towards an increasing economy of means and a conscious restraint and standardization. In this Giotto followed the same path as the masters of classical Greece and the High Renaissance. Every great style comes to fruition within its own self-imposed bounds.

The long disputed question of the date of the St Francis legend can therefore be taken as resolved. There is no longer any reason to doubt that Giotto began the designs for most of the scenes shortly after the accession of Giovanni da Muro to office, in 1296.[41] How long it took to complete the work is difficult to say: probably not much beyond 1300.

Giotto himself does not seem to have waited for the completion of the work. In 1300 at the latest, Pope Boniface VIII must have called him to Rome to paint the frescoes in the newly built Benediction Loggia in the Lateran. Only one badly damaged fragment, showing the pope with two companions blessing the populace, has been preserved.[42] The style of the fragment, now kept inside the Lateran basilica, is almost identical with that of the St Francis legend. Giotto evidently brought some of his assistants from Assisi to Rome, and here, too, he relied to a great extent on their work, even in the principal figures.

One panel-painting, the *Enthroned Madonna* of San Giorgio alla Costa in Florence, still belongs to Giotto's early period *(pls 62b, 64).*[43] It can probably be dated shortly before the beginning of the work in the St Francis legend and is of special interest because it is a preliminary version of the mature

VI GIOTTO,
*The Demons are Driven
from Arezzo* (detail)
Assisi, San Francesco

Ognissanti Madonna. Unfortunately only a fragment remains of the panel which was originally about six feet high. Wide strips on both sides and at the bottom have been sawn off, and the painting is extremely worn. However, the former spaciousness of the composition and the clear bright colours can be imagined, and the elegant throne in Arnolfo's Gothic manner can be approximately reconstructed.[44] The cloth hanging over the back of the throne is similar in pattern to materials that often appear in the Assisi frescoes. The charm of the heavily mutilated picture lies in the style of the Madonna and of the Child. Massive and yet delicate, the treatment of the Madonna is the first indication of a new realism, a new conception of conscious and refined monumentality. In particular, the solemn Christ Child with His royal dignity is indicative of Giotto's mature style, a preparation for the severity of the Child in the *Ognissanti Madonna.* The latter work can only be fully appreciated by reference to such earlier stages of development.

The obvious stylistic differentiation between the two Madonna panels corresponds to a time interval of more than ten years. But the road that Giotto travelled during this period is still unknown. He can be traced until 1300, when, having left Assisi, he designed the frescoes for the Benediction Loggia of the Lateran. Between this point and his activity in Padua, begun not later than 1305, there is a gap that for the time being can be filled only by supposition. Those first five years of the new century, the period between Assisi and Padua, saw the final consolidation of his style as manifested in the Arena frescoes.

The works done at this crucial time presumably also include the five-panelled retable with half-length figures under Gothic arcades, which originally came from the high altar of the Badia in Florence.[45] The central panel of the Madonna and Child is still reminiscent of the Madonna, also half-length, above the portal of the entrance wall at Assisi *(pl. 62a)*; but whereas here the round surface is organized strictly in verticals and horizontals, in the Badia retable steeply ascending diagonals are predominant, and relate the contours of the figures to the crowning gable. The effect is one of great monumentality; the strong sense of space conveyed by the figures is counteracted by the coloured inscription bands on the gold ground. The relationship of the figures to the ground and to the architectural elements of the frame, though not free from tension, is handled with confidence and a delicate sense of balance.

There is a similar subtle relationship between figure and surface in the Crucifix in San Francesco at Rimini, unfortunately in a fragmentary state of preservation.[46] The close connection of this work with the Badia altar is particularly noticeable in the Christ in Benediction on the newly discovered crowning piece on top of the cross.[47] If this connection with the Badia altar is accepted, the *Rimini Crucifix* must also belong to the pre-Padua period.[48]

The *Chronicle* of Riccobaldo records that Giotto was active in Rimini, working, as in Assisi, for the Franciscans.[49] On the other hand, there is no specific documentary reference to any particular work by Giotto in Rimini, or to this Crucifix. Its attribution to Giotto can be based only on stylistic grounds, and for this reason the question of dating is of crucial importance.[50] Riminese painting, on which Giotto's activity left a deep mark, is of some assistance. It has long been observed that Giotto's pre-Padua style produced a school in Rimini, but the explanation of this was sought in the presence at Assisi of Rimini painters. Recently Italian historians, rightly in our opinion, have reached the more likely conclusion that Giotto himself worked in Rimini before he went to Padua, between 1300 and 1305.[51] This would explain more clearly the course of his own development as well as the emergence of the Rimini school, to which we shall return later.[52] The *San Francesco Crucifix* conveys an idea of Giotto's style at the time when he produced the frescoes in Rimini that no longer exist.

7 Giotto and his pupils

Any attempt to assess Giotto's art as a whole must start with the fresco cycle in the Arena Chapel in Padua *(pls 66a, 66b, VII, VIII)*. It is pure chance that of the numerous monumental cycles that Giotto produced this particular one should have survived with hardly any damage.[1] There is a constant temptation to regard the little that has been preserved as the entire œuvre, or at least as its most important and characteristic part. We tend to forget that only a small fragment of Giotto's work, and indeed of all the painting of that time, is now extant. Many other works, both secular and ecclesiastical, were produced before and after those that happen to have survived.[2] Nevertheless we are justified in regarding the Padua cycle as a major work of the master done at the height of his powers, when he could turn to advantage the varied experience of his early years. In these frescoes his fully mature, classic style was formulated for the first time, and it remained the authoritative model for most of his pupils. The canon of form of the Padua frescoes became the storehouse of inspiration for the Giotto school, and to some extent all Trecento painting. Giotto himself went far beyond his Padua achievements, but very few of his pupils were able to follow his further development.

The modest, single-aisled building that houses this major work was founded in 1303 and consecrated as early as 1305. It is not recorded whether the frescoes were also completed by that date.[3] However, there is no practical reason why the work should have taken more than a year or two, for the workshop team which Giotto brought with him to Padua was now fully trained in his methods, and served as a perfect tool in his hand. Giotto must have designed most of the scenes and also executed the essential parts himself. This was possible only on the basis of a calculated division of labour that entrusted all the parts of secondary importance to assistants. Presumably all ancillary work – architectural motifs, ornaments, plants and flowers, landscapes – was done by particular, specialized members of the workshop, as was all preparatory work of a purely technical kind. This explains how a commission of this size could be completed so quickly. Assistants probably also executed many of the figures and even complete scenes, but they were so well trained that their work can hardly be distinguished from that of the master.

The only argument for a longer duration of the work depends on the considerable disparity of conception and handling between the three rows of pictures,[4] which indicates a remarkable stylistic development during the execution of the whole cycle. The structure of the scenes in the top row is more economic, and the expression of the figures more restrained. This may have been an intentional archaicism on the part of Giotto, a kind of abandonment of the experiments he had attempted but not yet fully solved in the St Francis legend. In the middle and lower zones the scenes are widened, and at the same time more densely filled. Perspective is used with greater confidence in the organization of the space; the figures become more solid, and the colours more vigorous and intense. But it is only in the last scenes of Christ's Passion, and especially in the Crucifixion and the Lamentation, that Giotto's style achieves its maturity, a complete harmony of monumental form and dramatic expression, of composition and intellectual content. However, firm conclusions about the duration of the work cannot be drawn from this. A master of Giotto's stature develops with each work, and his capacity for development cannot be measured in terms of time. We shall have to be content with the assumption that the Padua frescoes were painted around 1305.

The chapel, clearly designed from the start to include the paintings, was dedicated to the Virgin Mary. The story therefore begins in the upper zone with the *Expulsion of Joachim* and his *Encounter with Anna at the Golden Gate,* and continues with the life of Mary. The *Dispatch of the Archangel Gabriel,* who passes on to Mary the message of the Annunciation, is depicted on the triumphal arch. The middle and lower zones of the long walls give a detailed account of the life and Passion of Christ. The entrance wall in the west is devoted to the traditional *Last Judgment,* covering the whole area. Along the base, ornamental paintings done with remarkable skill show allegorical figures of the Virtues and Vices between painted marble panels, the first *grisailles* in Western painting. This, and the richly painted frames, serves to harmonize the pictures with the architecture. The separate scenes, thirty-six in all, are united according to a strict set of rules into an organic whole. This articulation also contributes to the narrative by providing a pattern of divisions and combinations, like the stanzas of a poem, so that a monumental rhythm is imposed on the compositions. The whole framework is carefully and subtly devised to serve the single purpose of giving full expression to each of the many pictures.

Giotto is the creator of the modern, autonomous picture. By virtue of his *disegno,* the compositions take shape within the surrounding frame, the rectangular form of which represents a specific proportion, and at the same time contains two basic architectural directions, the vertical and the horizontal. The inner architecture of the picture is completed and limited by its frame, thereby gaining both in freedom and in discipline. Indeed the picture dominates the real space, whereas until then it had been controlled by the architecture. Older medieval wall-paintings, taken on their own, look like fragments of a larger unit; they derive their character and monumentality from the structure and articulation of the room and its general decorative scheme. Giotto changed this. Such compositions as the *Flight into Egypt* and the *Lamentation,* in Padua *(pls 66a, VIII),* are monumental in their own right, and every figure and contour has this quality. The few panel-pictures that can be attributed to Giotto himself have the same independence. This also applies, for example, to the *Triumphal Crucifix* from the Arena Chapel, originally fastened to the beam separating the main room from the choir, and still extant.[5] Compared with the huge *Santa Maria Novella Crucifix* of Giotto's early period, it appears more refined and almost delicate. It is in fact less than half the height of the *Santa Maria Novella Crucifix* (2.23 meters as against 5.78), but it has an intrinsic greatness not inferior to the frescoes near which it stood. The *Ognissanti Madonna* in Florence, to which we shall refer again, conveys even more strongly this newly conceived monumentality. In its structure and the solidity of its forms it is incomparably superior to the older, and much larger, Madonna panels of Cimabue and Duccio.

The picture surface acquired a new internal order and independence, and also became suitable for three-dimensional illusionism. Giotto's pictures and his fresco cycles as a whole display a consistent, and to some extent systematic, 'perspective'. Although it is usual to ascribe the development of perspective to the painters of the following century, the Quattrocento, this is correct only in the sense that they were the first to employ an accurate system of perspective based on mathematical principles. Giotto's method of three-dimensional representation was not scientific, but it already exhibits the essential traits of Renaissance perspective: three-dimensional illusion and spatial depth, with a single viewpoint from which the entire pictorial space is comprehensible; and with this he introduced something entirely new in the Middle Ages, a concern for the relationship between picture and spectator. His inspiration was classical wall-paintings in Rome, then still preserved in large numbers. In these he found perspective effects achieved with masterly virtuosity, though in a peculiarly unsystematic fashion.[6] Giotto was the first to organize the entire pictorial decoration of a room on the basis of a single viewpoint. On the long walls of the Arena Chapel, all the pictures to the right of the middle axis have their viewpoint moved slightly towards the left; and on the left half of the walls the viewpoint is moved to the right. From the centre of the oblong chapel all the individual pictures and sculpturally conceived ornamental painted frames are seen in correct perspective. However, the optical illusion is not perfect; that was only achieved three hundred years later in Baroque ceiling paintings. Giotto used the central viewpoint primarily as a regulating principle, so that whenever foreshortening or distortion occur it is with reference to this point. He realized a completely illusionistic effect only in a few places, notably in the two Gothic choir lofts painted on the wall of the triumphal arch.[7] As a rule he avoided deep recession in his pictures, not through lack of skill in perspective, but for purposes of artistic economy. His feeling for space was still elementary and empirical, and the scientific methods adopted by the painters of the early Renaissance were beyond his range. The concept of an endless space was unknown to him. His pictorial space is more a 'pictorial relief', as it has been appropriately called,[8] and in this respect his work is still distinctly medieval in character.

However, there is another principle consistently applied in the Arena Chapel frescoes that was to have a far-reaching influence. The direction of light in all the narrative scenes, in the allegories of the base zone, and in the painted frames, corresponds with the natural source of light from the large tripartite window in the west wall. A rule to this effect, clearly derived from Giotto's teaching, is also found in Cennini's book (Chapter 9). In wall-painting the direction of light in the picture thus became closely related to the actual lighting of the room.

Giotto's contemporaries professed to see in his pictures nothing less than nature itself. Indeed he had a new and uncorrupted outlook on reality, and his pictures have all the freshness of a first encounter. In later times the Renaissance created an even richer, more variegated concept of nature, which is to a large extent still accepted today. In Giotto's work, however, the artistic form is more apparent: the bold, precisely calculated division of the surface, the clarity of the pictorial stage, the solidity of the figures and their

VII   GIOTTO *Adoration of the Kings* · Padua, Arena Chapel

controlled power of expression. His figures are like marble statues, and yet they have immense vitality. In his pictures nature is an extension of the human characters, and space exists only in relation to them. The light is concentrated on the figures in the foreground, and diminishes in the background of the landscape. The trees, leafy or bare, participate in the mood of the narrative, and other inanimate objects, especially the buildings, with which stone-masons and carpenters would find no fault, are delineated as clearly and precisely as the figures and the landscape. Interiors are not shown as views through the overlapping frame, but rather as views into complete buildings. Artificial lighting is exceptional, and is indicated with economy in those places where it is necessary for the narrative *(pl. 66b)*. Nothing is introduced for its own sake. Giotto is filled with the solemnity of the narrative, and tells it with an economy equal to that of the style. His attitude to nature is reverent and sober, and he is characterized by lucidity of mind and a strict devotion to reality. But above all else stands his unerring artistic drive to fasten on the dominant forms, and exclude whatever is accidental.

Three fruitful decades were to pass from the time Giotto completed the Padua frescoes until his death in 1337. His fame grew – we already find an echo of it in Dante's *Divine Comedy*[9] – and he became the busiest and most sought-after Italian painter. He had previously worked in Florence, Rome, Assisi, Rimini, and Padua, as we have said. In his later years he executed commissions for King Robert of Anjou in Naples, and for Azzo Visconti in Milan.[10] It is possible that he made a journey to Avignon, though the traditional account of this is not reliable.[11] Many Italian painters went to the papal court at Avignon, which even in exile remained a centre of artistic life.[12] The poet and humanist Petrarch, who had grown up in Avignon and eventually withdrew to the seclusion of Vaucluse not far from the city, owned a Madonna by Giotto, sent to him by a friend in Florence. Petrarch also knew Giotto personally, and refers to him as 'the foremost painter of our time' – *nostri aevi princeps*. Of the Madonna painting he says that its beauty is hidden from the ignorant, but astonishes the connoisseurs.[13] A commentary on Dante, known as the *Ottimo* and written in Giotto's life-time, expresses the same high regard.[14] The unknown author writes, 'Of all the painters past and present known to mankind, Giotto is the greatest.' It is remarkable that the true greatness of Giotto was recognized already in his own time. This verdict on his place in history was pronounced in an age that was far from a clear insight into historical relationships and at the same time not addicted to the abuse of the notion of greatness which arose only in modern times.

According to the records, Giotto produced numerous works in his post-Padua period, but few have survived. The frescoes of the Bardi and Peruzzi Chapels in Santa Croce, considered major works of his later years, do not provide a coherent picture of his development. (They will be referred to again later.) Of his panel-paintings of this period only the Madonna panel from the Ognissanti in Florence *(pls 63, 65; now in the Uffizi)* can be regarded as an authentic work of the master.[15] It was probably done directly after the Padua frescoes. In this picture the large solid forms and powerful proportions of the figures in the most mature compositions of the Arena Chapel are translated into the medium of panel-painting. The fine quality of the draperies, the lucidity of the spatial structure, the sure handling of perspective and surface in relation to each other, all correspond to the stage of development reached by Giotto in the bottom zone of the Padua frescoes. The same is true of the treatment of colour, where the most delicate tones are juxtaposed to glowing reds and greens; in the ornamentation of the finely articulated throne, beautiful white, gold, and red are used. The counterplay of these colours with the original cool ultramarine is unfortunately lost in the present condition of the painting, because the Madonna's cloak has turned dull and greenish. Yet despite this deterioration, the overall chromatic effect remains quite remarkable. The colours impose a brilliant jewel-like quality on the powerful forms and make the severely constructed composition light and transparent. Compared with the more sombre splendour of Duccio's and Cimabue's large Madonna panels, Giotto's work seems amazingly bright, crystal-clear, and almost cool.

Nowadays this clarity may have a disenchanting effect, but in fact it signifies a break-through to an entirely new mode of perception. Whereas earlier artists represented sacred images in an unworldly supranatural state, Giotto now portrays them as real beings, though raised to solemn eminence. Hitherto artistic form was only the image or reflection of a superior intellectual truth; it now became the direct expression of higher ideas to an extent not found in any pre-Giottesque painting. The beauty of art became instrumental in conveying the intellectual content, the vehicle for the divine.

A generation earlier, in his *Summa Theologica* of about 1270, Thomas Aquinas defined the essence of beauty as perfection *(integritas sive perfectio)*, proportion and harmony *(proportio sive consonantia)*, and lastly as clarity *(claritas)*.[16]

In this definition, found in a purely theological argument on the beauty of God, which is beyond human perception, beauty in art was probably furthest from the mind of the great theologian. For him earthly beauty existed primarily in nature, and he saw it as an analogy to the intellectual lucidity of reason. The faculties with which we realize beauty, according to him, are perception and cognition. In the early Middle Ages people were already convinced that divinity reveals itself in the symmetry of geometric forms, and in the richness of the material formed by the hand of the artist. In the glitter of gold, the gleam of pearls and precious stones, they saw a reflection of the divine light. They were conscious, however, that these were only a reflection of true beauty, which cannot be realized in material form. It was the richness of the material, the creation of nature rather than the artistic form, that gave value to a work of art; for the works of nature, which continue the divine process of creation, must be incomparably superior to anything that an artist can produce.

The ideas of Thomas Aquinas were still rooted in this interpretation, prevalent throughout the Middle Ages. His discussion of art is not concerned with beauty, but with the relationship between form and matter and with the skill of the artist, a proficiency that can be acquired and therefore cannot be regarded as a gift of the highest order.

It would certainly be wrong to consider Giotto's art as directly related to the Thomist definition of beauty, and still further from the truth to suppose that there was any actual connection, that the definition of the theologian, for example, was known to Giotto. And yet it is striking that it applies precisely to the new beauty realized in Giotto's art. Perfection, the first element in the definition, lies in the new strictness and compactness of the composition, which would be destroyed by any alteration, any shifting of a line or a figure. Proportion and harmony are also traits inseparable from Giotto's pictorial concept. Everything is reduced to simple basic forms, and all parts of the picture are in clear proportional relationship to each other. It is indeed by these specific artistic means that Giotto imparts beauty to his work. And finally there is clarity, the luminous, refined, chromatic scale, gradually dissolving into white. Pure strong colour is applied only in a few places; pale mixtures, lightened so that they become almost colourless, are predominant. Everything dull, heavy and earthy is avoided, as is everything excessively warm and fiery or having an unduly harsh impact on the senses. Giotto's art is directed at the intellect, not the emotions. Physical beauty is spiritualized and becomes 'form'. However, form limits, orders and subdues those aspects that relate merely to the elementary and emotional spheres. In this re-orientation of art towards the intellect, the rational faculty that regulates, distinguishes and evaluates lies the underlying connection between Giotto's art and the theory of beauty propounded by Thomas Aquinas. Just as Thomas

91

Aquinas refined the traditional medieval conception and raised it to a new level, Giotto realized a new concept of beauty in the practice of art. They have in common the emphasis on reason and the disposition to translate material and emotional elements into spiritual values.

Herein lies the special feature of the kind of beauty first encountered in Giotto's art. What we have described as 'form' is its governing principle, the rule controlling its novel realistic content. A strict discipline was required if the new fidelity to nature, which already drew the admiration of his contemporaries, was not to degenerate into naturalism. Giotto was certainly aware of this danger and took great care to avoid it. His grasp of the principles that impose order on the manifold aspects of what the senses perceive was as strong as his feeling for realism. The beginnings of these principles can be traced earlier, though in more elementary fashion, in Cimabue, but the obvious symmetry and massive structure of Cimabue's compositions are not found in Giotto's work. Here everything is infinitely more refined. The structure is light and atmospheric; it develops with the ease and inevitability of a crystalline formation. On the other hand, Giotto is not yet affected by the obtrusive logical consistency that is characteristic of Florentine painting of the Early Renaissance. As the parallel with Thomas Aquinas has indicated, the new element in his art is still within the frame of late medieval concepts.

Giotto was a highly conscious artist, who throughout his career deliberately accepted certain restrictions and observed a set of principles, modifying and developing them only slightly. This applies to the three-dimensional effects in his pictures in which he avoided all unnecessary depth, to the types of his figures and their restrained expression, and to his choice of subject in general; he excluded anything purely individual, portrait-like, or too naturalistic. He refrained from realizing many things that were easily within his reach. A few of his pupils and younger contemporaries, Taddeo Gaddi, Simone Martini, and the two Lorenzettis, overstepped the lines he had drawn, and made bold ventures into the field of realistic individual representation, but their efforts were not pursued in the fourteenth century, and were taken up again only in the Early Renaissance. Giotto himself remained true to his principles, and refrained from pressing his innovations to their final conclusions; this is the real basis of his influence on succeeding generations. As well as making substantial innovations, he set painting on a firm course for a whole century. The schools that developed later derived from Giotto and not from the radical 'modern' masters of the following generation. The establishment of norms and the standardization of types is fundamental to Giotto's art, and he himself no doubt considered the training of his school one of his most important tasks; but his subsequent influence was not by any means limited to the continuation of a Giotto school in the narrow sense of the concept. One can say that all Italian Trecento painting was based to some extent on Giotto's achievement, though sometimes it took a much inferior or cruder form. His personal style, compounded of traditional elements drawn from a variety of periods and places, grew beyond the personal and itself became the source of a wide tradition persisting through many generations.

This exciting drama, which takes place in the full light of history, is comprehensible to us today even in its details. The Middle Ages and modern times seem to meet at the point where the anonymous, supra-personal creative powers of a tradition-bound age, with its love of form, merge with the creative will and style of a single, outstanding personality, conscious of his mission and new artistic goals. Giotto, in fact, incorporates both the pioneering intentions of the individual and the powerful creative energies of the times.

We have already mentioned that Giotto started as a panel-painter, and that he was only introduced to the technique of monumental painting in Rome and Assisi. His Roman works have come down to us in mutilated condition or as sparse fragments;[17] but in Assisi it is possible to trace the development of his monumental style step by step and follow his new method of work, which culminated in the Padua frescoes. From then on his emphasis was on the monumental. The *Ognissanti Madonna,* his most important panel-painting apart from the *Santa Maria Novella Crucifix,* is filled with the spirit of monumental painting. On this one occasion the greatness of the new style overcame technical difficulties and imposed itself on panel-painting. None of the many altar panels produced in the Giotto workshop at a later date compares with the *Ognissanti Madonna* in inherent greatness and stylistic unity.

Three such altar panels bear inscriptions attributing them to Giotto, but in none of them can either the execution or the design (that is to say, the preliminary drawing on the underlying white panel) be ascribed to the master himself. The large panel, originally from San Francesco in Pisa and now in the Louvre in Paris, depicting the *Stigmatization of St Francis* with three predella scenes, seems the most archaic. The style of the whole work is dry and close to that of the St Francis legend at Assisi.[18]

The fine jewel-like altarpiece of the Baroncelli Chapel in Santa Croce in Florence belongs to a later period and could not have been done before 1328.[19] The many-figured composition, showing the *Coronation of the Virgin* in the midst of the heavenly host, unites the five panels of the polyptych into a uniform pictorial space. However, there is a discord, obviously deliberate, between the spatial unity and the formal arrangement of the figures in dense multiple rows behind and above each other. There is an interplay of depth and surface effects, which creates a tense relationship, by no means primitive, but rather calculated and subtle. The two principal saints of the Franciscan Order, St Francis and St Louis of Toulouse, placed precisely in the middle of each of the two outer wing panels, are plainly raised outside the schematic arrangement. The highly skilled perspective, which is basic to the whole composition, is particularly noticeable in the music-making angels kneeling in the foreground. The work, therefore, only seems to be archaic; in reality it uses all the techniques of spatial illusion developed by Giotto in order to create an artistic surface arrangement full of hidden tension. A mannerism of this kind cannot be attributed to Giotto himself. In fact, the Baroncelli altar shows the extensive scope of the Giotto workshop in the later years, and the broad interpretation Giotto gave to his function as its master. He could not otherwise have lent his name to a work in which the trend of his classical, monumental style is reversed. The inscription merely indicates that the altarpiece was done under Giotto's official supervision but by a painter of the younger generation who was clearly given a free hand.

The third signed work, also a five-panelled altarpiece, was originally in a church in Bologna, but is now in the Bologna Pinacoteca Nazionale.[20] The Enthroned Madonna in the centre panel is attended by the two archangels, Gabriel and Michael, on each side of her in the old Byzantine manner, and the Apostles, Peter and Paul, are on the outer panels. Each of the figures is in a different posture. Gabriel, the angel of the Annunciation, turns his profile towards the Madonna, and his counterpart, Michael, is seen full face as in an icon. The two apostles are standing in free space, in palpable opposition to the ideal gold ground which extends above and behind the figures. The common ground, which should accentuate the spatial unity of the five panels, heightens the effect of contradiction. The gold ground seems an anachronism in contrast to the emphatic modelling of the figures. The sharply outlined silhouettes stand in a vacuum, and the balance between surface and depth, so skilfully maintained in Giotto's works, is here upset. It is another typical workshop product in which isolated Giottesque elements are employed without producing a convincing homogeneous composition. The signature has the same significance as those of the Baroncelli altar and the Louvre panel: it is merely a workshop label.

At first glance this interpretation of the apparently unambiguous inscription, *opus magistri iocti de Florentia,* may seem strange, but it must be borne in mind that, although the modern conceptions of originality and authorship were just beginning to emerge, the traditional methods of team-work and

VIII GIOTTO *Lamentation* · Padua, Arena Chapel

workshop production were deep-rooted. In a few isolated cases, for example in the contract with Duccio for the Siena Cathedral *Maestà* of 1308, it was stipulated that the master should carry out the commission with his own hand – *suis manibus*.[21] This provision would not have been introduced if execution by the master himself were taken for granted, and it is significant that the requirement, *suis manibus,* only appears in the clause dealing with the fee. The contract begins with the provision that Duccio must execute the panel 'to the best of his ability and with the help of God'; then follow the usual conditions that he must complete the work without delay and undertake no other work before it is completed; finally the fee is fixed: sixteen *soldi* for each day of Duccio's work on the panel *suis manibus*. It was obviously understood that he could not work on it every day, as technical reasons alone made this impossible. There was no clear dividing line between the master's own part in the work and the purely technical operations, beginning with the preparation of the panel and ending with ornamentation, which were always left to assistants. In the fourteenth and fifteenth centuries this was a source of constant dispute between artists and patrons.[22] In the contracts with Perugino and Signorelli for the Orvieto frescoes the curious provision is introduced that all the figures 'from the waist up' must be done by the master's own hand.[23] Thus on the threshold of the High Renaissance division of labour was still common, and in this case in a form one would hardly expect to find even in the Middle Ages. It is well known that Raphael, too, made considerable use of the services of his pupils in his large fresco commissions as well as in his panel-paintings. We have a whole group of paintings bearing his signature, but largely or entirely executed by his pupils. If this liberal attitude still prevailed in the sixteenth century, it must have been even more common in Giotto's time.

Nearly all historians now agree that none of the three signed works we have referred to reveals Giotto's personal style,[24] and furthermore, no close stylistic links can be detected among the works themselves. It seems that a succession of assistants worked on them, which indicates the scale of the workshop activity, and also shows that the surviving works constitute only a small fragment of the whole production.

Other works of the Giotto workshop, unsigned, exhibit the variety of his assistants' individual styles. Among the works that can be attributed to the Giotto workshop on traditional or stylistic grounds are two multi-panelled altarpieces, and remnants of at least two others, now dismembered. The most important of these, and also the most controversial, is the double-sided triptych in the Vatican Museum, which is undoubtedly the altarpiece which was created by Giotto for Cardinal Jacopo Stefaneschi.[25] A number of artists participated in it, and Giotto himself seems to have been responsible only for the general composition. The five-panelled polyptych in the Florence Cathedral (formerly in the Zenobius Chapel) is a pure workshop product.[26] Both these works can be dated around 1320 at the earliest.

The half-length figure of St Stephen in the Museo Horne in Florence, a panel in an excellent state of preservation, is also a workshop product of great decorative beauty,[27] and was part of a polyptych of which the centre panel, a Madonna, is now in the National Gallery in Washington.[28] Two other panels, St John the Evangelist, and St Lawrence, are preserved in the Musée de Châalis, but it is doubtful whether they belong to the same polyptych as the Madonna and St Stephen, as was believed until recently.[29] Finally there is a series of seven small panels, depicting scenes from the life of Christ, that are all part of one polyptych. Three are in the Alte Pinakothek in Munich, and the rest are distributed among various collections.[30] Though typically Giottesque and close to the style of the Arena Chapel frescoes, they too can only be attributed to a gifted assistant, and not to Giotto himself.

When these paintings are compared with the corresponding scenes in Padua it becomes clear that Giotto's monumental style could not be reproduced in a small-scale work, except at the sacrifice of its special qualities. Although, as we have already observed, Giotto's monumental style became independent of external factors, this autonomy still had very definite limitations. He was not able to transpose the scale of his work from large to small or *vice versa,* as the Renaissance artists gradually learnt to do, and as artists now do as a matter of course. The monumental effect of a composition by Giotto is inseparably related to its size, and cannot be altered without impairing its artistic value. Unlike the Renaissance artists, who learnt to work from a small-scale design, the *bozzetto,* or preparatory drawing, and to produce from this, though not without difficulty, the finished work in full size, Giotto conceived and designed his compositions monumentally from the start, as was natural in an artist who always proceeded from the actualities of the given pictorial surface. He was primarily concerned with large conceptions, and only occasionally tried his hand at works on a small scale; yet how attractive these 'marginal observations' can be is seen in the two scenes of everyday life that appear in the allegories of Justice and Injustice in Padua. But any attempt to translate Giotto's monumental pictorial motifs into the medium of smaller-scale panel-painting was bound to fail. The reduction in scale appears to alter the proportions and upsets the relation of the parts, while the figures lose their impressiveness and become less refined. It seems that Giotto himself never attempted this. He left the transposition into small-scale works to his pupils, convinced from the start that a small panel-painting, a book illumination, or a drawing, could not convey the same value as a work of monumental painting.

It is, therefore, probably not mere chance that, although a number of small workshop panels have been preserved, none of them is by Giotto's own hand. One of these is the altar dossal, the *Death of the Virgin,* in the Berlin Staatliche Museen, which may well be the picture claimed by Ghiberti as one of Giotto's works in the Ognissanti in Florence.[31] It was natural for Ghiberti to adhere in his account to the traditional attributions, and not be concerned with the modern distinction between the master's own work and that of his workshop. His attitude to the question of authorship was basically not different from Giotto's. Indeed it is quite possible that the original frame (now lost) of the Berlin picture had a similar inscription to those on the three altarpieces mentioned earlier.

Here again the true authorship can be determined only on stylistic grounds. The first consideration is the inferior execution, particularly noticeable in the wide variations in scale and proportions of the figures. Some are excessively large, like the bearded Apostle on Christ's right; others have heads that are much too small, and shrunken limbs. This applies even to the principal figure, the Virgin, and is especially noticeable in the youthful Apostle standing to the left of St Peter. These observations enable us to say with certainty that not even the preliminary drawing was done by Giotto: the master of the Padua frescoes was incapable of such discrepancies. They are too marked to have been introduced in the course of the execution of the work and must already have been present in the preliminary drawing. Once this is realized, it becomes clear that we are dealing with the small-scale replica, with its inevitable deficiencies, of an original monumental composition by Giotto, a lost fresco. We can identify the original version of the *Death of the Virgin* with some certainty. The Tosinghi Chapel, on the left of the choir chapel in Santa Croce, contained a fresco cycle by Giotto depicting scenes from the life of the Virgin. All that is left today is a badly damaged Assumption scene above the entrance arch of the chapel.[32] The other scenes inside the chapel can be reconstructed to some extent from works that appear to be copies.[33] According to the sequence of the narrative, the death scene must have been in the lowest zone of one of the two walls, a position that enabled it to be frequently copied.[34] It is not surprising to find that a replica was produced in the Giotto workshop itself; this is quite in keeping with our idea of the activities of the post-Padua Giotto workshop.

We have little direct knowledge of Giotto's own style in these decades. The splendid monumental composition of the *Death of the Virgin*, which can be deduced from the workshop reproduction in Berlin, seems to have corresponded stylistically to the *Ognissanti Madonna*. The style of the figures must have been close to that in the lowest zone of the Arena Chapel, and the emphasis on symmetry and strict surface articulation are reminiscent of the slightly later *Ognissanti Madonna*. Many of the features follow the traditional iconography of the Dormition, including the figure kneeling in the foreground, as seen in the tympanum relief of the *Death of the Virgin* in Strasbourg.[35] The economic yet effective handling of the ornamentation in the rectangle of the bed is possibly an indication of new tendencies in Giotto's style. This brings us to the final and still unresolved question concerning Giotto's development, the problem of his monumental works in the post-Padua period.

To begin with, a pattern emerges similar to that of the panel-paintings of this period. The frescoes done in the period following the St Francis legend and the Arena Chapel are also predominantly workshop products. In the Lower Church of San Francesco at Assisi we come across a group of assistants working more or less in Giotto's style. The most independent of them is the Master of the 'Franciscan Virtues', an instructive and illustrative rather than monumental work, covering the vaults above the crossing of the Lower Church.[36] The traditional attribution of these celebrated allegories to Giotto himself is now almost universally rejected, and probably not even the designs can be attributed to him. The representations of the birth and childhood of Christ, and the *Crucifixion* in the vault of the adjoining north transept are elegantly done. They reveal an intimate knowledge of the forms and motifs of the Giotto workshop, and a considerable, though purely eclectic skill.

The painters of the frescoes in the St Nicholas Chapel (before 1307?) and the Magdalene Chapel were even more dependent on Giotto.[37] They were trained in the style of the Padua frescoes, and to some extent in the earlier style of the St Francis legend. In the St Nicholas Chapel the principles of Giotto's early compositions are applied in a free though clumsy manner. In the Magdalene Chapel, on the other hand, several of the scenes appear to be awkward, ill-conceived renderings of the corresponding scenes in Padua, which served as models: the *Raising of Lazarus, Noli me Tangere* and, here conceived in a different context, the *Wedding at Cana*. The more extensive landscape in the first two of these scenes no doubt reflects a change in the stylistic trend of the new generation, but as a result the dramatic tension is weakened and the essential figurative composition destroyed. Comparison with the originals reveals how far Giotto stood above his assistants, and demonstrates that attempts to reproduce his compositions even in their original size had little chance of success.

Such close dependence on Giotto must imply that all these frescoes were done at his direction and under his commercial responsibility, and were therefore regarded at the time as Giotto's works. One of the documents from records covering the years 1328 to 1333, and referring to commissions he did for King Robert of Anjou in Naples, gives an indication of the organization he set up to control such large-scale contracts.[38] From this document, a payment voucher of May 1331, it transpires that Giotto, described as the *proto-magister*, was collaborating with a number of masters, classified respectively as painters and craftsmen. The latter were chiefly masons and carpenters who were responsible for the construction of the scaffolding and the preparation of the plaster for the wall-paintings. In the Santa Barbara Chapel, i. e., the church of Castel Nuovo, the extent of the work to be supervised was enormous. The documents reveal that at the same time Giotto was also working in the private chapel of the king, and on a panel-painting commissioned by him; it is obvious that additional craftsmen were required for all these commissions. But our main interest is in the painters, who like the craftsmen are described as *magistri*. They received daily wages, whereas Giotto, as court painter, drew a fixed salary. The records do not tell where these painters came from, but here the fragments that have survived are of some assistance. The paintings in the private chapel of the king and the series of the Nine Heroes in one of the halls of Castel Nuovo are completely lost, but at least part of the decoration around the windows in the Santa Barbara Chapel has been preserved. It consists of ornamental friezes, interspersed with medallions of approximately life-size heads. These heads were all done by painters trained in Tuscany, though in many cases they may be loosely described as Giottesque. In a few of them, however, the well-known individual style of Maso di Banco can be recognized.[39] This distinguished pupil of Giotto, who will be referred to again later, was therefore one of the masters working under Giotto's direction. He had accompanied Giotto from Florence to Naples, whether as pupil or as a more or less independent collaborator is of little importance. It will be remembered that, according to Cennini, Taddeo Gaddi was Giotto's pupil for twenty-four years, which indicates that even fully qualified masters continued to work for Giotto.[40] It may therefore be assumed that Maso di Banco and other masters participated in the frescoes now lost.

The pictorial areas in the Santa Barbara Chapel are much larger than those of the Arena Chapel in Padua. The long high single-aisled room, built in the plain style of the Angevin Gothic, provided ideal conditions for wall-painting:

narrow windows, rising to the full height of the wall, leave the surfaces undisturbed and fill the room with bright, even light. It seems that from the start the building was designed with a view to decorative monumental painting.[41]

There is another notable church in Naples which once contained an extensive fresco cycle done under Giotto's direction. It was in the nuns' choir of Santa Chiara, which is enclosed on three sides by large walls, and well til from the west. A few remnants of the paintings, revealed beneath later decoration after a fire during the Second World War, give some idea of the original work. There are fragments of a Crucifixion, Giottesque in style, but the execution is crude, and certainly not by Giotto's hand.[42] Hopes of finding more fragments have unfortunately not been fulfilled, and the walls of Santa Chiara are as bare today as those of the chapel in Castel Nuovo. However, from the documentary evidence and the size of the walls, now stripped of their paintings, it is clear that Giotto's activity in Naples must have amounted to an impressive achievement; it could only have been accomplished by a man who, in addition to his artistic genius, possessed an exceptional organizing ability.

On his return to Florence, Giotto received the appointment, noted in a formal deed dated April 1334, of supervisor of the construction of the Cathedral.[43] In this capacity he began the building of the Campanile, and jointly with the sculptor Andrea Pisano undertook the relief decoration on the ground level of the tower.[44] But even this task, unusual for a painter, did not keep him in his home-town for any length of time. When he was almost seventy, he obtained the permission of the Florentine government to go to Milan to paint frescoes, probably on secular themes, for Azzo Visconti. Shortly after his return from Milan, he died in Florence on 8 January 1337.[45]

The last phase in the development of the Giotto workshop is reflected in the frescoes of the chapel in the Palazzo del Bargello, also known as the Palazzo del Podestà, now the Museo Nazionale in Florence. They were done in 1337, the year of Giotto's death, and thus give an idea of the kind of work produced by the Giotto school without the master's supervision.[46] They consist of a pictorial cycle depicting the life of Mary Magdalene, a representation of Paradise on the altar wall, and an Inferno on the entrance wall. The compositions are stiff and undramatic, and the individual forms have a routine polish. Nevertheless, Ghiberti included these frescoes without reservation in his catalogue of Giotto's works, and on account of this they were again accepted as Giotto's when they were rediscovered in the nineteenth century beneath the whitewash that had concealed them for centuries. It is, however, possible that Ghiberti was misled. Filippo Villani's chronicle, written in about 1400, refers to an altar panel in the Bargello chapel containing a portrait of Dante next to a self-portrait of Giotto. This altar panel seems to have disappeared shortly afterwards, because already in the middle of the Quattrocento the Dante portrait is referred to as being *in muro*, that is to say, in one of the wall-paintings,[47] a misconception that was faithfully handed on from generation to generation; even now the alleged Dante portrait is pointed out to visitors, though it is neither a portrait, nor by Giotto – as the date of the frescoes demonstrates.[48] Ghiberti's attribution of the frescoes to Giotto may have been the result of the same process that led to the confusion over the so-called Dante portrait. If the altar panel was by Giotto, the attribution of the frescoes to him was an error that easily followed; and when the panel disappeared, this false attribution remained. Even so, the unqualified inclusion of the Bargello Chapel among Giotto's works reveals Ghiberti's uncritical attitude.

We have dealt at length with Giotto's lost works and the unauthenticated works of his last period, rather than with those that are generally accepted as his, i. e., the two fresco cycles in Santa Croce in Florence. The reason is that there is no more certainty about Giotto's authorship of these frescoes than there is about the productions of his workshop that we have been discussing. There are no contemporary documents, no deed of donation, and no payment vouchers referring to the two fresco cycles. Even if there were any, it would not be possible to tell from them whether they relate to works by Giotto's own hand or to workshop products. We have seen that this distinction hardly existed at that time, and that Giotto's attitude in the matter was particularly liberal. Neither he nor his patrons had any objection to his name being given to obvious workshop products. The three signed altar panels, and in a different way the fresco fragments in Naples and the documents referring to them, are clear evidence of this. Later tradition only passed on what was accepted in Giotto's own time, and Ghiberti's *Commentarii*, our most important source, must be understood in this light. Since it is hardly likely that he attempted critical stylistic distinctions of his own, Ghiberti presumably did no more than record those works that were attributed to Giotto by his own contemporaries. It is true that in two places in his catalogue of Giotto's works Ghiberti adds the qualification '*di sua mano*': the Arena Chapel and a panel in Santa Maria Novella, unfortunately lost.[49] All the other works including the frescoes in the Bargello Chapel, and a scene of the *Death of the Virgin* (probably the Berlin panel), he records without comment. He mentions 'four chapels and four panels' in Santa Croce, and adds no further details.

One of the panels is undoubtedly the Baroncelli altar, and we have already noted the significance of Giotto's signature there. With the assistance of later records and surviving works in Santa Croce, the four chapels can probably be identified: the Tosinghi Chapel, mentioned earlier, with frescoes from the life of the Virgin, now lost; its counterpart to the right of the choir, the Bardi Chapel, containing six scenes from the St Francis legend, and a *Stigmatization* above the entrance arch; adjoining this the Peruzzi Chapel, with frescoes from the lives of SS. John the Baptist and the Evangelist; and finally the Giugni Chapel, with frescoes representing the martyrdom of the Apostles, also unfortunately lost.[50]

The frescoes in these chapels were Giotto's in the same sense as all the other works listed by Ghiberti, and the documentary evidence does not enable us to determine with any greater certainty the manner and extent of his personal participation. Indeed the only criterion we have lies in our own ability to draw distinctions on stylistic grounds. The external sources, the documentary records, can be misleading unless they are interpreted with careful regard to the prevailing attitudes and conceptions at the time when they were written.

The frescoes in the Bardi and Peruzzi Chapels, like those in the Bargello, were covered with whitewash at a later date, and replaced by new decoration. When discovered in the middle of the last century, they were readily accepted as works by Giotto, on the basis of Ghiberti's and Vasari's evidence, and were conscientiously restored in accordance with nineteenth-century ideas. Although the paintings had been severely damaged by the whitewash, the tombs that were mounted against them, and finally by the cleaning process, the restoration was not as radical and disfiguring as historians believed for a long time. A new restortaion, undertaken in 1960, has on the whole produced favourable results, and has shown that although the nineteenth-century restorers overpainted large sections, they left the iconographic content essentially intact.[51] The compositions, therefore, have survived without serious alteration, and remnants of the original painting now exist in a more or less damaged state.[52] The two bottom pictures in the Bardi Chapel have sharply defined blemishes, the marks of wall-tombs that were mounted there at one time,

IX GIOTTO, *Raising of Drusiana* (detail)
Florence, Santa Croce

but otherwise the work in this chapel is in surprisingly good condition, with parts painted in fresco almost intact, and only the *a secco* parts almost entirely obliterated.

The Peruzzi Chapel presents a more difficult problem. The usual technique of combining fresco and *a secco* was, for some unexplained reason, not used here, and instead the entire surface was covered with *a secco* painting over a light underpainting in fresco. In place of the relatively small plaster sections, typical of the fresco technique, the pictures in the Peruzzi Chapel are each divided into two large sections, corresponding to the level of the scaffolding on which the painters worked. The dividing line runs horizontally through the middle of the pictures, at the level of the figures' heads.[53] Because of the poor durability of the *a secco* technique, there is hardly anything left of the original top layer. A great number of the pictures can only be recognized in the outlines of the underpainting, but there are still enough coloured parts to give some idea of the original appearance of the work. As in the Bardi Chapel, the structure of the individual scenes, the formal substance of the compositions, is still clearly discernible.

Although the present condition of both chapels is rather unsatisfactory, it is not so bad as to make a stylistic judgment impossible. What has to be established is not only the relative stages of development that the two fresco cycles represent, and the dates of their composition, but also, and more important, the extent of Giotto's own share in the design and execution. This question has not yet been seriously considered by historians because of the authoritative nature of the sources attributing the Santa Croce frescoes to Giotto. Our answer, and the reasons for it, cannot be expounded here in full detail, and furthermore does not purport to be a complete solution to the numerous related problems.[54] It is intended as an encouragement to critical discussion and unbiased examination of the original works.

Our considerations so far have brought us to the view that the course of Giotto's development from the beginning to his maturity can be traced more clearly today than was possible even a short while ago. But the path ends with the frescoes in the Arena Chapel in Padua, and only the *Ognissanti Madonna,* and possibly the *Navicella* mosaic in Rome, give a slight indication of its further direction. For the rest, a period of more than twenty-five years, the story is obscure, and we have few facts to go on. We possess many workshop products of the period, uneven and dubious works preserved haphazardly; but from this comparatively rich store it is not possible to draw conclusions, even indirectly, about Giotto's own development and the characteristics of his style in those decades. This means that Giotto's share in the two Santa wide shoulders and hips, large hands and feet. The figures are generally heavy and block-like, and their outlines simple and large. They are wrapped in heavy folded draperies full of movement but always keeping to the contours of the figures. Every figure retains its separate physical identity; they are the essence of the picture, and action, grouping and composition are only developed on the firm foundation of these individual figures.

The overall impression is that nothing here is manifestly inconsistent with the style of the Arena Chapel. The looser structure of the composition, the colours, paler and yet more effectively used, the increased weight of the individual figures and their heavier proportions, may all be taken as a later development of the Arena Chapel style. Although it is likely that assistants also participated in the Peruzzi Chapel frescoes, the style appears distinctly Giottesque. However, before attempting to resolve the question of authorship and dating, we must consider the other cycle in Santa Croce.

In the Bardi Chapel, surface effects predominate. As far as possible the compositions are constructed symmetrically *(pl. 69a)*. Owing to their proportions, the figures appear small in relation to the whole picture, but in fact they are even larger than those in the Peruzzi Chapel. Their heads are small and narrow, and their movements sharp and angular. Striking gestures, like those of the sultan in the *Ordeal by Fire,* or of St Francis in the *Stigmatization,* produce the curiously unreal effect of a surface pattern, and although the figures can be impressive enough, their composition seems to be determined by such extrinsic factors as the requirements of pictorial symmetry and abstract geometric design. A figure is hardly ever seen in the round, standing free in space. Furthermore, most of the pictures present a stage-like space with the figures and action related to the foreground to a much greater degree than in Assisi or Padua. The architectural forms appear slender and insubstantial, and fit closely into the frames, whereas in the Peruzzi Chapel, roofs and towers are intersected by the frames, to give a sense of the space beyond. Such an extension beyond the limits of the picture would not have been suited to the abstract, two-dimensional mode of representation predominant in the Bardi Chapel.

As regards the colours, only a general description is possible on account of their present condition. The chromatic composition, the distribution of accents, can no longer be assessed. The blue, applied *a secco,* is frequently missing. Stronger colours, such as the brick-red of the disbelieving nobleman who kneels at St Francis' bier, are rare, and a creamy white with cool, faint shadows is used extensively. Most of the scenes are dominated by the dull tones of the monks' habits, brown and olive grey. The flesh-tints are pale and clear, and

This new freedom of composition is to a large extent due to a wider application of perspective, which is also used in the frontal representations of buildings and no longer confined, as in the Arena Chapel, to the receding side
walls. In Padua the horizontal cornices on the front of the buildings are generally parallel to the frame, and are therefore shown without foreshortening.
In Santa Croce they are markedly oblique. In the scene of the *Raising of
Drusiana,* the city wall in front of which the action takes place recedes in a
sharp, though rhythmically constructed line. At the crucial point of the composition the wall takes a right-angled turn to the front, and then resumes its
former direction. Two large structures extend above the wall, a twin-towered
city gate and the choir of a domed church, which are used, in Giotto's
customary manner, to strengthen and accentuate the grouping of the
figures.

The *Assumption of St John (pl. 71b)* is even richer and more elaborate in
its composition. The building is a three-aisled basilica seen from the side,
with one of the aisles cut away to give a view of the interior. In addition,
part of the nave is open, and from the tomb in the floor of this aisle St John
rises up to Christ and the Apostles, who lean down towards him. The flowing
upwards movement is convincingly portrayed, and has only one precedent
in post-classical painting, the *Allegory of Hope* in the Arena Chapel. Giotto was
the first to recapture the technique of depicting convincingly scenes in which
the laws of nature are suspended. The witnesses to the miracle are divided
into two wonderfully compact and yet animated groups. The drama is accentuated by means of the distribution of the colours, which in the present state
of the picture can only be reconstructed in their main tones. St John's cloak
is a delicate pink with light blue sleeves, and Christ and the Apostles are clad
in robes of pink and pale yellow ochre, colours that give an effect of weight-
lessness. Strong tones are used for those spectators who are most visibly affected by the event. The figure trembling on the floor is wrapped in a rich
red cloak, and the upright figure beside him was probably painted in a dark
blue. Various shades of red are used in the group in the left. On the right the
colours fade into the yellow-white surplices of the deacons, and this colour is
also used for the architectural features framing the pink surfaces.

In all the other pictures light colours, darkened only occasionally, predominate. The musician in *Herod's Feast (pl. 70)*, painted in pale grey with
lighter stripes, and with the delicacy of a watercolour, is placed in front of
the pink wall of the tower. The stripes on the drapery continue the movement of the musician's hand. The proportions of this figure, one of the best
preserved in the Peruzzi Chapel, are typical: a heavy head and broad face,

wide shoulders and hips, large hands and feet. The figures are generally heavy and block-like, and their outlines simple and large. They are wrapped in heavy folded draperies full of movement but always keeping to the contours of the figures. Every figure retains its separate physical identity; they are the essence of the picture, and action, grouping and composition are only developed on the firm foundation of these individual figures.

The overall impression is that nothing here is manifestly inconsistent with the style of the Arena Chapel. The looser structure of the composition, the colours, paler and yet more effectively used, the increased weight of the individual figures and their heavier proportions, may all be taken as a later development of the Arena Chapel style. Although it is likely that assistants also participated in the Peruzzi Chapel frescoes, the style appears distinctly Giottesque. However, before attempting to resolve the question of authorship and dating, we must consider the other cycle in Santa Croce.

In the Bardi Chapel, surface effects predominate. As far as possible the compositions are constructed symmetrically *(pl. 69a)*. Owing to their proportions, the figures appear small in relation to the whole picture, but in fact they are even larger than those in the Peruzzi Chapel. Their heads are small and narrow, and their movements sharp and angular. Striking gestures, like those of the sultan in the *Ordeal by Fire,* or of St Francis in the *Stigmatization,* produce the curiously unreal effect of a surface pattern, and although the figures can be impressive enough, their composition seems to be determined by such extrinsic factors as the requirements of pictorial symmetry and abstract geometric design. A figure is hardly ever seen in the round, standing free in space. Furthermore, most of the pictures present a stage-like space with the figures and action related to the foreground to a much greater degree than in Assisi or Padua. The architectural forms appear slender and insubstantial, and fit closely into the frames, whereas in the Peruzzi Chapel, roofs and towers are intersected by the frames, to give a sense of the space beyond. Such an extension beyond the limits of the picture would not have been suited to the abstract, two-dimensional mode of representation predominant in the Bardi Chapel.

As regards the colours, only a general description is possible on account of their present condition. The chromatic composition, the distribution of accents, can no longer be assessed. The blue, applied *a secco,* is frequently missing. Stronger colours, such as the brick-red of the disbelieving nobleman who kneels at St Francis' bier, are rare, and a creamy white with cool, faint shadows is used extensively. Most of the scenes are dominated by the dull tones of the monks' habits, brown and olive grey. The flesh-tints are pale and clear, and but otherwise the work in this chapel is in surprisingly good condition, with parts painted in fresco almost intact, and only the *a secco* parts almost entirely obliterated.

The Peruzzi Chapel presents a more difficult problem. The usual technique of combining fresco and *a secco* was, for some unexplained reason, not used here, and instead the entire surface was covered with *a secco* painting over a light underpainting in fresco. In place of the relatively small plaster sections, typical of the fresco technique, the pictures in the Peruzzi Chapel are each divided into two large sections, corresponding to the level of the scaffolding on which the painters worked. The dividing line runs horizontally through the middle of the pictures, at the level of the figures' heads.[53] Because of the poor durability of the *a secco* technique, there is hardly anything left of the original top layer. A great number of the pictures can only be recognized in the outlines of the underpainting, but there are still enough coloured parts to give some idea of the original appearance of the work. As in the Bardi Chapel, the structure of the individual scenes, the formal substance of the compositions, is still clearly discernible.

Although the present condition of both chapels is rather unsatisfactory, it is not so bad as to make a stylistic judgment impossible. What has to be established is not only the relative stages of development that the two fresco cycles represent, and the dates of their composition, but also, and more important, the extent of Giotto's own share in the design and execution. This question has not yet been seriously considered by historians because of the authoritative nature of the sources attributing the Santa Croce frescoes to Giotto. Our answer, and the reasons for it, cannot be expounded here in full detail, and furthermore does not purport to be a complete solution to the numerous related problems.[54] It is intended as an encouragement to critical discussion and unbiased examination of the original works.

Our considerations so far have brought us to the view that the course of Giotto's development from the beginning to his maturity can be traced more clearly today than was possible even a short while ago. But the path ends with the frescoes in the Arena Chapel in Padua, and only the *Ognissanti Madonna,* and possibly the *Navicella* mosaic in Rome, give a slight indication of its further direction. For the rest, a period of more than twenty-five years, the story is obscure, and we have few facts to go on. We possess many workshop products of the period, uneven and dubious works preserved haphazardly; but from this comparatively rich store it is not possible to draw conclusions, even indirectly, about Giotto's own development and the characteristics of his style in those decades. This means that Giotto's share in the two Santa

Croce cycles can be determined only on the basis of our knowledge of his earlier works, and therefore the crucial question of their attribution to Giotto must remain open for the time being except in so far as it can be answered on this basis.

Outwardly, what distinguishes the Santa Croce frescoes from those in the Arena Chapel is their much larger size. Whereas the figures in Padua are only about half life-size, those in Santa Croce are almost life-size. The pictures are in three rows one above the other, and fill the side walls of the chapels. The pictures in the Bardi Chapel are even larger than those in the Peruzzi, extending further downwards and with frames reduced to a minimum.

However, Giotto's monumentality does not depend on size. In the Padua cycle, although the dimensions of the pictures in all three zones are the same, there is a marked trend towards increasing monumentality. The figures in the bottom zone are heavier and more massive than those above, and yet they move more freely in the pictorial field, which now makes use of the whole available surface. The entire surface is converted into pictorial space, although, as always with Giotto, it is space limited in depth, rather like a relief. This is especially true of scenes like *Christ before Caiphas,* and the *Mocking of Christ,* where the action takes place in an architectural setting, but the same basic characteristic can be observed in the Crucifixion scene. Thus in Padua Giotto's development was in the direction of greater monumentality, which he achieved by means of added spatial and plastic values in his compositions. There is an interplay of depth and surface. The surface effects, far from being nullified, are heightened by the three-dimensional values. Furthermore, every picture has a subtle pattern of linear and surface relationships, each part being in correct proportion to the whole, and each line having its precise unalterable position. These characteristics also emerge distinctly in the *Ognissanti Madonna,* which consistently continues the same trend.

The figures in the Peruzzi Chapel *(pls 70, 71, IX)* move with greater freedom than those in the Padua frescoes. The pictures are larger and there is a looser connection between the frames and the architectural features in the pictures. The severe surface uniformity characteristic of the Arena Chapel frescoes is here replaced by flowing rhythms that enliven the pictorial planes, and divide them into distinct sections. This can be seen most clearly in the compositions that consist of two scenes with different settings, for example, the *Birth and Naming of St John,* and *Herod's Feast (pl. 71a).* Similarly, in the scene of the *Annunciation to Zachariah* there are two compact structures standing freely one beside the other. The pictorial space is full of animation, and the design is unconstrained but firmly organized.

occasionally even brownish; in some of the heads the pink cheeks stand out in lively contrast to the light green underpainting. The dark outlines and the lines of the drawing predominate. The powerful sculptural contours, characteristic of the figures in the Peruzzi Chapel, are absent here and the draperies lack the plastic fullness and rich modelling. The draperies, like the faces, are lightly modelled to conform to the surface pattern, except for the averted figures of the Saracens in the scene of the *Ordeal by Fire*; but even there the figures appear in frontal relief and not in the round.[55] The flat linear design is particularly apparent in the painting of the sultan on his throne in the scene of the *Ordeal by Fire* and of the angry father in the *Renunciation* scene, which is thus sharply and characteristically distinguished from its model in the corresponding scene at Assisi *(pl. V)*.

The comparison with Assisi is generally illuminating. The older St Francis legend was naturally taken as the model for all later versions of the theme produced in the Giotto workshop, and sometimes exact though inferior copies were made, for example in San Francesco in Pistoia.[56] In the Bardi Chapel, however, we find a deliberate attempt to break away from the model, and to create something entirely new. Comparison with the corresponding scenes illustrates the striking plastic content of the Assisi compositions, and reveals the deliberate attempt in the Bardi Chapel to produce an opposite effect of linear surface pattern. One further example will serve to illustrate this.

The scene of the *Apparition of St Francis in Arles* posed a difficult problem for a painter concerned with representing the event convincingly. The monks are gathered in the chapter-house of the Franciscan monastery in Arles to listen to a sermon by Friar Antonius of Padua. During the sermon one of the monks, Monaldus, and he alone, perceives St Francis hovering at the entrance of the hall and blessing the brothers with outstretched arms, although in fact the saint was a great distance away.[57] Two independent events, the sermon to the monks and Monaldus' vision, must therefore be depicted simultaneously, and at Assisi this is successfully achieved *(pl. 59)*. The left side-wall of the chapter-house and the ceiling supported by arches are visible exactly as far as the apex. The front of the room is cut away, but can readily be completed in the imagination. The monks sit in rows at the feet of the preacher, listening attentively, except for Monaldus, who sits by himself in the left corner, his eyes fastened on the vision of the saint. The cloister outside, covered by a simple lean-to roof, is seen through the door and the windows. The position of the chapter-house next to the cloister, and the arrangement of the door with two flanking windows, are in accordance with the ancient custom. The setting has the same realism as the rest of the scene; the story could not be told more vividly.

The spatial arrangement of the corresponding scene in the Bardi Chapel *(pl. 69 a)* would not be easy to understand without knowing the story and without the assistance of the representation at Assisi. The setting is reversed. The view is from the cloister garden through the intervening cloister into the chapter-house. The cloister also has a lean-to roof, which is seen in cross-section where the two side wings are cut off. Most of the monks sit on benches in the cloister, and only a few are in the chapter-house, where Friar Antonius preaches. St Francis is seen in the doorway, standing firmly on the raised floor of the chapter-house. Behind him, traces of a Crucifixion scene can be made out on the rear wall.

This highly artificial, one might almost say cryptographic, presentation of the scene, which nevertheless remains the same as that in the Assisi picture, clearly reveals the stylistic peculiarity of the Santa Croce frescoes. In addition there is the emphatic frontality and symmetry of their composition, and the surface pattern of the monks in the cloister and the figure of St Francis in the doorway. His raised arms and the curve of the arch form a circle in two dimensions, in contrast to Assisi, where the saint's arms extend beyond the door-posts. The structure of the space, arranged in numerous successive layers, one behind the other, is in strange contradiction to the severe two-dimensional pattern, and produces the most unexpected overlapping effects. The way in which only the tops of the heads of the monks seated inside the chapter-house are shown is almost ludicrous *(pl. 69 b)*. The virtuosity displayed in the use of perspective with an apparently flat surface design evokes a subtle charm, and produces a tension similar to that of the composition of the Baroncelli Altar.[58]

The Bardi Chapel scene has none of the naive freshness and narrative power of the Assisi fresco. Contrary to the tenor of the legend, most of the monks are looking towards St Francis, and it is impossible to distinguish brother Monaldus, who alone sees the vision. It is not even clear that we are present at a sermon, as there is hardly any connection between the monks and Friar Antonius, who is seen through the window. Such indifference to the narrative is typical of an eclectic, mannerist stage of stylistic development. The concern is not with the content but with the aesthetic aspect, which has great beauty, though of a cool and abstract kind, giving the impression of a vision rather than a drama. The powerful effect that this peculiar two-dimensional method of representation can produce is evident in the title scene of Santa Croce, *The Stigmatization of St Francis,* above the chapel's entrance arch and visible from the entrance to the church *(pl. 68).*[59]

1   Castelseprio, Santa Maria foris portas · *The Journey to Bethlehem*

2   San Vincenzo al Volturno · *Crucifixion*

3 a   Rome, Temple of Fortuna Virilis
St John Receiving the Apostles

3 b   Rome, San Clemente
Lower Church
Ascension (detail)

4   Galliano, San Vincenzo · *The Prophet Jeremiah*

5   Sant'Angelo in Formis · *Christ Enthroned*

ALLIS · QVATTVOR HILEGVM PIA MVNDO IVSSA DEĐ

DOMINIS ... R OBEDIIT: TVNC MAGI ... T ... MVNO ...

... NOMAE ... DEDIT ... VNC ...

... MINE DONAVIT TE SVS ...

7   Sant'Angelo in Formis · *The Archangel Michael*

6   Sant'Angelo in Formis · a *Christ and the Adultress* · b *Christ Healing the Blind*

ICCLIACEL.RELLIT   QVEPRÆVIAMATER

8 Rome, San Clemente, Lower Church · *The Miracle of St Clement*

9 Nepi, Sant'Elia · *The Elders of the Apocalypse*

10a   Tuscania, San Pietro · *Meeting of SS. Peter and Paul*

10b   Rome, San Giovanni a Porta Latina · *Creation of Adam*

11 Tuscania, San Pietro · *Ascension* (detail)

13   Sutri, Cathedral · *Christ Enthroned*

12 a, b   Tivoli, Cathedral · Triptych (side panels)

14 Civate, San Pietro al Monte
a *Angels Fighting the Apocalyptic Dragon*
b *Christ Enthroned in New Jerusalem*

15a, b Civate, San Pietro al Monte · *Angels*

16a,b Aquileia, Cathedral, Crypt · Paintings in the ambulatory and decoration on the dado

17   Aquileia, Cathedral, Crypt · *St Peter Ordaining St Hermagoras*

18 Rome, SS. Quattro Coronati, St Sylvester Chapel · *Entry of St Sylvester into Rome*

19a Grottaferrata, Abbey Church · *Moses with the Snake*

19b PIETRO CAVALLINI *Head of Christ*
(detail from the *Last Judgment*) · Rome, Santa Cecilia

19c PIETRO CAVALLINI *Apostles* (detail from the *Last Judgment*) · Rome, Santa Cecilia

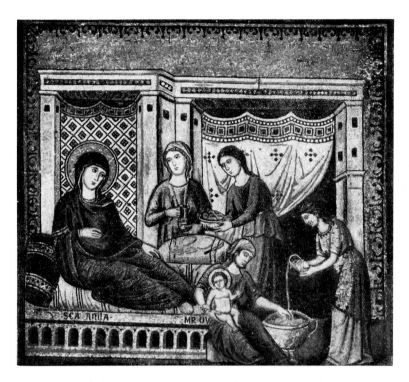

20 a   PIETRO CAVALLINI *Birth of the Virgin* · Rome, Santa Maria in Trastevere

20 b   PIETRO CAVALLINI *Presentation in the Temple* · Rome, Santa Maria in Trastevere

21 a JACOPO TORRITI
Coronation of the Virgin
Rome, Santa Maria Maggiore

21 b   Roman, *c.* 1290, *Prophet* · Rome, Santa Maria Maggiore

22   *Crucifix*, second half of 12th century · Pisa, Museo Nazionale

23   *Crucifix*, first quarter of 13th century · Pisa, Museo Nazionale

24 a *Washing of the Feet* (detail of pl. 22)

24 b *Women at Christ's Tomb* (detail of pl. 23)

25 *Head of Christ* (detail of pl. 23)

26 *Virgin* (detail of pl. 27)

27 GIUNTA PISANO *Crucifix*
Assisi, Santa Maria degli Angeli

28 ALBERTUS (1187) *Crucifix* (detail)
Spoleto, Cathedral

29 BERLINGHIERO *Crucifix* (detail)
Lucca, Pinacoteca

30a *Sermon to the Birds*
(detail of pl. 31)

30b *Healing of the Lame*
(detail of pl. 31)

31 BONAVENTURA BERLINGHIERI (1235)
St Francis · Pescia, San Francesco

32 SCHOOL OF LUCCA (*c.* 1260) *Madonna* · West Germany, private collection

33 COPPO DI MARCOVALDO
Madonna del Carmine
Florence, Santa Maria Maggiore

34 a   MASTER OF THE BIGALLO *St Zenobius Altarpiece* (detail)
Florence, Opera del Duomo
34 b   Detail of pl. 33

35   COPPO DI MARCOVALDO *Madonna*
Orvieto, Santa Maria dei Servi

36 GUIDO DA SIENA *Maestà*
Siena, Palazzo Pubblico

37 a   GUIDO DA SIENA *Retable* · Siena, Pinacoteca

37 b   *St John the Evangelist* (detail of pl. 37 a)

GUIDO DA SIENA *Annunciation* · Princeton, University Gallery

39   CIMABUE *Angel* (detail of pl. 40)

40 CIMABUE *Santa Trinita Madonna* · Florence, Uffizi

41 DUCCIO (1285) *Rucellai Madonna* · Florence, Santa Maria Novella

42 a   CIMABUE *Prophet* (detail of pl. 40)

42 b   CORSO DI BUONO (1284)
St John Raises Two Dead Men
(detail from *The Sorcerer Aristodemus
and the Proconsul*)
Montelupo, San Giovanni

43 DUCCIO *Angel* (detail of pl. 41)

44   CIMABUE *Crucifix* · Florence, Museo di Santa Croce

45 CIMABUE *St John* (detail of pl. 44)

46 Assisi, San Francesco, Upper Church
Choir and transept

47 a Assisi, San Francesco,
Upper Church · Nave
47 b *St Francis Legend*

48 CIMABUE *Women Lamenting* (detail of pl. 49)   49 CIMABUE *Crucifixion* · Assisi, San Francesco

50 CIMABUE *Angels* (detail of pl. 49)   51 CIMABUE *Spectators at the Cross* (detail of pl. 49)

52 FILIPPO RUSUTI *The Creation* · Assisi, San Francesco

53 Filippo Rusuti *Head of the Creator* (preparation, *cf.* pl. 52) · Assisi, San Francesco

54　Giotto *Esau and Isaac* · Assisi, San Francesco

55 GIOTTO *Head of Esau* (detail of pl. 54)

56 GIOTTO *Sermon to the Birds* · Assisi, San Francesco

57　Giotto *Confirmation of the Rule of the Order* · Assisi, San Francesco

58 GIOTTO *St Francis' Father* (detail of pl. V)

59 GIOTTO *Apparition of St Francis at Arles* · Assisi, San Francesco

60 GIOTTO *Crucifix* · Florence, Santa Maria Novella

61   Detail of pl. 60

62 a   GIOTTO *Madonna* · Assisi, San Francesco

62 b   GIOTTO *Enthroned Madonna* ·
Florence, San Giorgio alla Costa

63 GIOTTO *Ognissanti Madonna* · Florence, Uffizi

64 GIOTTO detail of pl. 62 b

65 Giotto detail of pl. 63

66a GIOTTO *Flight into Egypt*
Padua, Arena Chapel

66b GIOTTO *Christ before Caiphas*
Padua, Arena Chapel

67 Detail of pl. 66b

69 a, b
Master of the Bardi Chapel
Apparition of St Francis at Arles
Florence, Santa Croce

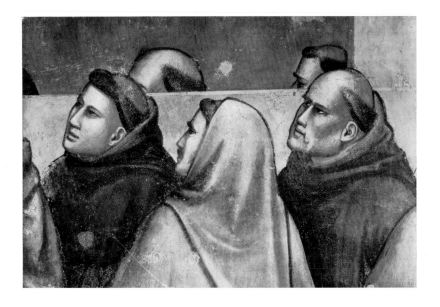

68   Master of the Bardi Chapel *Stigmatization of St Francis* (detail) · Florence, Santa Croce

70 GIOTTO *Musician* (detail of pl. 71 a)

71 a   GIOTTO *Herod's Feast* · Florence, Santa Croce
71 b   GIOTTO *Assumption of St John* · Florence, Santa Croce

72 BERNARDO DADDI (1333) *Madonna with Two Donors* (centre panel of a triptych) · Florence, Bigallo

All these are features that can hardly be ascribed to Giotto at any stage of
his extensive development. They would be a negation of everything he aspired to and accomplished in the first half of his life, and also of the free and
elevated style he achieved later in the Peruzzi Chapel. The Peruzzi frescoes
are deeply rooted in Giotto's earlier works, and as products of the post-Padua
period are a completely consistent development. But along the route between
the Arena Chapel and the Peruzzi Chapel there is no place for the Bardi
Chapel frescoes. Could they possibly be later than those in the Peruzzi Chapel?
This could only be so if, at the end of his life, Giotto had turned to a refined
eclecticism and himself became the creator of a 'Giotto mannerism'.

Such a supposition cannot be entertained. It is our conviction that the Bardi
frescoes do not fit into Giotto's work either before or after the Peruzzi Chapel
and that analysis on stylistic grounds alone makes it clear that they cannot
be attributed to him. The types and proportions of the figures are not his,
nor are the technique and colours compatible with his practice: the colours
are too heavy and opaque and the lines too hard and brittle. Giotto's style
was never heavy, and as the Peruzzi Chapel shows, in spite of its disfigurement, it became steadily lighter and easier in later years. The style and even
the types of figures of the Bardi frescoes could possibly be accounted for by
attributing the execution to assistants, as evidently several hands participated
in the work. But the designs and pictorial ideas as a whole are not Giottesque
either. The spirit and rhythm of the compositions are different from the start,
and are not the product of the elemental force of a unified sense of life that
informs Giotto's *œuvre*. The Bardi Chapel frescoes are the first great, characteristic manifestation of the spirit of the following generation.

Giotto's pupils were born into a situation similar to that in which the followers of the great High Renaissance masters found themselves. The towering
figure of Giotto, like Michelangelo's in the late Renaissance, cast a shadow
over all their work and inhibited the creation of a new style or the development of a new artistic synthesis. Until the end of the Trecento, Giotto's style
was the inevitable point of departure for his successors, with the result that
their work lost its freshness and became formalistic, eclectic, and artificially
archaic, or was reduced, for a time, to a premature, undisciplined naturalism.

The master of the Bardi Chapel was a formalist. He was familiar with the
methods of three-dimensional representation devised by Giotto, but he used
them for quite contrary purpose. For him the illusion of depth was merely
a piquant feature added to his elaborate surface pattern to give an even more
artificial effect. The extension of the pictures to the limits of the wall space
available, and the primary concern with surface effects are characteristic of

mid-Trecento painting. Formally this meant the reversion to two-dimensional composition. The tension between surface and depth was also used deliberately for artistic effect, as for instance in the work of Orcagna and others. The important pupil of Giotto, who, we believe, painted the Bardi Chapel frescoes, was one of the founders of this new style. Although trained in Giotto's workshop, he is closer to Orcagna than to Giotto. It is indeed probable that the Bardi Chapel was done as one of Giotto's commissions, like the Baroncelli Altar and many other works, and was therefore regarded by his contemporaries, and by Ghiberti, as Giotto's work. The date of the frescoes is probably considerably later than 1317, the date given by historians as the earliest possible. That was the year in which Louis of Toulouse, who is portrayed in the window wall of the Bardi Chapel, was canonized. Such an early date, however, is quite unacceptable. The stylistic reorientation which we have attempted to describe above indicates a date around 1330.[60] On the other hand, the Peruzzi Chapel, which really seems to give an example of Giotto's late style, was probably also painted not much earlier than 1330 – more precisely, before Giotto's departure for Naples in about 1328.[61]

A reflection of Giotto's great figurative and dramatic innovations is found in Andrea Pisano's reliefs on the bronze doors of the Baptistry in Florence, depicting the life of John the Baptist. Andrea Pisano, who shortly afterwards executed the reliefs on the Campanile after Giotto's designs, was already under his influence while working on the bronze door.[62] For these scenes he drew on the iconography of the Peruzzi Chapel frescoes, and the style of his work bears the stamp of the Giotto model. The strongly modelled figures with their richly folded draperies are Giottesque forms translated into the medium of bronze sculpture, although Andrea, following the current fashion, accentuated the flow of the folds, and at times lapsed into mere linear ornamentality. But the grouping, the restrained drama, the economy and clarity of architectural and landscape motifs are all inspired by Giotto. It is hardly possible that the single source of this dominant influence was the Arena Chapel frescoes, done at a much earlier date. A far more likely supposition is that Andrea was inspired by Giotto's current style, of which the Peruzzi Chapel may have been an example. The bronze doors were begun in 1330, and completed in 1336. Andrea became Giotto's closest associate in the construction and sculptural decoration of the Campanile, and after Giotto's death he was appointed his successor to the office of supervisor of the cathedral works.[63]

Ghiberti attributes the earliest Campanile reliefs to Giotto and Andrea.[64] Whatever Giotto's share may have been, these reliefs are even closer to the style of the Peruzzi Chapel frescoes than are the bronze doors. This is added support for the view that the frescoes represent Giotto's late style, to which Andrea Pisano could refer directly.

If our analysis is correct, the course of Giotto's development can now be traced from his beginnings in Assisi until the last years of his life. The style of the Peruzzi Chapel is an organic continuation of the Padua period. The principles of design clearly recognizable in Padua have acquired a new freedom without abandoning the distinctive structures of Giotto's pictorial conception. In beauty and rhythm the pictures surpass the Padua frescoes. Precision of form and economy of means, the governing principles of his earlier works, have given way to volume and size. Giotto has achieved that synthesis of monumentality and grace, the combination of autonomous individual figures and an unconstrained compact whole, that constitutes the essence of classical art. It was only in his later years that he became the creator of a style that was to persist for centuries, the foundation of the Italian style of the High Renaissance.

If the internal logical consistency of this development is understood, and its controlled genius recognized, a new yardstick becomes available for assessing Giotto's doubtful works. These will be seen as a reflection of the great personality of Giotto; and the peculiarities of his individual pupils, and their new aspirations, will also emerge more distinctly.

Like San Francesco at Assisi, Santa Croce, the great simple, spacious Franciscan church in Florence, is a monument of the fresco art of Giotto and his pupils. Apart from the two chapels to the right of the choir, which we have already discussed, there are five others in the transept where the original frescoes have been preserved. Three of these were painted by artists who were actually pupils of Giotto. In addition, there is the main choir chapel with a cycle of the legend of the Holy Cross painted by Agnolo Gaddi, a second-generation pupil, and the sacristy with a variety of frescoes by masters more or less dependent on Giotto. Finally on the end wall of the refectory – now the Santa Croce museum – there is an impressive work by Taddeo Gaddi and his pupils. Two other chapels contained paintings by Taddeo Gaddi,[65] and in the Tosinghi and Giugni chapels there were the fresco cycles, previously mentioned, by Giotto, all of which are now lost. And that was not all. The wall enclosing the monks' choir extended well into the nave, and was lined with altars and chapel-like structures, also decorated with monumental paintings. Large frescoes, of which only a few fragments remain, also extended along both walls of the nave, among them a major work by

Orcagna which we shall refer to later. The mere enumeration of these works gives an idea of the scale and exuberance of the Giotto school, which remained active until the end of the Trecento. All the works we have described, done in the course of three generations, were concentrated in a single, though very important church. The Dominican Church of Santa Maria Novella was just as heavily decorated, but there the share of Giotto and his school was much smaller. Most of the frescoes were done in about the middle of the Trecento by Orcagna and his circle.

The decoration in these two churches, unlike that in the Upper Church at Assisi, was not the result of a unified plan, but grew mainly from donations by wealthy families. In spite of this a remarkably uniform effect was achieved in Santa Croce. One part at least was properly planned, namely the huge east wall at the end of the centre aisle with its opening to the choir chapel. The model for this was probably the triumphal arch walls of the Roman basilicas decorated with mosaics or paintings. In Santa Croce this motif was worked out in an entirely new and original way. The upper part of the wall, flanking the choir, has splendid stained-glass Gothic windows, opening to the outside. Beneath these windows, and above the two side chapels, are the pictures of the *Assumption of the Virgin* and the *Stigmatization of St Francis*. There is a close connection between the subjects of these two pictures: in 1224, on 15 August, the day of Mary's Assumption, St Francis withdrew to the solitude of Monte La Verna where the winged Crucifix from which he received the stigmata appeared to him on 14 September.[66] Hence the façade of the choir became the focus of the varied decorative scheme and the entire space of Santa Croce.[67] The dominating role of the pictures shows the new importance painting had achieved in the arts – originating with Giotto.

The monumental painting on the end wall of the south transept in Santa Croce similarly produces the effect of a kind of internal façade, through which a large Gothic arched arcade leads to the Baroncelli Chapel. The decoration of the wall surrounding the arch is designed like a frame surmounted by a great frieze of consoles painted in perspective. Huge figures of prophets fill the areas on the sides of the archivolts, and beneath these there are smaller pictures. The creator of this impressive picture wall was Taddeo Gaddi, who was also responsible for the frescoes inside the chapel. In the past the frescoes were mistakenly connected up with records indicating a date between 1332 and 1337, but in fact they could have been begun as early as 1328, and in any case during Giotto's life-time.[68] Taddeo Gaddi, who worked in Giotto's workshop for many years, emerges here for the first time as an independent artistic personality, who quite deliberately overstepped the stylistic boundaries imposed by Giotto.[69] In the scenes from the life of Mary, on the left wall of the chapel *(pl. 73)*, he abandoned to a large extent the classical rhythm of composition and the idealized types to which Giotto always adhered, and painted instead colourful and animated crowds of people, boldly foreshortened architecture, and a steeply ascending, naturalistic mountain landscape. There are contemporary elements in the drapery, spectators look down from a high gallery, and birds nest in the carefully drawn foliage of trees overtopping a wall. These are all features that Giotto rigidly excluded from his monumental pictorial world. He never painted a scene as passionately animated as the *Expulsion of Joachim from the Temple,* nor did he indulge in such graceful interplay of foreshortening and intersection of lines as in the temple architecture of that picture. Taddeo Gaddi is at his boldest in the *Presentation of the Virgin in the Temple,* where the intricate construction of the building in a number of ascending levels results in a very unconventional distribution of the figures.[70] No earlier painter had dared to separate the participants in a ceremonial event by such distances, with the extreme reduction in size of some of the figures that this involved. We are reminded of Mannerist three-dimensional representations of the sixteenth century. Taddeo Gaddi's great Sienese contemporaries engaged in ventures of similar boldness, but none of them diverged from the recognized principles of design to the same extent as he did in this early phase of his independent activity.[71]

Inside the chapel, the side wall was clearly the first to be decorated. These frescoes are more closely related to Giotto in many of their individual forms than those on the window wall, where a new independent style is evident *(pls 74, 75a)*. This is especially noticeable in the treatment of the draperies – which in the window wall are simpler and more generous and powerful – and in the types of figures, which begin to resemble those in Taddeo Gaddi's later pictures. The work was probably not finished until around 1335, a conclusion supported by the absence of complete uniformity in the decorative scheme.[72] The six narrative scenes on the window wall – from the *Annunciation* to the *Adoration of the Kings* – are more mature and monumental than the uneven series on the other wall depicting the life of the Virgin, although even here Taddeo Gaddi did not confine himself to the Giottesque method of spatial representation.

Above all, however, it is Taddeo Gaddi's treatment of light that is new and original. As we have already noted, the direction of the light in Giotto's pictures always corresponds with the actual sources of light in the room; and we find this theory of the Giotto school propounded by Cennino Cennini in his manual for painters.[73] Taddeo Gaddi, however, used the actual lighting of the Baroncelli Chapel to create a new and very special effect. He started with the assumption that the light from the only window, on the south side, produced an effect of darkness on the surrounding wall, and compensated for this in several pictures by introducing supernatural sources of light, such as the ray of light emitted by the angels in the Annunciation scenes, and the light from the Christ Child hovering in the sky, who appears to the Three Kings in place of the traditional star. In the *Annunciation to the Shepherds (pl. 74),* a yellowish light illuminates the darkness, and shines softly on the mountain landscape. The Three Kings are similarly bathed in divine light. These supernatural sources of light are rendered with remarkable naturalism. The natural light in all the pictures comes, of course, from the direction of the window, and in the allegorical figures in the medallions on the vaults, which are lit from the window and from below, the fall of this natural light is accentuated and has a striking illusionistic effect.

In its overall results this solution had such logical consistency and was so suggestive of new possibilities that it served as model for centuries. Piero della Francesca, in his major work, the fresco cycle at Arezzo, used a similar supernatural source of light to illuminate the window wall in the scene of Constantine's Dream. Raphael took up the same problem in the *Liberation of St Peter* in the Stanze of the Vatican, and found a classical solution which became the inspiration for a whole line of Baroque painters.

It seems that the impetus for these important developments was given by Taddeo Gaddi, and not by Giotto himself. Giotto opened the way to the representation of light and developed the essential technique, but he never explored its possibilities to the same extent as his pupil, because his sure instinct warned him against the inevitable naturalistic consequences. Giotto's artistic theory was universal, systematic, and concerned with the harmonious balance of all the elements, like the *summa,* or universal systems, of the great theologians of the High Middle Ages. It was only the younger generation of his pupils who seized on isolated, specific problems, and pursued them without regard for the relationship of the whole.

In the history of medieval thought, mysticism co-existed with the study of the natural sciences with which Franciscan scholasticism, for example, was concerned. This was no accidental dichotomy but a deliberate attempt to maintain an unbridgeable gap between the temporal and spiritual world, and to accept the contradiction between the two. There is a parallel in Trecento painting where naturalistic and mystical elements co-exist, and are often found side by side even in the work of the same painter. It is in keeping with this outlook, which was becoming increasingly common, to hear that when

Taddeo Gaddi developed eye trouble from observing an eclipse of the sun he appealed in a letter to a clerical friend, Fra Simone Fidati, for spiritual help.[74] This would not be in accord with Giotto's personality as we know it, but it is very characteristic of his most devoted pupil, who became the leading Florentine painter during the three decades after the master's death.[75]

The Baroncelli Chapel is by far the most important of Taddeo Gaddi's surviving works, and historically the most interesting. It represents a phase of experiment, of bold ventures in unexplored fields, which came to an end soon after the completion of the frescoes. In his later works he reverted to more traditional ways. His *Last Supper* in the Santa Croce refectory is intentionally monumental, and the fresco of the *Crucifixion* in the sacristy is a composition of classical harmony and beauty.[76] The panel paintings of Taddeo and his school, which have survived in relatively large numbers, show that he relinquished all radical tendencies as his personal style and his position as custodian of the Giottesque heritage became more established.

It is indicative of the change in artistic attitude soon after Giotto's death, that panel-painting gained increasing importance as an independent form. Outwardly there was no decline in wall-painting but rather the reverse, in that the size and quantity of pictorial cycles increased more than ever in the course of the Trecento. But their monumentality did not keep pace with this growth. The intrinsic monumentality, on which the greatness of Giotto's own classical style rests, was never achieved by his pupils. Instead, an autonomous style of panel-painting emerged, which was not a mere derivative of monumental fresco painting. It was not beneath Taddeo Gaddi's dignity to execute personally a long sequence of narrative panels, which because of their small size cannot be viewed from any distance. Framed in Gothic quatrefoils, they once decorated the doors of the sacristy closet in Santa Croce. Twenty-six panels and two crowning scenes, in the shape of quadrants, have been preserved, some depicting the life of Christ and some the St Francis legend.[77] The scenes contain a fine variety of compositions of simple design and are skilfully set in the intricate Gothic frames. The ornamental effect of the quatrefoil with its inscribed rhombus extends to the pictures and evokes an attractive play of line and chromatic silhouette. The colours are smooth and glowing, often with gay heraldic tints, and sometimes, as in the *Transfiguration of Christ,* the pictures are illuminated by the same yellowish light we noticed in the master's frescoes. Surface and three-dimensional elements, and formal and naturalistic modes of representation, are mingled in a new way typical of the progessive movement in the Trecento. Undoubtedly, this very personal, intimate style of Taddeo Gaddi reached such maturity only after the completion of the Baroncelli Chapel, and not earlier, as historians have hitherto assumed.[78] The practical experience of the Baroncelli Chapel was put to use in these small panels, and fashioned into a personal, independent style. The process was typical of post-Giottesque painting.

Bernardo Daddi, also a pupil of Giotto and one of his closest associates, followed a similar path. The only surviving monumental works by his hand are two frescoes in a chapel in Santa Croce, showing the martyrdoms of St Stephen and St Lawrence. The events are depicted with true Florentine realism, in a style that is angular and brittle and goes back to the period of Giotto's Padua frescoes. Only the extension of the pictorial stage indicates an affiliation with subsequent development. The technique is dry and precise, and of a plain, craftsmanlike character.

This style and technique were better suited to panel-painting. Bernardo Daddi left many altarpieces, including a number of small tabernacles with folding panels, all painted between 1328 and 1348, and at some time in the 1330s he must have begun to employ an ever increasing number of assistants for such work.[79] It is thanks to him and his workshop that in the fourteenth century the new type of small devotional pictures, single panels, diptychs and triptychs, became popular in Florence, and soon appeared further afield. They were used for domestic worship and as travelling altars for people of rank, and they were also in demand for the numerous convents all over the country and the religious associations in the cities. At the beginning of the century Duccio had introduced this pictorial type in Siena, and produced small devotional pictures of high artistic quality. This was the start of an important development, which extended far beyond the Trecento, and which will be referred to again later. Also from Siena, Bernardo Daddi received some inspiration for his fine miniature altars, which immediately enjoyed great popularity in Florence. One of his most charming works of this kind, a tabernacle dated 1333 in the Loggia del Bigallo in Florence *(pl. 72)*, was reproduced a year later by Taddeo Gaddi, correct to the last detail.[80] The perfection of craftsmanship, which became Daddi's special care in the preservation of the Giotto-workshop tradition, reached its height in these small precious objects; they clearly reveal his forceful, precise, sculptural style and formal language. Daddi's colours, deep in earlier years, later become increasingly lighter and show that he was influenced by Sienese painting. On the whole, however, his style was based on that of his teacher, Giotto, and it is possible that as a young man he had worked on the frescoes in the Arena Chapel. This would be consistent with the tradition claiming that he was ten years older than Taddeo Gaddi and thus born in about 1290.

Both these artists were members of the older generation of Giotto's pupils. On the other hand, Maso di Banco, who, as we have seen, had assisted Giotto in Naples, was one of his youngest pupils. Apart from the fragments in Naples, Maso's only surviving works are one fresco cycle in Santa Croce, painted around 1340, and a few panel-paintings.[81] Although his powerful style developed under Giotto's teaching he was no immature copyist. He emerges as a vigorous though not very versatile personality, with a strong feeling for the monumental and a far greater independence as an artist than the older pupils of the master. He appeared at a stage when a direct continuation of the Giottesque tradition was no longer possible. We have seen that Giotto himself gradually outgrew his time, or rather lost touch with contemporary trends. With the exception of Andrea Pisano, who was not a painter, Giotto's late style had no emulators. The true modern style of the time was not that of the Peruzzi Chapel, but that of the contemporaneous or slightly later Bardi Chapel. There had been a return to the two-dimensional mode of representation, which Giotto as a young man had superseded, but it was a return on a higher level, for Giotto's innovations could not be ignored. The most powerful effects the master of the Bardi Chapel achieved arose from the tension between two-dimensional and three-dimensional vision. Giotto's methods were employed, but for contrary purposes.

This was also the point of departure for Maso di Banco, but it was not his way to add to the existing problems. The main feature of his art was a solemnity, an almost sombre suppression of mood and emotion. Although mere virtuosity in the use of artistic effects must have been repugnant to him, a far greater mastery of the modern methods of spatial representation is concealed behind the compact texture of his frescoes than in the works of Bernardo Daddi, or even the apparently progressive Taddeo Gaddi. In one of his pictures he goes beyond Giotto himself, conveying the mood of ruins in a Roman landscape, with decayed buildings of magnificent simplicity, the gaping windows evoking a lost grandeur *(pl. 102a)*. This mood was something entirely new. With Giotto there is no past; everything relates palpably to the present, and he never imparted this kind of significance to a setting. Maso does much more than set the necessary scene for the narrative. The events of the legend he is depicting take place in Rome: the pope, St Silvester, binds the dragon that had been harassing the Romans, and brings to life the two sorcerers who had been poisoned by the dragon's breath. Any other fourteenth-century painter would have been satisfied to indicate the locale by a few symbolic features. In Maso's picture the event becomes almost subordinate to the striking effect of the setting. The figures are skilfully related to the architectural elements, but the resulting interplay of depth and surface effects diminishes the dramatic content of the story, which in Giotto's hands would have been enhanced.

In Maso's work the scenery remains predominant even when the open landscape is almost completely obstructed by buildings. In the lunette picture of the *Baptism of Constantine,* the figures are placed within such a closely interlocking complex of buildings that their freedom of movement is severely restricted. The importance of the figures, which is already diminished by their small scale, is further reduced by the architecture. The autonomy of the forms, the basis of Giotto's dramatic narrative style, is sacrificed, as in the Bardi Chapel, to the encroaching principle of abstract composition. Yet the separate figures are more individually characterized here than in Giotto's work *(pl. 102b)*. We thus find in the work of Maso, possibly Giotto's most important pupil, an illustration of the same contradictory stylistic development as we have previously noticed.

But something much more significant becomes apparent, a profound change in the spirit of the age. The lofty plane on which Giotto had set human action and emotion could no longer be maintained by the generation that immediately followed him. It resorted to artistic virtuosity, attention to individual characteristics, and ultimately to the acceptance of new formal as well as intellectual restrictions. These are stylistic elements which do not exclude but rather complement and depend on each other. Giotto was not concerned with the individual, but with the essential qualities of recognized types, and it was this that gave his figures their autonomous existence. The diminished ability to perceive and render typical form was the underlying reason for the changed artistic direction in the decades after Giotto's death.

8 Duccio

When it turned away from Giotto, whose superior consistent style nevertheless continued to exercise a forceful influence, Florentine painting found itself in an oddly self-contradictory situation, which became most clearly apparent in the middle of the Trecento in the work of Andrea Orcagna. But before dealing with this we must return once more to the beginning of the century, when the new Trecento sense of style became predominant throughout northern Tuscany, and Florentine art asserted its supremacy. In Pisa and Lucca all the older artistic traditions were spent, and especially in painting the energies of these two cities, once so immensely productive, were exhausted. Only Pisan sculpture experienced a last burst of creativity in the brilliant achievement of Giovanni Pisano; however, he produced his most important works in Siena, and not in his native city. He accepted without reserve the Gothic ideal of form, which was spreading from the north. In his excitingly modern style, influenced by current trends and yet highly personal, all traces of the local pre-Gothic tradition were lost. In painting, no equals to this vigorous style emerged for the time being.

In Siena the course of development was different from that in Florence. Only in Siena can one talk of a genuine continuity, an organic development of tradition. The great painter responsible for this was Duccio di Buoninsegna. His *Madonna Rucellai* of 1285 has already been mentioned,[1] and we remarked that this work of his early manhood appears modern and progressive beside the similarly constructed Madonna of Cimabue. A first step towards overcoming the dependence of the Duecento on the archaic, it reveals faint traces of the Gothic style but at the same time belongs to the 'maniera greca'.[2]

Duccio was not a revolutionary artist. He created no new artistic system, and gave no new pictorial interpretation of reality. His virtue lay in maintaining the heritage of Byzantine art, thus preserving a valuable part of the medieval spirit and passing it on to the new era. His Madonnas are full of the melancholy, the solemnity, and the mature oriental beauty of the Byzantine world. Although he modernized the style, the technique, and the chromatic effects, he adhered closely to Byzantine models, especially those in manuscript illuminations. The spirit and content of his art remained unchanged: timeless, undramatic, and devoted to a single, strong emotion that places us under its powerful spell. This passion, this capacity for religious fervour and mystical absorption survived for a long time in Sienese painting, and frequently rose to the level of ecstasy. It is this that distinguished Sienese painting from all other Italian schools until well into the sixteenth century, as far as Sodoma and Beccafumi, so long as a Sienese school of any significance remained in existence.

The conservatism characteristic of Duccio's work was not merely a continuation of established tradition. His style was decidedly original. Its origins and sources are difficult to determine, but the essential lyrical strain in his art and his adherence to Byzantine models associate him with Guido da Siena, his most important predecessor, although there does not seem to have been a real pupil-master relationship between them. Attempts to detect Duccio's hand in the Assisi frescoes can be supported only by stylistic arguments,[3] for there is no documentary evidence that Duccio was ever engaged in wall-painting. His relationship to Cimabue, from whom he doubtless drew some inspiration without being fundamentally influenced, is also far from clear. Yet another unresolved question is whether Duccio made the designs for the stained glass of the large round window of the choir of Siena Cathedral. This work was commissioned in 1287–8, and the designs were probably by Duccio, but unfortunately the name of the artist who created them is not noted in the records. The paintings depict the *Death, Assumption,* and *Coronation of the Virgin,* and in addition the Four Evangelists, and four saints;[4] although there are unmistakable affinities with the *Rucellai Madonna,* especially in the *Coronation* scene, there is hardly anything that links them with the Assisi frescoes. The half-length Madonna figure from Crevole, now in the Opera del Duomo in Siena, also recalls the *Rucellai Madonna,* but it lacks the fluid line of Duccio's figures. His pure personal style appears again only in two small panels, painted almost with the delicacy of miniatures. They are devotional pictures, the *Madonna Enthroned with Angels* in the Kunstmuseum in Bern,[5] and the *Madonna with Three Franciscan Monks* in the Siena Pinacoteca Nazionale, both fervent

and mystical in mood and content. The *Bern Madonna,* doubtless belonging
in the 1290s, displays a strong Byzantine influence in its solemn melancholy
mood, but it also has a free, graphic and pictorial style, especially apparent in
the deeply emotional figure of the Madonna, clasping the Child to her bosom.
The *Siena Madonna* has the same qualities on a more mature stylistic level,
and was probably done after the turn of the century.

Duccio's major work is the *Maestà,* painted for the high altar of Siena
Cathedral. Commissioned in 1308 and completed in 1311, it was carried from
the master's workshop to the Cathedral in solemn procession to the accom-
paniment of drums and trumpets and the jubilation of the populace.[6] It is
now in the Opera del Duomo in Siena, the front and rear sides separated
from each other. Parts of the predella and the crowning panels are dispersed
among foreign collections.[7]

Maestà, Majesty, is the vernacular for the tabernacles and devotional pictures
still found in the streets and public places of Italian cities, referring in particular to representations of the Enthroned Madonna. In Siena the Mother of
God was revered as sovereign in a special sense: in gratitude for the victory
of Montaperti in 1260 the city submitted itself by solemn act to the sover-
eignty of the Heavenly Queen. Duccio created this work for the Cathedral
dedicated to her, as the highest tribute art could offer to her glorification.

The Madonna is seated on the throne, the divine Child in her arms, surrounded by angels, apostles and saints. The oblong panel, raised in the centre, is
treated as a single undivided surface, a bold undertaking for such a large
picture, and one that had no parallel for a long time, but there is no corresponding uniformity in the handling of the three-dimensional space. What
unites the figures is their common relationship to the Madonna. Each figure
is distinct and individual, and is depicted with unconcealed pleasure in its
beauty and sensuous quality *(pl. 76),* and yet together they form a rhythmic,
two-dimensional pattern. The grouping of the figures, arrayed towards the
centre, is masterly: the four patron saints of Siena[8] kneel in the foreground
and the other figures stand in rows behind and above one another. The two
female saints on each side, in fine flowing Gothic draperies, also face towards
the centre. However, one has the impression that the rows of figures could
continue indefinitely to the sides and upwards – which is in keeping with the
celestial setting.

The perspective plane is therefore fluid and without firm boundaries; this
also applies to the much smaller narrative scenes accompanying the main
pictures and to those painted on the back of the panel. The predella depicted
the story of the Birth and Childhood of Christ. Above the main panel were

scenes from the latter part of the Virgin's life, probably concluding with an Assumption, now lost. The back of the panel, like a huge page of miniatures, gave an account of the Life, Death and Resurrection of Christ *(pl. 77),* with special emphasis on the Passion. The sequence of the narrative, in four rows, starts from the bottom, the Appearances of Christ after the Resurrection filling the whole of the upper zone. In the centre is the Crucifixion, prominent on account of its size. The numerous figures and subsidiary scenes on the front of the panel form an unusually rich composition, but the abundance of figures and the variety of events portrayed on the back are overwhelming; and yet they convey no effect of drama or even of epic narrative, for the events all seem to be contemporaneous without any chronological order or specific locale. Landscapes, cities, and a diversity of buildings provide settings for the individual scenes, foreshortened and drawn with careful attention to the architectural detail. Occasionally a view is given into the interior of a building, as in the *Temptation of Christ on the roof of the Temple.*[9] But in all this there is a lack of logical coherence. The settings are mere backdrops for the figures: the landscapes, with rocks stylized in the Byzantine manner, are unrealistic, and the walled cities, as in the *Temptation of Christ on the Mountain,* resemble the completely interchangeable towns in medieval illuminated books. Yet there are also some surprisingly successful and advanced solutions: the scenery in front of the city gate in the *Entry into Jerusalem,* and the way the outdoor scene of *Peter denying Christ* is connected by a staircase to the interior scene above it of *Christ before Annas.*[10]

If we were not aware of the rich tradition behind Duccio's art, we might think that he worked to no system. His work does not seem to conform to any rule, and although the detail is often original and arresting, the overall effect is unsystematic, diffuse and without plan. Yet in each of the many scenes there is a focal point, and sometimes more than one, Christ or some other principal figure, or even a group of figures. The dominant motif is based on the figures, delineated according to the formulas prescribed by Byzantine art for centuries.[11] From these, Duccio derived complete, richly articulated configurations independent of the pictorial context as a whole, like the standardized *exempla* of medieval art. Sometimes they are single figures, or groups with their own linear and spatial unity, or sometimes landscapes or architectural settings. They are seldom more than isolated details, and only occasionally entire compositions. One could reconstruct the book of patterns from which Duccio worked. The figures are always primary, and have an inherent significance which can be interpreted as action; but above all is a permanent characteristic, the expression of an intellectual content. As a result, the scenes are not dramatic. The pictorial space is not fundamental, as it is with Giotto, and the form and boundaries of the perspective plane are not the starting point for the composition but its more or less accidental outcome. The way in which the pictures on the back of the panel are placed next to each other with very little framing is indicative of this. Many scenes are overloaded, and in others, as in the *Descent from the Cross,* the distribution is lopsided. The figures are frequently crowded together, one head next to the other, with the feet of only a few showing. The human forms seem to displace no space, and the mass of each is determined solely by its relative importance in the theme of the picture.

There would be no point in drawing attention to all these purely medieval features if they did not stand side by side with the new, rational mode of representation evolved by Giotto. The Arena Chapel had been completed when Duccio began his *Maestà*. Duccio's art is unmonumental and he has no understanding of structure. The influence of his style was confined almost entirely to his native town, Siena, and its immediate domain. Nevertheless he is undoubtedly one of the great masters of all time. Even Ghiberti recalls him with high esteem, and refers to him as a '*nobilissimo pictore*'.

Duccio's continued undisputed eminence derives from the virtues of medieval art, which owed its greatness to a creative conservatism, that is to say, the preservation of a genuine living tradition. These virtues Duccio possessed to the highest degree, together with an original artistic temperament, acute sensibility and vivid perception, qualities that can be sensed but hardly described or analyzed. This aspect of his art is most directly revealed in his colours,[12] which glow against the bright ground, especially the red tones, cherry-red and carmine, threaded with the gold of the hems. These are used in combination with deep blue, a wide range of closely related colours from pink to violet and pale blue, and a cool clear sea-green. Green is also found in all the underpainting of the flesh, which has a pink tint in the female figures and a strong brownish tint in the male figures. Everything is softly moulded by means of colour rather than by the use of white highlights for the modelling, and thus the plastic values appear animated, and not abstract as in the works of the Florentine masters. Although most of the tones are cool, the effect is of rich glowing colour, and the overall impression that of a work in mosaic or precious enamel. Duccio could justifiably claim to have a close affinity with the painters of an older culture, the masters of Byzantine sacred art. Compared with Giotto's rational system of representation, ordered in every detail, his method seems arbitrary; and yet it followed the guiding principle, inherent in medieval painting and persisting in Eastern Orthodox

Duccio religious art almost up to our own time, of embodying a spiritual vision in concrete pictorial terms. It also had certain characteristic formal elements: a two-dimensional pattern, ornamentality, the main figures presented frontally, and corporeal and spatial values expressed simultaneously from multiple viewpoints.

This method of representation enabled Duccio to incorporate a mass of realistic observation, and it gives his art its fairy-tale, dream-like quality, with reality and mystery intermingled. The narrative scenes are full of life, often passionate in expression, and suffused with sensitive, human feeling; and yet in spite of this they are never realistic. Duccio's Madonnas, though they bend tenderly over the Child, and gaze with mild penetration on the faithful, are not mortal creatures. What realism they have is subsidiary. Duccio appeals directly to the emotions, and himself creates emotionally; and any attempt to interpret his works by rational analysis cannot hope to penetrate this central core of his creative impulse.

So personal a style could not, like Giotto's, become the foundation of an extensive school. Artists wanting to model themselves on Duccio had to renounce their own personalities and follow him as disciples. This is precisely true of two of his pupils, Ugolino da Siena and Segna di Buonaventura, both of whom had only one ambition, to acquire completely the style of their master. Ugolino's style is somewhat harsher, and Segna's smoother and more elegant.[13] A third artist, known as the Master of Città di Castello after his major work, a *Maestà,* has an even more externalized style.[14] Of greater importance was the painter of the *Madonna* in the church of Badia a Isola, not far from Siena, who used very archaic elements with striking precision and lucidity. This, together with the sharpness of line and the hard vitreous colours, show that we have here the work of a gifted eclectic painter, who adhered to Duccio's early style and long remained unaffected by the master's later development.[15]

Duccio died in 1318 or the first half of 1319. The *Maestà* is his last dated work. He lived to see the rise of younger masters in Siena with new aspirations, who outgrew the world he was familiar with. Two great artistic influences now imposed themselves with increasing effect on Sienese painting: the monumental style created by Giotto in neighbouring Florence, and the new Gothic style, which spread through Italy from various sources. The cathedral in Siena itself, under construction already for half a century, proclaimed the triumph of the new Gothic style. Giovanni Pisano, the creator of the cathedral's façade and its grandiose sculptural decoration, had long been

working in Siena, and provided a direct link with the source of the Gothic, *Duccio*
the Ile-de-France.[16] But the builders of the cathedral were by no means alone in their acceptance of the Gothic. Apart from the cathedral, churches and secular buildings, simpler but equally Gothic in style, were built in Siena, and to an increasing extent determined the character of the city. The Palazzo Pubblico, under construction since 1297, was much more Gothic than the Palazzo Vecchio in Florence, begun a year later.

9 Simone Martini

It took an exceptionally long time for Sienese painting to come under the pervading influence of the Gothic style. Duccio shows only faint traces of the Gothic, which did not affect the fundamental character of his art. But in the second decade of the Trecento there was a sudden change.

Simone Martini's fresco in the Palazzo Pubblico, a *Maestà* painted in about 1315,[1] is permeated with Gothic sentiment *(pl. 78)*. The throne of the Queen of Heaven, a delicate structure of pure Gothic form, stands beneath an airy baldachin supported by slender vertical posts. The figure of the Madonna herself, with fleur-de-lis crown and wide, gold-embroidered cloak, is evidently based on a Gothic model, probably of northern France. Slender and proud, and displayed in richly plastic draperies with linear folds, she sits in truly royal state, conforming to the courtly ideal celebrated at that time in the art of the entire Western world. The facial types of the Madonna and Child bear no resemblance to the Byzantine. A large retinue of angels and saints surrounds the throne in a well-composed semicircle. The four patron saints of Siena kneel in the front row, as in Duccio's *Maestà,* but this is the only tangible link with the older master's work, completed a bare four years earlier. The two angels kneeling at the steps of the throne and holding up bowls of roses and lilies, are a new motif. Giotto had also assigned two such angels holding gold vases with lilies and roses to his *Ognissanti Madonna,* but their reverent postures and offerings are much more restrained; Simone's kneeling angels strike a true Gothic note. Among the other figures in his *Maestà* there are indeed some that recall the old Byzantine type, but this applies only to the faces; the figures themselves and the draperies are all imbued with the new Gothic rhythm.

These traces of Byzantine types and several other indications suggest that Simone Martini came from Duccio's workshop.[2] If so, he made the break with his master's ideals very quickly and determinedly. The sheer monumental size of his *Maestà*, with figures larger than life-size, exceeds anything that had hitherto been customary in Siena. The Gothic trend is only one of the elements in the new style encountered here. Equally important, though possibly less obvious, is the affinity with Giotto. Already, in this first major work, Simone shows that he could handle spatial representation with the logical consistency of Giotto, for a great deal of rational thought is concealed behind the apparently loose arrangement and general tapestry-like effect of the *Maestà*. The perspective of the baldachin, seen from below, is clear and convincing, and the distribution of the figures in receding rows is accomplished with equal skill. Closer examination reveals an ordered symmetry in the apparently informal arrangement. The spatial problem is handled with greater ease than one finds in Giotto's work, but it was the pictorial system of representation created by Giotto that made the animated rhythmic solution possible. In addition, the lighting of the figures from the direction of the window conforms to the rule established by Giotto. The carefully delineated frame, also lit from the same side, is separated from the picture by a frieze of tiny consoles, foreshortened in perspective when seen from the middle and from below. This perspective system and centralized method of representation could not have been derived from Duccio nor from any impetus received from French art. It could have come only from Giotto, and there is no doubt that at this early stage, before 1315, Simone was already familiar with and versed in the new style of Florentine painting.[3] Obviously he cannot be considered one of Giotto's pupils in the narrow sense. Simone's personality was too strong for him to be content with mere emulation of the master. He sought, and already realized in his *Maestà*, a synthesis of the Duccio legacy and Giotto's deliberate, systematic style. Emotional fervour, graceful and sometimes passionate linear expressiveness, delicate and sensuous beauty of colour were the heritage of his Sienese origin. From Giotto he derived monumentality, rational order, and the new unifying vision. Something of both he probably sensed in Gothic art, which also combined rational order with transcendental elements, and it was perfectly natural for him to substitute the Gothic of his time and environment for the Byzantine style. This was not a renunciation of local tradition, but indeed the only way of preserving it. Through a deep affinity with the new style, Siena became the most 'Gothic' Italian city in the fourteenth century, and Simone Martini its most ardent disciple in painting. At the same time he was the most systematic and logical of

Sienese painters, and the only one of them whose fame, like that of the Florentine Giotto, soon spread far beyond the boundaries of his native city.

Simone Martini was summoned to Naples by King Robert of Anjou more than a decade before the same distinction was conferred on Giotto.[4] In 1317, or shortly after, he completed a large panel in Naples in honour of Louis of Toulouse, the king's brother, who had just been canonized *(pl. 79)*. The picture, now in the Naples Museo di Capodimonte, was also a political gesture: the saint, having himself renounced the crown of Naples, places it on the head of the king, shown on a much smaller scale kneeling beside him,[5] thus legitimizing the coronation beyond any possibility of worldly protest. At that time the secular power of a dynasty was still closely related to its divine authority. Beneath his magnificent bishop's cope the saint wears a Franciscan habit tied with a cord. The eyes in the pallid, enraptured countenance, by no means handsome yet full of inner fervour, are fastened on things not of this world; and in the presence of this fixed and lustreless gaze the splendid trappings so lavishly displayed by the painter lose all their brilliance. The irregular features are stripped of all conventional stylization. Though it is certainly not an actual portrait, it is an extremely personal and portrait-like representation. The glitter of the gold, the rich Gothic linear play, the almost barbaric abundance of ornamental and heraldic motifs, do not detract from the central religious significance of this saintly figure. Naturalistic and decorative elements, intensified to a degree hitherto unknown, are used side by side. The two belong together because the desired effect is achieved through the tension between the real and the unreal, the temporal and the divine. There is hardly another work of painting in which the essence of saintliness has been realized so convincingly in the form of an historical figure, human and frail.

Simone Martini produced other works in Naples; but as none has survived our only knowledge of them is by inference from occasional indications in Neapolitan painting. The clearest is an apparently reliable copy of a Madonna panel in San Domenico in Naples.[6] The original was presumably the archetype of a new kind of Madonna that Simone repeated on the portal of Avignon Cathedral. The Madonna is no longer shown in state on a high throne, but is seated on a cushion on the floor, where she nurses the Child. Thus the old Byzantine interpretation, which conceived the Madonna not as a ruler, but as the humble mother of the Divine Child, appears here in the new, purely Western, pictorial type of the *Madonna dell'Umiltà*. This is possibly the most characteristic and intimate theme of the new devotional pictures of the Trecento, produced for purposes of private worship. All the indications suggest that Simone was the creator of this new pictorial type, which soon spread throughout Italy, above all in Tuscany, and remained popular until the first decades of the fifteenth century. No doubt Simone produced similar representations of the Madonna seated on the floor in Siena itself. A small picture in the Berlin Staatliche Museen, done by one of his closest associates, is a particularly unpretentious, expressive version of the same theme, belonging stylistically to the 1333 *Annunciation,* which will be referred to later.[7]

A multi-panelled altarpiece from Santa Caterina in Pisa, now in the museum there, gives an idea of the style of the master and his workshop in the years around 1320.[8] Between 1322 and 1326 there is no evidence of his presence in Siena, and presumably during those years he was engaged on his major work, the frescoes in the St Martin Chapel in San Francesco at Assisi *(pls 80, 82c, 82d, X).*[9] The harmony between this painting and the architecture of the chapel, and the uniformity of the whole conception, represent an unparalleled achievement in stylistic synthesis. Everything in this unique room, from the perspective of the legendary scenes to the last decorative motif, is done with careful attention to the structure of the Gothic building. Like the great architects of the French Gothic, Simone Martini combined logical thought with the most refined sensuousness and a sure sense of the organic. Just as the strict geometric ground-plan in no way detracts from the animation of the room, the still abstract illusionism of the painting does not impair the consistent surface design. The delicate chromatic pattern, extending like tapestry between the pillars of the chapel and the groins of the ceiling, everywhere maintains its independent consistency. Simone's work is one of the peaks of Italian Gothic. As a pictorial interpretation of a Gothic room it has no equal.

The south facing chapel, filled with warm light, is entered from the gloomy nave of the Lower Church of San Francesco. The Gothic architecture, of noble, almost classical, proportions, gains warmth and life from the alternating red and yellowish-grey stone-work. The forepart, rectangular in plan, has a plain, arched vault. The inner portion has a five-ribbed vault, and its end walls, containing the windows, form three sides of an octagon. The keystone marks the approximate centre of the room, from which the frescoes are intended to be viewed. The legendary scenes are placed in pairs next to each other along the side walls, and the viewpoint for the architectural structures within the scenes lies in each case on the central dividing line of the wall, except for the single scenes at the top of each wall. Altogether there are ten scenes, five on each wall. On the wall opening to the nave a surprising effect is produced by illusionistic means: painted above the Gothic arched arcade there is a kind of gallery that has the appearance of a bridge over the opening below. On this gallery, beneath a baldachin, the donor of the chapel, Cardinal Gentile da Montefiore (d. 1312), kneels before his patron saint, St Martin.[10] The forceful prelate, accustomed to authority, is depicted with bold realism. His cardinal's hat lies on the balustrade next to him. The face of St Martin, bending down to the kneeling man, has all the features of true piety, steadfastness, kindliness and religious zeal. Behind the two figures on the gallery stretches the blue background of the sky. The perspective of the baldachin, though not of the figures, is correct for a scene high above the spectator's viewpoint. As in Giotto, this is not true illusionistic painting but only a demonstration of the principle of illusionism, the employment of a central viewpoint. Even the half-length figures of saints painted in Gothic niches in the window recesses are included in the perspective system, so that they are correct when viewed from the centre of the chapel. The direction of the light in the picture also follows a uniform rule: it falls from the window wall in the scenes in the chapel itself, and in the figures of saints in the archway to the nave and in the painted Gothic arcades in which they stand. Whereas here, as in the legendary scenes, the light in the pictures falls from the side, the donor group above the arch is lit from the front.

Oddly enough, this elaborate scheme has hardly been remarked upon,[11] whether because it was considered too obvious to be worth mentioning, or because the observance of such rules was taken for granted. But neither of these views is justified: at the time when the frescoes were done the systematic method employed here represented a significant intellectual achievement. Simone Martini is once more following Giotto's lead, but again as an independent artist, freely and creatively interpreting the artistic theory of the Florentine master. Occasionally, as in the perspective of the gallery with the donor groups, and of the niches in the window recesses, he goes much further than Giotto, while at other times he shows greater restraint. In the narrative scenes, with the exception of the two upper ones, which were evidently the first to be painted, the perspective lines, although clearly indicating the oblique view, all run in the same direction *(pl. 80)*. The pictures must be looked at in pairs in order to elicit the common viewpoint. This was done deliberately so that the consistency of the surface effect should not be impaired more than necessary. Giotto, on the other hand, preferred a centralized recession of lines for each of the scenes at Assisi, and also in the Arena Chapel. It was only in the Peruzzi Chapel, presumably for reasons similar to Simone Martini's, that he reverted to receding lines running more or less parallel.

Two conclusions can be drawn: first, that Simone's art was essentially based on Giotto's achievement, and second, that he nevertheless emerges as an artist

X   SIMONE MARTINI, *St Martin Rejecting the Weapons* · Assisi, San Francesco

intellectually independent and playing a creative part in elucidating the rationale of Trecento painting at that stage of its development. The tendency to centralize the composition, which manifests itself in the strict single viewpoint, is in keeping with the main aesthetic feature of the chapel and with the principles of Gothic architecture in general. In a Gothic building all the parts are related to a central axis, and so in Simone's fresco cycle everything is organized from a central point and referred, as far as possible within the limitations of the technique available at the time, to a spectator standing in the middle of the room.

In comparison with this basic affinity to the Gothic approach, all the other features of the frescoes, which are usually described as Gothic, are of secondary importance. The magnificent decorative quality, the two-dimensional harmony, the exquisite silky texture of the colours are all superficial features in themselves, and not the basis but simply the expression of the underlying sense of style. Yet they too contribute to the unique compact effect of the whole work. The same applies to the specifically 'Gothic' naturalism of this painting, which is not, as in Giotto, based on form, but on visual, external aspects. Although, unlike Giotto, Simone Martini was not primarily concerned with standardized and accepted form, he had his own compendium of recognized types. Thus a youthful figure of almost childlike delicacy recurs in his work, reflecting the current courtly aspect of the contemporary style. However, side by side with these idealized types, he depicts highly individualized characters, men fat and thin, knights and commoners, elegant men of the world and humble monks. The musicians in the *Knighting of St Martin (pl. 80)*, the chanting clergymen in the *Service for the Dead,* are portrayed with a penetrating realism which was not seen again until a century later in Jan van Eyck and Pisanello. In depicting such figures, Simone Martini was not subject to the restrictions that Giotto imposed on himself. Nevertheless, throughout the entire pictorial sequence he preserves a pious, charming, legendary tone and a sparkling fairy-tale quality, which still lend an air of enchantment to the peaceful chapel.

On his return to Siena, Simone Martini painted another fresco (dated 1328) in the Palazzo Pubblico, on the wall opposite his *Maestà,* but quite different in theme and character. It is a tribute to the victorious general of the Sienese Republic, Guidoriccio da Fogliano.[12] The long horizontal picture shows a single continuous landscape, a rocky region, in which stand a walled city, a castle, a tented camp and a stockade. There are lances and fluttering banners, but not a single combatant. The only figure is the general who, with fixed gaze, and baton in hand, rides in the foreground of the landscape, which is seen through his eyes, the eyes of a soldier. The gold saddle-cloth of his charger, inlaid with a bizarre pattern, is like a fanfare in the bleak, unpeopled landscape, the oppressiveness of which is only partly alleviated by the toy-like effect of the precise Gothic drawing. By eliminating all distractions the artist displays the fascinating distinctive personality of the general with supreme skill. It is primarily the representation of an individual, and anticipates subsequent developments in portrait painting. Whether it is an actual likeness is impossible to say, but in any case only the general characteristics of the subject are delineated.[13]

At about the same time Simone probably also painted the altarpiece for Sant'Agostino in Siena, with St Agostino Novello as the main figure, surrounded by four scenes from his life.[14] The airy quality that had reached its height in the Assisi frescoes begins here to give way to a more severe manner and a denser disposition of the pictorial elements. Surface and depth effects are no longer in simple harmony, but are skilfully combined to accentuate each other. The figures have become more massive, and their movement and fluid outlines contrast with the gold ground and the smooth surfaces and sharp edges of the architecture. Although the general effect has become more abstract and the pictorial structure more taut, the realism of the representation is actually increased. In the legendary scenes, the scale of the figures to the architecture is more natural than in Assisi. Simone Martini's development thus took a similar turn to that observed in Florentine painting around 1330, though in his work it manifested itself quite differently. It may seem surprising, in this respect, to place the Sienese master, one of the great creative figures of his time, on a level with an eclectic artist like the painter of the Bardi Chapel. However, the formative influence of the contemporary style, predominant all over Europe, also had its effect on him. His famous *Annunciation* of 1333 (now in the Uffizi in Florence, *pl. 81*) is a splendid example of this style, even though it could have been painted nowhere but in Siena.[15] The slender, fragile figures are by no means incorporeal images: on the contrary they are conceived with a fine feeling for movement resulting from accurate observation of anatomical relationships. Unlike Giotto's figures, however, their artistic vitality does not have its source in physical action, but in the flowing linear movement imposed on them, which expresses their inner emotions and gives them reality. In this they resemble such works of northern art, as, to give only one example, the statues of the Apostles installed in the choir of Cologne Cathedral shortly before 1322.[16]

Reference to these affinities with the northern Gothic does not by any means give a complete description of Simone's complex style. He made full use of Giotto's new, three-dimensional, pictorial method even in the *Annunciation,* which has the appearance of an entirely linear and flat composition. In fact Simone creates a pictorial relief with its characteristically abrupt boundary, noticeable here at the sharp line where the marble floor meets the gold ground. The background fills four-fifths of the pictorial area, but everything that lies in front of it has a distinctive spatial character. The carefully drawn perspective of the throne and the golden amphora containing lilies shows how thoroughly Simone had mastered the representational method created by Giotto. The subtle relationship of the Virgin to the angel, expressing both her attraction and her withdrawal, also postulates an understanding of Giotto's sense of the dramatic, even if only in the general presentation of an active interplay between the figures. To Duccio such a relationship was hardly known. Needless to say, however, Simone's treatment of it is quite different from Giotto's. Instead of restrained power and slight yet positive action, Simone depicted hesitation and cautious insistence on the part of the angel, and in the Virgin stifled alarm merging into deep humility; in place of straightforward drama there is an ambiguity of gesture and lightness of movement, as of figures mysteriously arrested in motion. Of the various formal devices used to produce this effect, the subtle tension between the visual space and the gold ground is one of Simone's most important means of expression. There are similar tensions between different parts of the surface area, irrespective of their spatial relationship, and between linear elements. The gold ground is at times intersected by sharp silhouettes, and occasionally it merges with forms that are close to it in colour. With great skill and imagination Simone has assembled a variety of different hues of gold, especially in the figure of the angel, in his wings and flowing cloak, and used glazed colours and various ornamental techniques. As a result, the figure of the angel, an emissary of heavenly light, appears to be part of the gold ground in concentrated form. There is the further tension between the real and the unreal, from which derive the impulse and constant unrest of the mystic perception. Few works of pictorial art have expressed this mystic quality as directly as Simone's *Annunciation.*

The last stage of Simone's development is seen in a picture, now in the Walker Art Gallery in Liverpool, depicting the *Return of the Young Jesus from the Temple (pl. 83).*[17] The figures are more compact than in the *Annunciation,* and the forms more severe and almost too sharply chiselled. Although there is greater stress on the dramatic aspect of the event, the figures appear to be acting not of their own volition, but under an anguished hypnotic compulsion. The tension between the space occupied by the figures and the gold ground is heightened to become a violent, acute contrast, and except for the haloes embossed on the gold ground there is no transitional area. The strong colours – three different shades of red in the figures of Joseph and the young Jesus – have an overheated quality, and stand out sharply against the shining gold. The figures themselves seem confined in their own dark outlines, whose abstract, wilful contours inhibit any freedom of movement. Only in the figure of the Virgin are the contours gentler and more fluid; but she is firmly fixed in her position in the lower left corner of the picture, seated curiously close to the ground as in the *Madonna dell' Umiltà*. The characteristic petrified appearance of the whole composition is reminiscent of the contemporary devotional pictures in which the simplified forms were raised to a kind of symbolic level. This attempt to transform an intimate, individual narrative scene into a standardized mould was bound to fail, but it is indicative of the spirit of the time, which always sought a synthesis between the actual subject and the idealized type.

The picture is dated 1342, and was therefore probably painted in Avignon, where Simone was summoned towards the end of his life[18] and where he died in 1344. His major work in these last years was the fresco decoration in the vestibule of Avignon Cathedral, Notre-Dame-des-Doms, presumably commissioned by Cardinal Jacopo Stefaneschi. The main part, a representation of *St George and the Dragon,* is unfortunately lost,[19] but remnants of the paintings in the tympanum of the main portal and the gable above it, have survived. They were lifted from the wall in 1961–2, and the preliminary drawings were revealed underneath in several layers, one above the other as the work had progressed. The layers were successfully separated and removed from the wall.[20] These monumental drawings are of unique beauty, and their sequence enables us to follow the creative process by which Simone Martini arrived at his final design. The gable above contained a half-length figure of *Christ in Benediction,* surrounded by angels. The face of Christ preserved in the *sinopia* combines sublimity and Gothic sensitiveness.

The theme of the tympanum picture is a *Madonna dell' Umiltà,*[21] a pictorial type probably originating, as mentioned above, with Simone Martini himself. But on account of the dominant position in which the picture is placed, the excessively intimate aspect of the motif of the Madonna nursing the Child is avoided. The Child sits upright in her lap. An angel kneels on each side: one commends the donor, whom he supports with a gentle movement of his right arm; the other draws aside the curtain of the throne with a wide and reverent gesture. The elegance and true Gothic sweetness of all the forms might appear to be in strange contrast to the severity of the small Liverpool

picture; but the surviving parts of the coloured top layer show the same
precision of contour, and the same goldsmith-like finish and smooth modelling as the panel painting. The ornamentation of the surrounding arch has a
similar severe elegance.[22] This is not, therefore, an example of a late stylistic
phase in the usual sense, implying a loosening of the linear structure and a
decrease in opacity. It is rather a final stage in which the linear severity and
opaque metallic corporeality we have already observed in Simone Martini's
work are combined.

Another work plainly done at this late stage of the master's development
was a small polyptych, of which six panels are preserved, each approximately
25 cm. high and painted with the delicacy of miniatures. Two of the panels
depict the *Annunciation,* and the others show scenes from Christ's Passion.[23]
The figures in the *Annunciation,* strongly modelled like painted statues in front
of the gold ground, give an idea of the appearance the frescoes on the portal
of the Cathedral must originally have had. The scenes from the Passion *(pls
82a, 82b)* are densely filled with expressive figures, often passionately animated. The stocky proportions, the detailed execution of the numerous faces
crowding one beside another, the violent pathos of the gestures, all add to the
jostling, overcrowded impression. The colours, bright and jewel-like, seem
exaggerated and outdo each other in intensity. Although the details are plastic-
ally conceived, everything is restricted to the surface of the picture without
regard to depth or volume. In one scene, the *Descent from the Cross,* the gestures of the crowd surge in a common direction, but for the most part there
is a confusion of isolated motifs, each as if seen separately through a magnify-
ing glass. To some extent this is due to the small size of the panels; but it
also indicates a new pursuit of realism that did not hesitate to multiply closely
observed and unexpected detail, and attached importance to the realistic portrayal of each separate facet of the subject. Simone was as yet unable to trans-
mute the mosaic of details into a uniform vision. But his minute pictures
already contain the germ of the revolution in painting that occurred in the
fifteenth century. The radiant, poetic naturalism of the Assisi frescoes gives
way in these later works to a more radical, realistic secular conception. It
is therefore no accident, but a logical and characteristic development, that the
awakening realistic painting of the north repeatedly drew on works of Simone's last phase. The composition of the *Road to Calvary* was reproduced
with fair accuracy as late as the second decade of the fifteenth century in the
Chantilly Book of Hours, the *Très Riches Heures* of the Duc du Berry. This
important work of Franco-Flemish court art also contains a copy of Taddeo
Gaddi's fresco of the *Presentation of the Virgin in the Temple.*[24] That a work of

Florentine monumental painting, no doubt transmitted only indirectly through a drawing, could serve as an inspiration for northern art should warn us against over-estimating the influence of the Italian masters active in Avignon, and should remind us that there were many channels of communication between north and south, including direct access across the passes of the Alps. It is also wrong to suppose that Sienese painting was the only, or even the principal, influence on the north.[25] The main currents in Europe have the same source as those in Italy itself: Giotto is the key figure. Between him and the van Eyck brothers there is a definite connection, although we can no longer comprehend its complex implications.[26] It is true that the unsystematic and still medieval realism of Simone Martini's last years struck a particularly responsive chord in the northern painters, but this was by no means the only Italian inspiration. More important was the control of space and the strict organization of the pictorial composition into a unity of form and content, that is to say, the innovation that began with Giotto and was to become the common property of all Western painting in the fifteenth century.

Another work of Simone Martini's that has survived is a miniature, probably done at Avignon. It is the frontispiece of a Virgil manuscript, which was owned by Petrarch.[27] The miniature, skilfully painted in pastel shades, shows Virgil accompanied by his commentator Servius and characters from his poems: Aeneas, and two peasants at work, a reference to the *Eclogues* and the *Georgics*. Presumably Petrarch, who lived in Avignon, himself chose the subject of the illustration. It is clear from the two sonnets to the portrait of Laura, painted for him by Simone, that he knew and admired the painter. In another passage Petrarch links Simone with Giotto among the greatest painters of the age.[28]

The portrait of Laura was *in carte,* i. e., on parchment, and thus also a miniature. The Virgil miniature is exceptional in that it is bolder, and at the same time more delicate, than any of the works of the professional illuminators of the time, and yet it does not give the impression of an isolated production. Presumably there were more miniatures by Simone's hand done in Avignon, and it is possible that the art of Books of Hours that began to flourish around 1400 owed much more to him than can be deduced from the slender evidence we have today.

It would be in line with this surmise that one of the best Italian miniature painters, the Master of the St George Codex, was a pupil of Simone Martini in Avignon. The manuscript from which he derives his name is a life of St George written by Cardinal Stefaneschi.[29] One of the miniatures is a youthful idealization of the cardinal composing his work. The miniature depicting

St George and the Dragon is a reflection of Simone's fresco at Avignon, which, as already noted, was also probably commissioned by Cardinal Stefaneschi. The common patron, the resemblance to the fresco and, finally, the style of the miniatures suggest a close relationship between the two artists. The master of the St George Codex, however, translated Simone's style into a typical miniature style, with dainty, naive figures. A series of small panels, attributable to him, reveal the same characteristics: delicate, slender figures with gentle child-like expressions, soft, pale colours, and a dream-like and rather precious ambience. It is tempting to associate these works with the International Style, which first emerged around 1380 in the Parisian court and in the tapestries of the Angers *Apocalypse*. However, the true Trecento slenderness and elegance of the figures, and, for all its delicacy, the rigorous structure of the composition, leave no doubt as to the true date of the works. They could not have been done much later than the middle of the century. The Master of the St George Codex probably returned to Italy after Simone Martini's death.

This painter of miniatures was one of the most gifted and original of Simone's pupils. More famous, but not so independent, was Lippo Memmi, who, together with his father, Memmo di Filipuccio, made a full-scale copy of Simone's *Maestà* in the San Gimignano town hall as early as 1317.[30] All his mature works seem to be derived in greater or lesser degree from Simone's models, which he reproduced faithfully, though without deep feeling. Nevertheless, his graceful and decorative Madonnas are among the finest and most characteristic works of Sienese painting. The small panel in Altenburg *(pl. 84)*, signed by Lippo Memmi, with its subdued colours and gleaming brocade lined with ermine, which forms the transition to the gold background, is one of the most successful works of his eclectic art.[31] There is hardly any other period in which devoted craftsmanship reached a level where it approached so closely to true artistic genius.

Another pupil of Simone Martini, and a much stronger personality, was the painter of the fresco scenes from the New Testament in the Collegiate Church of San Gimignano *(pl. 85)*. His name, Barna, handed down by Ghiberti, is not completely authenticated, but his artistic characteristics are clear.[32] Like Lippo Memmi, he adopted a style based on a relatively early style of Simone's. His simple spatial presentation, with a relief-like quality, is combined with strong emphasis on two-dimensional elements; vanishing lines, which occur frequently, are incorporated in the surface pattern, thus maintaining a firm link with the picture surface. The harsh and angular movements of his figures are also drawn into the two-dimensional scheme, and their powerful plasticity is neutralized by the predominant abstract linear structure. Barna's gripping, robust style is far removed from the airy delicacy of Simone's work in Assisi, but his frescoes are among the few examples in Sienese painting of the true monumental style essential to wall-painting.

Barna's San Gimignano frescoes were probably not done before the middle of the century and show that Simone Martini's influence in Siena was still effective long after his departure. In Avignon, on the other hand, although Simone left works that were later to have important consequences, he founded no school and had no direct followers.

Before Simone's death in 1344, Matteo Giovannetti of Viterbo, a painter of an entirely different character, had already become prominent among the numerous artists working for the Curia in Avignon.[33] Born probably about 1300, he is already mentioned in papal letters in 1322 and again in 1328; in 1343 we hear of him for the first time in Avignon. His earliest work there, still extant, is the decoration of the chapel of St Martial in the Papal Palace, with lively narrative legendary scenes. This was followed, probably around 1347, by a pictorial cycle in the chapel of St John, and later, in about 1353, by a series of twenty figures of prophets in the vault of the Audience Hall. Finally, there are the paintings in the Carthusian monastery of Villeneuve-les-Avignon, which are also attributable to him. According to documents published some time ago but only recently connected with the Villeneuve chapel, Matteo painted these works in 1355–6. These wall paintings in Avignon have made it possible to recognize Matteo's style in a small number of panel paintings.[34] He died in 1368 or 1369 in Rome, where he was summoned by Pope Urban V for work in the Vatican.

Whereas Simone Martini still conformed to the last phase of the High Gothic, to the courtly, idealized style of the beginning of the fourteenth century, Matteo Giovannetti's encounter with Gothic art and the influences he was subject to during his early years in Italy were entirely different. He appears to have been quite unaffected by Giotto's regularizing concept of art. The dominant influences in his formation were the work of Simone Martini, which he must have known in his early years in Orvieto and Assisi, and the versatile, experimental style of Pietro and Ambrogio Lorenzetti. The international atmosphere in which he found himself at the Papal Court in Avignon intensified these features of his style and he seized eagerly on the naturalism of the Late Gothic. His strong and very modern interest in physiognomy led him to create types of figures, gestures and heads types that broke all current conventions. They are less portrait-like than was previously thought, but were conceived as somewhat anecdotal popular folk-types, often bordering on caricature, like characters in Boccaccio. These odd, animated figures are placed in boldly designed spatial settings, in which surprising perspective effects are achieved. The multiplicity of motifs frequently appears confused and unsystematic, and the mixture of stylistic elements is somewhat hybrid. His style, which is neither French nor Italian, is the first example of International Gothic, and yet it is very personal and attractive. It reached its peak in the hurried, nervous *intonaco* drawings for the *Crucifixion* in Villeneuve.[35] Compared with the carefully worked monumental drawings of Simone Martini for his frescoes on the portal of Notre-Dame-des-Doms, they are, however, mere hasty improvisations.

10 Pietro and Ambrogio Lorenzetti

The brothers Pietro and Ambrogio Lorenzetti, more or less contemporaries of Simone Martini and of equal artistic stature, worked in Siena quite independently of him.[1] Little is known of their lives. Their dates of birth, like that of Simone Martini, can be determined only approximately, between 1280 and 1295. Pietro was probably a good deal older than Ambrogio, perhaps by as much as ten years. Both may have been victims of the plague of 1348, but this is no more than a conjecture. A relatively large number of their works, some of them dated, have survived; others, now lost, are known from the descriptions of Ghiberti and Vasari. Nevertheless, the course of their development is still a subject of controversy. The numerous chronological and stylistic problems still requiring solution can be considered here only in broad outline. Furthermore, the question of the brothers' intermittent collaboration and the artistic relationship between them cannot be resolved here. But all this is fundamentally of secondary importance. The artistic personalities of both brothers are well established, and their position in Trecento painting can be precisely defined.

The earliest datable work by Pietro Lorenzetti is the polyptych of the high altar of the Arezzo parish church, which was commissioned in 1320 *(pls 86, 87, 91a)*.[2] The centre-piece is a half-length Madonna surrounded by a number of saints, also in half-length figures but varying in size. Above the Madonna is a delicate and tranquil Annunciation scene, and also an Assumption. The basic elements of Pietro's style are clearly revealed here: his indebtedness to Duccio, the deep and deliberate study of Giotto, and finally a very personal affinity, surprising in a painter, to the passionate style of Giovanni Pisano, the greatest of the contemporary sculptors. Pietro himself had a passionate, emotional temperament. The demeanour and expression of his Madonna leave no doubt that he was fascinated by the sculptures of Siena Cathedral and other works of the Pisan master. We are witnesses to a silent dialogue between Mother and Child that has none of the warmth and intimacy of human relationship, but is suffused with awareness of divine power and the premonition of the future supra-human sacrifice and passion. Giovanni Pisano was the first to convey this in his Madonnas, and Pietro Lorenzetti translated it into the medium of paint. On the other hand the types of the saints are a heritage of Duccio. Giotto's influence is perceptible in the free yet determined movements of the figures, and in the firm grip of the hands grasping a book or bishop's staff, or gathering up a piece of drapery. The hands of the Madonna, boldly but not quite successfully foreshortened, are no longer referable to Duccio, nor to the Gothic; the crucial feature is the functional, three-dimensional vision, which, once again, could have been derived only from Giotto. To the new concept Pietro brought his own personal contribution, an almost feverish sensibility and agonized intensity of expression. It is this that sharply distinguishes his figures from those of Giotto; they are completely lacking in the self-sufficiency and tranquillity of Giotto's monumental forms. They are always tense, and in constant acute agitation, filled with the inward glow of a single dominant emotion. Contact with Florentine art had no effect at all on this central Sienese mood, which is the essence of Pietro's creations. It pervades all his later works and gives his style its unmistakable personal character.

The only larger picture attributable with certainty to an even earlier phase of Pietro's development than the Arezzo polyptych is the Madonna panel in the cathedral of Cortona. It was painted around 1315, or even slightly earlier. Its only reference to Giotto, whose influence is as yet barely apparent, is in the classic and quite non-Byzantine youthful face of the Madonna. The influence of Duccio is much stronger, especially in the angels beside the throne, but the traditional forms are here already imbued with the glow of his personal emotion. In this early work gentleness and restrained passion are mingled most impressively. The apparently Gothic linear effect is full of vibrant tension, uncontrolled emotion and energy.

The unmistakable characteristics emerging in this painting, and already present in the Arezzo polyptych as an established mode of expression, become more pronounced in Pietro's later work. Surviving records show that in 1329 he was paid for a grand altarpiece in the Carmelite Church in Siena.[3] The centre panel, now in the Siena Pinacoteca Nazionale, depicts the Madonna seated, with proudly raised head, on a simple, solidly designed throne. Four angels, St Nicholas, and the prophet Elias are arranged around her in strict symmetry. The Child, with a somewhat awkward, constrained movement, turns towards Elias and blesses him. The prophet and the bishop, both in long draperies with stiff, vertically falling, tubular folds, stand at the front corners like two sturdy fluted columns. The whole design is regular and frontal. The approximately square ground plan of the pictorial stage is clearly apparent, but the two-dimensional pattern nearly obliterates the depth effects.

The unusual shape of the panel, almost square, is surely not accidental, and is clearly related to the centralized tapestry-like composition. From entirely different starting points, the Sienese painter and the Florentine master of the Bardi Chapel arrived at surprisingly similar results at more or less the same time. The question arises whether this was only a prevailing contemporary trend, a latent intrinsic logic of development, or whether it is evidence of an actual connection between the two artists. The artistic relationships between Florence and Siena at this time were plainly fairly close. Pietro's brother, Ambrogio Lorenzetti, was active in Florence as early as 1320, and presumably again on several occasions between 1327 and 1332. The resulting influences were reciprocal, like those between Cimabue and Duccio a few decades earlier. We shall revert to this at a later stage.

Pietro's *Carmelite Madonna,* a Maestà of solemn, formal character, was a progressive work, in the forefront of the contemporary trend, and stylistically far in advance of the 1320 altarpiece. But the restrained tension of his earlier works is still maintained and, in purely formal terms, even increased. The figures are more strict and compact in contour, more economic in movement, and the forms have become more severe and ample. The resilient lines acquire a distinct abstract expressiveness beyond their organic relationships. This becomes even clearer in three panels of a polyptych, dated 1332, also in the Siena Pinacoteca Nazionale.[4] In particular the half-length figure of St John the Baptist *(pl. 91b)* invites comparison with the corresponding figure in Arezzo *(pl. 91a).* Whereas in the Arezzo figure there is a pronounced contrapostal movement, the 1332 St John is rigid, almost like a figure in an icon. His look and gesture, directed to the Christ Child in the centre panel, now lost, appear cramped and exaggerated. The same transformation can be seen in the folds of the drapery; in the Arezzo polyptych they are relatively full and flexible, flowing in wide Gothic curves; here they are hardened into a few, parallel sets of lines, which intersect the bodily forms and give them a solid, rigid appearance.

Thus Pietro Lorenzetti's work shows a development similar to that of Simone Martini and of Florentine painting from about 1330. The free movement, and the organic and functional concept of the human body that had already been achieved, are abandoned and replaced by an abstract crystalline rigidity. The lively, well-articulated forms become stiff and hard. The vitality of the figures and the subtle tension of their emotions disappear in the determination to achieve solid compactness and an emphatic fixed expression. Just as the figures have become standardized, almost formalized, the composition as a whole also frequently reverts to a symmetrical and ornamental formula.

It is true that the faculty of representing three-dimensional space, having been acquired, could not be ignored, and together with the two-dimensional effects, bold and surprisingly successful experiments in perspective appear; but the tension between surface and depth is not always successfully controlled or brought to satisfactory artistic expression. Because of this, there is a curiously contradictory element in the general aspect of Sienese painting in the second quarter of the Trecento, which has resulted in a striking uncertainty among present-day historians with regard to the dating of a number of important works of that time and in particular some of the works of Pietro Lorenzetti.

From the observations we have already made, two distinct chronological stages emerge as points of departure for our study of Pietro's development: the style of the early 1320s, represented by the Arezzo polyptych begun in 1320, and the group of pictures painted in Siena between 1329 and 1332. This latter group includes the predella panels of the Carmelite Altar, five narrative scenes in which the severity of form and stereometric elucidation of pictorial space are as evident as in the *Carmelite Madonna*.[5] We believe that with the help of these two fixed starting points the most controversial question regarding Pietro's work, the dating of his Assisi frescoes, can be answered.[6] For this purpose we must return once more, and for the last time, to the monumental pictorial complex of San Francesco. Pietro was entrusted with the decoration of the south transept of the Lower Church, which required a representation of the last stages of Christ's life, from the Entry into Jerusalem to the Resurrection, as the logical complement to the frescoes of his Birth and Childhood in the north transept. The recent cleaning of Pietro's frescoes has exposed their high artistic quality anew, and enabled their many absorbing and original details to be appraised at their true worth.

Consideration of a purely external factor, indispensable for the clarification of their sequence and chronological order, is a necessary preliminary to the study of Pietro's frescoes. In the decoration of the transept it was natural to start from the crossing, i. e., the vault which stretches above the high altar and the saint's tomb; and it can therefore be assumed that work on the Franciscan Allegories was already in hand, and possibly even finished, when Pietro started on his section. The luxuriant decorative framework surrounding his frescoes is of the same general character as the borders of the frescoes in the centre vault, and corresponds almost exactly – with the addition of a few, unimportant embellishments – to the scheme of the north transept. Although it cannot be established with certainty, the close ornamental similarity between these parts makes it probable that all three sections were done at approximately the same time, or at least in close succession. As regards the sequence of the frescoes in the south transept, it is almost certain that, for practical reasons, the scenes at the top of the barrel-vaulting were done first. These are the Passion scenes, considered by most of the earlier critics to be the work of assistants and not of Pietro himself. However, as the entire programme was uniformly planned by Pietro, there was no reason for him to start with the frescoes on the side walls and lower zones of the vaults, since they are the last scenes in the cycle. Even if we assume that he entrusted a large part of the execution of the frescoes on the vaults to his pupils, the design would in any case have been done by him; and these frescoes are as much his as the St Francis legend is the work of Giotto. 'Design' in relation to Trecento wall-painting practice refers to the monumental drawing on the pictorial surface itself, and this too would normally begin at the apex of the vault. It would therefore be entirely artificial to assume that the upper zone was left completely empty at first and filled with pictures only at a later stage by Pietro's pupils.

The frescoes *(pls 88, 89, 90a, 90b, XI and XII),* abundant in detail and colourful as a fairy-tale, begin the story with true Sienese delight in narrative. In the first scene the people rush joyfully and excitedly out of the city to welcome the Lord on his *Entry into Jerusalem.* But in the midst of the crowd, and heard by all, the Pharisees are already inveighing against Him *(pl. 90b),* and Judas, evil-eyed and tight-lipped, the only disciple without a halo, walks close behind Christ's donkey. The next scene, the *Washing of the Feet,* is filled with apprehensive whispers and anxious, questioning looks; Judas, the betrayer withdrawn into the corner, broods menacingly. In the *Last Supper (pl. XI),* the uneasiness is alleviated. Judas sits among the disciples and reaches for a piece of bread that Christ is handing him. The painter was absorbed not so much with the psychological content of the scene as with its external aspects: the festively lit round table, the landlord and his servant, the cook at the blazing log-fire conversing with his mate as he cleans the plates. The close attention to ancillary matters, trivial and incidental details, is almost a profanation; but there is an astonishing freshness of observation, and the representation of the scene, the interior of a hexagonal room, and the treatment of the lighting, are also very unusual. There was no other example of a hexagonal room in the whole range of Italian painting of interiors since the end of the thirteenth century.[7] Possibly Giotto's *Wedding at Cana* in the Arena Chapel could be regarded as a hesitant step in this direction; and there may have been another picture by Giotto, now lost, which provided a stimulus for Pietro, as Taddeo Gaddi also portrayed a hexagonal building in a small panel in Santa Croce, the *Presentation in the Temple.* There can be no doubt that despite the novelty and daring of Pietro's perspective technique

XI PIETRO LORENZETTI *The Last Supper* · Assisi, San Francesco

in this picture, he could not have succeeded without Giotto's prior example. Apart from the hexagonal shape of the room, the composition is Giottesque, and so too is the positioning of the building in the picture, with the narrow strips of night sky at the top and along the right side. Pietro has added only the stars and crescent moon, and heightened the effect of the artificial light, coming from no visible source in the room, to an extent far beyond anything that Giotto would have considered acceptable: Giotto's treatment, for example, in the scene of *Christ before Caiphas* in the Arena Chapel *(pl. 66b)*, is infinitely more discreet and unobtrusive. Giotto's self-imposed restraint, his economy in the use of illusionistic techniques – the secret of the grand style – are here abandoned as heedlessly as in Taddeo Gaddi's frescoes in the Baroncelli Chapel. Faithfulness to life is achieved at the cost of monumentality in a way that jeopardizes the dignity of the holy scene.

The scene of Christ's Apprehension is suffused with uncontrolled passion. Stooped, but with a large purposeful stride, Judas approaches Christ, who turns only slightly away, not resisting the traitor's kiss. Peter approaches Malchus threateningly while the disciples flee, one of them turning his fearful face to look back once more. The agonizingly realistic scene is followed by a formal, stage-like Flagellation. The scene takes place in a low room, with sumptuous but somewhat petty decoration. The curious, over-large roof distracts the eye; a child and a young girl, who look out of a Gothic window high above, are playing with a monkey that runs at the end of its chain along the cornice. The lucid, playful fantasy of the whole scene has considerable charm, and its artistic excellence cannot be denied. Finally, in the Road to Calvary, the over-ornate description of the city again distracts from the main theme, but some of the figures are of great beauty, and the event as a whole is vividly depicted.

In the Crucifixion, which is four times larger than the scenes described so far, the story finally rises to the height of tragedy. Here too there is an almost unmanageable crowd, above which the bodies of the crucified men rise against the deep ultramarine of the sky. For the first time in a monumental composition the two robbers are shown together with the Son of God. They hang on their crosses with arms distorted in agony, their nakedness pitilessly exposed.[8] Twelve mourning angels, each of them a shrill lament, hover over the huge central figure of Christ. The dying Saviour, with closed eyes and noble countenance deeply bowed in pain, is here transformed from Christ in Agony to Christ Triumphant. He becomes the mighty symbol of redemption. The restless crowd at his feet, the many horsemen with their gleaming weapons and colourful costumes, the grief, the hatred, the indifference and the doubt, all pale and dwindle in the presence of the tremendous sacrifice. Not one of the numerous figures is superfluous, and in the mass of realistic detail there is nothing that does not contribute to the grand and simple conception. Many other versions of Calvary were produced by Trecento painters and later painters in the North, but none of them is filled with such feverish agitation and such consciousness of the solemn significance of the event as Pietro Lorenzetti's fresco.

On the wall opposite the Crucifixion, and in close inward relationship with it, the Stigmatization of St Francis is painted in the same intense linear style, as an addition to the cycle of the Passion. The cyle concludes with the pictures on the end wall of the transept, the Descent from the Cross, the Entombment, the Descent into Hell, and the Resurrection. Here again the emphasis is on the central tragedy, and all ancillary distractions are avoided. In the endeavour to achieve monumentality the forms have been enlarged and simplified, and the spatial illusion reduced as far as possible. The Descent from the Cross *(pls 88, 89)*, with its pain-racked figures interlocked by sharp lines, is a thoroughly two-dimensional composition, in front of an empty background. In the powerful movement of the man pulling out the last nail with a pair of pliers to free the feet of the dead body, we recognize the same vigour with which Judas approaches Christ in the Mount of Olives, or the soldier pushes back the women in the Road to Calvary. The uniformity of concept and of movement and form underlying the whole pictorial cycle is unmistakable, and yet the painter appears to have undergone a profound change since the time he started work in the vault with the Entry into Jerusalem. It is as though he was deeply affected by the moving events he had to illustrate. From then on his style never lost the harsh, agonized character it assumed in Assisi. The *Madonna with St Francis and St John the Evangelist (pl. 90a)*, on the north wall of the transept, next to the Crucifixion, is also infused with the same mood. The three half-length figures in front of the gilded ground form a monumental retable for an altar that stood at this position. It is evidently the last work Pietro did in Assisi.[9]

In this respect it would appear that Pietro's Assisi frescoes were designed according to a uniform plan, and executed in their narrative sequence and without notable contribution from assistants. The development which we profess to recognize in them could only have taken place in the period between 1320 and about 1330. The Passion scenes at the top of the vault postulate the existence of the style of the Arezzo polyptych.[10] The only fresco of Pietro in Assisi that was probably done before the Arezzo polyptych is the *Madonna with St John the Baptist and St Francis* in the St John Chapel on the south side of the transept, which we have not yet mentioned.[11] It is a compositon of half-length figures, like the picture on the north wall just described, but the pictorial surface is divided in the Cosmati manner into three painted arcades. Stylistically this fresco triptych marks the point of Pietro's closest approach to Giotto, and at the same time still clearly shows an affinity with the *Madonna* in the cathedral at Cortona. Pietro must therefore have already been in Assisi before 1320; he probably returned a few years later, perhaps immediately after completing the Arezzo polyptych, in order to undertake the execution of the Passion cycle. The path that led from Arezzo to the *Carmelite Madonna* can now be clearly traced. The *Descent from the Cross* in Assisi marks the turning point, the reversion to a two-dimensional, severely linear style. Perhaps there was another interruption in his work between the frescoes on the vaults and those on the end wall, but there is no compelling reason for this assumption. The explanation of the change in Pietro's style can be found in Assisi itself. It was the result of his struggle with the great monumental task, and probably also of the impression made on him by the older frescoes in San Francesco, which were constantly before his eyes. The somewhat artificial two-dimensional character of the last scenes, though in line with the general trend of the time, can nevertheless be attributed to some extent to such impressions. This development could have taken place within the space of a few years, probably still in the first half of the 1320s. The Arezzo polyptych, commissioned in 1320, was presumably finished within a year or two. It is likely that the Carmelite altar was started by Pietro in 1328, or even earlier, and there is evidence that in 1326 he painted four historical scenes, probably frescoes, in Siena. According to a doubtful record he was also in Siena in 1324.[12] It follows that the years 1322–3, and possibly 1325 or 1327, would have been the periods available for the Assisi frescoes. It is possible, therefore, to regard the frescoes as having been done in two stages. In any case, we find ourselves in the third decade of the Trecento, to which the Franciscan allegories of the Maestro delle Vele are usually also assigned. Furthermore, this would be the most fitting date for the frescoes in the north transept, in which Simone Martini and his pupils participated.[13]

Pietro Lorenzetti's naturalistic experiments in the Passion scenes thus take their proper place in the overall development of Tuscan painting – prior to Taddeo Gaddi's work on the same lines around 1330, for which Sienese influence has always been assumed. They followed directly on Giotto's achievement, as an inevitable consequence, once the aesthetic boundaries he had imposed were no longer respected. To a painter not endowed with a natural feeling for monumentality and raised on Duccio's undramatic simultaneous narrative style, Giotto's new modes of pictorial expression were a dangerous temptation. The somewhat archaic character of Pietro's compositions in Assisi is noticeable not only in their abundance of closely observed details, but also in the formal relationship of the size of the figures to the architecture and to the pictorial space, which still corresponds approximately to the norm established by Giotto in the Arena Chapel. This relationship only changes fundamentally in the predella scenes of the Carmelite altar of 1329. The figures become smaller and move more freely in the larger, more open spaces. The excessive decorative detail gives way to an almost ascetic economy of architectural forms, and the landscape takes on a large uniform aspect.[14]

The Assisi frescoes also provide us with a valuable guide to the rest of Pietro Lorenzetti's works. The severe, expressive fresco of the *Crucifixion* in San Francesco in Siena could only have been done after the much richer and more animated version of the theme in Assisi, though not much later because the style of the figures still bears a close resemblance to that of the figures in the *Descent from the Cross* and the *Entombment;* the composition, monumental and two-dimensional, also corresponds to the last stage of development reached in the Assisi frescoes.

The frescoes in Santa Maria dei Servi, probably not executed by Pietro himself, are undoubtedly later. The relationship of the figures to the architecture is approximately the same as that in the Carmelite predella. The appearance of isolated motifs from Giotto's frescoes in the Peruzzi Chapel gives further support for a date around 1330 at the earliest.

A major joint work of the Lorenzetti brothers, four frescoes depicting scenes from the life of the Virgin, done in 1335, decorated the façade of the Ospedale della Scala in the cathedral square of Siena. Their destruction in the eighteenth century was one of the worst losses suffered by Sienese painting and Trecento painting in general. They can, however, be reconstructed with some accuracy from later copies.[15] A panel-painting by Pietro, the *Birth of the Virgin,* in the Opera del Duomo in Siena, dated 1342, appears to have preserved the main features of the monumental version[16] which, according to Ghiberti, was done by Ambrogio.[17] This would account to some extent for the idyllic mood, unusual in Pietro's work, although, on the other hand, the subject itself demands this kind of treatment. The rich warm beauty of the colours, the harmony of yellow, vermilion and pale blue in the left side of the picture, and the dark lilac and ochre of the mother's gown, may have been derived from Ambrogio's fresco. The arrangement of the pictorial space, which takes up an idea that was partly realized by Pietro in the Annunciation scene of the Arezzo polyptych, is of special interest: the actual frame of the panel is used as part of the structure of the open front of the buildings seen in the picture. In the *Annunciation* of 1320 *(pl. 87),* although the panel is divided into only two sections, and the rooms adjoining the frame are of simple rectangular shape, the principle is nevertheless clearly displayed. Giotto does not seem to have been familiar with this device, but it is quite in line with the developments he initiated. Pietro is again following in Giotto's footsteps, not as an imitator, but as an original and consistent interpreter of his ideas. There is no reason, therefore, to assume that Ambrogio was the originator of this device, especially as his picture of the *Presentation in the Temple* of 1342, arranged in a similar way, does not show the same connection between the pictorial architecture and the frame. On the contrary the intersections are rather sharp and unaesthetic. Pietro, however, in the *Birth of the Virgin,* handles this with great virtuosity; the Gothic forms of the frame in the shape of a triptych continue the vaults of the painted rooms in the most natural manner: one of the posts of the frame cuts across the figure of the guest beside the bed, so that a direct effect of spatial depth is created. On the left side of the picture, the view opens into a much loftier room of Gothic character, probably a palace courtyard. The incorporation of the frame into the pictorial illusion is an idea that was to have far-reaching effects on Western painting. Jan van Eyck took it up in the Annunciation scene in his *Ghent Altar,* Robert Campin and Konrad Witz made use of it, and so did Rogier van der Weyden with great skill and striking effect in his *Altarpiece of the Sacraments.*

Two further works of Pietro done at this time give a good idea of the course of his development, which corresponds closely to the prevailing trend in Europe towards increased rigidity of form and tautness of line. They are the *Madonna with Angels,* bearing the date 1340 (as far as it can be deciphered), and the altar panel of the *Beata Umiltà* dated 1341, both now in the Uffizi in Florence.[18] The Madonna, though barely life-size, gives the appearance of a highly monumental work owing to the simple pyramidal structure and compact outlines together with equally compact rounded bodily forms, which are also noticeable in Simone Martini's work of that time. The symmetrical arrangement of the figures, the cool colours (especially the many shades of blue), the simple forms of the throne, all add to the crystalline, timeless and solemn effect. This was the new ideal that emerged in Trecento art towards the middle of the century, in architecture and sculpture as well as in painting. Pietro Lorenzetti was one of the leading figures in this movement, which was to reach its maturity with Orcagna and his circle in Florence. In the figure of the *Beata Umiltà* the flow of the lines and the modelling of the bodily forms attain an almost metallic hardness and smoothness. Together with in-creased stylization there was also a trend towards naturalism, and this re-sulted in a noticeable, and almost irreconcilable, contradiction. In the small legendary scenes *(pl. 91c)* surrounding the main figure this produces a curious and attractive tension. There is a conflict between the harsh plasticity, severe line, deliberately simple architectural and landscape elements, and the refined, psychologically acute art of narrative and sophisticated skill in pictorial com-position. The pious tone of the legend, and the asceticism of cloistered life are so aptly expressed that the apparently archaic manner is still sometimes mistaken for a genuine archaic style. The opinion that the date, written in Roman numerals (and renewed), should be read as 1316, has its supporters even now.[19] However, a comparison of the two interiors in the legendary scene *(pl. 91c)* with those in the Arezzo *Annunciation* of 1320 *(pl. 87)* shows that such an early date is indefensible. That a mistake of this kind is possible is due to the characteristics of Pietro's late style, and to the general eclectic tendency beginning in Trecento painting at that time.

Ambrogio Lorenzetti, probably the younger of the two brothers, had an even greater sensitivity and a gentler, more pliant temperament than Pietro.[20] He does not appear to have felt the burden of tradition, so that there was no need for him to struggle laboriously to free himself from it. His earliest sur-viving work, a *Madonna* of 1319 in Sant'Angelo in Vico l'Abate (near Greve, south of Florence), shows that at this time he was already an accomplished and confident artist perfectly adjusted to the spirit of the age *(pls 92, 93)*. He had left Duccio's world far behind him, and although Giotto's new art was well known to him, he did not allow it to divert him from his course. Decades before his brother Pietro and the other masters of the 'second gene-ration', he reverted to the severer solemnity of the Duecento, while retaining his modern outlook, his subtlety and sensitivity. The Vico l'Abate *Madonna*, almost completely filling the narrow frame, is presented full face, and holds the plump, motionless Child in her powerful hands. The throne, of simple geometric form, is three-dimensional, but also seen frontally, with seat and arms in steeply rising perspective. Ambrogio avoids the slight obliquity that Giotto introduced into his Madonna paintings to accentuate the three-dimen-sional effect. Only the Madonna's left knee is slightly raised and turned out-wards, and the lines of the neck and the top of the dress waver from their

XII Pietro Lorenzetti *Crucifixion* (detail)
Assisi, San Francesco

rigid course in an inimitable, circular movement. These are the sole sources of vitality in this mature female figure. The full, proud face is immobile, but not with the supra-natural solemnity characteristic of the popular craftsman-like Madonnas of the Magdalene Master and the Master of Bagnano, although there can be no doubt that Ambrogio had those works in mind when he painted his picture. His style is archaicizing, but in a very sophisticated way: he does not abandon his own special qualities nor relapse into an artificial austerity. However, Ambrogio's interpretation in this picture is unique and was never repeated.

The *Madonna* in the chapel of the Archbishop's Seminar in Siena, done about ten years later, suggests that at that time Ambrogio was attempting to emulate the severer style of his brother, but the motif of the Madonna nursing the Child immediately creates an entirely different atmosphere from that of Pietro's Madonnas. The prevailing mood, intimate and human, expresses maternal care and tenderness, childish innocence and lack of self-consciousness; and a faint melancholy pervades the scene. Pietro's passionate temperament, his alert, tense spirituality, were alien to Ambrogio. Whenever he tries to achieve the same effects as Pietro, for example in the triptych of the *Madonna with Two Saints* in half-length figures, now in the Uffizi in Florence, the result is uneven. The exquisite preciousness of colour and ornament is more impressive than the harsh expressions on the faces. These three panels are part of an altarpiece that Ambrogio did in 1332 for San Procolo in Florence.[21] There are four more panels in the Uffizi with scenes from the legend of St Nicholas, which also come from San Procolo, and were probably done at the same time as the triptych. The scenes are vividly depicted, and the imaginative spatial arrangement and architectural features are similar to those of Simone Martini's legendary scenes from the life of St Agostino Novello. Ambrogio's handling of perspective illusion is even freer than Simone's, especially in the scene of the harbour, busy with ships and rowing-boats, which, with its high horizon, anticipates effects not found again until the fifteenth century.

As early as 1327 Ambrogio was admitted into the Florentine guild of physicians and apothecaries, to which painters also belonged. Whether he really lived and worked in Florence for the required five years, from 1327 to 1332, is questionable; it is more likely that he frequently stayed in Florence, which was within easy reach of Siena. The style of the Vico l'Abate *Madonna* indicates that at an early stage he had first-hand knowledge of Florentine art, and there is support for this in a documentary record of 1321 that appears to refer to him.[22]

In spite of this relatively firm evidence of his association with Florence, Ambrogio's relationship to Florentine art is by no means clear, for it is difficult to determine what each owed, and what each contributed to the other. Ambrogio's frescoes in San Francesco in Siena may have been done before his stay in Florence in 1332, although the traditional date for them, 1331, is by no means certain.[23] In the *Martyrdom of the Franciscans in Ceuta,* the central figure of the sultan on his throne is very similar to that in the fresco of the *Ordeal by Fire* in the Bardi Chapel. Ambrogio's much richer, livelier composition appears to be the more original work. It may have been known to the painter of the Bardi Chapel through a drawing, but it is more likely that a lost fresco by Giotto was the common source of both works.[24]

The counterpart of the *Martyrdom in Ceuta* is the *Admission of St Louis of Toulouse into the Franciscan Order (pls 94, 95).* Before the assembled curia and in the presence of his brother, King Robert of Naples, the saint kneels to Pope Boniface VIII and takes his vows. It was a memorable scene from recent history, with the lay witnesses in realistic contemporary dress crowding into the side aisle of the hall behind the partition. The two linked youths, one with folded arms, on the left are evidently taken from the two spectators in *Herod's Feast* in the Peruzzi Chapel *(pl. 71 a).*[25] The design of the room corresponds, but in reverse, to that in the predella picture depicting the *Confirmation of the Carmelite Order,* painted, as previously mentioned, by Pietro Lorenzetti around 1329. But Ambrogio left out the front aisle, so that the observer feels himself to be standing in a position corresponding to that of the spectators in the opposite aisle. The pictorial idea, which Pietro made use of but did not fully exploit in his predella panel, is here developed most effectively; and this could in fact suggest a date for the fresco not much later than 1329. But again no firm conclusion can be drawn, because there is always the possibility that there were other, now lost, interpretations of this idea, and that the predella panel itself was derived from an earlier monumental model.

The chronology of Ambrogio's works presents further difficulties. Our picture of his development would certainly be clearer if the frescoes on the façade of the Ospedale della Scala, which he did in conjunction with his brother in 1335, had survived.[26] An important panel painting by Ambrogio, the *Maestà* of Massa Marittima, now in the Municipio there, probably belongs to the same period.[27] The oblong retable, over two meters wide, shows the Madonna Enthroned with the three theological Virtues and surrounded by angels and numerous saints. The figures, crowded together, are arranged in three rows behind and above each other, a curiously abstract, two-dimensional form of composition, which reduces the effect of the three-dimensional elements in the foreground. Such crowded pictorial surfaces are not found in Sienese painting in the 1320s. Many of the individual forms, especially those of the angels playing musical instruments and offering flowers, appear heavy and opulent, as in Ambrogio's mature works. Other features, like the draperies of the seated Virtues, are hard and brittle. This unconventional picture can thus be given a relatively late date, towards the end of the master's middle period.

Ambrogio's best known frescoes are in the Sala della Pace – so-called after the frescoes – in Siena's Palazzo Pubblico *(pls 96, 97)*.[28] Their date, 1338–9, is authenticated by documents recording payments made. On the rear wall there is an elaborate allegory of *Good Government*, symbolized in a colossal enthroned male figure, *Il Buon Governo*, accompanied by the seven cardinal Virtues, here increased to eight by the addition of Magnanimity.[29] Soldiers guard a group of captured evil-doers; at the feet of the *Governo* is the she-wolf suckling the twins, the ancient Roman emblem of government, which medieval Siena had also adopted. Justice, already shown at the extreme right among the Virtues, appears again in the left side of the picture, inspired by Wisdom and supported by Concord, who holds her rather drastic attribute, a huge carpenter's plane, on her knee. Two angels lean outwards from the pans of a gigantic pair of scales, held by Wisdom, and kept in balance by Justice. One of the angels hands out reward and punishment, while the other upholds the rule of law. From the symbol of Justice a long cord leads to the rulers of the city, a procession of twenty-four men in the apparel of notables and important burgesses. In the middle of the picture the goddess of Peace, holding an olive branch, reclines on a richly decked couch, wearing a classical white robe that falls in narrow folds *(pl. 96)*. The fresco on one of the side walls, illustrating the results of good government in town and country, gave full scope for Ambrogio's sensuous talent as a story-teller. The view of Gothic Siena *(pl. 97)*, with its tiers of brick-red houses, its high towers and airy terraces, its busy life, and girls dancing in the streets, is the most vivid and complete picture of contemporary life left to us by the Middle Ages. On the opposite wall, preserved only in fragments, is the allegory of *Bad Government*. Here the principal figure is Tyranny, surrounded by Vices. At her feet Justice lies in chains. Fear, a half-naked hag, reigns over the devastated landscape, whereas in *Good Government* the flourishing countryside around Siena is ruled by Security, who prepares a gallows for the wrongdoers, while under her protection the farmers cultivate their fields, and the merchants go about their business unmolested. The hilly Sienese countryside is depicted with remarkable naturalism and extends into distances not previously represented by any painter. There is no work of secular monumental painting that can compare with this fresco of Ambrogio Lorenzetti in historical and documentary value, or in the artistry of its interpretation of the spirit of the Italian city-republics of the Trecento.

The Madonna with SS. Mary Magdalene and Dorothy, three fragments of an altarpiece from Santa Petronilla in Siena, now in the Siena Pinacoteca Nazionale, was probably painted only after the Palazzo Pubblico frescoes, about 1340.[30] Despite the division of the surface into separate panels, the three plastic figures in fluid movement form together a single group owing to the painter's feeling for the new three-dimensional, which prevails over the traditional partitioning of the polyptych. The reverent upwards gaze of the two saints, both in three-quarter profile but in quite different postures, is unique in the Trecento, and goes beyond all conventional rules; and the splendid handling of the colour, of great beauty and delicately harmonizing with the warm glow of the gold ground, is also very personal to the artist.

Two other panel paintings have inscriptions dating them in the first half of the 1340s: the *Presentation in the Temple* of 1342, in Florence (already mentioned), and the *Annunciation* of 1344, in Siena.[31] In both pictures Ambrogio displays a knowledge of perspective that again seems to be in advance of his time. But the appearance is misleading, for in both cases the perspective is arrived at by empirical means, and has no mathematical foundation. This is evident in the scene of the *Presentation in the Temple:* although the three-aisled Gothic building, above which rises the exterior of a high dome, recedes into considerable depth, the various architectural components are not in proper proportion, and the figures are placed only in the foreground. In the *Annunciation* the perspective is quite different: it is restricted to the representation of the floor, which ends abruptly at the gold ground. The pattern of this tiled floor is drawn in centralized foreshortening, but notwithstanding repeated assertions to the contrary, the vanishing lines do not meet exactly at one point, nor are the distances between the transversals accurately foreshortened. We are dealing, therefore, not with an elementary stage in the development of the system of central perspective invented in the Early Renaissance, but with an astonishingly close approximation achieved, however, by purely empirical means.[32] The resulting tension between the tiled surface, conceived in perspective, and the large areas of the gold ground, is even more pronounced and disquieting than in Simone Martini's late works. The contours of the two figures are also harsher, and the figures themselves more solid and massive, than in Simone's small panel in Liverpool. The characteristic tension and the heaviness of the form, clearly deliberate, are in keeping with the deep, melancholy mood and powerful urgency that raise the events to the level of the symbolic and the permanent. The personal note that persisted in Ambrogio's work since the early stage of Vico l'Abate has thus not disappeared in the 1344 *Annunciation*, but asserts itself there for the last time and with difficulty. Meanwhile the forms have become increasingly more rigid, and a new, hieratic severity is apparent in the whole composition.

Two further works belong to the late period of Ambrogio's creative activity: the lunette fresco of the *Madonna with Saints* in Sant'Agostino in Siena,[33] discovered about twenty years ago, and the frescoes in the round chapel of Montesiepi near San Galgano, south-west of Siena, which have been known for much longer.[34] The fresco in Sant'Agostino is a *Maestà*, with the Virgin enthroned in the midst of eight kneeling saints, who turn to her in adoration. The painting, parts of which still retain their original freshness, could have been executed by an assistant. The main theme of the Montesiepi frescoes is also a *Maestà*. At the Virgin's feet Eve, the type of sinful humanity whose guilt was expiated through the Virgin and her divine Son, gazes coolly from the picture. A group of saints fill the lunette above the wall on the right. On the left wall, done by an inferior hand, the legend of St Galganus is illustrated. To the left of the window, and beneath the *Maestà*, kneels an angel with mighty wings outstretched. Facing the angel was the *Madonna Annunciata*, badly restored and repainted as early as the fourteenth century. The two frescoes were detached from the wall in 1966, whereby the preliminary design on the *arricciato* came to light. It is a quick sketch drawn with the brush, and perhaps the most ingenious of all monumental drawings hitherto discovered. It discloses Ambrogio's original idea, which was altered by an insignificant painter of the next generation – probably because the design of the Virgin appeared too bold and unusual. Greatly astonished at the sight of the angel, she draws herself together and clings desperately to a slim column. In this respect Ambrogio goes far beyond Simone Martini, who had already represented the frightened Virgin in his *Annunciation* of 1333.[35] Unlike the Madonna, the kneeling angel, a figure of inspiring simplicity, appears to hover in spite of his monumentality – an achievement possible only for a great artist. The other frescoes are also much damaged and over-painted, and in addition have faded badly during the last decades; but the better preserved parts, like the figure of Eve in the centre picture, show it to be a work of Ambrogio, assisted by pupils after the custom of the time. In spite of the damage, the boldness of the composition is still clearly visible, not only in the *Maestà* but also in the preserved part of the lunette above the right wall. The master's individuality is also apparent in the type and posture of many of the figures. A fervent, devoted spirit is discernible in the delicate curve of a neck, the lifted profile of a youthful face, and Eve's eyes gleam with cunning and unfathomable evil. Nowhere is Ambrogio's style so light and grandiose as in the best parts of these frescoes, evidently painted rapidly and with great skill.

The last documentary reference to Ambrogio Lorenzetti is dated November 1347. He must have died shortly after, possibly in 1348, the year of the plague. None of the great masters, whose work laid the foundations of a new era in Western painting, survived the middle of the century. From now on the situation in Siena was the same as that in Florence since the death of Giotto: until the end of the Trecento, and a generation beyond, artists stood in the shadow of the towering personalities of the first half of the century. It was as though all the possibilities of the new pictorial style had been explored and exhausted; and the limitations of the new style and the hazards of an excessively individualistic mode of representation, had become apparent. Above all, no further important advances were possible in the field of perspective and naturalistic representation without jeopardizing the monumental and idealistic character of the style itself. The result was a resort to the established convention, and forms, once wrested directly from nature, deteriorated into uninspired formulas. The only scope for the expression of individuality lay in the choice and application of the prescribed material. The presentation of reality was quantitatively enriched, without any essential change in interpretation, so that in this respect a decline set in that lasted till the end of the century.

But even an eclectic art, keeping itself alive on a great tradition, can aspire to a character of its own, and in the absence of outstanding personalities the prevailing style of the time becomes more marked. The return to a formal, two-dimensional mode of representation brought about a stylistic standardization in Sienese painting towards the middle of the Trecento, and also seemed to eliminate to a large extent the old contrast between Florence and Siena. The artistic relations between the two cities were never closer and more fruitful than between 1330 and 1360, and whereas Florence had hitherto made the greater contribution, Siena now assumed the leading role. Its technical excellence and sense of colour, its grace and idealism, which preserved a breath of the Byzantine spirit, were more satisfying to the needs of the time than the cool formalism of Florence. A new specifically religious painting was sought, in order to express the re-awakened sense of mysticism and piety. Three-dimensional effects and dramatic situations were no longer required of this art, but sublimity of theme and confirmation of the validity of the mystical vision.

This is what Sienese art had to offer, and it had no difficulty in renouncing the newly acquired range of representational possibilities. Supported by the tradition they had inherited, even artists of only secondary rank now succeeded in producing important works, and the level of pictorial production was higher here than in any other Italian city. We have many pictures from that time of high technical standard together with numerous names and dates, but it is difficult now to distinguish the individual artistic personalities. We shall mention briefly only the more important of these. To characterize them all in detail would involve us too deeply in specialized research.

The relatively important and independent painter usually known as the Master of the Madonna in San Pietro a Ovile, in Siena, belonged to the circle of Pietro Lorenzetti. He may have been the painter Bartolomeo Bulgarini, frequently mentioned in the records.[36] He was active between the second and third quarters of the century. A contemporary of his, Lippo Vanni, was an artist whose eclectic style showed the influence of the Lorenzettis and that of Simone Martini. Another artist, Niccolò di Ser Sozzo Tegliacci, well known as a painter of manuscript miniatures since 1336, emerged as a distinctive artistic personality. His panel-paintings had considerable influence in Pisa as well as in Siena. Closely associated with him, and slightly younger, was the technically accomplished Luca di Tommè.[37] The last generation of Trecento painters is represented by Andrea Vanni, Bartolo di Fredi and Paolo di Giovanni Fei. Although all three did not die until 1410, they were not able to free themselves from the representational methods of the Trecento. The first artist to accomplish this was Taddeo di Bartolo, born about 1362. His work marks the transition to the International Style, the last Gothic stylistic movement of European importance, which injected new spirit into the lustreless, anaemic painting of Siena and indeed of all Europe. It offered a new interpretation of reality, although obscured for the time being by the pervasive ornamentality of line and the abstract standardized modelling of all the forms. Taddeo's *Adoration of the Shepherds* of 1404, in Santa Maria dei Servi in Siena, is typical of this discordant style, which nevertheless went far beyond the Trecento tradition. In his huge altarpiece of 1401, in the cathedral of Montepulciano, Taddeo included a remarkable likeness of himself in the figure of his patron saint, the apostle St Thaddæus.[38] This is the earliest surviving genuine self-portrait in painting, a significant sign of the profound change in the artists' view of themselves, which had begun with Giotto.

11 Orcagna and his circle

Giotto's supremacy, and the absence of any comparable successor, were already recognized in Florence in the latter part of the Trecento. In one of his short stories Franco Sacchetti gives a lively account of a meeting of Florentine painters in the Convent of San Miniato above the city. One of the masters, Andrea Orcagna, puts the question, 'Who is the greatest painter next to Giotto?' The aged Taddeo Gaddi expresses the opinion, plainly shared by all present, that the art of painting is daily declining. Eventually the problem is resolved with a joke: the best painters are the Florentine women, who with the aid of cosmetics are able to repair the errors of the greatest painter of all, the Lord Himself.[1]

Andrea di Cione, called Orcagna, who is merely mentioned along with the others in Sacchetti's story, was the outstanding artistic personality in Florence in the middle of the Trecento.[2] The date of his birth is not known, but he died in the second half of 1368, or a little later. He was the eldest of several brothers, of whom two others, Nardo and Jacopo di Cione, were also painters. Orcagna himself was active as a sculptor and architect as well, and in 1359 he completed the splendid marble Tabernacle in Or San Michele with scenes in relief of the life of the Virgin. As a painter he was head of a busy workshop, but few of his own works have survived. The only panel painting that can be attributed to him with certainty is the altarpiece, dated 1357, in the Strozzi Chapel in Santa Maria Novella *(pls 103, 105a)*. The work was commissioned in 1354. Admirable as an achievement of absolute technical perfection, it is the most important illustration we have of the singular stylistic situation that had evolved in Florence two decades after Giotto's death. The figures still conform to the canon laid down by Giotto, but the composition as a whole deviates radically from the Giottesque principles. The forms have a metallic stiffness and severity, and a peculiarly abstract plasticity, as though in the absence of any spatial medium. It would be pointless to attempt to discover the source of the light that moulds the hard, glassy forms and gives the colours their intense glow. A rigorous geometric form keeps the figures firmly in a two-dimensional plane and overcomes any tendency towards spatial illusion. The basis of the composition is an equilateral triangle uniting the three main figures, Christ surrounded by an aureole of angels, and the kneeling, voluminous figures in profile of St Peter and St Thomas Aquinas. St John the Baptist stands behind St Peter, staring fixedly to the front in the same way as Christ, so that these two figures are brought together in a separate spiritual association. The Virgin, commending St Thomas, is shown in three-quarter profile, equally severe and immobile. The rigidity that marks the central design is relaxed in the two pairs of saints on the right and left. All the figures, except the two kneeling saints, are related to the gold ground through the gold interwoven in their draperies. A piece of brocade, shown without foreshortening, serves as a floor for the figures, and prevents even the limited effect of depth that might be described as pictorial relief. On the other hand, there is a good deal of foreshortening and overlapping in the figures, and changing directions and sometimes violently salient or receding forms. Orcagna could not entirely disclaim the mode of spatial representation introduced by Giotto, but he tried to create a kind of non-perspective space governed, as it were, by rules not applicable to a finite world. With a sure instinct he seems to have sensed the danger to religious art of referring everything in the picture to a single human viewpoint, and therefore deliberately and patently rejected Giotto's three-dimensional method of representation. What pre-Giottesque painters did naturally without artifice, Orcagna attempted to achieve by calculated means and consciously conservative intellectual effort: the creation of a transcendental reality superior to that of the temporal world. The success of the style he evolved shows that it satisfied a deep need of his time.

The development of Orcagna's stylistic aims in wall-painting can unfortunately only be inferred from fragmentary remnants, and we shall come back to this later. By good chance, however, one complete fresco cycle has been preserved that conforms in general style to Orcagna's principles; it is the decoration of the Strozzi Chapel in Santa Maria Novella. It was executed not by Orcagna himself but by his brother Nardo di Cione *(pls 106a, 106b)*.[3] The entire decoration was doubtless based on a uniform plan, and the frescoes were probably painted in the same years as the altarpiece, that is to say, 1354–7. The chapel of the Strozzi family is in the south transept of the church, and each of its large walls is covered by a single picture, a *Last Judgment* on the window wall, and representations of Paradise and of Hell on the side walls.

The subject itself is appropriate to a two-dimensional form of representation, and indeed the Paradise scene has the effect of a huge tapestry with innumerable figures. The Blessed, arranged in regular rows one above the other, occupy the greater part of the picture. High in the centre, and in scale matching their importance, Christ and the Virgin are seated on a throne of Gothic design. The disproportionate size of this group produces an effect of reversed perspective: even if the rows of the Blessed are seen in recession one behind the other, the two main figures place everything firmly on the foreground plane. This artificially imposed two-dimensional pattern is completely in the spirit of Orcagna's work, and may have been based on a design prepared by him. However, closer examination of the apparently schematic arrangement of the Blessed reveals a surprising freedom of movement and softness of line and form, far removed from Orcagna's severe manner. In many cases the figures combine to form lively groups, and spatial effects emerge, but the composition as a whole has no unified perspective. Nardo di Cione was an artist of much gentler, more pliant temperament than his brother, and this abstract pictorial schematism appears even more forced in his work, as if it were a burden unwillingly accepted.

This contradiction between the natural inclination of the artist and the stylistic rule imposed on him becomes apparent in a most interesting manner in the counterpart of the Paradise scene, the picture of Hell. It is crowded with small animated figures, most of which are naked. They reveal a remarkable knowledge of the human form and its possibilities of expression – quite contrary to what would be expected in view of the two-dimensional character of the composition as a whole. The complicated movements are depicted with apparent ease, and impinge on the surface with three-dimensional effect (*pl. 106b*). Hovering figures, running, falling, and violently entangled with each other, pass across the picture like a flight of birds; it was within the almost unlimited capacity of this Trecento painter to illustrate every aspect of the torments of the damned. Time and again he succeeded in creating isolated scenes that have the atmosphere of Dante's *Inferno*, although he lacked the poet's comprehensive vision to give unity and order to his composition as a whole. It is also possible that he did not wish to shape his *Inferno*, after Dante's model, into an intelligible and transparently clear spatial presentation. The fresco is in fact a 'detailed and faithful illustration' of Dante's *Inferno*.[4] Even for a Renaissance painter, however, it would have been an almost impossible task to illustrate such a profusion of separate scenes, and at the same time to give a comprehensive single view of Dante's funnel-shaped image of Hell. The failure to accomplish this here cannot be attributed simply

to lack of artistic ability. Nardo di Cione depicts numerous scenes, isolated
places of punishment separated by narrow rocky ridges; and the circular structure of the infernal landscape with its zones rising one above the other is also indicated. But a greater recession in depth was hardly possible if the compactness of the huge surface pattern was to be preserved, and therefore the only practicable solution was the development of individual motifs on the same plane. In these separate scenes the painter reveals that his knowledge of spatial representation was much more extensive and sophisticated than the tapestry-like, seemingly primitive, view of Hell would lead one to suspect.

It is surely not a coincidence that these tensions and contradictions, usually masked by the idealizing tendencies of the contemporary style, became so marked in a representation of Hell. A similar manifestation is already seen in Giotto's work: uncontrolled demonic and human passions, breaking through all stylistic conventions, emerge in the scenes of Hell in the Padua *Last Judgment*. The torments of the damned are illustrated with frightening realism. Although there are precedents in medieval and Byzantine iconography, Giotto's representation of Hell achieves a degree of realism beyond anything previously attempted. The crude intensity of the description was to some extent necessitated by the subject, but even more remarkable is the licence Giotto permitted himself in the rendering of movement and naturalistic detail. An abundance of realistic observations, imaginative features, and expressive motifs, which had no place in his high formal style, are here displayed, and reveal more clearly than anywhere else the degree of artistic discipline Giotto imposed on himself to produce his distinctive creation, the grand, monumental style. There is a good deal of additional evidence to prove that his imaginative power was far greater than his executed works might suggest. The painted choirs in the Arena Chapel indicate that he could easily have created a complete perspective illusion. His 'style' can in no sense be equated with his 'vision'. The representational elements with which he constructs his pictorial world are only a conventional vocabulary, chosen according to the requirements of his monumental style. What Dante called the *freno d'arte* kept his artistic powers in check, and any infringement of this principle resulted in a loss of monumentality.[5]

In his scenes of Hell, Nardo di Cione goes far beyond Giotto in the free and imaginative handling of form. The Padua *Inferno* appears archaic and inhibited beside the Strozzi Chapel fresco. The figurative motifs and spatial vistas, occasioned by the special requirements of the subject, that are realized here on a small scale and by a Trecento painter, are only encountered again centuries later on the grand scale in Mannerist and Baroque art. It is as though the natural, unaffected vision of the painter were glimpsed behind the characteristic forms of the monumental style; verse is transformed into free-flowing, expressive prose. The contrast between these two modes of representation had become sharper in the two decades since Giotto's death. This is clearly apparent when one compares Nardo's scenes of Hell with the other Strozzi Chapel frescoes and with his own panel paintings,[6] which are even more consciously primitive than the works of the contemporary Sienese masters. Nardo di Cione is meticulous in avoiding any suggestion of spatial depth. As in Orcagna's Strozzi Chapel altar, the floors are usually indicated by a two-dimensional brocade pattern, and it is never possible to tell what supports the seated figures; at best a piece of brocade implies some sort of throne. The deliberate renunciation of perspective devices is carried to its final conclusion. In the mild, vacant faces there is no sign of the rich range of expression that the painter demonstrated in the scenes of Hell in his fresco. An unrealistic, Nazarene calm and impersonal mood envelops these pictures, and we sense that the painter is not conveying everything he is capable of expressing. It is unquestionably an example of the impoverishment that always follows when the wheel of progress is turned back. Whenever religious art ceases to be a natural product of the life around it, it becomes retrospective and archaicizing; and it loses its substance as soon as it no longer employs the full artistic capacity of its time. The painting of the Orcagna circle is a striking early example of this phenomenon in the history of post-classical art.

In view of the problematic nature of Nardo di Cione's style, it is the more regrettable that Orcagna's major monumental work, the decoration of the main choir chapel of Santa Maria Novella, has been almost entirely obliterated. He received this commission in 1350, when he must already have been an experienced and recognized master.[7] It was a cycle depicting the life of the Virgin, and was replaced towards the end of the Quattrocento by the famous frescoes of Ghirlandaio. Only a number of medallions containing half-length figures, part of the vault decoration, have recently come to light. The solid, powerful forms are clearly distinguishable from the softer, more delicate work of Nardo di Cione. It is very unlikely, however, that they were executed by Orcagna himself.[8]

The huge fresco of the *Crucifixion* in the refectory of Santo Spirito in Florence is a work of high, though somewhat cold, monumentality.[9] The composition of this large and powerful work is based on the contrast between the compact mass of scarcely articulated figures and the empty background, visible over a large area. The figure of Longinus on one side, and that of the centurion with his distinct, sweeping gesture, on the other, are deliberately introduced as effective features. Both are mounted and shown with haloes.[10] Figurative and two-dimensional elements dominate the composition, and the recession of the landscape and the rising slope of the hill of Golgotha are hardly perceptible. It seems that Orcagna was responsible for the general conception, but here again the execution must be ascribed to his pupils.[11]

There is another major work of Orcagna which must have been much more impressive than the *Crucifixion,* with its impersonal mood and contrived setting. Unfortunately it has survived only in fragmentary condition. Three large frescoes extended along the wall of the south aisle of Santa Croce, depicting related subjects: the *Triumph of Death,* the *Last Judgment,* and the *Inferno.* Ghiberti numbered them among Orcagna's works, and Vasari's description, linking them together with very similar representations in the Campo Santo in Pisa, attributes both groups to Orcagna.[12] However, at about the time the enlarged edition of his *Lives* appeared, Vasari recklessly sacrificed Orcagna's frescoes in Santa Croce, as well as a number of other important Trecento works, in favour of a plan of his own for the redecoration of the church. This was carried out between 1566 and 1584. The screen, containing numerous works of art, was demolished,[13] and the walls of the aisles whitewashed and furnished with the Late Renaissance altars that are still there today. Only a few specially valuable monuments of the Early Renaissance were spared. All traces of Orcagna's frescoes seemed to have been lost, until a fragment of the *Triumph of Death* was discovered behind one of Vasari's altars: the group of beggars vainly invoking Death *(pl. 104).* A second fragment, the left half of the *Inferno (pl. 105b),* was found, badly damaged, behind another altar, and after careful search remnants of the painted frame were also uncovered. All these fragments are now in the Museo di Santa Croce.[14] These parts of the original frescoes, together with Vasari's description and the analogous representations in Pisa, enable us to reconstruct the monumental 'triptych' with some accuracy. The entire work was seven meters high and not less than eighteen meters wide. Great painted columns, strongly plastic on account of their spiral shafts, divided the pictorial surface, in the Cosmati manner, into three sections. It is the same illusionistic architectural motif that Giotto had used in the St Francis legend at Assisi. Orcagna further heightened the illusionistic effect by omitting the frames alongside the columns, so that the scene appears to continue without interruption behind them. The solid effect produced by the bizarre shape of the columns is strongly emphasized, but as far as can be gathered from the fragments, there was hardly any spatial depth. The beggars, at whose feet the dead lie in a tangled mass, are surrounded by large areas of empty background, and their bold abstract forms are combined with the inscription, written diagonally across the surface, into a two-dimensional entity. The composition seems to have been entirely confined to the figures placed in the foreground. In the *Inferno,* a certain degree of spatial depth was unavoidable owing to the scenic elements, but even here the non-perspective picture-book character is still more distinct than in Nardo di Cione's scene of *Hell.* Orcagna's version is more primitive than his brother's fresco in the Strozzi Chapel both as a whole and in its detail, for example in the scenes of torture, which have a crude savagery. Orcagna's experience as a sculptor in marble is seen in the powerful modelling of the nude figures and the angular, unconventional movements. Strident colours, shining out against the prevailing chalky, stone and earth tones accentuate the infernal negation of the divine order and the general impression of violence. Here also there is a deliberate renunciation of idealized forms, justified by the nature of the subject, which releases the artist's creative force and reveals his naturally powerful temperament. The 'prose' style is vivid and elemental, and directly reminiscent of Giotto's scenes of *Hell* in the Arena Chapel in Padua. In comparison Nardo di Cione's style is much softer, more flexible and rhythmic, more capable of genuinely poetic effect: and he alone of the Trecento painters succeeded in finding a language for his vision of Hell that does not appear ill-judged or pedestrian beside Dante's poem. No doubt the difference was mainly one of temperament, but it is impossible to avoid the conclusion that in his conception Nardo had progressed far beyond Orcagna.

As far as can be judged, therefore, from the surviving frescoes, Orcagna's frescoes in Santa Croce are in some respects more archaic than those of Nardo in Santa Maria Novella, but in spite of this they seem to have been done later, possibly in the 1360s.[15] Compared with that of the *Strozzi Altar* Orcagna's style had now become freer and more versatile, and his grasp firmer and more realistic. He commanded a wider range of expression, not necessarily just dictated by the very different subject-matter.

The Triumph of Death in Santa Croce was not the first illustration of this theme, but was probably derived from the frescoes by Francesco Traini in the Campo Santo in Pisa, which will be discussed in the next chapter.[16] When the Santa Croce beggars *(pl. 104)* are compared with those in Pisa *(pl. 100a),* it becomes clear that in addition to iconographic elements Orcagna drew considerable artistic inspiration from the Pisan master. None of this affected Orcagna's dominant influence, both as a painter and a sculptor, on Florentine art of the second half of the Trecento. His grave virile style, his austere forms, and his characterization of types, provided a firm foundation on which even the weaker artists were able to build.

12 The Triumph of Death

Orcagna's presentation of the *Triumph of Death* corresponds to a comparatively familiar pictorial type in Trecento art. A fresco of Bartolo di Fredi in San Francesco in Lucignano is a model of the complete composition.[1] The main figure, *La Morte,* in female form, is placed in the centre of the picture, with savage features and fair hair streaming in the wind, galloping on a black horse. She draws her bow, and levels the fatal arrow at two fashionably dressed youths strolling unsuspectingly in the hilly countryside. Under the horse's hooves lie strewn the dead bodies that have already fallen to her. On the left of the picture, beggars vainly entreat the ferocious rider for death. The beggars and the dead are strikingly similar to those in Orcagna's picture.

In another fresco, in the Sacro Speco monastery near Subiaco, the direction of the movement is reversed.[2] Death, a skeleton characterized as a woman by her long flowing hair, rides towards the young men standing at the left of the picture, while the beggars remain behind her to the right; dead bodies again lie in heaps on the ground. Although there is no direct link with Orcagna's fresco, the elements of the representation are the same. As already mentioned, Orcagna himself did not invent the motif, but took it from an existing model, the fresco in the Campo Santo in Pisa, where he had already found the allegory of Death associated with the Last Judgment and the Inferno. It was this association that gave the allegory its full significance, and provided it with the religious justification necessary at the time.[3]

It is often forgotten that the *Triumph of Death* in itself is not a Christian theme. The concept of Death as a female figure is of classical origin. The gruesome harbingers of Death, the *Keres,* who snatched the souls of fallen warriors, were familiar figures in Greek mythology; and Horace, well known in the Trecento, describes Death as a goddess hovering on sable wings. The fair hair, which we noticed in the Lucignano fresco and which reappears in the Campo Santo fresco, also has a classical derivation, the golden hair of Proserpina, mistress of the underworld. On the other hand no prototypes of Death are found in the art of the Early and High Middle Ages. The death of the body had little importance for the faithful, whose eyes were fastened on eternal life. They knew that the final decree, life or death, would be made when the Lord returned on the Day of Judgment, and their fear was only of the 'second', the ultimate death, the everlasting damnation of the soul. For this reason references to death are found only in association with the Crucifixion, a skull at the foot of the cross, sometimes a whole skeleton, or, on rare occasions, a demonic figure with the inscription *Mors*.[4] But the symbolism was quite different from that of the later allegories of Death: the implication was that Christ had conquered, and death had lost its sting. There was no way in which medieval art could conceive the representation of death except in the role of the vanquished.

The vivid and terrifying scenes of death depicted in Trecento art were therefore a startling innovation. Death in its most fearful forms was no stranger to the people of that period. Time and again, above all in the dreadful year 1348, the Black Death swept over Italy claiming thousands of victims and depopulating whole cities. This wholesale slaughter is impressively described by Boccaccio with grandiose realism at the beginning of the *Decameron*. Yet this was not a pessimistic book; on the contrary, it expressed a new worldliness in which every aspect of human reality was described in colourful anecdotal or sober realistic terms, including death, the most inexorable fact of all.

The allegories of death are therefore by no means fully accounted for by the terrible experience of the plague. The new image of death had deeper roots; it was the counterpart of the increasing awareness of the value of human life, which made the prospect of death correspondingly more real and frightening. The signs of this change can be seen throughout Europe from the beginning of the fourteenth century, especially in the field of sepulchral art. The youthful, idealized images of the dead 'sleeper' that adorned most tombs were increasingly replaced by actual likenesses, and in time, soon after the middle of the century, even by representations suggesting the decomposition of the flesh.[5] Although elements of the Christian admonition of the necessity for self-communion and soul-searching were also involved, a new and unmistakable emphasis was placed on the physical aspect of death. In the early Middle Ages there had been no need to draw attention to the transience of life, since the only real existence lay beyond the grave.

Independently of the change manifested in sepulchral art, death in itself, without any religious connotations, now became a subject for pictorial art. The most popular motif, the *Dance of Death,* is of northern origin, and appears in Italian art only in the third quarter of the fifteenth century.[6] It should be mentioned here, however, because it demonstrates that the secularization of the concept of death was a phenomenon common to the whole of Europe.

73 TADDEO GADDI Frescoes of the Baroncelli Chapel · Florence, Santa Croce

74 TADDEO GADDI
Annunciation to the Shepherds
Florence, Santa Croce

75 a TADDEO GADDI *Allegory of Poverty*
Florence, Santa Croce
75 b TADDEO GADDI *Shepherd with His Flock*
(detail of the *Annunciation to Joachim, cf.* pl. 73)
Florence, Santa Croce

76 DUCCIO *St Catherine* (detail of the *Maestà*)
Siena, Opera del Duomo

77 DUCCIO *Women at the Tomb of Christ*
Siena, Opera del Duomo

80　SIMONE MARTINI *The Knighting of St Martin* · Assisi, San Francesco

81 SIMONE MARTINI (1333) *Angel* (detail of the *Annunciation*) · Florence, Uffizi

82 a–d SIMONE MARTINI a *Road to Calvary* · Paris, Louvre   b *Descent from the Cross* · Antwerp, Musée Royal
c, d *St Martin Shares His Cloak with a Beggar* (sinopia and fresco) · Assisi, San Francesco

83　Simone Martini (1342) *Return of the Young Jesus from the Temple* · Liverpool Museum

· LIPPVS · MEMMI · DE · SENIS · ME · PINXIT ·

84   LIPPO MEMMI *Enthroned Madonna* · Altenburg,
Staatliches Lindenau-Museum

85   BARNA DA SIENA *Road to Calvary*
San Gimignano, Collegiata

86   PIETRO LORENZETTI (1320) *Madonna*
Arezzo, Pieve di Santa Maria

87   PIETRO LORENZETTI (1320) *Annunciation*
Arezzo, Pieve di Santa Maria

88   Pietro Lorenzetti *Descent from the Cross* · Assisi, San Francesco   89   Detail of pl. 88

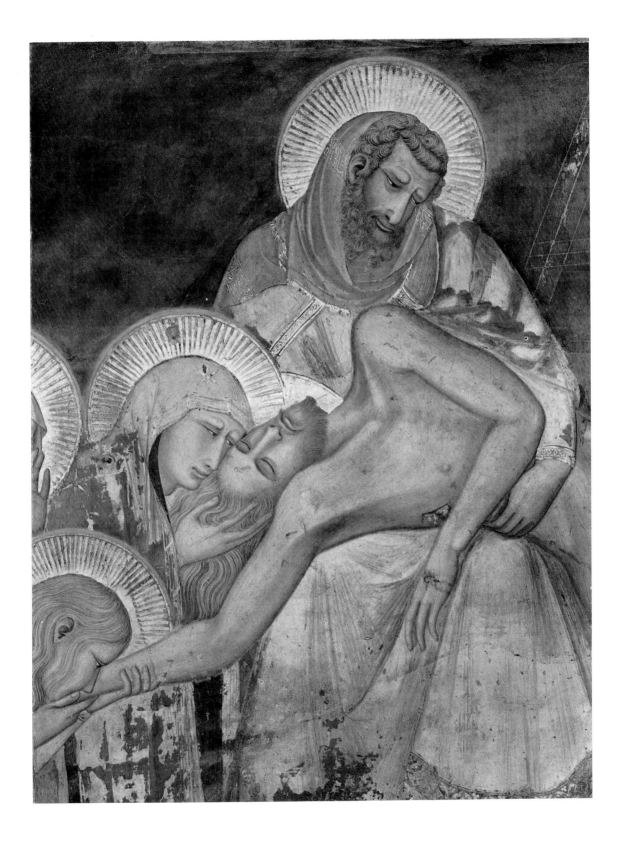

90 a PIETRO LORENZETTI *Madonna with SS. Francis and John the Evangelist* · Assisi, San Francesco
90 b PIETRO LORENZETTI *Entry into Jerusalem* (detail) · Assisi, San Francesco

91 a   PIETRO LORENZETTI
St John the Baptist (1320)
Arezzo, Pieve di Santa Maria
91 b   PIETRO LORENZETTI
John the Baptist (1332)
Siena, Pinacoteca

91 c   PIETRO LORENZETTI
Legend of the Beata Umiltà
Berlin-Dahlem, Staatliche
Gemäldegalerie

94 AMBROGIO LORENZETTI *Admission of St Louis of Toulouse into the Franciscan Order* · Siena, San Francesco

95 *King Robert of Naples* (Detail of pl. 94)

96 AMBROGIO LORENZETTI *Allegory of Peace*
Siena, Palazzo Pubblico

97 AMBROGIO LORENZETTI *View of Siena* (detail)
Siena, Palazzo Pubblico

98 FRANCESCO TRAINI *The Three Living and the Three Dead*
Pisa, Museo Nazionale

99 Detail of pl. 98

100a, b FRANCESCO TRAINI a *Group of Beggars*
(detail of *Triumph of Death*) · Pisa, Museo Nazionale
b *Temptation of a Hermit* (sinopia) · Pisa, Museo Nazionale

101 a, b FRANCESCO TRAINI Details of the
Triumph of Death and *The Last Judgment*
Pisa, Museo Nazionale

102a MASO DI BANCO
Legend of St Sylvester
Florence, Santa Croce
102b Detail of pl. 102a

103   ANDREA ORCAGNA (1357) *Strozzi Altar* · Florence, Santa Maria Novella

104   ANDREA ORCAGNA *Beggars* (detail of *Triumph of Death*) · Florence, Museo di Santa Croce

105a ANDREA ORCAGNA
St Peter (detail of pl. 103)

105b ANDREA ORCAGNA *Inferno* (detail)
Florence, Museo di Santa Croce

106 a, b NARDO DI CIONE *Head of Christ* and
The Damned (details of *The Last Judgment*)
Florence, Santa Maria Novella, Strozzi Chapel

107 ANDREA DA FIRENZE *Resurrection*
Florence, Spanish Chapel

108 ANDREA DA FIRENZE *Heretics* (detail of the *Triumph of the Church*) · Florence, Spanish Chapel

109 ANDREA DA FIRENZE *Dancers* (detail of the *Triumph of the Church*) · Florence, Spanish Chapel

110　Giovanni da Milano *Christ with the Virgin and St Martha* (detail) · Florence, Santa Croce

111 GIOVANNI DA MILANO *Birth of the Virgin* · Florence, Santa Croce

112   GHERARDO STARNINA *St Benedict* (fragment) · Florence, Santa Maria del Carmine

113a   AGNOLO GADDI *Legend of the Holy Cross* · Florence, Santa Croce
113b   Detail of pl. 113a

114a Riminese Master (c. 1317) *The Last Supper*
Pomposa, Refectory
114b Riminese Master (c. 1310–20) *The Last Judgment*
(detail), Rimini, Palazzo dell'Arengo
(from Sant'Agostino)

115 Riminese Master (c. 1310–20)
Presentation in the Temple
Rimini, Sant'Agostino

116 Riminese Master (*c.* 1330) *Deposition and Lamentation* (from an altar-retable) · Rome, Palazzo Barberini

117　Paolo Veneziano *Coronation of the Virgin* · Venice, Accademia

118 VITALE DA BOLOGNA
Madonna 'dei Denti' (1345)
Bologna, Galleria Davia Bargellini

119 VITALE DA BOLOGNA
Legend of St Anthony
Bologna, Pinacoteca Nazionale

120 VITALE DA BOLOGNA *Nativity* (detail) · Bologna, Pinacoteca Nazionale

121　Barnaba da Modena (1369) *Madonna* · Formerly Berlin, Kaiser-Friedrich-Museum

122　Tomaso da Modena (1352), *Albertus Magnus* · Treviso, San Niccolò

123 TOMASO DA MODENA *Madonna* · Karlstein Castle near Prague

124 Tomaso da Modena *Legend of St Ursula*
Treviso, Museo Civico

125 Guariento *Angel* · Padua, Museo Civico

126 Altichiero *Crucifixion* (left side) · Padua, Santo

127 ALTICHIERO *Beheading of St George* · Padua, Oratorio di San Giorgio

128 ALTICHIERO *Presentation in the Temple* · Padua, Oratorio di San Giorgio

Literary models of the *Dance of Death* motif occur as far back as the thirteenth century. In its original form it was a procession of living people on their way to death, their leader not Death, but a man already dead. The constantly recurring theme was *Vado mori*. Pope and Emperor led the dance, and representatives of all walks of life followed behind them. The emphasis on the inevitability of death had the social and political connotation – cold comfort for the wretched – that in death all are equal.

Another motif is the *Encounter of the Three Living and the Three Dead*. This allegory appeared in the cathedral of Atri and in other places in southern Italy as early as the middle of the thirteenth century, and soon afterwards in the north.[7] Three kings while out hunting come upon three dead men, shown as skeletons or half-decayed corpses. In the words addressed by the dead to the living there is no suggestion of a spiritual message. 'What you are, we were; what we are you will be', is the formula used, with variations, in literary works from the eleventh century onwards. Oriental epigrams since pre-Islamic times contain references to the allegory of the encounter the dead,[8] and its early appearance in southern Italy, as well as the pictorial form it took, could indicate an Eastern derivation. Its original significance was simply *Memento mori,* without any Christian implication. It was only later that an attempt was made to turn it into a Christian motif by the inclusion of the hermit, St Macarius.

The third of these pictorial types, the Triumph of Death, was a purely Italian creation, of classical origin as already mentioned. Furthermore the view that Death spares the wretched who long for him, and carries off the young and healthy instead, also has a classical tradition.[9] Strange to say, the seemingly typical medieval picture of death ruthlessly taking life in its prime, is actually a sign of the revival of humanism, not only because of its general sense of a secular approach to the conception of death, but also in its explicit reference to classical motifs. However, the artistic form it assumed was not in the least classical, but distinctly medieval, of the Trecento. There is only one literary work, Petrarch's poem, *Trionfi,* in which a classical form, the Triumphal Procession, is given to the allegory of Death. The name, the *Triumph of Death,* is taken from this poem, although it is not strictly applicable to fourteenth-century painting. It was only in the fifteenth century that pictorial art also adopted this classical motif, and showed Death, among other allegorical figures, driving her chariot in a triumphal procession.

The most splendid Trecento pictorial representation of the allegory of Death was in the Campo Santo in Pisa until the end of the Second World War.[10] The frescoes were badly damaged in the fire of 1944, which destroyed the roof of the famous building, and the entire huge pictorial cycle had to be removed from the walls to prevent its complete deterioration. At least the most important part of the frescoes, the *Triumph of Death,* can now be seen in the Museo Nazionale di S. Matteo in Pisa, in addition to the *Last Judgment,* the *Inferno,* and the *Anchorites of the Thebaid.* The transfer has been remarkably successful, but the fire caused considerable damage and, even more important, the effect of the frescoes in their original setting has been irrevocably lost.

However, this disaster involving one of the great works of Italian monumental painting had one unexpected beneficial result. Beneath the upper layer of the frescoes, the large preliminary drawings have come to light in a remarkably clear and complete condition.[11] These have also been transferred, in part, to the museum, where they can be compared directly with the paintings under which they had been concealed. They are strikingly fresh and bold brush drawings, sketched with sparse strokes, yet monumental and powerful. Together with their monumentality and emotional content they have considerable delicacy and elegance, as for instance in the figures of the young woman vainly trying to seduce a hermit *(pl. 100b).*[12] Their graphic style has great confidence and seemingly effortless power. The disparity between these designs and the finished paintings, for the most part executed by assistants, is plain to see. These finds in Pisa clearly confirm the view of the important creative function of the monumental drawing in Trecento painting already discussed in connection with Giotto's method of work. The illustrative material in the Campo Santo in Pisa covers an uninterrupted period from the middle of the Trecento right into the second half of the Quattrocento, that is to say, to Benozzo Gozzoli's frescoes in the north arm. It is surprising to see how long the old type of monumental drawing continued in use. Even Gozzoli's designs, drawn directly on the wall, are usually fresher and more impressive than the finished painting, which shows that the making of monumental drawings was not an occasional practice but the normal and traditional procedure. It is also apparent, however, that Gozzoli's drawings are far less monumental than those of the older masters, and that the direct link between the original design and the pictorial surface, to which Trecento wall-painting owed its sureness of style, was lost in the Quattrocento. The most effective of the preliminary drawings are the ones done for the early frescoes painted shortly after the middle of the Trecento.

The marble buildings of the Campo Santo, situated next to the cathedral, form the cloistered quadrangle of the cemetery, 126 meters long and 52 meters wide. The windowless walls, more than nine meters high in the interior and protected by the roof of the cloister, provided a more extensive area for frescoes than is found in even the largest churches. To cover these immense walls with pictures was a gigantic task, which could have been contemplated only at the end of the Middle Ages. The work extended over more than a hundred years, and what the Trecento had left unfinished, the Renaissance faithfully completed. The fresco sequence stretched around the four arms of the cloister, like a huge picture-book compiled for those unable to read, until the final scenes joined up with the beginning.

The earliest paintings were in the south-east corner of the Campo Santo: the *Crucifixion,* the *Resurrection,* and the *Ascension* on the east wall, and the *Last Judgment* cycle at the beginning of the long south wall. The fresco that is now usually known as the *Triumph of Death* was evidently the first to be done. It combines the two principal motifs of the Italian iconography of death: the encounter of the three living and the three dead *(pl. 98),* and the gruesome figure of Death, with great bat's wings, hovering over a pile of corpses and wielding her murderous scythe. Behind her a crowd of beggars and invalids, vainly craving for death, present an unforgettable picture of human suffering and utter despair *(pl. 100a).* In front of Death her next victims are gathered, a fashionable group, full of life, gossiping and playing music *(pl. 101a).* This elaborate and dramatic *Memento mori,* painted in strident colours, is followed by a *Last Judgment,* done according to the old medieval formula: Christ sits in judgment, with the Blessed on his right and the Damned on his left *(pl. 101b).* The Virgin, given equal prominence with her Son, and seated next to Him on the same side as the Blessed, is a new feature introduced into the traditional representation. The gesture with which Christ damns the sinners, 'Ite Maledicti', has such menace that it even inspired Michelangelo's magnificent conception of the wrathful figure of Christ the Judge in the Sistine Chapel. The third picture in the series is the *Inferno,* a crude catalogue of the tortures of the Damned, dominated by the colossal, grotesquely repulsive figure of Satan.[13] The arrangement is thus similar to that of Orcagna's three frescoes in Santa Croce, except for the addition of the allegory of the meeting of the dead and the living. On the right of the *Inferno* there was a fourth large picture, the *Anchorites of the Thebaid.* It is the counterpart of the first picture, in which the theme is the danger of sudden death to those engaged in active life. Withdrawal from life and pious contemplation take the sting from death. This was the answer offered by the Middle Ages to the inevitability of death.

But the dominant theme is the one stated in the first picture. The horror of death was the real innovation in the series, and must have deeply affected and gripped people at that time. One feels that the painter himself was passionately concerned not so much with death as with the flamboyant cavalcade of life he so strikingly portrayed – kings, cavaliers, and fashionable ladies out riding. The vivid colours, rounded contours and taut lines display a virile, joyous love of life, subjected, however, to a highly disciplined sence of decorative form. The same virility is seen in the group of beggars *(pl. 100a)*; their unanimous shrill lament echoes like the wailing of a Greek tragic chorus. The sharp contrasts between the rich and the wretched in which life abounded at the time, are depicted without compassion, and the scenes of misery with dead bodies piled carelessly on top of each other are taken directly from contemporary experience. There is nothing in the contemporary records that tells the circumstances in which these frescoes came to be painted or give any clue to their authorship. Vasari's attribution to Orcagna has long been recognized as untenable. More recent studies have associated the frescoes with an altarpiece from Santa Caterina in Pisa, signed by the Pisan painter Francesco Traini, and completed, according to documentary evidence, in 1345. The panel, now in the Pisa Museum, depicts St Dominic and eight scenes from his life. The same passionate temperament is revealed in these scenes, despite their small, almost miniature, size, as in the *Triumph of Death* and the three adjoining pictures in the Campo Santo in Pisa. Notwithstanding contrary opinions, the attribution of the frescoes to Francesco Traini and a group of assistants working under him remains the most convincing solution to this controversial problem.[14] As to the time of their composition, a date roughly in the middle of the 1350s could be appropriate. They must have been painted some time after the St Dominic panel, because the style of the frescoes, despite the close affinity with the panel, is more precise and ornamental. Orcagna's cycle in Santa Croce, undoubtedly a later work, affords no firm latest date for the Campo Santo frescoes.[15] The inscriptions, which are in part repeated in Santa Croce, refer only to the subject-matter of the paintings.[16] Some external evidence is possibly provided by the tombstones in the Campo Santo, the earliest of which is dated 1359. It seems that about this time the grounds of the Campo Santo began to be used for burials. But whatever answers are given to the question of dating and attribution, the painter of these frescoes in the Campo Santo was one of the great artistic personalities of the Trecento. He may appear somewhat provincial beside Orcagna, and almost crude and rustic beside the Sienese masters, to whom he owed much, but he surpassed all his contemporaries in elementary vigour and comprehension of the life around him.

13 The end of the Trecento in Florence

The apparent paradox, that the representation of death expresses a new zest for life, reflects the ambiguous character of an age that saw the spread of intellectual activity in many fields, and yet was unable to rid itself of medieval trammels. The new awareness of life that was gradually emerging could express itself only within the traditional forms, and its first innovations were confined to the introduction of novel subjects. The allegory of Death and its complement, the description of life as it was then lived, were indeed new pictorial themes that evidently aroused general interest, but iconographically and formally they were firmly linked to tradition, and therefore could not be presented otherwise than in conjunction with the *Last Judgment,* the Christian concept of the hereafter. Thus they were given a kind of indirect sanction by official ecclesiastical doctrine. Above all, the gradually awakening humanism was for many generations incapable of evolving an adequate artistic form of expression. That was accomplished only in the Early Renaissance, almost a century after Giotto's death, and until then the stylistic foundation of painting, the categories of artistic concepts, and the standards of formal design remained essentially unaltered. Even though Orcagna reversed the elements of the Giottesque style and turned them into a system of tensions between depth and surface, and other masters attempted to go beyond the limits established by Giotto by extending the pictorial depth and introducing new motifs, fundamentally his spatial relief, abstract plasticity and standardized figurative types remained unchanged. Naturally there were individual and local variations within the set limits, but in general the Giottesque canons remained valid until the end of the Trecento, either because they persisted as a conscious tradition, or simply because they appeared more modern and effective in comparison with older forms. By the middle of the century there existed no local school of painting anywhere in Italy that was not to some extent influenced, at least in outward form, by the Tuscan style that Giotto had originated.

Strictly speaking, this completes the artistic development which we have sought to elucidate. There was no substantial advance in medieval painting in Italy after the middle of the Trecento. The gradual decline of the Giottesque tradition was a process whose details are a subject for specialized research. The new characteristics that occasionally manifested themselves at the end of the Trecento and the beginning of the Quattrocento were of little historical significance. They were hesitant, sporadic beginnings of an attempt to overcome the medieval stylistic conventions, and although indicative of the ambivalent character of the time, which was both traditionalistic and progressive, their part in the birth of the Renaissance was negligible. Of much greater importance was the International Style, which originated not in Italy but at the court of France. The intrusion of this international stylistic movement, although disrupting the course of Italian painting, prepared the ground for the re-awakening of its intrinsic creative forces, which occurred with the abruptness of a revolutionary upheaval, and was based on entirely different principles of representation. It is true that Masaccio drew on the great native tradition, and was indebted to Agnolo Gaddi, two generations older than himself, and above all to Giotto. But this was a purely personal predilection, a deliberate recourse to a past age, and not the organic outcome of a live and continuing tradition. That tradition, in spite of its tenacious hold and seemingly permanent status, was already condemned to extinction by the middle of the Trecento.

The inner exhaustion of artistic forces in the second half of the Trecento was nowhere so pronounced as in Florence itself, the fountainhead of the Giottesque tradition. The painting of large fresco cycles continued, and panel paintings were produced on an almost industrial scale. The size of the paintings became larger than ever before, and the variety of the decorative schemes increased; but the immediacy of perception was lost, and the style became more and more eclectic. What development there was, was confined to iconographical motifs, but even here it is significant that the stimulus was frequently external, that is to say, it was given by ecclesiastical or even secular patrons. Throughout the Middle Ages artists had accomplished creative achievements in iconography: the small devotional pictures of the early Trecento were in the first place products of a vivid imagination that succeeded in giving pictorial form to certain religious conceptions. A striking change now took place. Art became the *ancilla theologiae* in the service of learned allegory, illustrating intellectual concepts rather than visual themes. Didactic pictorial representations began to appear in addition to the customary Biblical and legendary pictures, especially in the churches and monasteries of the Mendicant Orders. The Franciscans had initiated this movement already in the first half of the century. A typical motif in their monasteries was the Tree of St Bonaventure, Christ's cross represented as the Tree of Life, after the book of St Bonaventure entitled *Lignum Vitae* (*see* the Revelation of St John 22, 2).[1] The tree has twelve branches, each bearing four fruits representing events in the life of Christ. This was the arrangement of the book that artists now tried to illustrate pictorially. The idea did not lend itself to pictorial description, but required a kind of allegorical diagram, which could be made comprehensible only by means of numerous inscriptions. The most detailed representation of this specifically Franciscan theme is in a panel painting by Pacino di Buonaguida, now in the Florence Galleria dell'Accademia.[2] Taddeo Gaddi and his workshop produced a monumental version for the Santa Croce refectory, and succeeded to a remarkable degree in integrating the branches, shaped like tendrils, and the profusion of inscriptive scrolls into a highly decorative pattern.[3] But even Gaddi could not create a real picture out of this non-pictorial theme.

An even more elaborate, didactic scheme was produced by the Dominicans for the decoration of the chapter-house in Santa Maria Novella, called the Spanish Chapel since the sixteenth century.[4] The frescoes, painted by Andrea da Firenze between 1366 and 1368, are a penetrating, well-devised illustration of Dominican ecclesiastical doctrine, with the Dominican Order represented as the most important organ of the Church for purposes of spiritual guidance and religious teaching, having its roots in the principal events of the story of the Salvation. The artistic realization is as uniform and compact as the logical structure of the theme. Architecture and painting form a single artistic entity, and doubtless the building was designed from the start with the pictorial decoration in mind. The large, plain room is roofed by a single cross-vault supported by powerful ribs. The pictures, framed by wide ornamental borders, extend over the whole surface of the walls, and also cover the four huge vaults. The complete domination of the room by the paintings goes beyond anything known until then. The whole work has undeniable verve, and the confident handling of the enormous surfaces is remarkable. The style of the frescoes, which are well preserved, is the product of an impersonal academic skill placed unconditionally at the service of the theological patrons. The only personal trait is a certain brittleness of forms, which appear dry and sober beside Giotto's monumental yet lively style, and even beside

Orcagna's austerity. The purpose of the frescoes is predominantly illustrative; although thematically they are wholly devoted to expounding the theological doctrine and mission of the Dominican Order, in formal terms they reveal a rapidly encroaching secularization of artistic expression. The form is no longer inspired by the spirit of the work, which is not surprising when one considers the heavy load of ideas with which the pictures are burdened. The *Triumph of St Thomas Aquinas,* on the left wall, is a schematic arrangement of allegorical figures. Fourteen female figures, personifying the Liberal Arts and the Spiritual and Temporal Sciences, are seated on thrones one beside the other, each with her leading exponent at her feet – a subject that would have taxed the capacity of greater artists than Andrea da Firenze. The picture on the opposite wall, in which mankind is shown the path to faith and salvation, also remains cold and rigid. Numerous additional themes were included in this densely packed composition: at the top is the Saviour in Glory with choirs of angels and the symbols of the evangelists; at the bottom the representatives of the religious and secular vocations arranged in strict order of rank in front of a Gothic church, an idealized version of Florence Cathedral as it was then planned. Finally, in the same picture, a major task of the Dominicans is also depicted, their struggle against the heretics *(pl. 108).* While the Dominicans dispute with the infidels, white and black spotted dogs, the *domini canes,* hurl themselves, in a vividly symbolic attack, upon the wolves that have penetrated the fold of the faithful. It is the harshness of the style that produces the gripping effect of this representation, and even gives an unobtrusive charm to the dance of the young girls, abandoning themselves to the joys of worldly life *(pl. 109).*

The front wall of the chapter-house, interrupted below by the arched opening of the small sanctuary, is also treated as a single surface, depicting the events of the Crucifixion and containing a multitude of figures. The story begins in the lower left corner with a *Road to Calvary,* and ends with *Christ's Descent into Hell,* in the lower right. In the vaults there are four scenes from the New Testament, corresponding in subject to the respective scenes on the walls below. The *Resurrection (pl. 107)* in a new iconographic conception, symmetrical in form and with a strict hierarchical structure, is placed above the *Crucifixion.*[5] In the right vault, above the picture of the Church Militant, is the *Navicella,* the small ship of the church, tossed by the storm, with Peter saved by Christ from drowning. The left vault contains the *Descent of the Holy Ghost at Pentecost,* the divine complement to the Glory of St Thomas, the inspired teacher of the church. Finally, above the entrance-hall and opposite the *Crucifixion,* is the *Ascension of Christ.* The white-clad, hovering figure of Christ thus appears twice, in the *Resurrection* scene and in the *Ascension,* each time on the central axis of the room. The main emphasis is placed on the inner logic of the work as a whole, and the real merit of the painter lay in the co-ordination of the architectural features of the room with the complicated scheme devised by the theologian.

The chancel of the sacristy of Santa Croce, the so-called Rinuccini Chapel, was also decorated with a fresco cycle at about the same time as the Spanish Chapel, and there is evidence that in the year 1365 a Lombard painter, Giovanni da Milano, was working on this commission. The left wall depicts the story of Joachim and Anna and the life of the Virgin up to her marriage, and on the right wall the legend of Mary Magdalene and the Raising of Lazarus. The evangelists are portrayed on the vaults and figures of saints on the curve of the entrance arch. Giovanni da Milano, however, did not finish the cycle. The frescoes on the lower zone are by an anonymous successor of Orcagna, the Master of the Rinuccini Chapel,[7] and are dry, unimaginative, and technically mediocre, while Giovanni's contribution ranks with the best work produced in Florence at that time. His style displays the north Italian talent for decoration and ornamental pictorial construction, together with a sensitive feeling for colour. His narrative scenes have a silent, undramatic quality *(pls 110, 111),* the movements fusing with the gentle flow of the contours and remaining arrested in the dense texture of the delicately chromatic surface. The spell is not broken even by the motifs taken from contemporary life, which are completely transposed into the prevailing poetic mood. Even in the *Expulsion of Joachim from the Temple,* a large lunette fresco with numerous figures, the dramatic element is still subordinate to the formal presentation.

Although the severe hierarchical structure, intended to emphasize the timeless nature of the events, was in conformity with the prevailing stylistic trend, Giovanni's personal contribution, the legacy of his Lombard origin, must not be underestimated. The exquisite glowing colours of his panel paintings distinguish them from all other Florentine productions of that time, and give them animation and a delicately substantial quality in harmony with the rounded linear contours. The richly articulated polyptych that Giovanni da Milano painted for the high altar of the Ognissanti Church in Florence is unfortunately preserved only in part. Five of the original six side-panels together with their predella pieces are in the Uffizi. The sixth panel and the centrepiece are lost. The impression this magnificent All Saints' Altar must have made beside the works of Orcagna's followers may be compared to that made by Gentile da Fabriano's altarpieces two generations later beside

313

those of Bicci di Lorenzo. But there was this difference, that Masaccio appeared in Florence at the same time as Gentile, whereas Giovanni da Milano had no contemporary of comparable stature. His north Italian sense of colour made no noticeable impact on Tuscan painting.

In the second half of the Trecento the weight of tradition lay heavily on Florentine painting, where Giotto's strictly ordered world of form had a petrifying effect. Already in the first generation of his followers it became evident that Giotto's idealized, self-sufficient style left only few possibilites open for development. Every 'system' is prone to stagnation. As soon as a measure of perfection is achieved further development stops, and instead there is only reproduction, until the system is ousted, overcome and replaced by another. This would have required another creative personality of Giotto's stature. But Orcagna had constricted and formalized Giotto's system still further, and transposed it into a personal idiosyncrasy. The essence of Orcagna's Giotto-interpretation was the internal tension, and when this was relaxed all that remained was the formalization. This is seen very clearly in the work of Jacopo di Cione, the younger brother of Orcagna and Nardo di Cione. He produced a number of altarpieces and small devotional pictures between the 1360s and the end of the century.[8] The severity of his forms, in which the types developed in the Orcagna workshop were reproduced, has a charm of its own, but only rarely is the emptiness of this eclectic style concealed, as in the large *Coronation of the Virgin* of 1373, now in the Florence Galleria dell'Accademia, by the splendour and severity of the overall decorative effect.

With Giovanni del Biondo, whose work, covering a wide range of subjects, extended from 1356 to 1392, the Orcagna manner was finally reduced to a mere technical skill.[9] The fixed expression of his figures and careless gaiety of colour may have been irritating even to the people of his time, for the critical approach to art had become steadily more discerning since Giotto, even in secular circles. We have a drastic contemporary verdict on another painter of the end of the century, Niccolò di Pietro Gerini, in a letter of the year 1395, which says of his figures that they look 'as though they were done with an axe'.[10] Naturally the painter did not share the opinion of his patron. He says that his Crucifix is so well drawn that it could not have been better 'even if it had been drawn by Giotto himself.'[11] Niccolò Gerini was in fact one of the chief representatives of the still surviving *maniera giottesca*, as can be seen from his cold, classic *Entombment of Christ,* in San Carlo dei Lombardi in Florence.[12] This tenacious adherence to a tradition that had long since lost its vitality inevitably brought about a reduction of monumentality. This is clearly seen in the frescoes in the sacristy of Santa Croce – the *Road to Calvary*, the *Resurrection*, and the *Ascension of Christ*, which were placed around the earlier *Crucifixion* of Taddeo Gaddi in about 1400. All three were probably painted by Niccolò Gerini and his pupils.[13] Beside Taddeo Gaddi's austere and strictly tectonic *Crucifixion*, done half a century before, they seem paltry and restive, a decorative surface ornament without monumental power.

There is another Florentine master of the late Trecento whose style is livelier and less constricted, although he too was a second-generation pupil of Giotto. Agnolo Gaddi, the son of Taddeo, could with justification consider himself heir to the Giottesque workshop tradition, and Cennino Cennini, his pupil, expressly emphasizes this relationship.[14] Agnolo's style, however, was far less subject than Niccolò Gerini's to the dictates of the Giottesque formula; on the other hand there is no doubt as to its derivation from Taddeo Gaddi. Agnolo's major work is the imposing, well-preserved fresco decoration of the main choir chapel of Santa Croce, done in about 1380, a huge work depicting in a manner more epic than dramatic the whole detailed *Legend of the Holy Cross (pls 113a, 113b)*. It consists entirely of a succession of crowd scenes shown, as in a book of pictures, within landscapes rising in the background and extending in considerable depth. The light penetrates into the depth until it is finally lost in the distant darkness. The Giottesque pictorial stage is substantially enlarged, but remains essentially unaltered. Space and figures are not brought into harmony; the various elements have only a surface unity like that of a tapestry, without tension or contrast. These frescoes are monumental only in actual size. The supple lines, the flow of the draperies, and the bright colours are already suggestive of the new decorative sense of the International Style. This tendency is even more pronounced in the frescoes portraying the life of the Virgin, in the cathedral of Prato, the last work of Agnolo Gaddi and his workshop (1392–5). Agnolo died in 1396, and had he lived longer, he might well have associated himself with the new stylistic movement of the International Gothic. It was left to his pupil, the Camaldolensian monk, Lorenzo Monaco, to take this step.[15]

This brings us to the limits of our enquiry. The International Style in painting was not just the end of the Trecento tradition, but something entirely new: it was the first attempt to unify all the elements of a picture, though for the time being still based on a single ornamental motif. This prepared the way for the next, truly revolutionary step, the optical unification, which treats the picture as a section of infinite, homogeneous space, seen from a single viewpoint. We have previously noted that Giotto had already established the foundation for this, but he had stopped in midstream. He never discarded the medieval hierarchy of pictorial values that was prescribed by the subject-matter. For him the primary element was the figure, to which space was merely ancillary. It is only in the Early Renaissance that this relationship is reversed: space becomes the given medium, in which everything is basically of equal value.

This is what we mean when we talk of the consistently traditional Giottesque character of Florentine painting up to the end of the Trecento. There were of course differences in personal styles and changing trends with the passing generations, although these may reveal themselves only on close examination, and sometimes only to the experts. In this kind of approach several other names would have to be mentioned: Niccolò di Tommaso, who painted amiable, naive frescoes in Pistoia in the Convento del T; the presumably Venetian Antonio Veneziano, whose soft lethargic style contrasts with that of his Florentine contemporaries; the prolific and versatile Spinello Aretino, who painted many frescoes and panels in Lucca, Pisa, Florence, Siena, and in his native Arezzo.[16]

Finally we should mention a great artist, whose work unfortunately is almost entirely lost. The few remnants that have survived, however, are enough to show that grave nobility and true monumentality had not completely disappeared even in this last phase of post-Giottesque painting. In 1404 Gherardo Starnina completed a fresco cycle in the chapel of St Hieronymus in Santa Maria del Carmine in Florence. All that has been recovered of these frescoes are fragments of isolated figures *(pl. 112)*.[17] The light colours, already touched with the sweetness of the International Style, and the large powerful forms, reveal a true painterly style, and the precise hatched technique of Agnolo Gaddi, who was probably his teacher, is almost completely overcome. Beside these fragments, preserved by chance, all the painting done in Florence since Orcagna seems insignificant. To find works of comparable standard we must go back to the most disciplined and virile of Giotto's pupils, Maso di Banco. There is another comparison that forces itself on our attention: in the same church, Santa Maria del Carmine, Masaccio painted his major work, the Brancacci Chapel frescoes. It was from Starnina, if indeed from anyone, that Masaccio could have learnt to construct form from colour alone, without linear contours (as Alberti later demanded) and without ornamentation.[18] It would certainly be wrong to regard Starnina as a founder or even a precursor of the Renaissance, but in a general sense he was one of its spiritual ancestors. He stands at a critical point in time between Giotto and Masaccio, as custodian of the most valuable heritage of Florentine painting, its great monumental tradition.

14 Trecento painting outside Tuscany

Of the Tuscan schools, whose rise and decline we have here traced over a period of more than two centuries, only the two most important still survived at the eve of the Renaissance, those of Florence and Siena. All the other Tuscan cities, including the once powerful and prolific Pisa, had sunk in the course of the Trecento to provincial insignificance. Except for Francesco Traini, who was probably a native of the city, painters from other parts of Italy had to be engaged for the decoration of the Campo Santo in Pisa: Taddeo Gaddi, Andrea da Firenze, Antonio Veneziano, Spinello Aretino and Benozzo Gozzoli. The conquest of Pisa by the Florentines in 1406 only put the final seal on a course of development that in the artistic field had long since come to an end. Outside Tuscany, in the north and south of the Italian peninsula, Giotto's ideas had been planted, germinated and borne fruit according to the receptiveness of the local soil. In addition, the Sienese influence had a far-reaching effect. Under the impact of the new Tuscan style, local modes of expression evolved especially in northern Italy, and though they differed, they bore the same relation to each other as the dialects of a language.

There was one place, however, where Giotto's seed fell on barren ground – in Rome. The *Navicella* mosaic and the frescoes in the Lateran and the choir of St Peter's evoked no noticeable response. In 1309 the papal court had moved to Avignon, and in its absence almost the entire artistic life of Rome withered throughout the whole century. It was only with the return of Pope Martin V in 1420, that art too was restored to the city.

The situation in Naples was more favourable. The House of Anjou expressed its authority in splendid ecclesiastical and secular buildings, and Italy's

317

most famous painters were brought to adorn them: Cavallini, Simone Martini, and Giotto.[1] All three were active in Naples over a number of years, helped by assistants, some of whom they brought with them, and others whom they probably trained in Naples itself. They made a deep mark, and left behind them a syncretic kind of art that continued even in the later Trecento to receive new stimuli from the north. The most important creations of Neapolitan painting in the third quarter of the Trecento are the frescoes on the vaults of Santa Maria Incoronata, representations of the *Seven Sacraments* and the *Triumph of Religion*.[2] Nothing is known of the artists who painted these frescoes. One of them was possibly Roberto di Oderisio, whose style is known to us from a signed panel painting, a *Crucifixion,* in Eboli near Naples.[3] His style is basically Sienese with local features barely noticeable, a description that applies in greater or lesser degree to everything painted in Naples during the Trecento. Even the exuberant spread of marble sculpture, which developed above all in the royal tombs, is essentially attributable to Tuscan masters. Notwithstanding its political importance, the kingdom of Naples was, as far as art is concerned, only a colony, and on the whole this status did not alter during the period of the Renaissance.

Further north also, in Latium, Umbria and the Marches, Trecento painting did not rise above a provincial level. Regional characteristics were confined almost exclusively to iconographic motifs, and in these districts, where piety tended towards mysticism, some individual, sensitive pictorial themes were evolved, especially in connection with the cult of the Virgin, and in representations of the Birth of Christ. Stylistically this art received its inspiration mainly from Siena. Further north, notably in the Marches, Florentine influence was dominant. Allegretto Nuzi, who was active in Fabriano in the third quarter of the Trecento, was doubtless apprenticed in a Florentine workshop, in the school of Bernardo Daddi or of Maso di Banco.[4] His style, which never conceals this provenance, is similar to that of Nardo di Cione, but it also has distinctive personal characteristics. His soft lines, mild sweet colours, and quiet, reticent temperament anticipate the art of Gentile da Fabriano, his junior by a generation or two. The link between them was possibly a pupil and follower of Allegretto Nuzi, Francescuccio Ghissi, who left a number of Madonna panels, all of the Madonna dell'Umiltà type. They are true devotional pictures, homely and pious, and most of them, still in their original settings, are worshipped to this day by the local inhabitants.

A well-defined school with its own character never emerged in Umbria or in the Marches. But in Romagna, the region north of the Marches, a proper local school established itself at an early stage, and as far back as 1300

we find there a gifted painter of miniatures, Neri da Rimini, a follower of
the Bolognese tradition of manuscript illumination. This school received a
further stimulus from Assisi, where a unified Italian style seemed already to
be evolving in the last decade of the Duecento out of the encounter between
Roman and Tuscan masters. This might well have come about if Giotto had
not impelled painting in an unswerving direction along his own prescribed
path. Rimini was one of the places where he worked, as we read in the contemporary chronicle of Riccobaldo da Ferrara.[5] The frescoes Giotto painted
there for the Franciscans probably perished when their Church of San Francesco was converted into the Tempio Malatestiano.[6] The *Crucifix* painted on
wood which, as mentioned earlier, takes its place among the works done
by Giotto immediately after the turn of the century,[7] is still to be seen there.
This raises the chronological question of Giotto's presence in Rimini. It would
be natural to start with the assumption that the *Crucifix* was painted in Rimini,[8]
and as recent Italian research has shown, there is a good deal of evidence
indicating that Giotto must have been in Romagna before his stay in Padua.[9]
It was doubtless a specific commission that brought him there, probably the
fresco cycle for the Franciscans in Rimini. Perhaps it is not by accident that
Riccobaldo lists Giotto's works *'in eclesiis minorum'* in the following order,
'Assisij Arimini Padue'. The frescoes painted for the Franciscans in Padua are
also lost, and all that remains of the work is some scant remnants in the
chapter-house of the 'Santo' (the church and monastery of St Anthony),
which cannot be attributed to Giotto himself.[10] If this trail has been followed
aright, Giotto's activity in Rimini can be placed in the first five years of the
Trecento, and his 'Rimini style', like that exemplified by the *Crucifix* in the
Tempio Malatestiano, would take an intermediate place between his Assisi
style and that of the upper zone in the Arena Chapel in Padua. We believe
that acceptance of this chronology would throw new and valuable light on
the development of Riminese painting, but specialized research has so far not
attempted to draw the conclusions from this well-grounded hypothesis.[11]

It has hitherto been assumed that the earliest products of Riminese panel
painting were at the same stylistic stage of development as the works done
in Assisi in about 1300 or shortly thereafter. The major example of these
early Riminese panels is an altar dossal (now in the Isabella Stewart Gardner
Museum in Boston) from Urbania, the former Castel Durante, not far from
Urbino. It bears the date 1307 and the signature of Giuliano da Rimini,[12]
and depicts the enthroned Madonna, adored by kneeling women, flanked by
eight saints beneath painted arcades in the Cosmati style. Roman and Tuscan
elements are combined in this work in a way found only in Assisi – except

that here Giotto, coming from Rome soon after 1300, may himself have introduced both elements to Rimini, in which case his 'Rimini style' would have been Giuliano's direct inspiration. It has been observed that the St Clara of the Boston dossal closely resembles the figure of the same saint in the St Nicholas Chapel in Assisi.[13] One may postulate a common Riminese model for these two figures, for the painters who executed the frescoes of the St Nicholas Chapel in 1306 or slightly later were presumably Giotto's assistants not only in Padua, but also earlier in Rimini, and had available to them examples of both phases of the master's development. However this may be, there is much to support the hypothesis that Giotto was in Rimini before he went to Padua. On the other hand, Giotto's Padua style, i. e., the style of the Arena Chapel, was in turn to have a marked effect on Riminese painting. The link, once established, seems to have persisted for some time, just as it did in Assisi, where pupils of the Giotto school continued to work on new commissions for several decades.

However, Giotto's influence, though it was brought to bear at an early stage and lasted for a long time, never completely determined the character of Riminese painting. It was only for its stock of forms that the distinctive local school drew on Roman-Florentine art. For its general artistic character it looked to those north Italian stylistic trends of which Venice was later to become the centre. Its predilection for elongated proportions and numerous long verticals, and for abstract, intersecting diagonals, make this style somewhat mannered, but also give it dignity and elegance *(pl. 116)*. They are devices that appear later, in a completely different stylistic context, in Tintoretto and Veronese. All the constituent elements serve to hold the composition in a two-dimensional plane, and Giottesque ideas, frequently recognizable, are re-interpreted by the Riminese masters back into two-dimensional values. The cool colours, carmine and sea-green, lilac and pale blue, pink and white, also produce a detached shallow effect. The inclination to two-dimensional design was thus not a sign of an archaicizing approach, but a lasting indigenous feature. Nor can this art be accused of eclecticism, for the borrowed forms are only the raw material, which is treated in a highly original way. Oddly enough this style was employed with most assurance by those painters who adhered closely to Giotto. The artist, who painted the frescoes of the life of the Virgin in the chapel beneath the Campanile in Sant'Agostino in Rimini, was doubtless at one time a pupil and assistant of Giotto; this is clear from his technique, the type of his figures, and his decorative motifs.[14] And yet without effort he transposes everything into a two-dimensional design. The severe verticality of his composition is reminiscent

of the solemn remoteness of Byzantine mosaics, and his pictorial space achieves
an indeterminate, suspended quality. The transparent and strictly symmetrical architecture of the temple in the *Presentation in the Temple (pl. 115)*
seems to conform closely to Giotto's 'Rimini style' and, though over-elon-
gated, to be intermediate between the abstract architecture in the last scenes
of the St Francis legend and the economically constructed buildings in the
upper zone of the Arena Chapel. The huge fresco of the *Last Judgment,* which
has been removed from Sant'Agostino to the Palazzo dell'Arengo *(pl. 114b),*
is also reminiscent of Giotto's pre-Padua style. Both works were probably
done in the second decade of the Trecento, possibly even in the last years
of the first decade. On the other hand the frescoes in the choir chapel of
Sant'Agostino, scenes from the life of St John the Evangelist, are less monumental, and appear to have been done later. The diffuse, prolix narrative,
the reversion to a scale of sizes to indicate the relative importance of the
figures, the continuous progression of the scenes without separation on the
large picture surface, all these are old-fashioned and provincial features, and
show a lack of understanding of Giotto's stylistic principles. The *Enthroned
Madonna,* on the rear wall of the choir, seems to have been derived from a
Giottesque model, but its style also indicates a later date.[15]

The frescoes in the refectory of Pomposa Abbey are yet another work of
the early Romagnese monumental style, showing influences of Giotto and
also traces of Cavallinesque types.[16] In one of the scenes Christ and the disciples are gathered for the Last Supper at a round table. Figures and table are
united in a two-dimensional pattern of circling lines *(pl. 114a).* The colours
are unusually cool and light, and the technique remarkably bold. The date,
'about 1317', suggested by an inscription of doubtful authenticity, now obliterated, seems entirely convincing.[17]

All the other surviving monumental works in Romagna belong, without
exception, to the second or even third quarter of the century. The frescoes
in Santa Chiara in Ravenna, now the chapel of the Almshouse, were possibly
painted in the 1330s. They show evangelists and Fathers of the Church on
the vaults, after the model of the Doctors' Vault at Assisi, and in addition
a *Crucifixion* of deep pathos, and other New Testament scenes. The characteristic style of these paintings justifies their attribution to Pietro da Rimini,
whose style is known to us from a large signed crucifix in Urbania.[18]

The chapel of St Nicholas in Tolentino is the counterpart of the Spanish
Chapel in Florence in the shape of the room and the profusion of pictures,
although the scheme is not so systematic and uniform. The representations
consist of the life of the Virgin, the life of Christ, and the legend of St Nicholas,

with a Doctors' Vault above. The frescoes have many charming individual details, but now it is clearly apparent that the first fruitful impact of the Roman-Tuscan sense of form on north Italian painting had lost its force, and with the passing of time mannered and provincial elements predominated.

More important on account of their distinctive character and severity of form were the frescoes in Santa Maria in Porto, near Ravenna, unfortunately destroyed in the Second World War. But from the stylistic evidence, the date proposed by local historians, 'between 1314 and 1319', is much too early, for the implication would be that the specific features of the Riminese style had already reached full maturity in the second decade of the Trecento.[19]

In panel painting the best work of this Romagnese school was done in its very small-scale productions. The polyptych form was only rarely used for altarpieces, and for a long time the old-fashioned square *paliotto,* divided into numerous separate pictures, was preferred. In addition there were small diptychs and tabernacles, and also triumphal crosses painted on wood, similar in type to Giotto's *Crucifix* in San Francesco in Rimini. Few of the artists are known to us by name. In addition to Giuliano and Pietro da Rimini we should mention Giovanni Baronzio, whose signature, with the date 1345, is found on a retable in the Urbino Gallery. Some important authorities contend that he is the artist who in that same year painted the large Giottesque crucifix in San Francesco in Mercatello, and signed it 'Johannes pictor', but this has not been established.[20] On the other hand, there is no doubt that the unsigned altarpiece in the same church in Mercatello is closely related to the Urbino retable. Perhaps Giovanni Baronzio was head of a busy workshop, and his signature covered the work of several artists. Despite intensive efforts, the relatively numerous panel paintings that have survived in Romagna have not yet been satisfactorily classified according to their authorship or even to their dates. The local tradition of this remote district, especially notable for its craftsmanlike character, had died out by the end of the Trecento.

Bologna, the capital of Emilia, north-west of Romagna, was closely connected with Tuscany in the thirteenth century. Altar panels and crucifixes in Bologna's churches came from the workshops of Pisa, Lucca and Florence, and wall-paintings were done by Tuscan artists.[21] In wall- and panel-painting no specific Bolognese school is discernable in the Duecento. Only manuscript illumination achieved a degree of importance through the encouragement it received from the university, which was famous throughout Europe for its law faculty. From the turn of the century Tuscan influence in Emilia gradually declined. It is true that as late as 1330 the altarpiece bearing Giotto's signature, which was mentioned earlier, was commissioned for the Church of Santa Maria degli Angioli in Bologna, but this was only a workshop product, and on the whole Giotto's art had remarkably little influence in Bologna.[22] The new Tuscan style found its way there only indirectly through Riminese painters and in an attenuated, provincial form.[23]

In the second quarter of the Trecento a local style emerged for the first time, closely dependent at first on the style of Romagna. The first local artist of great stature was Vitale da Bologna, who is known to have worked in San Francesco as early as 1330.[24] His earliest known work, the fresco of *The Last Supper,* preserved in a fragmentary condition, and now in the Bologna Pinacoteca Nazionale, was also originally in San Francesco, and can be related to a payment voucher of 1340. Another painting by Vitale, an authenticated major work signed and dated 1345, is the *Madonna dei Denti,* in the Museo Davia Bargellini in Bologna *(pl. 118).*[25] It has a grave demure charm. The delicate Gothic type of figure has undergone an odd transformation, and has acquired a quality not merely bourgeois but almost rustic, revealing a highly original creative power. The angular, strongly modelled forms, the awkward yet vigorous movements of the Child, and the lively rhythm of the Madonna's cloak, all seem to be a reaction against the courtly elegance and remote idealism of the Gothic style. In a later work, the polyptych of 1353 in San Salvatore in Bologna, Vitale painted a *Coronation of the Virgin* with moving restraint and grace. The sweet, melodic linear rhythm of this picture is difficult to reconcile with the austere style of the 1345 Madonna, and even more with the vehemence of expression in the four panels depicting the legend of St Anthony, which were transferred from Santo Stefano to the Bologna Pinacoteca Nazionale *(pl. 119).* Yet these small, crowded legendary scenes reveal the characteristic style of Vitale at every point, and the dispute over their attribution to him is unfounded. On the other hand their chronological position is difficult to determine, but it is probably close to the *Madonna dei Denti.* They seem to have been done soon after 1345, at about the same time as a wall-painting that belongs to the same extremist stage of the master's development. The huge fresco, *The Nativity,* from the desecrated church of Santa Maria (or Sant'Apollonia) di Mezzaratta, now also in the Bologna Pinacoteca Nazionale *(pl. 120),* shows spirited figures in graceful, dramatic movement. The bold triangular composition of the principal scene accentuates the gable form of the entrance wall and can be understood only in relation to it; and the animated style may also have been partly determined by the effect the fresco would have in its setting in the room at a considerable height. Primarily, however, this work reveals the presence of a creative talent

323

expressing itself with remarkable freedom, and makes other paintings in Florence of that time seem dull and artificial in comparison. The analogy with Tintoretto again suggests itself, not only in the linear structure and two-dimensional effect, but also in the direct affinity of artistic temperament.

In the 1350s the decoration of Mezzaratta was continued with narrative scenes along its side walls by pupils and followers of Vitale.[26] Vitale himself seems to have participated only intermittently. In 1348–9 he was in Udine, where he decorated a chapel in the cathedral with scenes from the legend of St Nicholas. Of the exuberant temperament in the Mezzaratta fresco hardly a trace remains, but from now on his painterly qualities emerge with increasing strength. His frescoes take on light and warm colours, and soft impasto, as in the St Eustace scenes in the abbey church of Pomposa (about 1351),[27] and in the frescoes in Santa Maria dei Servi in Bologna, unfortunately now in very bad condition;[28] so that the San Salvatore altarpiece of 1353 is by no means unique in its exquisite decorative effect. In his last years Vitale produced works of rarefied beauty, for example the small panel of the *Adoration of the Kings,* now in the National Gallery of Scotland in Edinburgh, in which the figures with their gentle gestures are incorporated into a strict two-dimensional pattern. When he died, between 1359 and 1361, his style left a deep impression on Bolognese painting.

Among the painters of the younger generation we should note Jacopino di Francesco, who emulated the personal and expressive linear style evolved by Vitale in his Mezzaratta frescoes.[29] Jacopino's polyptych containing a *Coronation of the Virgin,* No. 161 in the Bologna Pinacoteca Nazionale, has an animation unusual in Trecento works: flashing glances and abrupt turnings of the head, and stiff and haughty elegance of features. The figures have a hieratic dignity, and are presented frontally in the archaic manner. The technique is lush and sensuous, and the colours strong and passionate – glaring red, yellow, white, a harsh brown, and nacreous flesh tints. The brownish underpaint, evident everywhere, is characteristic of the entire Bolognese school. It is also present in their wall-painting as a base for the strong colours, the rosy flesh tones, and the white highlights.

The most comprehensive surviving work of monumental painting is not found in Bologna itself, but in the abbey church of Pomposa, east of Ferrara.[30] The ancient building, dating from the early Middle Ages and situated in a remote lagoon district, is a large basilica with a lofty campanile visible from far away. The decoration, covering the whole of the nave, the apse and the entrance wall, was done around 1351 by various Bolognese masters, among them, as already mentioned, Vitale. Taken separately, the frescoes often have a rustic crudeness, but they are drawn together by a single gold-brown tone, and the overall effect is impressive. The iconography of the apse representation and the huge *Last Judgment* on the west wall suggest that the work was only a restoration of an older decorative scheme, possibly of the eleventh century.[31] The division of the walls of the nave is reminiscent of Sant'Angelo in Formis. The solid, robust narrative painting of the Bolognese Trecento artists thus interpolated in the medieval scheme produces an odd effect, and the anachronism is hardly concealed by the decorative unity of the work as a whole.

The second half of the Trecento in Bologna was prolific in craftsmanlike productions, and many multi-panelled polyptychs with elaborately carved frames still survive. The painters, Simone and Cristoforo da Bologna, Jacopo di Paolo, and Lippo di Dalmasio show little individuality, but they all display the common character of the school – its heavy, prosaic temperament, sturdy forms, and earthy colours.[32]

The style of Barnaba da Modena is similar, though it originated in a different background. Emilian ponderousness and earthiness are combined in his work with a precise knowledge of Sienese painting, and even more with a sense of the Byzantine tradition, which at that time had not yet been forgotten in northern Italy. Something of the solemnity of the old icons persists in the measured rhythm of his Madonnas, although the opulent splendour of the gold highlights and the indiscriminate solidity of the colours have little in common with Byzantine art *(pl. 121)*.[33]

The downright, earthy feature of Emilian art was essentially more modern and forward-looking than anything produced in other parts of Italy in the Trecento. In the hands of one of the leading artists, Tomaso da Modena, this realism was raised to a high creative level.[34] In Tomaso's frescoes in the chapter-house of San Niccolò in Treviso, dated 1352, the characterization of the figures is so penetrating that at first glance they might appear to be the work of a fifteenth- rather than a fourteenth-century artist. The same theme is presented in as many as forty variations: the principal figures of the Dominican Order are shown reading, writing, or meditating, each seated in a narrow, wooden cell. The ability to depict the nature of the intellectual activity without external symbolism is even more remarkable than the skill in representing objective facial characteristics *(pl. 122)*. The theme itself was an old one in medieval art, repeated thousand of times in pictures of the evangelists and portraits of authors in manuscript illumination. Medieval artists knew how to illustrate vividly the intellectual stature of such figures, but the specific nature of the intellectual activity was always indicated by purely external means, for instance by the act of writing, or of sharpening the quill. In the Doctors' Vault in Assisi, and especially in the emulation of this motif by the Romagna school, such external symbols were prominent. Tomaso da Modena's portraits of the Dominicans, on the other hand, were a decisive step towards the portrayal of intellectual activity without symbolism, of an inward psychological process. It would be wrong to see the new realism only as a more acute observation of the external aspect of reality, although in this, too, Tomaso surpassed all his predecessors. Occasionally he still resorted to the old motifs of writing or examining the quill, but he gave a new and lively interest to these practical tasks.

In the naturalism of his painting and its penetration to new psychological depths, Tomaso da Modena resembles his great and enigmatic fourteenth-century contemporary, Theodoric of Prague, whose half-length figures of saints and Fathers of the Church in the Chapel of the Cross in Karlstein Castle are comparable achievements. It was probably not mere coincidence that Emperor Charles IV also provided Tomaso da Modena with commissions. Two of his works are still in Karlstein, a triptych showing the Madonna and two saints, and another Madonna *(pl. 123)* and an *Ecce Homo*, probably designed as a diptych, and not, as is sometimes thought, the remnants of a larger altarpiece. Tomaso presumably executed these works in his home town; a journey to Bohemia seems very unlikely.[35] On the other hand Theodoric might well have visited northern Italy, and possibly it was he who established the contact between Tomaso and the emperor. It is tempting, however, to speculate on the course Bohemian and German painting might have taken if Tomaso had himself worked in Prague and painted a large fresco cycle there. He seems to have been familiar with the courtly atmosphere. In his fresco of the legend of St Ursula, now in the Museo Civico in Treviso, a worldly mood and sensuous enjoyment of contemporary life predominate *(pl. 124)*. It brings to mind the famous St Ursula legend painted by Carpaccio more than a century later, and the voluptuous female types are like a Trecento preparation for the figures of Palma Vecchio and Sebastiano del Piombo. The fashionable '*miparti*' of the draperies and the splendid brocade designs, now badly damaged, must originally have been highly decorative. The colours, as far as they can be seen in the present state of the pictures, are bright and warm, as if already infused with Venetian light,[36] and the linear rhythm and the two-dimensional unity of the forms also have a Venetian appearance. A number of figures, or heads, are often brought together by means of a simple large contour. The wide neckline of the women's dresses emphasizes the horizontals.[37] Tomaso, who attached such importance to two-dimensional unity in his pictures, was not greatly concerned with depth effects. Already in the portraits of the Dominicans in San Niccolò, the lines of perspective have unwittingly been converted into the diagonals of a surface pattern, and in the frescoes of the St Ursula legend the three-dimensional elements have diminished even further. However, the natural mobility of the figures, and their inward life and fine psychological gradations have increased, and in this respect Tomaso da Modena, who died in 1379, was one of the most progressive artists of the century. If one looks for a comparable achievement it can be found once again in Bohemia: the busts of Peter Parler in the triforium of Prague Cathedral, done between 1379 and 1393. Naturally there is no question of an actual connection, but the comparison clearly demonstrates that the highest achievements of north Italian painting in the second half of the Trecento were superior to and more advanced than those of Tuscan art, which had stagnated in its own great tradition.

Trecento painting outside Tuscany

In addition to the new progressive aspects discussed above, Tomaso da Modena's style exhibited with exceptional purity those characteristics of north Italian painting that were to be present for centuries. A fine sense of colour and of decorative surface values, and a feeling for beautiful materials, are generally considered to be the special and permanent attributes of Venetian painting. But these 'Venetian' traits, recognizable from the Renaissance on, have a history of their own, and their origin is to be found as much on the Italian mainland as in Venice itself. A glance at Trecento painting in Venice shows that at the beginning its development took a course of its own, in no way parallel to that of other north Italian districts. The adherence to Byzantine tradition was nowhere so close as in Venice, and nowhere else so firmly grounded in history and contemporary associations. For centuries Venice looked to the East, and in its sanctuary of St Mark it possessed a major work of Byzantine monumental art, visible proof of the long historical connection.

The latest medieval mosaics in St Mark's, those in the baptistry and the chapel of San Isidro in the north transept, were done only in the middle of the Trecento, in a strange and often contradictory mixture of eastern and western stylistic elements. And long before this, the collaboration between Byzantine mosaicists and their local pupils had evolved a 'syncreticism of typical Venetian character'.[38] Panel painting followed a similar course, but took as its models icons and manuscript illuminations, which were technically more closely related to it than mosaics. From these models it derived the Byzantine figure type, the smooth metallic modelling, the cold refined colours, and the brownish flesh tints over green under-paint.

327

Paolo Veneziano, the leading Venetian painter of the first half of the Trecento, conformed closely to the Byzantine models in some of his works, but in spite of this the essentially Italian, and more particularly Venetian, character of his style is unmistakable. In the early part of his career he came under the influence of Giotto's ideas, communicated in all likelihood through the painters of Romagna. One example is his altar dossal, dated 1321, originally in a church in Venice and now in Dignano in Istria.[39] His leaning towards the Byzantine was a later development seen at its most pronounced in the painting of the *Death of the Virgin,* of 1333, in the museum of Vicenza. Still later, Italo-Gothic influence became increasingly important. In the *Coronation of the Virgin (pl. 117),* painted around 1350, in Venice (formerly in the Brera Gallery, Milan), two angels playing musical instruments kneel in the foreground in a posture that is also found in the work of Vitale da Bologna.[40] The flowing linear style of the hems of the gowns draping the principal figures is also Gothic rather than Byzantine. The decorative splendour of the gold pattern, spread flat across the draperies without regard to the flow of the folds, is truly Venetian, although it follows the Byzantine manner. In the *Madonna* in Carpineta near Cesena (1347), a delicate enchanting figure, the robe and mantle are decorated with gold and jewelled arabesques that give a precious quality to the pale colours.[41] This is typical 'Venetian Gothic'. In the last works of the master, who died between 1358 and 1362, Byzantine influence plays a minor part.

In Lorenzo Veneziano, who was active in the third quarter of the Trecento, the encroachment of the International Style, the last and most opulent flowering of the Gothic, is already perceptible. His *Enthroned Christ handing the Keys to St Peter,* in the Museo Correr in Venice, a panel of 1370 with warm transparent colours and undulating play of line, is one of the earliest examples of this stylistic movement, which spread through the whole of western Europe.[42] It is once again a specifically Venetian interpretation: the broadly conceived pattern of Christ's gown, sprinkled with gold, envelops the forms in a glittering aura, quite unrelated to the actual atmosphere of Venice. It is rather the mysterious lustre of the mosaics in St Mark's that is here recaptured by means of a completely different technique. And even much later, when Venetian painters discovered the essentially watery atmosphere of their city and illuminated their pictures with the golden light of Venice, the deep glow of these mosaics remained the source of their inspiration.

But the influences and conditions we have just described do not in themselves account for the subsequent brilliant development of Venetian painting. The contribution of the mainland was necessary to give Venetian art its full

lasting radiance. Many of its greatest masters came from Veneto, Verona and Bergamo, or, like Titian, from the lower Alps, and even in the Trecento there are instances of painters being summoned from the mainland to work in Venice. Guariento, who painted the huge fresco of the *Coronation of the Virgin* in the Palazzo Ducale between 1365 and 1368, came from Padua,[43] where he is known to have worked since 1338. He died around 1370, possibly in Venice. His style plainly shows the influence of Giotto, whose powerful monumentality he translated, however, into graceful and elegant forms. The effect that Venice had on him, and the influence of Byzantine art are also clearly seen in his work. A charming blend of the various stylistic elements in Guariento's style is displayed in a series of panels, remnants of the wooden ceiling from the Cappella Carrarese, now in the Museo Civico in Padua, depicting the Madonna and the divine hierarchy of the angels *(pl. 125)*.[44] His major work in Padua was the decoration of the main choir chapel in the Eremitani, which was unfortunately badly damaged in the last war.[45] The decoration of the base, with representations of the planets and the ages of man painted in monochrome, are particularly fine. The narrative scenes on the left wall, which is still standing, are somewhat crude, and their execution is probably attributable to his assistants. The composition, however, reveals the hand of a confident artist. The figures and the groups are convincingly matched to the skilfully foreshortened buildings, and the perspective is surprisingly progressive. These frescoes were probably painted in the first half of the 1360s, and they served to demonstrate Guariento's qualifications for the large commission in the Palazzo Ducale in Venice. His fresco of Paradise with the Coronation of the Virgin in the centre made a lasting impression on Venetian painting. Although now in very poor condition, it shows that Guariento's style in its final phase had become more restrained and more monumental.[46] The types of the figures had become almost classical, very different from the mobile Gothic figures of his earlier works. The large beautiful *Madonna* in the Metropolitan Museum, New York, expressing warm, restrained feeling, also probably belongs to this late phase of the master's work.[47]

After Guariento's death another master appeared in Padua, Giusto de' Menabuoi, also called Giusto Padovano.[48] He came from Florence, and the basic elements of his style were formed there. There is some evidence, unauthenticated yet credible, that in 1376 he completed the decoration of the Baptistry in Padua, one of the most ambitious undertakings of Italian monumental painting.[49] The Romanesque structure encloses a large square room, vaulted with a dome. At the top of the vault Giusto designed a colossal half-length figure, in the Byzantine manner, of Christ the Redeemer, surrounded by the heavenly host in concentric circles. Prominent among them is the Virgin characterized as Queen of Heaven in Western fashion by her cloak and crown, but her demeanour, that of *Maria orans,* conforms to the Eastern type. The profusion of figures and the almost uninterrupted sequence of scenes from the Old and New Testaments in the dome and on the walls give an oppressive and overcrowded effect. It is strange that this Florentine painter should have given so little consideration to the architectural structure of the room he was decorating. The scenes are divided from each other by very narrow painted frames, quite inadequate to define them as separate pictures, and even less adequate for the purpose of giving a firm structure to the general decoration of the room. And yet there in Padua, Giusto had before him in the Arena Chapel a supreme example of a masterpiece of painted frameworks that give full value to both room and pictures. It is true that Giotto reduced the width of his frames in the Peruzzi Chapel, and that his followers preferred an even lighter, more two-dimensional treatment; but even the two-dimensional, highly decorative painted – and again very wide – borders used by Andrea da Firenze in the Spanish Chapel are conceived in relation to the architecture and the setting; they give emphasis to the dynamic structure of the ribs, and at the same time clearly define the pictorial surfaces. Giusto attempted nothing of this kind, and his treatment is feeble and uninspired. He was apparently trying to achieve an effect similar to that of a Byzantine room entirely decorated with mosaics, which ignore the architectural features and produce the effect of a uniform and continuous surface. However, its hard opaque colours, earthy shadows, and brittle Florentine style vitiate any idea of a room worked in mosaics. The details, too, frequently give the impression of a mixture of stylistic elements that have not been fully integrated. Although there is considerable charm in some of the compositions, for example in the highly stylized and yet sensitive Annunciation scene, the overall effect is unconvincing.[50] In his representation of interiors Giusto found some surprisingly modern solutions, but they lose their effectiveness owing to the lack of autonomy and compactness in the individual scenes.[51] Giusto was important as the intermediary who transmitted Florentine stylistic elements to north Italian painting, but he was not capable of achieving a proper synthesis.

There was, however, a painter who had this ability, Altichiero, a native of Verona. Influenced by the painting of Giotto, and possibly also that of Giusto, he produced in Padua works of true monumentality, which were north Italy's greatest contribution to Trecento painting. In fifteenth- and sixteenth-century sources he is mentioned together with Jacopo Avanzo, whose actual role is disputed. Altichiero was evidently the principal master

with overall responsibility, and Avanzo only one of the collaborators, whose different style appears here and there in the two surviving fresco cycles.[52] Both were done in the 1370s and '80s, one shortly after the other. The frescoes in the chapel of St James, now San Felice, in the 'Santo' in Padua, were the first to be painted. Altichiero received payment for this work, possibly the final payment, in 1379. The arrangement of the pictures was dictated by the architectural design. The room is rectangular in shape, spanned by three cross-vaults with eight ogival lunettes containing scenes from the legend of St James. Only one of the end walls provides space for two more scenes on rectangular surfaces. On the main wall, facing the entrance arcades, which open into the church, is a large *Crucifixion* divided into three sections. Whereas the legendary scenes were plainly executed by assistants acting more or less independently, the *Crucifixion* is painted in a grave mature style that can be attributed only to Altichiero himself. Even the colour tones are different here from those in the legend scenes where bright local colours, such as yellow and carmine, are applied on a rather dull turbid base. In the *Crucifixion* such contrasts are avoided, and everything is lighter and more transparent. Soft tender colours are used with a fine sense of harmony, and blended to give a firm texture: mild yellow, orange, pink and lilac in rich gradations, light green, and a warm solid white. Blue is introduced with marked restraint, in contrast to Giusto's frescoes in the Baptistry, where it is applied crudely and to excess. Altichiero is equally restrained in his use of gold patterns, which in Venice tended to be displayed on an extravagant scale. He is a colourist of high rank and in this respect the true precursor of the great Venetians. He was concerned not merely with the material, absolute beauty of colour as such, but also with the creative use of colour, the mastery over a rich range of graduated shades and their overall effect; and he succeeded in evoking those hidden values that come to light only through a proper relationship of chromatic tones.

The advanced stage he reached in his treatment of colour and his anticipation of future achievements can be seen clearly in Padua itself. The frescoes painted by the young Titian in 1511 in the Scuola del Santo leave no doubt that there was a close connection here. Titian made a thorough study of Altichiero's painting, and not only with regard to his handling of colour. The massive proportions of the figures, their broadly conceived, somewhat slow-flowing contours reappear in Titian's work. There is even a similarity in the rhythm of the grouping, an aspect of composition in which Altichiero was also a precursor in his time: his groups are two-dimensional rather than plastic, but within the general structure of the pictures they are each individually defined and full of vitality. In the grouping of his figures he shows a subtle command of composition that matches his feeling for harmony of colour. The group of women in the left of the *Crucifixion* fresco *(pl. 126)* could be an invention of the High Renaissance, and indeed the memory of it still seems alive in Titian's *Presentation of the Virgin in the Temple,* where the figure of St Anne in profile looks like a paraphrase of Altichiero's woman with the child.

It is impossible to tell precisely how much of this is due to actual continuity and recollection, and how much merely to artistic affinity and a native sense of colour and form. However, as to Altichiero's importance in the development of Venetian painting there can be no doubt. His specifically painterly treatment of colour is not found in any Venetian Trecento painter, still less his mastery of monumental composition – the easy rhythm of the pictorial structure, fluid and yet firmly contained in the surface pattern. These features emerged in Venice only in the course of the fifteenth century, and from the High Renaissance onwards they have been regarded as typically Venetian.

Altichiero's second fresco cycle in Padua is in the Oratory of St George, which stands beside the Scuola del Santo in the forecourt of the 'Santo'. It is a barrel-vaulted, oblong symmetrical room, designed from the start with a view to the fresco decoration. The building was begun in 1377, and in 1384 Altichiero received final payment for the frescoes, which cover all four walls with the uniformity of a tapestry.[53] The upper of the two pictorial courses partially extends, as in the Arena Chapel, into the barrel vault, divided into three sections by wide borders containing medallions. However, the painted borders, unlike Giotto's in the Arena Chapel, which extend right down to the floor, are limited to the vault region. With the exception of the end wall, which has two painted columns, there are no special illusionistic elements in the framework of the frescoes. On the other hand, the pictures themselves have many richly developed architectural motifs, and also an internal architectural structure that gives pictorial expression to the compact surfaces and solidity of the walls. The stocky figures, like Giotto's, are always outlined by a large, simple contour, even when they are in vigorous movement or strongly foreshortened. Emphatic verticals and horizontals provide the surface pattern. The design for the entrance wall, five scenes from the childhood of Christ, from the Annunciation to the Presentation in the Temple *(pl. 128)*, is particularly uniform. Compared with Giotto's corresponding compositions, the scale of the figures in relation to the landscape and architecture has plainly become more correct and realistic. Altichiero knew how to enlarge the spatial values without impairing the compactness of the picture surface. Here too

his work is entirely in line with Giotto's, and can be considered as a direct continuation of the development we have observed in the Arena Chapel. The temple in the Presentation scene, a three-aisled basilica of Gothic design, is a masterpiece of perspective: the depth and structure of the building are perfectly clear, and yet everything remains firmly related to the picture surface. The receding lines are hardly apparent, and the façade of the building is presented as a flat design, which imposes a powerful rhythm on the composition as a whole. The stable in the *Nativity* and the *Adoration of the Kings* follows the same principles. Even more elaborate architectural features are seen on the side walls, where the legends of Sts George, Catherine and Lucy are illustrated. The altar wall has a *Coronation of the Virgin* and a *Crucifixion*. Altichiero did not himself execute all the scenes, but the general design and spirit of the whole work were undoubtedly his. An innovation such as the motionless upright lances in the *Beheading of St George (pl. 127)* reveals the presence of an artist of the highest rank and originality. The surprisingly portrait-like character of some of the figures that has been frequently noticed (for example, in the *Burial of St Lucy*) does not disturb the harmony of the grand, tranquil style of the whole work, and they too display a true sense of monumentality as well as of realism. The use of colour differs considerably from that in the *Crucifixion* fresco in the chapel of San Felice. A greater part is played by the duller, brownish-yellow, and smoky-grey tones, to which are added the white and pink of the architectural features. The wealth of colour in the earlier work is rarely evident. Nevertheless, despite some differences in scale of certain scenes, and the variety and turbulence of the events portrayed, a homogeneous surface uniting all the pictures is achieved here too. Everything is related to the surface, the figures, the buildings, and even the landscape features. This is the art of northern Italy, and yet it falls within the definition propounded by Giotto. No Trecento artist ventured so far ahead of Giotto as Altichiero, and still remained so faithful to him.

Altichiero had no direct followers. He left no school of any importance either in Verona or in Padua. As in other parts of Italy, there was an interlude when the International Style prevailed in the north, where artists came more completely under the spell of this courtly French movement than anywhere else. Its decorative character and playful, mannered grace were eagerly taken up in Verona, Milan and Venice. It is only in the middle of the Quattrocento that we find works that are a belated vindication of what Altichiero aspired to and realized within the limitations of his age. Some of Jacopo Bellini's drawings, with their architectural vistas and spatial depth, preserving nevertheless a surface unity, could have been derived directly from Altichiero's frescoes. There is only one novel aspect of his art in which Bellini surpassed Altichiero: the representation of space by means of central perspective. But the Venetian masters of the Early Renaissance took the new Florentine principles of spatial representation and re-interpreted them, in the same sense as Altichiero had re-interpreted Giotto's pictorial conception. When Venetian painting subsequently merged more and more with the main stream of Italian art, it nevertheless succeeded in retaining its special heritage, and this was largely attributable to the work of Altichiero. Italian painting had achieved almost complete stylistic unity by the end of the Trecento. That the struggle had to be resumed again in the following century was due solely to the pressure exerted by the explosive development that was to take place in Florence.

Notes on the text

Abbreviations of the works most frequently referred to

Anthony: Edgar Waterman Anthony, *Romanesque Frescoes*, Princeton 1951

Bologna: Ferdinando Bologna, *La pittura italiana delle origini*, Rome/Dresden 1962

Borsook: Eve Borsook, *The Mural Painters of Tuscany from Cimabue to Andrea del Sarto*, London 1960

Brunetti/Sinibaldi: *Pittura italiana del Duecento e Trecento*, Catalogo della Mostra Giottesca di Firenze del 1937, a cura di Giulia Sinibaldi e Giulia Brunetti, Florence 1943

Coletti: Luigi Coletti, *I Primitivi. Vol. I.: 'Dall'arte benedettina a Giotto'*, Novara 1941; Vol. II: '*I Senesi e i Giotteschi*', Novara 1946; Vol. III: '*I Padani*', Novara 1947

Garrison: Edward B. Garrison, *Italian Romanesque Panel Painting*, an Illustrated Index, Florence 1949

Ghiberti: *Lorenzo Ghibertis Denkwürdigkeiten (I Commentarii)*, edited by Julius von Schlosser, Berlin 1912

Gnudi: Cesare Gnudi, *Giotto*, Milan 1958

Hager: Hellmut Hager, *Die Anfänge des italienischen Altarbildes / Untersuchungen zur Entstehungsgeschichte des toskanischen Hochaltarretabels*, Munich 1962

Kleinschmidt: Beda Kleinschmidt O. F. M., *Die Basilika San Francesco in Assisi*, 3 vols, Berlin 1915–28; Kleinschmidt, *Die Wandmalereien der Basilika San Francesco in Assisi*, Berlin 1930

Ladner: Gerhart Ladner, 'Die italienische Malerei im 11. Jahrhundert', in *Jahrbuch der Kunsthistorischen Sammlungen in Wien*, new series, vol. V, 1931, p. 33 *ff.*

van Marle: Raimond van Marle, *The Development of the Italian Schools of Painting*, 19 vols, The Hague 1923-38; van Marle, *Le scuole della pittura italiana*, vols I, II, L'Aja/Milan 1932 & 1934

Offner, Corpus: Richard Offner, *A Critical and Historical Corpus of Florentine Painting*, New York 1930 *ff.*

Salvini: Roberto Salvini, *Giotto, Bibliografia*, Rome 1938

Toesca, Storia: Pietro Toesca, *Storia dell'arte italiana I, Il Medioevo*, Turin 1927

Toesca, Trecento: Pietro Toesca, *Storia dell'arte italiana II, Il Trecento*, Turin 1951

Vasari: *Le vite de' piu eccellenti pittori scultori ed architettori scritte da Giorgio Vasari*, 9 vols, edited by Gaetano Milanesi, Florence 1878-85

Wilpert: Joseph Wilpert, *Die römischen Mosaiken und Malereien der kirchlichen Bauten vom IV. bis XIII. Jahrhundert*, 4 vols, Freiburg 1916

Notes on the text

Introduction

1 (p. 9) The earliest evidence for Giotto's influence on the painting of the north is the monumental copy of the *Navicella* in Jung-St Peter in Strasbourg of about 1320 (W. Körte, *Oberrheinische Kunst X,* 1941, p. 97). In the third decade of the 14th C. (1324–9) Giottesque compositions from the Padua frescoes were reproduced on the altar wings of Klosterneuburg (O. Pächt, *Österreichische Tafelmalerei der Gotik,* 1929). There are Giottesque elements in the stained-glass windows of Königsfelden in Switzerland of about the same date, *c.* 1325–30 (*cf.* M. Stettler, *Königsfelden, Farbenfenster des XIV. Jhs,* Laupen near Bern 1949). An Austrian panel-painting in the Staatliche Gemälde-galerie in Berlin-Dahlem (*c.* 1350) is derived from the composition of the *Nativity* in Padua (Pächt *op. cit., pl. 4*).

2 (p. 11) Salvini No. 19. Filippo Villani's biographies of painters are reprinted in their entirety in C. Frey, *Il libro di Antonio Billi,* Berlin 1892, p. 73; also in J. v. Schlosser, *Quellenbuch zur Kunstgeschichte des abendländ. Mittelalters,* Vienna 1896, p. 37 *ff.*

3 (p. 11) Salvini No. 17. Cennino d'Andrea Cennini, *Il libro dell'arte,* text and English translation edited by D. V. Thompson, New Haven 1932–3 (2 vols). German translation by A. Ilg, *Quellenschriften f. Kunstgeschichte I,* Vienna 1871.

4 (p. 11) Ghiberti p. 35. Schlosser, *Quellenbuch* (*cf.* note 2), p. 375. The theory of the three periods of art can be traced back from Ghiberti to the Trecento, *cf.* W. Paatz, *Die Kunst der Renaissance in Italien,* Stuttgart 1953, p. 12.

5 (p. 11) Vasari, Milanesi's edition (*cf.* Abbreviations). For the genesis of Vasari's work and his sources see W. Kallab, *Vasaristudien, Quellenschriften f. Kunstge-schichte,* new series, vol. XV, Vienna 1908. See also Vasari, *Künstler der Renaissance,* edited by H. Sieben-hüner, Leipzig 1940 (selected biographies in German translation with detailed introduction).

6 (p. 12) J. Kollwitz, 'Zur Frühgeschichte der Bilder-verehrung', in *Römische Quartalschrift,* vol. 48, 1953, p. 1 *ff.* H. Schrade, *Vor- und frühromanische Malerei,* Cologne 1958, p. 47 *ff.* ('Das Tafelbild des Frühmittel-alters'). Hager, p. 33 *ff.*

7 (p. 12) See especially Wilpert; also van Marle I (1923) and his Italian edition *Le scuole della pittura italiana,* vol. I, Milan 1932; also Anthony; for the 11th C. see Ladner.

8 (p. 13) W. Goetz, *Italien im Mittelalter,* 2 vols, Leipzig 1942.

9 (p. 14) J. v. Schlosser, *Quellenbuch* (*cf.* note 2), p. 149 *ff;* also P. Toesca, *La pittura e la miniatura nella Lombardia,* Milan, 1912, p. 40 note 40 and p. 60 note 4. For a detailed account see P. Clemen, *Die romanische Monumentalmalerei in den Rheinlanden,* Düsseldorf 1916, pp. 15, 16.

10 (p. 14) J. v. Schlosser, *Quellenbuch* (*cf.* note 2), p. 188.

1 The early Middle Ages

1 (p. 15) Wilpert I, p. 413 *ff.*, III, *pls 8–28, 53–74*; Wilpert dates the mosaics in the nave of Santa Maria Maggiore around the mid–4th C. Presumably, however, they were done at about the same time as those on the triumphal arch, which have an inscription dating them in the reign of Pope Sixtus III (432–40). This date is also proposed by R. Kömstedt, *Vormittelalterliche Malerei,* Augsburg 1929, p. 14 *ff.* (with an impressive analysis of the style). Finally for the dating, see G. Matthiae, *Pittura romana del medioevo,* I (secoli IV–X), Rome 1965, p. 46 *ff.*; with additional literature (C. Cecchelli, P. Künzle).

2 (p. 15) The frescoes in St Paul's, destroyed in the fire of 1823, are known through copies commissioned by Cardinal Francesco Barberini in 1634 (Wilpert II p. 565 *ff.*). The frescoes of Old St Peter's are recorded in drawings, commissioned around 1610 by the papal notary Giacomo Grimaldi, and made before the demolition of that part of the basilica (Wilpert I, p. 376 *ff.*); all the drawings are now in the Vatican Library. *Cf.* J. Garber, *Wirkungen der frühchristl. Gemäldezyklen der alten Peters- und Pauls-Basiliken in Rom,* Berlin/Vienna 1918; Garber, like E. Müntz before him, started with the assumption that both cycles were done at the time of Pope Leo I (440–61), *i.e.* in the middle of the 5th C., and showed that they were restored in part by Cavallini at the end of the 13th C. *Cf.* p. 59. A comprehensive catalogue has recently been published, of the copies done in the baroque period: S. Waetzoldt, 'Die Kopien des 17. Jhs. nach Mosaiken und Wandmalereien in Rom', *Röm. Forschungen der Bibliotheca Hertziana,* vol. XVIII, Vienna/Munich 1964. According to Waetzoldt (p. 56 *ff.*) the paintings found by Cavallini in the nave of St Paul's had probably been restored once in the early Middle Ages, *c.* 700, closely following the originals of the 5th C. Cavallini, too, evidently remained faithful to the iconography of the older paintings, which were apparently in need of renovation, though by no means completely obliterated. Grimaldi also commissioned copies of the St Peter cycle in the vestibule of St Peter's; *cf.* Wilpert, I, p. 402 *ff.*; Waetzoldt *op. cit.* p. 66 *ff.*, and *pls 465–472.* Illustrations of two original fragments of these frescoes were published by A. Muñoz in *Nuovo Bullettino di Archeologia Cristiana,* 1913, p. 175; Wilpert I, *pl. 144;* the fragments date from the third quarter of the 13th C.; Toesca (*Storia,* p. 1034 note 38) associates them with Jacopo Torriti. For the frescoes of the nave of St Peter's see Garber *op. cit.* p. 27 *ff.*, who dates them in the time of Leo the Great. Waetzoldt (*op. cit.* p. 70) considers the time of Pope Formosus (891–6) more probable; also G. Matthiae, *Pittura romana* (*cf.* note 1), p. 57 *ff.*, who treats the problem of the Leo dating with lucid and critical reservation.

3 (p. 15) The most important examples are listed by Garber (*cf.* note 2), p. 28 *ff.* Also G. Matthiae, 'Note di pittura laziale del Medioevo', in *Bollettino d'Arte* 36, 1951, p. 112 *ff.*

4 (p. 16) Garber (*cf.* note 2) p. 44/45. – Kleinschmidt p. 63 *ff.* – also *cf.* p. 56.

5 (p. 16) W. de Grüneisen, *Sainte-Marie-Antique,* Rome

1911. Wilpert II, p. 653 *ff.* Anthony p. 17 *ff.*, *pls 23–31.* E. Kitzinger, *Die römische Malerei vom Beginn des 7. bis zur Wende des 8. Jhs.,* Diss. Munich 1934. P. Romanelli and P. J. Nordhagen, *S. Maria Antiqua,* Rome 1964. G. Matthiae, *Pittura romana* (*cf.* note 1), p. 116 *ff.*

6 (p. 16) Wilpert IV, *pls. 133, 134.*

7 (p. 16) Wilpert IV, *pl. 135;* Anthony *pl. 25.*

8 (p. 16) G. P. Bognetti, A. de Capitano d'Arzago, G. Chierici, *Santa Maria di Castelseprio,* Milan 1948 (the basic work that proposed a date around the middle of the 7th C. for the frescoes). For other opinions see following note.

9 (p. 17) *Cf.* G. P. Bognetti, *Castelseprio, Guida storico-artistica,* Venice 1960. B. gives a concise and lucid account of the controversy and the conclusions of current research. From B's numerous bibliographical references (p. 66 *ff.*) the following may be stressed: K. Weitzmann, *The Fresco Cycle of S. Maria di Castelseprio,* Princeton 1951 (dating them in the second quarter of the 10th C.); Meyer Schapiro (discussing Weitzmann's book in *The Art Bulletin* 34, 1952, p. 147 *ff.*) places the frescoes in the second half of the 8th C.; C. R. Morey in *The Art Bulletin* 34, 1952, p. 173 *ff.*: second half of the 7th C.; A. Grabar in *Gazette des Beaux-Arts* 1950, p. 107 *ff.* comes closest to Weitzmann's view; according to him the Castelseprio style should be regarded as an early stage of the Renaissance in the middle of the Byzantine period, and not as a parallel or derivative.

10 (p. 17) For earlier discoveries see J. Zemp & R. Durrer, 'Das Kloster St. Johann zu Münster in Graubünden', in *Mitt. der Schweiz. Ges. zur Erhaltung histor. Kunstdenkmäler,* Geneva 1906–10. For discoveries since 1947 see L. Birchler, 'Zur karolingischen Architektur und Malerei in Münster-Müstair', in *Frühmittelalterliche Kunst, Akten zum III. Internationalen Kongreß für Frühmittelalterforschungen,* Olten and Lausanne 1951, pp. 167–252.

11 (p. 17) Géza de Francovich, 'Il ciclo pittorico della Chiesa di San Giovanni a Münster (Müstair) nei Grigioni', in *Arte Lombarda* II, 1956, pp. 28–50.

12 (p. 18) For Milan as the probable centre, see Francovich *op. cit.,* p. 36.

13 (p. 18) G. Panazza, 'Le scoperte in S. Salvatore a Brescia', in *Arte Lombarda* V, 1960, p. 13 *ff.* G. Panazza, 'La Chiesa di S. Salvatore in Brescia', *Atti dell'ottavo Congresso di studi sull'arte dell'alto Medioevo* [1959], vol. II, Milan 1962. Panazza (*op. cit.,* p. 110 *ff.*) dates the decoration of the centre aisle 'soon after 816'. H. Torp's attempt to date the paintings of San Salvatore in the

third quarter of the 8th C., *i.e.* a date still in the Langobard period, has met with strong opposition (H. Torp, 'Il problema della decorazione originaria del Tempietto Langobardo di Cividale del Friuli – La data ed i rapporti con San Salvatore di Brescia', in *Quaderni della FACE* No. 18, Udine 1959). For a discussion of these theses see following note.

14 (p. 18) G. de Francovich prefers a later date, see *Atti dell'ottavo Congresso di studi sull'arte dell'alto Medioevo,* vol. I, 1962, p. 65*ff.*

15 (p. 18) See p. 70*ff.*

16 (p. 18) The monastery was destroyed by the Saracens in 882; only scanty remnants of the nine churches and chapels that existed at that time have been preserved. The frescoes are in the cruciform Lawrence Chapel, now half underground, on the left bank of the Volturno, near Castellone, north-west of Isernia. A vivid description and evaluation by G. Graf Vitzthum in *Handbuch der Kunstwissenschaft* (Vitzthum-Volbach, *Die Malerei u. Plastik d. Mittelalters,* Wildpark-Potsdam 1924, p. 49*ff.*). Toesca, *Storia,* p. 408*ff.* E. Bertaux, *L'art dans L'Italie méridionale* I, Paris 1904, p. 93*ff.* M. Avery, *The Exultet Rolls of South Italy,* Princeton 1936, 13 ills, on *pls* CXC–CXCIV. C. Brandi, 'Gli affreschi della Cripta di S. Lorenzo a S. Vincenzo al Volturno' (report on state of preservation) in *Bollettino dell'Istituto Centrale del Restauro,* No. 31/32, 1957, p. 93*ff.* Janine Wettstein, *Sant'Angelo in Formis et la peinture médiévale en Campanie,* Geneva 1960, p. 69*ff.* (detailed description and discussion). Photographs: Gabinetto Fotografico Nazionale, Rome; and Soprintendenza, Aquila.

17 (p. 18) van Marle I, p. 122*ff.*, especially p. 126. H. Belting has pointed out that the representation of the Crucifixion goes back to Carolingian models (*Die Basilica dei SS. Martiri in Cimitile,* Wiesbaden 1962, p. 66, note 117).

18 (p. 19) H. Belting, *Die Basilica dei SS. Martiri in Cimitile und ihr frühmittelalterlicher Freskenzyklus,* Wiesbaden 1962.

19 (p. 19) H. Belting *op. cit.* p. 132*ff.*

20 (p. 19) J. Wettstein *op. cit.* (*cf.* note 16), p. 82*ff.*: '2nd half of 9th C. or beginning of 10th' (also further information). See, however, the earlier dating by Bologna, p. 26*ff.* (with 3 colour pls): '*c.* 762–800'.

21 (p. 19) Colour plate in Wilpert IV, *pl. 210;* van Marle I, *pl. 56;* Ladner p. 90*ff.* and *pl. 53;* Anthony *pl. 46;* G. Matthiae, *Pittura romana* (*cf.* note 1), p. 223; colour plates on pp. 228, 232.

22 (p. 19) A. Muñoz, *Il Restauro del Tempio della Fortuna Virile,* Rome 1925. Ladner p. 94*ff.*, *pls 54–59;* van Marle, Italian edition vol. I, p. 14; Anthony p. 68, *pls 59, 60;* G. Matthiae, *Pittura romana* (*cf.* note 1), p. 228*ff.* All 25 scenes and fragments were published together for the first time by Jacqueline Lafontaine, 'Peintures médiévales dans le temple dit de la Fortune Virile à Rome' *Etudes de philologie, d'archéologie et d'histoire anciennes publiées par l'Institut Historique Belge de Rome,* vol. VI, Brussels-Rome 1959. The increasing atmospheric danger to the frescoes has recently necessitated their removal from the temple's walls. It has not yet been decided where they will be kept in future.

2 The eleventh and twelfth centuries

1 (p. 20) P. Toesca, *La pittura e la miniatura nella Lombardia,* Milan 1912, p. 42*ff.* Ladner, p. 128*ff.* Anthony, p. 98*ff.*, *pls 149–154.* G. R. Ansaldi, *Gli affreschi della Basilica di S. Vincenzo a Galliano,* Milan 1949; also detailed study of the paintings in the nave of S. Vincenzo, which Ansaldi dates in the last 11th C. (the story of Samson, legends of SS. Christopher, Vincent, and Margaret, unfortunately preserved only in incomplete state). Discussion by C. R. Morey in *The Art Bulletin* 34, 1952, p. 163, and by A. Grabar in *Cahiers archéologiques* VI, 1952, p. 177*ff.* (according to Grabar the paintings in the nave could possibly also have been done as early as the beginning of the 11th C.). G. de Francovich, 'Arte carolingia ed ottoniana in Lombardia', in *Röm. Jahrb. f. Kunstgeschichte* VI, 1942/44, p. 113*ff.* (for Galliano p. 158, 159). Bologna p. 32*ff.*, *pls 8–11.*

2 (p. 20) At the founding of S. Vincenzo Aribert was sub-deacon of S. Ambrogio. His portrait as donor holding a model of the church was in the apse and is now in the Ambrosiana in Milan (Anthony, *pl. 154*).

3 (p. 20) The words *petici(o)* and *postulatio* are allusions to Psalms 119, V, 169, 170; *cf.* H. Schrade, *Vor- und frühromanische Malerei,* Cologne 1958, p. 247. The line-drawing of the apse representation in Schrade, p. 245, is not complete because it omits the figures

339

standing on the left of the archangel Michael; *cf.* on the other hand Schrade *pl. 103* and Anthony *pl. 151.*

4 (p. 21) At first in the apse of SS. Cosma e Damiano (526–30), Wilpert III, *pl. 102;* Anthony *pl. 20; cf.* also p. 28 (Tuscania, San Pietro).

5 (p. 21) As in the Carolingian mosaics in the dome of Aachen Cathedral, *cf.* P. Clemen, *Die romanische Monumentalmalerei in den Rheinlanden,* Düsseldorf 1916, p. 14 and 25 *ff., pls 5, 8.* The origin of the enthroned Christ *(Majestas Domini)* is to be found in the Ascension representations of Syrian-Palestinian and Coptic art, *cf.* Anthony p. 32 *ff.*

6 (p. 21) S. Bastianello (= Sebastianello), also called S. Maria in Pallara: Wilpert II, p. 1075 *ff.*, IV, *pl. 224.* According to Ladner (p. 100 *ff.*) '*c.* 970'. Anthony p. 69: 'end of 10th or beginning of 11th C.' The paintings of Sant'Urbano alla Caffarella, near Rome (*c.* 1011, Ladner p. 105 *ff.*, Anthony p. 71 *ff., pls 60, 71*) with their meagre linear style cannot be compared with the style of Galliano.

7 (p. 22) Anthony p. 100 and *pl. 158.*

8 (p. 22) *Cf.* pp.14, 337, notes 9, 10.

9 (p. 23) F. X. Kraus, 'Die Wandgemälde von S. A. in F.', in *Jahrb. d. preuss. Kunstsamml.* XIV, 1893, pp. 3 *ff.*, 84 *ff.* E. Dobbert, 'Zur byzantin. Frage, die Wandgemälde in S. A. in F.', in *Jahrb. d. preuss. Kunstsamml.* XV, 1894, pp. 125 *ff.*, 211 *ff.* Ladner p. 76 *ff.* Anthony p. 90 *ff.* O. Morisani, *Bisanzio e la pittura Cassinese,* Palermo 1955; Morisani, *Gli affreschi di S. Angelo in Formis,* Cava dei Tirreni/ Naples 1962 (with numerous illustrations mostly in colour). Janine Wettstein, *Sant'Angelo in Formis et la peinture médiévale en Campanie,* Geneva 1960 (with a complete description of the frescoes and full discussion of the research up to date).

10 (p. 23) Ascended the papal throne in 1086 unter the name Victor III but died in 1087. Sant'Angelo in Formis was given to the convent on 1072, and Desiderius immediately began the building of the new church. In 1089 the church is said to have been '*nuper constructa*' (Morisani, *Gli affreschi . . .;* p. 77 and notes 13, resp. 4). The decoration can also be dated about this time.

11 (p. 23) *Cf.* the extracts from the '*Chronicon monasterii Casinensis*' in J. v. Schlosser, *Quellenbuch zur Kunstgeschichte des abendländ. Mittelalters,* Vienna 1896, p. 200 *ff.*

12 (p. 23) A. Boeckler, *Abendländische Miniaturen bis zum Ausgang der romanischen Zeit,* Berlin and Leipzig 1930, p. 74 *ff. pls 71, 72.* Ladner p. 38 *ff.* D. M. In-

guanez and M. Avery, *Miniature Cassinesi del sec. XI illustranti la vita di S. Benedetto,* Monte Cassino 1934. P. Baldass, 'Disegni della scuola Cassinese del tempo di Desiderio', in *Bollettino d'Arte* 37, 1952, p. 102 *ff.*

13 (p. 23) Unfortunately there is no inscription identifying the donor, but historians now generally accept that the figure represents the abbot Desiderius.

14 (p. 23) As early as about 800 in St John at Müstair, *cf.* p. 17 *ff.*

15 (p. 23) For the iconography of S. Angelo in Formis see also F. X. Kraus, *Die Wandgemälde der St.-Sylvester-Kapelle zu Goldbach am Bodensee,* Munich 1902. Supplementing Kraus and Dobbert (*cf.* note 9): G. de Jerphanion, *La voix des monuments,* Paris and Brussels 1930, p. 260 *ff.*

16 (p. 24) The fresco was in danger of deterioration and was removed from the wall in 1956; the angel on the right had already been restored in the 17th C. See also following note.

17 (p. 24) *Cf.* M. Bonicatti, 'Considerazioni su alcuni affreschi medioevali della Campania', in *Bollettino d'Arte* XLIII, 1958, p. 12 *ff.* After the removal of the fresco plaster it was revealed that the original semicircular wall surface had been heightened to connect with the pointed arch vaulting. The joint was hidden by the fresco. This invalidates the speculation in the first edition of this book that the frescoes in the vestibule were still part of the original structure preserved during the restoration.

18 (p. 24) Toesca (*Storia,* p. 936/37) had already suggested a date in the 13th C. for the artistically inferior hermit scenes on the curved surfaces on the sides of the vestibule.

19 (p. 27) *Cf.* S. Bettini, *Pittura delle origini cristiane,* Novara 1942; and Coletti I, p. V. *ff* especially p. X.

20 (p. 27) *Cf.* esp. van Marle I, p. 129 *ff.*, also L. Coletti, 'Arte benedettina' in *Enciclopedia Cattolica* II (1949), col. 1225 *ff.; cf.* the qualifying remarks of E. Carli ('Affreschi benedettini del XIII secolo in Abruzzo', in *Le Arti* I, 1932, p. 442 *ff.*) who says: a true Benedictine 'style' has never existed.

21 (p. 27) A. Boeckler, (*Abendländische Miniaturen,* 1930 p. 72) sees in the oldest Exultet Rolls of the Benevento school (2nd half of the 10th C.) an indigenous southern Italian tradition, and no direct connection with *contemporary* Byzantine art. Rich illustrative material for this in M. Avery, *The Exultet Rolls of South Italy,* Princeton 1936. For the miniature-painting in Monte Cassino under Desiderius: Boeckler, *op. cit.* p. 74/5; *cf.* also our note 12.

22 (p. 27) Other wall-paintings of the Monte Cassino school are, or were, to be found in the following places: Cassino, Chiesa del Crocefisso (a classical domed tomb at the foot of Monte Cassino converted into a church in the Middle Ages); the frescoes, a half-length figure of Christ in Benediction and three medallions with portrait busts of saints, were removed in 1950 to the Abbey of Monte Cassino; J. Wettstein, *op. cit.* (*cf.* note 9) p. 94, *pl. 19 a* (and further references). S. Maria di Trocchio, now in ruins (the apse painting of the Ascension was also transferred to Monte Cassino), *cf.* A. Pantoni, 'S. Maria di Trocchio e le sue pitture', in *Bollettino d'Arte* 38, 1953, p. 14*ff.*; J. Wettstein *op. cit.* p. 97, 98. Ausonia (north of Minturno), S. Maria del Piano, crypt, *cf.* Anthony p. 93, *pls 139, 140;* J. Wettstein *op. cit.* p. 96, 97. Foro Claudio (between Sessa and Carinola), S. Maria della Libera, apse decoration, *cf.* van Marle, Italian edition I, p. 142, *pls 70, 71;* Anthony p. 93, *pl. 141;* J. Wettstein *op. cit.* p. 93, 94. All these paintings were manifestly done later than the frescoes inside Sant'-Angelo in Formis.

23 (p. 27) The frescoes consisting of scenes from the lives of SS. Clement and Alexis are painted on the surface of the walled-up arcades of the present lower church of S. Clemente; the date of these walls is disputed. Scholars have so far usually connected them with the reported destruction or damage by Robert Guiscard in 1084; this date has been taken by some as the *terminus ante quem* and by others as the *terminus post quem* for the frescoes. Vitzthum *op. cit.* (*cf.* p. 339 note 16) p. 46*ff.* considers them earlier than 1084 (with a careful description and analysis of the frescoes); Coletti I p. XIII, to the same effect. Wilpert II, p. 535*ff.*, IV, *pls 239–42.* Ladner, p. 61*ff.* Anthony p. 73/4 *pls 73–6* ('after 1084'). Recently E. B. Garrison has stressed that there is no evidence for the supposed destruction in 1084; he declares this date irrelevant and dates the frescoes in the first decade of the 12th C.; the construction of the new upper church, which presumably began at this time should be considered as *terminus ante quem* (*Studies in the History of Medieval Italian Painting* I, 1953, p. 1*ff*); supplements and rectifications: *op. cit.* II, 1955–6, p. 173*ff.*, also III, 1957–8, p. 113*ff.*, and IV, 1960–2, p. 210*ff.* *Cf.* also the closely associated miniature in Cesena dated 1104, *op. cit.* II, p. 179, *pl. 193.*

24 (p. 28) Also called 'Castel Sant'Elia', after the place situated near the church. C. J. Hoogenwerf, 'Gli affreschi nella chiesa di Sant'Elia presso Nepi', in *Dedalo* VIII, 1927/28, p. 331*ff.* Ladner p. 69*ff.* Anthony p. 69*ff.*, *pls 63–6.* E. B. Garrison, *Studies in the History of Medieval Italian Painting* III, 1957–58, p. 5*ff.* ('first quarter of the twelfth Century').

25 (p. 28) Tuscania, the Toscanella of the Middle Ages, lies north of Viterbo. The paintings were probably done not long after the ciborium in the church choir, which bears the consecration inscription of the year 1093. C. A. Isermeyer, 'Die mittelalterlichen Malereien der Kirche S. Pietro in Tuscania, in '*Kunstgeschichtl. Jahrb. d. Bibliotheca Hertziana* II, 1938, p. 289*ff.* Anthony p. 75, *pls 77, 78.*

26 (p. 28) The frescoes in the convent oratory behind the apse of S. Pudenziana in Rome are probably of the first half of the 12th C. Wilpert IV, *pls 234–6;* Anthony p. 75, *pls 79, 80;* Garrison p. 26; Garrison, *Studies in the History of Medieval Italian Painting III,* 1957–58, p. 5*ff.* ('Second Quarter of the twelfth Century'); W. Paeseler dates them in the second quarter of the 13th C., undoubtedly too late ('Die römische Weltgerichtstafel im Vatikan', in *Kunstgeschichtl. Jahrb. d. Bibliotheca Hertziana* II, 1938, p. 388). The paintings from the Grotta degli Angeli near Magliano-Pecorareccio, removed in 1939 and now in the Corsini Gallery in Rome, are closely connected: *cf.* P. Rotondi, 'Gli affreschi di Magliano Romano nella Galleria Corsini a Roma', in *Le Arti* II, 1940, p. 288*ff.*; Ladner, p. 82*ff.*; Anthony p. 74, 75; Garrison, *Studies op. cit.* p. 198*ff.* ('c. 1125 or shortly after').

27 (p. 29) Wilpert IV, *pls 252–9;* Anthony p. 77 *pls 82, 83.*

28 (p. 29) Near Terni in Umbria. Described in detail by A. Schmarsow in *Repertorium f. Kunstwiss.* 28, 1905, p. 391*ff.*; supplementing this: Garber *op. cit.* (*cf.* p. 214, note 2), p. 30*ff.*; Anthony p. 77, 78, *pls 84, 85.* Wall-paintings of similar stylistic trend dating from the beginning of the 13th C. in Viterbo, S. Andrea di Pianoscarano and elsewhere; *cf.* G. Matthiae, 'Note di pittura laziale del Medioevo', in *Bollettino d'Arte* 36, 1951, p. 112*ff.*

29 (p. 29) According to Toesca, *Storia,* pp. 972 and 1033, note 37, dating from the 'early 13th C.'; van Marle I, p. 158*ff.* gives a date much too early '*c.* 1100'; Anthony p. 71, *pls 68, 69;* Garrison p. 26: 'second quarter of the 13th C.'

30 (p. 29) Garrison No. 279; Colletti I, *pl. 16;* illustration of the centre panel in Hager, *pl. 37;* colour plate in Wilpert IV, *pls 244, 245.*

31 (p. 29) Entire triptychs: Garrison 278, 279, 280, 299; centre panel only: Garrison 288, 289, 290, 292, 305. *Cf.* W. F. Volbach, 'Il Cristo di Sutri e la venerazione del SS. Salvatore nel Lazio', in *Atti della Pontif. Accad. Romana di Archeologia, Rendiconti*, XVII, 1940/41, p. 97*ff.* Garrison, *Studies* (*cf.* note 24) II, 1955–6, p. 5*ff.* ('The Christ Enthroned at Casape with Notes on the Earlier Redeemer Panels'). The original of this popular Christ-icon in Latium is the so-called 'Achiropoites', the representation of Christ in the Sancta Sanctorum Chapel in Rome, which 'was not done by human hands'; *cf.* Wilpert II, p. 1103*ff.*, and IV, *pl. 135;* Wilpert, 'L'Achiropoite della Cappella Sancta Sanctorum', in *L'Arte* 10, 1907, p. 161*ff.* The panel-painting, now badly damaged, was mentioned for the first time in connection with a votive procession in 752 or 753, when Pope Stephen II carried it from the Lateran to Santa Maria Maggiore; *cf.* Hager p. 35. Such processions, regularly held, were a Christian derivative of the classical processions in which the emperor-portraits were carried.

32 (p. 29) The datings of the Tivoli Triptych vary by more than a century. According to Garrison, *Studies* (*cf.* note 24) III, 1957–8, p. 198*ff.*: 'between the 1st and 2nd quarter of the 12th C.'). Hager, p. 36: '2nd half of the 12th C.'. Paeseler *op. cit.* (*cf.* note 26) p. 382/3 dates the triptych (probably too late) shortly before 1234; in this year the chapel in which the triptych was to be kept was consecrated.

33 (p. 30) *Cf.* W. W. S. Cook and J. Gudiol Ricart, 'Pintura e Imaginería Románicas' in *Ars Hispaniae*, VI, Madrid 1950.

34 (p. 30) Painted or moulded decoration on the frame, representation of the main figure in low relief; *cf.* the antependium in Siena of 1215 (Hager *pl. 142*) and the Madonna in Santa Maria Maggiore in Florence (our *pl. 33*); also see pp. 30 and 344, note 4.

35 (p. 30) Hager p. 44*ff.*, *pls 44, 45* (and further bibliographical references).

36 (p. 30) C. Bertelli, *La Madonna di S. Maria in Trastevere*, Rome 1961. Hager p. 52, 53, *pl. 56*.

37 (p. 30) E. Sandberg-Vavalà, *La Croce dipinta italiana e l'iconografia della Passione*, 2 vols, Verona 1929, gives a detailed account of all the crucifixes discussed by us, and many illustrations. Hager p. 75*ff.*, *pl. 86ff.*

38 (p. 30) For the origin of the panel crucifix and its antecedents *cf.* Hager p. 77. and earlier G. de Francovich, 'L'Origine du crucifix monumental sculpté et peint', in *Revue de l'art ancien et moderne* 67/68, 1935, p. 185*ff.*

39 (p. 30) One of the scenes in the St Francis Legend at Assisi has such a crucifix together with two other panel-paintings on the triumphal beam; another scene shows a stone screen from behind with pulpit and crucifix (Hager *pls. 86, 87*).

40 (p. 30) Garrison No. 498. Bologna p. 53; *pl. 20*. The figure of Christ was overpainted in the 13th C.; an X-ray of the head revealed the original layer beneath, *cf.* A. Morassi, *Capolavori della pittura a Genova*, Milan–Florence 1951, *pls 1–13* (many further details of the parts that were not overpainted).

41 (p. 30) Garrison No. 456. The inscription of the crucifix is damaged, the artist's name Alberto 'di Sotio' is not certain.

42 (p. 31) See p. 24. The old political association between the Duchy of Spoleto and the principality of Benevento could easily explain the art-historical link with the Monte Cassino district. The wall-paintings of the late 12th C. in Spoleto also point to such a link. *The Martyrdom of SS. John and Paul* in the crypt of SS. Giovanni e Paolo (van Marle I, *pl. 90*) is still strongly reminiscent of the style of the miniatures of Desiderius' time. ('Vita S. Benedicti' in Toesca, *Storia, pls 725–7*). Even closer to the Spoleto frescoes is the coarser provincial late style of the Monte Cassino miniatures, *cf.* the *Regestum of S. Angelo in Formis* of about the mid-12th C. (A. Boeckler, *Abendländ. Miniaturen*, p. 104; reproductions in D. Mauro Inguanez, *Regesto di S. Angelo in Formis*, Monte Cassino 1925, *pls I, II* in text.

43 (p. 31) D. G. Polvara, 'Il monastero benedettino di S. Pietro al monte sopra Civate', in *Arte Cristiana* 29, 1941, pp. 177*ff.*, 30, 1942 p. 1*ff.* P. Toesca, 'Gli stucchi di S. Pietro al monte di Civate', in *Le Arti* V, 1942/43, p. 55*ff.* P. Toesca, 'Monumenti dell'antica abbazia di S. Pietro al monte di Civate', in *Artis Monumenta fotografice edita* I, Florence 1951. G. Bognetti and C. Marcora, *L'Abbazia benedettina di Civate*, Civate 1957. R. Salvini, 'Romanico o Alto Medioevo? Il problema cronologico della decorazione di S. Pietro al monte', in *Arte Lombarda* IX, 1964, p. 61*ff.*

44 (p. 31) Published with many illustrations, some in colour, by G. Bognetti and C. Marcora *op. cit.* (*cf.* note 43). Most of the paintings of S. Calocero are above the vault on the upper walls of the centre aisle.

45 (p. 32) The dating (*c.* 1180) suggested in the first edition of this book (1953) with reference to Toesca cannot be sustained. For the earlier dating *cf.* Bognetti/Marcora, and Salvini *op. cit.* (*cf.* note 43). Salvini points to the relationship of the frescoes with other

342

Lombard paintings some of which can be dated (Como, S. Giorgio di Borgo Vico, possibly 1082; Oleggio, S. Michele) and also with the stucco decoration in Civate itself, which was probably done at the same time as the paintings. A. Grabar (*cf.* Grabar/Nordenfalk, *Die romanische Malerei,* Geneva 1958, p. 46) stressed the Byzantine element in the frescoes of Civate and dates them 'not earlier than the first half of the 12th C.'. For the dating of the stucco at the end of the 11th C. see G. de Francovich, 'Arte carolingia ed ottoniana in Lombardia', *Römisches Jahrb. f. Kunstgesch.* VI, 1942-4, p. 113*ff.*, and before him A. Feigel, in *Monatshefte f. Kunstwiss.,* II, 1909, p. 206-217.

46 (p. 32) The paintings, which were almost inaccessible for a long time, were first published by E. Arslan, 'Affreschi romanici Pavesi e una scultura lignea', in *Studi in onore di Aristide Calderini e Roberto Paribeni,* vol. III, Milan/Varese 1956. p. 833 *ff., pls 1-6.*

47 (p. 35) P. Toesca, 'Gli affreschi del duomo di Aquileia', in *Dedalo* VI, 1925/6, p. 32*ff.* A. Morassi, in *La basilica di Aquileia,* Bologna 1933, p. 299*ff.* Anthony p. 108*ff., pls 183-7.* L. Magnani, *Gli affreschi della basilica di Aquileia,* Turin 1960.

48 (p. 35) The iron grill between the gallery and centre part of the crypt, still visible in our illustration, has since been removed. *Cf.* Magnani *op. cit. pl. 5.*

49 (p. 35) P. Muratoff, *La pittura bizantina,* Rome, n.d., *pls 153-6.* R. Hamann-Mac Lean and H. Hallensleben, *Die Monumentalmalerei in Serbien und Makedonien vom 11. bis zum frühen 14. Jhdt.,* Giessen 1963, p. 17*ff., pls 29-45.* Magnani regards this relationship with the frescoes of Nerez as too close and too direct.

3 Early Tuscan painting

1 (p. 36) Pisa, Museo Nazionale, No. 15. Brunetti/Sinibaldi No. 130. Garrison No. 520. W. Arslan, 'Su alcune croci pisani', in *Rivista d'Arte* 18, 1936, p. 217*ff.* Bologna p. 54 without explanation dates the crucifix to the early 13th C.

2 (p. 37) Pisa, Museo Nazionale No. 20. Brunetti/Sinibaldi No. 14. Garrison No. 521.

3 (p. 37) For the origin of the Dead Christ on the Cross in Byzantine art (since the 1st half of the 11th C.) *cf.* L. H. Grondijs, *L'Iconographie byzantine du Crucifié mort sur la croix,* Leyden, n.d. (Bibliotheca Byzantina Bruxellensis 1).

4 (p. 38) Garrison No. 501. Brunetti/Sinibaldi No. 1. Bologna colour plate *21.* From S. Maria dei Servi in Lucca, now in the Lucca Pinacoteca.

5 (p. 38) Lucca, Pinacoteca, No. 226. Garrison No. 476. Brunetti/Sinibaldi No. 2. For Berlinghiero and his school, *cf.* E. B. Garrison, 'Toward a new History of early Luchese Painting', in *The Art Bulletin* 33, 1951, p. 11*ff.*, and Garrison, 'A Berlinghieresque Fresco in S. Stefano, Bologna' in *The Art Bulletin* 28, 1946, p. 211*ff.*

6 (p. 38) We do not share the rather emotional, belittling opinion of Byzantine influence on Italian Duecento painting expressed by R. Longhi and recently also by F. Bologna. This influence was also felt in countries north of the Alps, and it is indisputable that it was of great importance in the French High Gothic. One has only to think of the Byzantine motifs in the patternbook of Villard d'Honnecourt. However, the overall view of Italian painting becomes distorted when one tries to exclude especially those masters, who like Berlinghiero, were particularly related to the Byzantine models. The far-reaching influence of the Berlinghiero school on Tuscan painting of the 2nd quarter of the century is the best proof of the fruitfulness of the encounter with the East. *Cf.* R. Longhi, 'Giudizio sul Duecento' (1939), in *Proporzioni* II, 1948, p. 5*ff.*; F. Bologna, *La Pittura italiana delle origini,* Rome/Dresden 1962.

7 (p. 38) Garrison No. 402. Brunetti/Sinibaldi No. 5. Hager p. 94.

8 (p. 38) Painted before 1228, the year of the canonization of St Francis, and still with the title 'Frater Franciscus'. van Marle I, *pl. 246* and plate, p. 424; Anthony *pl. 97.* Hager p. 88, *pl. 115.* According to R. Offner (*Gazette des Beaux-Arts* 94/39, 1952, p. 132) dateable after *c.* 1218 (St Francis' visit to Subiaco) and probably before 1224, as the stigmata are not yet shown. A panel-painting with a full-length figure of St Francis, done only slightly later, was discovered by Offner in the storage-vaults of the Louvre in Paris (*op. cit.* p. 129*ff.*).

9 (p. 39) Formerly in S. Miniato al Tedesco. Garrison No. 140. Hager p. 94 *pl. 128.*

10 (p. 39) Hager pp. 91, 93-5; *pls 129-33.* Garrison Nos. 361, 371, 394, 400, 405, 408, 409, 411.

11 (p. 39) The Antependium is to be regarded as the 343

precursor of these early altar-retables; *cf.* Hager pp. 91*ff.*, 103*ff.* The horizontal rectangular panel, dated 1215, with the Enthroned Christ in the Siena Pinacoteca (Garrison No. 357), was, as Hager proves on p. 105, not yet a retable, but an antependium. The liturgical requirement for the appearance of the retable was the custom, which developed in Italy only gradually, that the priest no longer celebrated mass behind the altar *(versus populum),* but in front of it with his back to the congregation. For the earliest forms of the retable *cf.* Hager pp. 91*ff.*, 101*ff.*, Hager stresses the importance of the Mendicant Orders for the emergence of panels as highaltar retables.

12 (p. 39) Hager, *pls 122ff, 134ff.*

13 (p. 39) P. Bacci, 'Juncta Pisanus pictor', in *Bolletino*

d'Arte 1922/23 p. 145*ff.* E. Carli, *Pittura medievale pisana,* Milan 1958, p. 30*ff.*, *pls* III, *32–37.*

14 (p. 39) *Cf.* R. Oertel in *Zschr. f. Kunstgesch.* VI, 1937. p. 229/30. A hitherto unnoticed reference to the Frate-Elia Crucifix is found in D. Nicolo Catalano, *Fiume del Paradiso, diviso in Quattro Capi,* 1651, p. 298; 'una gran mole d'un Crocifisso, posto nell'alto sopra una trave, avanti l'altar maggiore ... nella Chiesa Superiore.'

15 (p. 39) Assisi, S. Maria degli Angeli (Garrison No. 543; Brunetti/Sinibaldi No. 15). Pisa, S. Ranierino (Garrison No. 578). Bologna, S. Domenico (Garrison No. 546; Brunetti/Sinibaldi No. 16); C. Brandi, 'Il Crocifisso di Giunta Pisano in Domenico a Bologna', in *L'Arte* 1936, p. 71*ff.*

16 (p. 40) See p. 349, note 11.

4 Florence and Siena in the Duecento

1 (p. 41) R. Oertel, 'Ein toskanisches Madonnenbild um 1260', in *Mitt. des Kunsthistor. Inst. in Florenz* VII, 1953, p. 9*ff.* Also E. B. Garrison, in *Bolletino d'Arte* 41, 1956, p. 303*ff.* (with the dating between 1270 and 1287, in our opinion too late).

2 (p. 41) Garrison No. 363; Brunetti/Sinibaldi No. 52; Hager pp. 91, 92, *pl. 122.*

3 (p. 41) Garrison No. 219; Brunetti/Sinibaldi No. 61.

4 (p. 41) This connection is especially clear in the antependiums (*cf.* p. 343, note 11). Originally, these were done as a rule by goldsmiths. According to Hager (p. 59) all antependiums not done in precious metal are to be regarded as substitutes.

5 (p. 41) Garrison No. 1. C. Brandi, 'Il restauro della Madonna di Coppo di Marcovaldo nella Chiesa dei Servi di Siena', in *Bolletino d'Arte* 35, 1950, p. 160*ff.* G. Coor-Achenbach, 'A Visual Basis for the Documents relating to Coppo di Marcovaldo and his Son Salerno', in *The Art Bulletin* 28, 1946, p. 233*ff.*

6 (p. 42) For the increase of popularity of the 'Seated Hodegetria' *cf.* V. Lasareff, 'Studies in the Iconography of the Virgin', in *The Art Bulletin* 20, 1938, p. 46*ff.* ('The Seated Hodegetria'); for further information about the emergence of this type of Madonna in Tuscan painting *cf.* R. Oertel, 'Ein toskanisches Madonnenbild um 1260', in *Mitt. d. Kunsthistor. Inst. in Florenz* VII, 1953, p. 9*ff.* esp. p 26*ff.*

7 (p. 42) Garrison No. 25 ('1265–70'); Brunetti/Sinibaldi No. 58 (with good illustrations after the restoration).

8 (p. 42) For full account *cf.* J. H. Stubblebine, *Guido da*

Siena, Princeton 1964 (with catalogue of works, many illustrations and extensive bibliography).

9 (p. 42) Garrison No. 297 ('about 1270'); Hager pp. 137, 138. Stubblebine *op. cit.*, Cat.-No. IVa, b ('about 1280'). Originally in S. Domenico in Siena. The heads of the Madonna and Child were repainted early in the 14th C. like those of Coppo's *Madonna* of 1261; in this case the throne was also repainted.

10 (p. 42) The long standing controversy, still not settled, over the dating of the Guido *Maestà* is a typical example of the conflict between the specific art-historical approach, based on stylistic evidence, and the supposed 'historical' method, based on external data. R. Offner ('Guido da Siena and A.D. 1221', in *Gazette des Beaux-Arts* 1950, p. 61*ff.*) dates the picture with convincing stylistic argument around 1275–80. C. Brandi (*Duccio,* Florence 1951, p. 94*ff.*) gives a comprehensive account of the history of the picture and the controversy relating to it; supported by technical observations made during the 1949/50 restoration, he firmly accepts the date 1221 on the inscription. As Offner, however, convincingly demonstrates, this could not possibly have been the actual date when the picture was painted. Thus, if the date on the inscription is, as accepted by Brandi, intact and authentic, an explanation is required that would be consistent with the stylistic evidence. It is, for instance, not entirely inconceivable that the date of an older Madonna which was replaced by Guido's panel was adopted; such an assumption would, how-

ever, contradict the general character of the inscription which is a typical 'artist's' inscription. According to J. H. Stubblebine (*Guido da Siena*, 1964, p. 39*ff*.) the inscription is undoubtedly part of the overpainting done at the beginning of the 14th C., and its text is derived from the inscription of the polyptych No. 7 in the Siena Pinacoteca (*cf.* note 12). On this occasion only the date, '1221', was added, and could refer to the date, transmitted by an unreliable account, of the first establishment of the Domenican Order in Siena. These considerations are all, however, fundamentally irrelevant to the stylistic assessment of the work. Our present view of Duecento painting, arrived at after decades of research, cannot be completely repudiated on the basis of an isolated date. As long as no convincing explanation can be given for the date 1221, the doubt regarding the inscription of Guido's *Maestà* must remain. Possibly the technical evidence needs to be re-examined. On the results of the restoration *cf.* E. Carli and C. Brandi, in *Bollettino d'Arte* 36, 1951, p. 248*ff*.

11 (p. 43) Garrison No. 378. Hager *pl. 145*.

12 (p. 43) Siena Pinacoteca, No. 7. Garrison No. 430. Brunetti/Sinibaldi No. 27. Stubblebine Cat.-No. II.

13 (p. 43) The twelve panels (c. 35 × 46 cm) come from the Badia Ardenga near Siena, and are now dispersed in the museums of Altenburg, Princeton, Siena and Utrecht, as well as in the Stroelin collection in Paris (Garrison Nos. 660–2, 671, 687, 696–100, 702; Stubblebine Cat.-No. IVc, p. 43*ff*., *pls 18, 20–30*). They were sawn apart at the beginning of the 19th C. and their original connection is disputed. C. Weigelt ('Guido da Siena's Great Ancona: A Reconstruction', in *The Burlington Magazine* LIX, 1931, p. 15*ff*.) was the first to attempt to identify them with the so-called *aliae* (side-wings), which are reputed to have belonged to Guido's *Maestà*. It is, however, by no means certain that they were indeed part of these *aliae* mentioned in the 16th C. Neither the reconstruction by Weigelt, nor the one recently suggested by Stubblebine (p. 54*ff*., *pl. 16*) is convincing. *Cf.* R. Oertel, *Frühe italienische Malerei in Altenburg*, Berlin 1961, p. 57*ff*. (with an attempted reconstruction, *pl. 5*). Judging by the horizontal direction of the joints between the wooden boards, which can be detected in several parts of the series, it was probably a large, wide altar-panel, the centre-piece of which is missing.

14 (p. 43) The major work, the Magdalene panel, is in the Florence Accademia (Garrison No. 404. Brunetti/Sinibaldi No. 70). For an analysis of the master *cf.*

Garrison p. 22, and G. Coor-Achenbach, 'Some Unknown Representations by the Magdalen Master', in *The Burlington Magazine* 93, 1951, p. 73*ff*.

15 (p. 43) Madonna in Bagnano near Florence, S. Maria: Garrison No. 35; Brunetti/Sinibaldi No. 74; other works: Garrison Nos. 7, 10, 191.

16 (p. 44) J. Strzygowski, *Cimabue und Rom*, Vienna 1888. A. Aubert, *Die malerische Dekoration der San-Francesco-Kirche in Assisi. Ein Beitrag zur Lösung der Cimabue-frage*, Leipzig 1907. E. Benkard, *Das literarische Porträt des Giovanni Cimabue*, Munich 1917. A. Nicholson, *Cimabue*, Princeton 1932. R. Salvini, *Cimabue*, Rome 1946. E. Battisti, *Cimabue*, Milan 1963. Also Brunetti/Sinibaldi p. 253*ff*. and the bibliographical appendix. Battisti *op. cit.* p. 111*ff*.

17 (p. 44) Garrison No. 186. Brunetti/Sinibaldi No. 33, containing a full list of references.

18 (p. 44) Reprinted in G. Milanesi, *Documenti per la storia dell'arte senese* I, 1854, p. 158*ff*. Supplemented in R. Oertel: *Zschr. f. Kunstgesch.* VI, 1937, p. 221. Vasari's attribution of the *Rucellai Madonna* to Cimabue was the reason for the relatively late acknowledgment of Duccio's authorship and the long dispute concerning it. Duccio's authorship can now be accepted.

19 (p. 44) Cimabue is mentioned in the records for the first time in 1272 as witness to a contract in Rome (*cf.* p. 48). He must have been already a master of some renown at that time; the date of his birth was thus probably between 1240 and 1250, presumably in the first half of the decade. Duccio is mentioned for the first time in 1278 in connection with a modest commission in Siena to paint chests containing the municipal records. *Cf.* C. Brandi, *Duccio*, 1951, p. 77. He was probably born between 1250 and 1260. On his artistic origins and reputed participation in Assisi *cf.* pp. 56 and 196, and further p. 347 notes 22, 23.

20 (p. 48) The document was discovered and published by J. Strzygowski, *Cimabue und Rom*, Vienna 1888, p. 158*ff*.

21 (p. 48) Colour plate of the figure of St John in Battisti, *op. cit. pl. 68*. In 1302 Cimabue also received the commission for the high-altar retable in Santa Chiara in Pisa (now lost); Hager p. 113, including an attempted reconstruction *pl. 164*.

22 (p. 48) Garrison No. 540 ('workshop or school of Coppo di Marcovaldo, with the participation of the young Cimabue, *c.* 1270–5'). A good illustration in Brunetti/Sinibaldi No. 81 ('1260–1270?'). Battisti *op. cit. pls 1–6* (of which four in colour).

23 (p. 49) Garrison No. 182 ('1285–90'). Sinibaldi/

Brunetti No. 82. Hager p. 142 ('after 1285, already influenced by the *Rucellai Madonna*').

24 (p. 49) *Cf.* P. Beye, *Cimabue und die Dugentomalerei*, Diss. Freiburg i. Br. 1957 (typescript).

25 (p. 49) Garrison No. 560 (with the dating '1280 to 1285', doubtlessly too early). Brunetti/Sinibaldi No. 83. A curious reversal of Cimabue's chronology is proposed by R. Longhi ('Giudizio sul Duecento', in *Proporzioni* II, 1948, p. 5 *ff.*), according to which the S. Croce Crucifix would stand at the beginning of Cimabue's development; supported by Bologna p. 100 *ff.* ('before 1274'); further E. Battisti *op. cit.* (*cf.* note 16), p. 62 *ff.* ('before 1288'). The alleged dependence of Salerno di Coppo's Crucifix in Pistoia (1274) on Cimabue's work is no more convincing than the dependence of Deodato Orlandi's Crucifix dated 1288 in Lucca. There were doubtlessly other crucifixes by Cimabue and his workshop, now lost, from which

the Cimabuesque elements in the works mentioned could have been derived. Equally untenable is the early dating of the large Madonna panel from S. Francesco in Pisa (Louvre, Paris), which is also based on R. Longhi 'Giudizio sul Duecento', pp. 15, 16); also Bologna pp. 100, 101, 105. The dependence of this picture on Duccio's *Rucellai Madonna* has always been remarked upon. This applies both to the composition with the oblique view of the throne and to the frame, which is a cruder imitation of the *Rucellai Madonna* frame (photograph of the frame of the Louvre Madonna: Alinari 23082; *cf.* also Bologna pl. 70). *Cf.* the analysis of the frame by M. Cämmerer-George, *Die Rahmung der toskanischen Altarbilder im Trecento*, Strasbourg 1966, pp. 32, 45 and note 65 ('product of the Cimabue school between 1288 and 1296').

26 (p. 49) Garrison *op. cit.*: 'Cimabue, largely assisted'.

5 Assisi and Rome

1 (p. 50) For the overall scheme of S. Francesco (architecture and painting) reference can always be made to Kleinschmidt. Further illustrative material for the paintings in L. Coletti, *Gli affreschi della Basilica di Assisi*, Bergamo 1949. Photographs of the frescoes in the nave of the Upper Church were, after the restoration of 1942/43, published in P. Toesca, 'Gli affreschi della Vita di S. Francesco nella Chiesa Superiore del Santuario di Assisi, in *Artis Monumenta photographice edita* III, Florence, Bencini e Sansoni, 1946; P. Toesca, 'Gli affreschi dell'Antico e del Nuovo Testamento nel Santuario di Assisi (*idem*, IV, 1947); both publications have valuable introductions. Further Gnudi, *Giotto* (1958), with many colour plates. Comprehensive survey of the sources and literature in L. Martius, *Die Franziskuslegende in der Oberkirche von S. Francesco in Assisi und ihre Stellung in der kunstgeschichtl. Forschung*, Berlin 1932.

2 (p. 50) W. Schöne, 'Studien zur Oberkirche von Assisi', in *Festschr. Kurt Bauch*, Munich 1957, p. 50 *ff.*, esp. pp. 54, 55.

3 (p. 50) The wooden consoles that once supported the beam designed for the triumphal cross are still preserved on the first and last frescoes of the St Francis Legend, next to the pillars of the crossing: *cf.* the representation in the fresco of the *Funeral of St Francis*

(Gnudi pl. 58). For the choir screen *cf.* Schöne *op. cit.* (*cf.* note 2), pp. 64, 65.

4 (p. 51) E. Hertlein (*Die Basilika San Francesco in Assisi*, Florence 1964) has given the first analysis of the construction and a convincing examination of the type and style of S. Francesco. He points out the French influence, which asserted itself after the election of Giovanni Buralli da Parma (1247) as general of the Franciscan Order. The patronage of Louis IX of France, who was a tertiary in the Order, was of special importance. Schöne, *op. cit.* (*cf.* note 2) p. 59 expresses a similar view.

5 (p. 51) I. B. Supino's supposition (*La basilica di S. Francesco di Assisi*, Bologna 1924) that at the consecration in 1253 only the stone structure of the roof of the Upper Church existed, and that the vault was added later, is incorrect. *Cf.* W. Krönig in *Kunstgeschichtl. Jahrb. d. Bibl. Hertziana* II, 1938, p. 37 *ff.* In fact the stone rafters were actually built in the 15th C., as has been proved by Italian scholars (*cf.* Hertlein *op. cit.*, p. 48).

6 (p. 51) Gnudi p. 235 *ff.* discusses fully the question of sources and the hypotheses of dating that arise from it.

7 (p. 51) Hertlein *op. cit.* (*cf.* note 4), p. 10, thinks that the south portal was built after the severe earthquake

of 1279. Possibly the buttresses to the nave, which were not part of the original building, were also added at that time. *Cf.* Kleinschmidt I, p. 130.

8 (p. 51) The identification of the Capitol for the first time in C. Brandi (*cf.* note 10). The conclusions that Brandi draws from his observations, and which we also adopted in the first edition of this book, cannot, however, be sustained.

9 (p. 51) *Cf.* Battisti (*cf.* note 10), *pl. 9*, in which the escutcheons can be clearly seen.

10 (p. 52) J. Strzygowski (*Cimabue und Rom*, Vienna 1888, p. 84 *ff.*) was the first to deal thoroughly with the Roman view of Cimabue, although his interpretation of the single buildings is in part incorrect; a controversy lasting several decades arose out of his thesis. C. Brandi (*Duccio*, Florence 1951, p. 127 *ff.*) was the first to recognize the building with pinnacles and escutcheons as a representation of the Capitol. He connected the coats-of-arms with the Orsini senators who were in office in the years 1288–92, and deduced from this that Cimabue's activity in Assisi is to be dated at about this time. Differing with Brandi, J. White 'The Date of the "Legend of St. Francis" in Assisi', in *The Burlington Magazine* 98, 1956 p. 344 *ff.*) stresses that from 1277 on members of the Orsini family had served repeatedly as senators. That the Orsini emblems could refer to Pope Nicholas III had been suggested earlier, *e.g.* Kleinschmidt II, pp. 59, 60. For our summary of the historical situation we are indebted to D. Gioseffi (*Giotto architetto*, Milan 1963, pp. 108, 109), and E. Battisti (*Cimabue*, Milan 1963, p. 38 *ff.*). The early dating of Cimabue's activity in Assisi (*c.* 1277 to 80) is already found in Longhi, 'Giudizio sul Duecento', (*cf.* p. 343, note 6), p. 15; also in Gnudi p. 41, Bologna p. 101, and C. Volpe, in his otherwise controversial discussion of Battisti's Cimabue monograph, in *Paragone* XV, 1964, No. 173 p. 61 *ff.*

11 (p. 53) The repeated reversal of the black-and-white values gives a rough impression of the original effect, *cf.* our *pls 48–51* and the numerous excellent reproductions in Battisti *op. cit.* For *pls 48* and *50* we are deeply grateful to Prof. E. Battisti and Dr E. Sindona.

12 (p. 53) Kleinschmidt *pls 12–15*.

13 (p. 54) *Cf.* Battisti *pl. 7* and the grandiose *Angels of the Winds*, *op. cit. pls 19, 20*.

14 (p. 54) R. Salvini, *Cimabue*, Rome 1946, p. 21/22.

15 (p. 55) The barrel-vaulted choir is on the ground floor of the tower; under the window of the rear wall is the signature CORSVS ME PINXIT and the year 1284. Published by G. Castelfranco in *Bollettino d'Arte* 28, 1935, p. 322 *ff.* Bologna p. 101.

16 (p. 55) Also Bologna p. 101. No direct pupil-master relationship between Corso di Buono and Cimabue seems to have existed. The stylistic connection is of a rather general nature, and Corso's technique is still wholly traditional.

17 (p. 55) Blue vaults strewn with stars are found in almost all churches of the Italian Gothic that contain pictorial decoration. Over large surfaces in Assisi the blue (azurit = copper carbonate) has changed into malachite of typical green colour through the effects of humidity and the presence of carbon dioxide in the atmosphere.

18 (p. 55) Gnudi's assumption (p. 237) that the Doctors' Vault in its present form was a relatively late addition – after 1297 – as a subsistence for an earlier vault decoration, appears convincing. According to traditional iconographic conceptions one would expect a representation of the prophets as counterpart to the evangelists in the vault over the crossing. For the question of dating see p. 349 note 17.

19 (p. 56) See pp. 15, 16 and notes 2, 3.

20 (p. 56) See Strzygowski, *Cimabue und Rom*, Vienna 1888, p. 176; also A. Nicholson in *The Art Bulletin* XII, 1930, p. 270; and L. Lochoff in *Rivista d'Arte* XIX, 1937, p. 250 likewise Bologna p. 120.

21 (p. 56) For technique of painting and work practices see p. 70 *ff.*

22 (p. 56) R. Longhi, 'Giudizio sul Duecento', in *Proporzioni* II, 1948, p. 18; likewise Bologna p. 126; Gnudi p. 238.

23 (p. 56) A series of panel paintings reveal stylistic features of both masters. For Duccio's beginnings *cf.* C. Volpe, 'Preistoria di Duccio', in *Paragone* V, 1954 (No. 49) p. 4 *ff.* and F. Bologna, 'Ciò che resta di un capolavoro giovanile di Duccio / Nuovi studi sulla formazione del maestro', in *Paragone* XI, 1960 (No. 125), p. 3 *ff.*; also Bologna (1962) pp. 126, 127.

24 (p. 57) Anthony p. 81, *pls 100, 101*. Wilpert IV *pls 268, 269*.

25 (p. 57) Wilpert IV, *pl. 300*. Garber *op. cit.* (cf. p. 214, note 2) pp. 43, 44. Anthony pp. 82, 83, *pls 104, 105*

26 (p. 58) P. Muratoff, *La pittura bizantina*, Rome n.d., *pl. CLVII*. Colour plates of Cavallini's frescoes in Wilpert IV, *pls 279–96*. Bologna *pls 96–9*.

27 (p. 59) *cf.* p. 338, note 2.

28 (p. 59) The frescoes of the story of the Apostles on the north wall of St Paul's at the time of Abbot John VI (1270–79); the Old Testament scenes on the south wall

347

at the time of Abbot Batholomew I (1282–97). Garber *op. cit.* (*cf.* p. 338, note 2) p. 76. According to J. White, 'Cavallini and the Lost Frescoes in S. Paolo', in *Journal of the Warburg and Courtauld Institutes* XIX, 1956, p. 84 *ff.*, the period of Cavallini's activity can be determined with even greater accuracy: 1277–9 for the north wall, between 1282 and 1290 for the south wall. This dating is confirmed by White's analysis of the compositions transmitted in the baroque copies, from which a convincing picture of Cavallini's stylistic development emerges.

29 (p. 59) C. Cecchelli, 'S. Maria in Trastevere', in *Le Chiese di Roma illustrate* 31/32, Rome, n.d., pp. 39/40, 149. A. Prandi, 'Pietro Cavallini a S. Maria in Trastevere', in *Rivista dell'Istituto Nazionale d'Archeologia e Storia dell'Arte*, N.S.I., 1952 pp. 282–97.

30 (p. 60) See Toesca, *Storia*, pp. 985 and 1035, note 39. F. Hermanin in *Le Gallerie Nazionali Italiane* V, 1902, p. 61 *ff.* first published the frescoes of S. Cecilia with good illustrations. Also on Cavallini: F. Hermanin, 'Il maestro romano di Giotto', in *Almanacco di Roma per l'anno 1924*, Spoleto 1924, p. 154 *ff.*; A. Busuioceanu, in *Ephemeris Dacoromana* III, 1925, p. 259 *ff.*; L. Coletti, 'Nota sugli esordi di Giotto', in *La Critica d'Arte*, 1937, p. 124 *ff.* and 129 note 26. E. Sindona, *Pietro Cavallini*, Milan 1958.

31 (p. 60) Considerable remnants are preserved; *cf.* the reconstruction of W. Paeseler in *Kunstgesch. Jahb. d. Bibl. Hertziana* II, 1938, p. 375.

32 (p. 60) *Cf.* O. Morisani, *Pittura del Trecento in Napoli*, Naples 1947, p. 26. 1320 is the date of the consecration of the church. After 1316 Cavallini was again in Rome, where he executed the mosaic for the façade of S. Paolo fuori le mura, commissioned by Pope John XXII (1316–34); *cf.* Garber *op. cit.* (see p. 338, note 2), p. 77. The date of his death is unknown.

33 (p. 63) The apse of S. Maria Maggiore: Wilpert II, *pls 121–4.* For Torriti see van Marle I p. 482 *ff.*; M. Soldati, 'Nota su Jacopo Torriti', in *L'Arte* 31, 1928, p. 247 *ff.*

34 (p. 63) The apse mosaic in Santa Maria in Trastevere in Rome (*c.* 1145) is an early development of this, *cf.* Toesca, *Storia, pl. 622* (detail); complete illustration in Cecchelli *op. cit.* (*cf.* note 29) *pl. 13.* Christ still occupies the centre of the apse surface, the Virgin has been moved to his right. It is not a representation of her coronation, but of her enthronement. It is conceivable that the French type of the 'Coronation of the Virgin' was derived from this early Roman type, and that the motif thus travelled via France, where it received its final Western form, and then returned to its point of origin.

35 (p. 63) *Cf.* in particular the two angels bearing torches, van Marle I, *pl. 283.* Rusuti's signature is at the foot of the Enthroned Christ, and thus possibly refers only to this part of the mosaic. It is doubtful wheter the narrative representation in the lower part of the facade is by him. There is evidence that in 1308 and 1317 Rusti was in the service of Philip the Fair of France. Toesca, *Storia*, pp. 987 and 1035, note 40. For Rusuti's alleged activity in Assisi see pp. 56 *ff.*

36 (p. 63) Wilpert IV, *pls 270, 271, 276–8.*

37 (p. 63) P. Toesca, in *Il Trecento*, 1951, p. 451. *Cf.* also M. Salvini, 'Le origini dell'arte di Giotto', in *Rivista d'Arte* XIX, 1937, p. 193, esp. p. 207 *ff.*, and *pls. 9–13.*

6 Giotto: the early years

1 (p. 64) This is mainly true by comparison with the older wall-paintings in Assisi itself. *Cf.*, however, the explanation of W. Schöne (*Über das Licht in der Malerei*, 1954, p. 32 *ff.*), who uses the frescoes of the *St Francis Legend* to analyze the chromatic effect of light in medieval churches with stained-glass windows.

2 (p. 65) The many attemps at attribution and division cannot be considered here. The best account is in L. Lochoff, 'Gli affreschi dell'antico e del nuovo testamento nella basilica superiore di Assisi', in *Rivista d'Arte* XI, 1937, p. 240 *ff.* L. Martius *op. cit.* (*cf.* p. 346 note 1), p. 116 *ff.*

3 (p. 65) *Cf.* Gnudi pp. 236, 237.

4 (p. 65) R. Offner, 'Giotto, Non-Giotto', in *The Burlington Magazine* 74, 1939, and 75, 1939, p. 96 *ff.*, expressed a different view. M. Meiss (*Giotto and Assisi*, New York 1960) attributes the two Isaac scenes and the Lamentation to the young Giotto, the *St Francis Legend* to a follower of Giotto.

5 (p. 65) Salvini No. 2. P. L. Rambaldi, 'Postilla al passo di Riccobaldo', in *Rivista d'Arte* XIX, 1939, p.

349 *ff*. P. Murray, 'Notes on Some Early Giotto Sources', in *Journal of the Warburg and Courtauld Institutes* XVI, 1953, p. 58 *ff*. Gnudi, pp. 242, 243.

6 (p. 65) *Cf.* F. Rintelen, *Giotto und die Giotto-Apokryphen,* Munich and Leipzig 1912 (2nd edition Basle 1923). Despite the criticism of Rintelen's book that can now be made, it remains, together with the monographs of P. Toesca (*Giotto,* Turin 1914) and C. Gnudi (Milan 1958), the most comprehensive and artistically adequate monograph. *Cf.* R. Salvini, *Einleitung zur Giotto-Bibliographie* p. XXIV *ff.*, and R. Oertel, 'Wende der Giotto-Forschung' (*cf.* note 8), esp. p. 2.

7 (p. 66) Thode, Toesca, *cf.* note 9.

8 (p. 66) Brunetti/Sinibaldi No. 96, with comprehensive bibliography. The numerous scholarly contributions occasioned by the Giotto Exhibition of 1937 are listed by R. Oertel, 'Wende der Giotto-Forschung', in *Zschr. f. Kunstgesch.* XI, 1943/44, p. 1 *ff.* Further K. Bauch, 'Die geschichtliche Bedeutung von Giotto's Frühstil', in *Mitt. d. Kunsthist. Inst. in Florenz* VII, 1953, p. 43 *ff.*

9 (p. 66) H. Thode (*Giotto,* Bielefeld and Leipzig, 1899, p. 136) already identified the crucifix correctly as an early work of Giotto. P. Toesca (*La pittura fiorentina del Trecento,* Verona 1929, p. 23) considered it to be a work of Giotto's done shortly before the Padua frescoes; the same view in *Giotto* (Turin 1941) p. 78/79. Until 1937 the majority of the critics, on the other hand, considered the crucifix to be a workshop product and did not accept its identity with the piece mentioned in the document of 1312. The 'rediscovery' is due to L. Coletti, 'Note giottesche', in *Bollettino d'Arte* XXX, 1937, p. 350 *ff.* For the dating of the crucifix *cf.* R. Oertel, 'Giotto-Ausstellung in Florenz', in *Zschr. f. Kunstgesch.* VI, 1937, p. 224 *ff.* According to Gnudi p. 58, it was done about or shortly after 1290.

10 (p. 66) In all probability Giotto was born in 1266, *cf.* P. Toesca, *Giotto,* 1941, p. 9.

11 (p. 66) A similar earlier type in the pulpit relief of Nicola Pisano, *cf.* Oertel *op. cit.* (*cf.* note 9). For the development of Italian crucifix panels in pictorial form *cf.* W. Schöne, 'Giottos Kruzifixtafeln und ihre Vorgänger', in *Festschrift für Friedrich Winkler,* Berlin 1959, p. 49 *ff.*

12 (p. 67) F. J. Mather, *The Isaak Master,* Princeton 1932.

13 (p. 67) M. Meiss (*Giotto and Assisi,* New York 1960, p. 12) demonstrates clearly that this figure cannot be a representation of Rebecca, as was previously thought. In the left picture Rebecca is shown looking considerably older and wearing different clothes.

14 (p. 68) It is hardly likely that Giotto was Cavallini's pupil. More probable is the supposition that there was a 'dialogue' (Gnudi), *i.e.* a reciprocal relationship. In no circumstances, however, could Cavallini have been Giotto's pupil as Vasari states (*Vasari-Milanesi* I, p. 537).

15 (p. 68) *Cf.* L. Lochoff *op. cit.* (*cf.* note 2) p. 266 *ff.* Toesca (*Giotto,* 1941, p. 67 *ff.*, and *Il Trecento,* p. 446 *ff.*) recognizes the hand of the young Giotto in the *Lamentation,* the *Ascension,* and the severely damaged *Baptism of Christ, the Pentecost,* the two Joseph scenes and the Isaac scenes. *Cf.* also Gnudi p. 45 *ff.*

16 (p. 68) We do not share Gnudi's view that the Old and New Testament scenes in the first bay were painted before the Isaac scenes. The Isaac scenes are still closely connected with the Roman tradition; they surpass it in their more striking and consistent design, but do not display new ideas of composition. On the other hand we subscribe to Gnudi's view that the Doctors' Vault could have been executed without technical difficulty after the frescoes on the side walls had been completed (*cf.* p. 347 note 18).

17 (p. 68) At that time the doctrine of the 'Four Fathers of the Church', the *doctores,* was officially declared in the *Decretals* of 1297 (Gnudi p. 237). This probably led to the representation of this theme in the Doctors' Vault. However, a conclusive *terminus post quem* cannot be drawn from this as the intentions of the Curia could have been known in Assisi sometime before. According to P. Murray (*cf.* note 5) there is no evidence that Vasari's statement that Giovanni da Muro was Giotto's patron in Assisi is based on reliable sources. The close connection between the *St Francis Legend* and the Doctors' Vault, however, supports the view that both works were done at more or less the same time, *i.e.,* around 1297. For the perspective elements in the Doctors' Vault *cf.* M. Sperlich, *Die Stellung der Fresken der Franzlegende in der Oberkirche von San Francesco in Assisi in der Geschichte der Perspektive,* thesis Hamburg, 1955 (typescript).

18 (p. 69) Kleinschmidt, II, p. 96, rightly says: 'The master of the St Francis Legend was also the creator of the Doctors' Vault'. *Cf.* R. Oertel, *Zschr. f. Kunstgesch.* XI, 1943/44, p. 14 *ff.*

19 (p. 70) *Cf.* the vivid description given by Didron in his edition of the painters' handbook from Mt Athos (*Das Handbuch der Malerei vom Berge Athos,* edited by G. Schäfer, Trier 1855).

20 (p. 73) The process is accurately described in Cennino Cennini (*cf.* p. 337 note 3), chapter 67. The word

sinopia is, however, used by him only as a colour term and not in the wider sense of a preliminary drawing on the rough plaster.

21 (p. 73) *Cf.* R. Oertel, 'Wandmalerei und Zeichnung in Italien. Die Anfänge der Entwurfszeichnung und ihre monumentalen Vorstufen', in *Mitt. d. Kunsthistor. Inst. in Florenz* V, 1940, p. 217 ff. Also recently, U. Procacci, *Sinopie e affreschi*, Florence 1960 (with a catalogue of all the *sinopie* known until then).

22 (p. 73) See pp. 305 and 365, note 11. The progressive decay of many of the surviving Italian frescoes led to the removal of numerous wall-paintings in other places. During the process of detaching 14th and early 15th C. frescoes *sinopie* were often discovered, and in many cases also removed to safety.

23 (p. 73) The Italien terms are: *arriccio* or *arricciato,* and *intonaco.*

24 (p. 73) No blue dye was known that could withstand the carbonization that occurred when the fresco dried. Until the 15th C. the blue was therefore nearly always applied after the fresco was dry *(a secco)* in tempera. Except for a few traces, the blue on these parts is now lost, *e.g.* in Giotto's Padua frescoes (the cloaks of Christ and the Virgin). *Cf.* our *pl. VII.*

25 (p. 74) Our *pl. I* shows the division of the apse surface into sections of plaster, whose intersections cut across the figure of Christ below the knee. The blue ground is unevenly preserved in the different sections. The Italian term for these divisions, made necessary by the height of the scaffolding, is *pontata*. Sketched underdrawings for wall-paintings are already present in S. Salvatore in Brescia, *i.e.* in the Carolingian period. As the surfaces are not too large, these are true *sinopie*. Illustrations in Panazza, *cf.* p. 338 note 13.

26 (p. 74) Kleinschmidt *pl. 8.* Very sketchy underdrawings directly on the wall surface became visible when the picture of the *Creation* was lifted (according to a verbal report by P. Gerhard Ruf, Assisi). The brush-drawing of the head of the Creator (our *pl. 53*) was painted on an relatively thick plaster directly underneath the coloured layer, and is thus a preliminary drawing done *a fresco, i.e.,* an underpainting for the *a secco* execution in lime painting.

27 (p. 75) The fresco technique and the 'man-days' division connected with it were already known in classical times, *cf.* Tintori/Meiss *(cf.* note 28) pp. 6, 7, and *pl.* p. 4/5. A continuous tradition of this technique in wall-painting cannot be established; however, the Roman painters of the end of the 13th C. were familiar with the mosaic technique and they could easily have adapted it to the medium of wall-paintings.

28 (p. 75) L. Tintori and M. Meiss, *The Painting of the Life of St. Francis in Assisi, with Notes on the Arena Chapel,* New York 1962.

29 (p. 75) A few unimportant missing portions were plastered at an early stage. On the other hand in Cavallini's frescoes in S. Maria Donnaregina in Naples there were large areas, up to the time of the last restoration, where the paint had come away revealing the monumental underdrawings on the bottom layer. *Cf.* Oertel *op. cit. (cf.* note 21) *pls 17, 18.* On the basis of the technical findings of Tintori and Meiss, underdrawings on one of the unterneath layers of the St Francis Legend must also be assumed, although until now none have been found. Work on separate and often numerous sections presupposes the existence of a preliminary drawing of the entire composition on the wall. The number of man-days within the whole cycle varies between six *(The Prayer in San Damiano)* and as many as fifty-four *(The Death of St Francis)* – which indicates that painters with very different technical habits took part in the execution.

30 (p. 75) Toesca 1946 *(cf.* p. 346, note 1); see also *Studies in the History of Art Dedicated to William E. Suida,* London 1959, p. 21 ff.). He considers the ochre-coloured underdrawing to be the only one, and that the actual fresco-ground (fine plaster) was applied in a very thin layer on top of this drawing. This would be a very unusual technique, found nowhere else. The plaster sections that have since been revealed, and Cavallini's analogous technique, *(cf.* note 29) support the view that the *St Francis Legend* was painted in the two layer technique we have described.

31 (p. 75) For the Arena Chapel, *cf.* Tintori/Meiss *(cf.* note 28) p. 157 ff. and *pls 56–8.*

32 (p. 75) *Cf.* p. 107.

33 (p. 75) For the *St Martin sharing his Cloak* scene in Assisi see C. Brandi, 'Una sinopia di Simone Martini', in *Arte Antica e Moderna,* Nos 13–16, 1961, p. 17 ff. At the sinopia stage the painter already made a crucial alteration in his composition: the city gate was originally to be on the right side. Other alterations were made during the execution of the painting, the most striking being the postures and gestures of the beggar. Thus, in this case there could have been no definitive small-scale drawing preceding the work on the wall. For the monumental drawings found at Avignon see p. 212.

34 (p. 75) The wall-paintings of Corso di Buono in

Montelupo dated 1284 (see p. 55) were executed in a lime secco medium in the true medieval manner.

35 (p. 76) L. Venturi, 'La Navicella di Giotto', in *L'Arte* 25, 1922, p. 49 ff. W. Paeseler, 'Giotto's Navicella und ihr spätantikes Vorbild', in *Röm. Jahrb. f. Kunstgesch.* V, 1941, p. 49 ff., pls 85, 93. C. Virch, 'A page from Vasari's Book of Drawings', in *The Metropolitan Museum Art Bulletin* March 1961, p. 185 ff.

36 (p. 76) Many examples in B. Degenhart, 'Autonome Zeichnungen bei mittelalterlichen Künstlern', in *Münchener Jahrbuch der bildenden Künste*, 1950, p. 93 ff.

37 (p. 77) Cf. Oertel, 'Wandmalerei und Zeichnung' (cf. note 21); also H. Tietze and E. Tietze-Conrat, *The Drawings of the Venetian Painters in the 15th and 16th Centuries*, New York 1944, introduction. M. Meiss (Tintori/Meiss, *The Painting of the Life of St Francis in Assisi*, New York 1962, p. 20 ff.) has tried to prove that in the Trecento small-scale drawings were already used in the preparation of wall-paintings. He admits, however, that the examples he gives could be considered as drawings submitted to the patron. The earliest known drawing that can be regarded with some certainty as a preliminary sketch for a fresco is the drawing by Spinello Aretino of c. 1407 in the Pierpont Morgan Library, although this particular design was never actually executed (Oertel op. cit., p. 248 and pl. 11). But probably even in this case the main purpose of the drawing was to provide the patron with a specification, especially as the subject was a historical representation for which no iconographic precedent existed. The question of the role played by such drawings in the creative process is decisive; and yet for the Trecento it still remains open. However, the problem is gradually losing importance as a result of our increasing familiarity with monumental drawings, about which little was known until recently.

38 (p. 77) Cf. A. Romdahl 'Giotto und die Franziskus-legende in der Oberkirche in San Francesco in Assisi', in *Tidskrift för Konstvetenskab* XVIII, 1934/35, p. 33 ff. (Swedish with a German synopsis). Gnudi's attempt to separate the different groups appears to be the most convincing. Useful indications of the style of the individual collaborators in Tintori/Meiss op. cit. (cf. note 28).

39 (p. 78) The Master of St Cecilia, so-called after the altar-panel showing St Cecilia surrounded by scenes from her life, in the Uffizi in Florence, was a relatively independent contemporary of Giotto, whose work combines archaic features with a skilful treatment of colour (cf. his late work, the St Margaret Altar in S. Margherita a Montici near Florence). R. Offner, *A Corpus of Florentine Painting*, Section III, vol. 1, New York 1931; Brunetti/Sinibaldi Nos 117–120; Toesca, *Il Trecento*, p. 605 ff., with bibliography. For the Madonna in S. Giorgio alla Costa in Florence, which is sometimes attributed to him, see pp. 78, 81 and note 43. The style of the Master of St Cecilia is probably also discernible in the fragments of Old Testament scenes on the right wall of the nave of S. Cecilia in Rome. Cf. A. Parronchi, in *Rivista d'Arte* XXI, 1939, p. 193 ff. For the masters' activity in Assisi cf. A. Smart, in *The Burlington Magazine* CII, 1960, pp. 405 ff., 431 ff.

40 (p. 78) These were probably monumental drawings that Giotto executed on the prepared wall surface (the *arricciato*) prior to his departure from Assisi. It is, however, possible that in the *St Francis Legend* small-scale drawings were made before work was begun, as no iconographic models existed for many of the scenes. But these would have had a predominantly iconographic importance and would not be conclusive for the artistic solution. For the content of the legendary sequence cf. H. Schrade, *Franz von Assisi und Giotto*, Cologne 1964.

41 (p. 78) Cf. p. 68 and note 17. – For the question of dating cf. also J. White, 'The Date of the *The Legend of St Francis* at Assisi', in *The Burlington Magazine* 98, 1956, p. 344 ff.

42 (p. 78) Gnudi pls 64, 65. C. Mitchell, 'The Lateran Fresco of Boniface VIII', in *Journal of the Warburg and Courtauld Inst.* XIV, 1951, p. 1 ff. C. Brandi, 'The Restauration of the St. John Lateran Fresco', in *The Burlington Magazine* 94, 1952, p. 218; C. Brandi, 'Giotto ricuperato a San Giovanni Laterano, in *Scritti di storia dell'arte in onore di Lionello Venturi* I, Rome 1956, p. 55 ff. It is not certain whether the fresco, by portraying the pope, is intended to represent the proclamation of the church jubilee, which only occurred on 22 February 1300. From the form of the papal crown the fresco must, however, have been completed in 1301 at the latest.

43 (p. 78) Brunetti/Sinibaldi No. 109 ('Giotto school'). Ghiberti p. 36 mentions 'una tauola' and a crucifix by Giotto in S. Giorgo. Published as a work of the Master of St Cecilia by R. Offner, in *The Burlington Magazine* 50, 1927, p. 91 ff. Attributed to Giotto by R. Oertel, in *Zschr. f. Kunstgesch.* VI, 1937, p. 233 ff.; also by R. Longhi, in *Proporzioni* II, 1948, p. 19. R. Offner later modified his original opinion and

attributed the panel to a supposed 'Master of the Santa-Maria-Novella Crucifix' (Offner, *Corpus*, sec. III, vol. IV, p. 3 *ff.*).

44 (p. 81) *Cf.* the reconstruction in Offner, *Corpus*, sec. III, vol. IV *pl.* Ia.

45 (p. 81) Gnudi, *pls* XVII, *68a–71.* U. Procacci, 'La tavola di Giotto dell'altar maggiore della chiesa della Badia fiorentina', in *Scritti di storia dell'arte in onore di Mario Salmi* II, Rome 1962, p. 9 *ff.* Although the high altar was consecrated only in 1310, the retable was probably executed shortly after 1300; stylistically it belongs to the period 'between Assisi and Padua' (Procacci). Analysis of the extremely well-proportioned frame supports the early dating, *cf.* M. Cämmerer-George, *Die Rahmung der toskanischen Altarbilder im Trecento,* Strasbourg 1966, p. 50 *ff.*

46 (p. 81) Gnudi, *pls* 153–5 and *pl.* L. M. Bonicatti, *Trecentisti riminesi,* Rome 1963, *pls 22–5,* text pp. 26, 27.

47 (p. 82) F. Zeri ,'La cimasa del Crocefisso del Tempio Malatestiano', in *Paragone* VIII, 1957 (No. 85), p. 79 *ff.* The fragment is in London, Lady Jekyll collection.

48 (p. 82) The Rimini Crucifix was attributed to Giotto by H. Beenken (in *Zeitschr. f. Kunstgesch.* V, 1936, pp. 197, 198). and L Coletti (in *Bollettino d'Arte* XXX, 1937, p. 350). L. Coletti in *I Primitivi,* I, Novara 1941, pp. LIII, LIV, dates the crucifix in the period of the Padua frescoes, before the fresco of the *Crucifixion,* one of the last to be painted in the Arena Chapel. It might be added that the panel-painting showing God the Father Enthroned, covering the opening to the rafters on the triumphal-arch wall of the Arena Chapel, also belongs to a more mature stage of development than the Rimini Crucifix (photo: Museo Civico, Padua, No. 2447). G. Sinibaldi (in *Zeitschr. f. Kunstgesch.* X, 1941/2, p. 289) rejects the attribution of the Rimini Crucifix to Giotto. Our own earlier rejection of Giotto's authorship of the Crucifix (in *Zeitschr. f. Kunstgesch.* VI, 1937, p. 232,

233) can no longer be sustained. For the early dating *cf.* note 50.

49 (p. 82) For the *Chronicle of Riccobaldo ('Compilatio cronologica') cf.* note 5. The passage about Giotto was, according to Gnudi (p. 243), written in 1312/13, and certainly not later than the beginning of 1314. *Cf.* also Gnudi, 'Il passo di Riccobaldo Ferrarese relativo a Giotto e il problema della sua autenticità', in *Studies in the History of Art Dedicated to William E. Suida,* London 1959, p. 26 *ff.*

50 (p. 82) Gnudi (p. 193) dates Giotto's stay in Rimini *c.* 1312/13, and the Crucifix 'between *c.* 1312/13 and *c.* 1316/17', and points out the great disparity between the conception of the theme in Rimini and that of the crucifix of S. Maria Novella. Giotto probably moderated the bold realism of his youthful work to achieve a solemn monumental restraint of style and expression. But this also applies, *mutatis mutandis,* to the Badia polyptych, and is entirely in keeping with Giotto's developemnt 'between Assisi and Padua'. The ornamentation of the Rimini Crucifix is still very much like that of the Madonna panel from S. Giorgio, and thus belongs to the same stylistic stage as the *St Francis Legend.* The figure of Christ in Rimini is very closely connected in its essential features with the earlier crucifix: in the three-quarter profile of the head, which in Padua is turned more to the side, and in the shading of the face, which gives both works their solemn mood; furthermore in the position of the hands, which is quite different in Padua, both in the Crucifix fresco and in the crucifix panel. The same is true of the modelling of the legs in large shaded areas, and of the treatment of the torso which, although stylized in Rimini, is still comparable in structure with the earlier work.

51 (p. 82) D. Gioseffi, 'Lo svolgimento del linguaccio Giottesco da Assisi a Padova: il soggiorno Riminese e la componente Ravennate', in *Arte Veneta* XV, 1961, p. 11 *ff.*

52 (p. 82) *Cf.* p. 311 *ff.*

7 Giotto and his pupils

1 (p. 83) It is thanks to Pietro Estense Selvatico that the Arena Chapel was saved from demolition (*cf.* his book, *Sulla Cappellina degli Scrovegni nell'Arena di Padova e sui freschi di Giotto in essa dipinti,* Padua 1836). Selvatico was also responsible for the fact that the frescoes were restored and preserved on strict scientific principles, without any pictorial retouching. Probably for the first time in the history of the care and maintenance of monuments, photographs (by Naya, Venice 1869) were used as a method of control; *cf.* P. E. Selvatico, *Sulle riparazioni dei celebri affreschi di Giotto detti dell'Arena in Padova,* Pisa 1870. Also, more recently: A. Prosdocimi, 'Il Comune di Padova e la Cappella degli Scrovegni nell'Ottocento/Acquisto e restauri agli affreschi', in *Bollettino del Museo Civico di Padova* XLIX, 1960, pp. 1–225; also Prosdocimi, 'Restauri alla parete di facciata della Cappella degli Scrovegni', *ditto,* XLVI–XLVII, 1957–58, pp. 720. G. Fabbri Colabich / A. Prosdocimi / G. Saccomani, *I recenti lavori di restauro alla Cappella degli Scrovegni, 1961–63,* Padua 1964.

The frescoes of the Arena Chapel are in fact still almost untouched by restoration. Only a few unimportant blemishes, mainly in the ornamental parts of the triumphal arch, have been mildly retouched. The blue grounds are also in the original colour. Only the absence of a large part of the perishable tempera, done *a secco,* is noticeable, and confuses the spectator who lacks technical experience. The allegations of bad preservation and overpainting that are found in the Giotto literature since Rumohr (*Ital. Forschungen* II, 1829) are incorrect.

2 (p. 83) Astrological representations in the Salone in Padua (*cf.* G. F. Hartlaub, 'Giotto's zweites Hauptwerk in Padua', in *Zschr. f. Kunstwissenschaft* IV, 1950, p. 19 *ff.*). Representations of the Nine Heroes in Castel Nuovo in Naples, *cf.* pp. 101 *ff.* and probably also in Azzo Visconti's palace in Milan (Salvini 135) *cf.* p. 102.

3 (p. 73) The donor was Enrico Scrovegni, whose palace stood on the grounds of the classical Arena, not far from the Oratory. As early as 9 January 1305 the monks of the neighbouring Eremitani monastery lodged a complaint with the bishop against the extravagance of the chapel's decoration and especially against the installation of bells (O. Ronchi, 'Un documento inedito del 9 gennaio 1305 intorno alla Cappella degli Scrovegni', in *Memorie della R.a Accad. di Scienze, Lettere ed Arti in Padova* 52, 1935/36). On 25 March 1305, the chapel was dedicated to the Virgin Annunciate. A portrait of the donor is included in the lower part of the Last Judgment fresco. For the dating of the frescoes *cf.* Gnudi p. 243 *ff.* and D. Gioseffi, *Giotto architetto,* Milan 1963, pp. 34 *ff.,* 114 *ff.*; Gioseffi argues convincingly that the design of the chapel itself was also by Giotto. Some of the compositions in the Arena Chapel, including the last scenes to be painted, served as models for the miniatures in a sixvolume antiphonary in the cathedral library in Padua. Existing payment vouchers reveal that the first three volumes were probably already completed in 1306, and the remainder possibly shortly afterwards. *Cf.* M. Walcher Casotti, *Miniature e miniatori a Venezia nella prima metà del XIV secolo,* Trieste 1962, p. 31, *pl, 38;* also Gioseffi *op. cit.,* pp. 117, 118, *pls* VI, VII.

4 (p. 84) H. Jantzen, 'Die zeitliche Abfolge der Paduaner Fresken Giottos', in *Jahrb. d. Preuss. Kunstsamml.* 60, 1939, p. 187 *ff.*

5 (p. 85) In 1937 the crucifix was temporarily set up again on a reconstructed beam beneath the choir arch in the Arena Chapel. The effect was one of impressive beauty and convinced everyone that this was also Giotto's original solution. It is to be regretted that the crucifix was recently transferred to the Museo Civico. The crucifix was probably painted at the same time as the last frescoes in the main room of the chapel. We do not accept the late dating (*c.* 1317) suggested by R. Longhi, and recently also by Gnudi (p. 188 *ff.*).

6 (p. 86) *Cf.* however D. Gioseffi, *Perspectiva artificialis,* Trieste 1957, in which an attempt is made to show that constructions with an accurate vanishing point were already used in classical wall-painting; but it seems that this applies only to small sections and not to paintings covering a whole wall. For a full discussion and especially for the development of perspective in Italian painting of the 13th and 14th C., *cf.* J. White, *The Birth and Rebirth of Pictorial Space,* London 1957.

7 (p. 86) Gnudi *pls 130/131.* For the illusionistic elements in Giotto *cf.* R. Oertel, in *Zschr. f. Kunstgesch.* XI, 1943/44, p. 16 *ff.* R. Longhi, 'Giotto spazioso', in *Paragone* III, 1952 (No. 31), p. 18 *ff.* D. Gioseffi, *Giotto architetto,* Milan 1963, p. 53, *pls 52, 53.* U. Schlegel ('Zum Bildprogramm der Arenakapelle', in *Zschr. f.*

Kunstgesch. XX, 1957, p. 135 *ff.*) would like to interpret the two mock galleries as burial rooms, dedicated
to the memory of the donor Enrico Scrovegni and his
father Rinaldo, thus the balustrades demarcating the
front of the painted rooms would be painted cenotaphs.
But there is no reliable evidence for such an assumption. The lights on the vaults of the painted rooms
could be regarded as funerary lights, if they appeared
in conjunction with other sepulchral motifs. However,
this is not so: the supposed cenotaphs are nothing
but balustrades (*cf.* Longhi *op. cit.*: 'due vani gotici . . .
riparati da un *parapetto* a lastra rettangolare.'). As
balustrades their size is in scale with the figures in the
adjoining frescoes. Giotto was, however, careful not
to paint figures in these galleries and on the whole
did not attempt to define the rooms more specifically.
If the crucifix panel was originally fastened in the
choir arch as a triumphal cross (*cf.* note 5), its place
would have been exactly between the two galleries
and this would explain the strange emptiness of the
galleries. Their artistic function would then have
been to accentuate the crucifix and bring it into harmony
with the room as a whole.

8 (p. 86) H. Jantzen, 'Giotto und der gotische Stil',
in *Das Werk des Künstlers* I, 1939/40, p. 441 *ff.*

9 (p. 89) *Purg.* XI, 94–96. Also Benkard, *Cimabue* (*cf.*
p. 345 note 16); P. L. Rambaldi, 'Dante e Giotto nella
letteratura artistica sino al Vasari', in *Rivista d'Arte* XIX,
1937, p. 286 *ff.*

10 (p. 89) *Cf.* pp. 100–102 and notes 38, 45. Vasari also
mentions Verona, Ferrara, Urbino, Arezzo and Lucca
as places where Giotto worked. Altogether a picture
emerges of indefatigable activity covering almost
the whole of Italy, and of unusual business ability.
For Giotto as a business man *cf.* R. Davidsohn, *Geschichte von Florenz* IV, part 3, Berlin 1927, p. 233,
and F. Antal, *Florentine Painting and its Social Background,* London 1947, p. 160 *ff.*

11 (p. 89) *Cf.* P. L. Rambaldi, 'Vignone', in *Rivista d'Arte*
XIX, 1937, p. 357.

12 (p. 89) For the Italian artists in Avignon *cf.* Toesca,
p. 542 *ff.*, with bibliography. It appears that even
before the Curia moved to Avignon a pupil of Cavallini
was summoned to the South of France, and some
frescoes of high quality by his hand are preserved in
the cathedral of Béziers (M. Meiss, 'Fresques italiennes
cavallinesques et autres, à Béziers', in *Gazette des
Beaux-Arts* 79, 1937, p. 275 *ff.*). E. Castelnuovo,
'Avignone rievocata', in *Paragone* X, 1959 (No. 119),
p. 28 *ff.*

13 (p. 89) Salvini Nos. 9, 10, 11.

14 (p. 89) Salvini No. 4.

15 (p. 90) Gnudi *pls 141–4,* and colour *pls* XLVI, XLVII.
L. Marcucci, *Gallerie Nazionali di Firenze | I dipinti
toscani del secolo XIV,* Rome 1965, No. 1, p. 11 *ff.*
(with bibliography). The frame of the picture is
original, *cf.* the careful examination and analysis
by M. Cämmerer-George, *Die Rahmung der toskanischen Altarbilder im Trecento,* Strasbourg 1966, p.
31 *ff.*

16 (p. 90) *Summa theologica* I, 39, 8. A. Dyroff, 'Zur allge-
meinen Kunstlehre des hl. Thomas', in *Festgabe zum
70. Geburtstag Clemens Baeumkers (Beitr. z. Gesch. d.
Philosophie d. Mittelalters,* Suppl. vol. II), Münster
1923, p. 197 *ff.* M. Grabmann, *Thomas von Aquin,*
Munich 1935, p. 186 *ff.*

17 (p. 93) For the Benediction fresco in the Lateran *cf.*
p. 78. For the Navicella mosaic: L. Venturi, W. Paeseler
op. cit. (see p. 351, note 35); also W. Körte, 'Die
Navicella des Giotto', in *Festschr. f. Wilhelm Pinder,*
Leipzig 1938, p. 223 *ff.* The angel medallion from the
frame of the Navicella in Boville Ernica (Brunetti/
Sinibaldi No. 97) must be treated with extreme
caution for purposes of stylistic analysis, on account of
its present condition; *cf.* the illustration prior to the
touching-up in A. Muñoz, 'I restauri della Navicella
di Giotto etc.', in *Bollettino d'Arte* 1924/25, p. 433 *ff.*
The second angel medallion in the Grottos of the
Vatican, Rome (Gnudi *pl. 145c*) is in better condition.
The mosaic was probably done *c.* 1310, as Paeseler
correctly realized.

18 (p. 93) O. Sirén, *Giotto and some of his Followers,*
2 vols, Cambridge 1917, *pls 62, 63.* C. Weigelt, *Giotto
(Klassiker der Kunst),* Stuttgart 1925, *pl. 184.* Gnudi,
pl. 66.

19 (p. 93) Brunetti/Sinibaldi No. 107. The date 'February
1327' (*stile fiorentino*) is the date of the marble tomb
of the Baroncelli family on the right of the entrance
arch of the chapel; *cf.* p. 188 and note 69. Recently
F. Zeri discovered the gable of the centre panel of
the Baroncelli Altar, showing God the Father adored
by angels (in *Paragone* VIII, 1957, No. 85, p. 75 *ff.*),
now in the museum in San Diego (Calif.); Gnudi, *pl.
176.*

20 (p. 94) Brunetti/Sinibaldi No. 108.

21 (p. 97) C. Brandi, *Duccio,* Florence 1951, p. 84.

22 (p. 97) *Cf.* the complaints of a patron in Perugia in
1451 that Fra Filippo Lippi had not himself executed
the commissioned picture (W. Bombe, in *Repertorium
für Kunstwiss.,* 34, 1911, p. 115 *ff.*)

23 (p. 97) L. Fumi, *Il Duomo di Orvieto*, Rome 1891, pp. 398, 407.

24 (p. 97) *Cf.* however W. and E. Paatz, *Die Kirchen von Florenz* I, Frankfurt 1940, p. 559, on the Baroncelli Altar: 'Despite all the objections the composition must be considered as Giotto's, and regarded as the most important point of departure of his late style.'

25 (p. 98) A double-sided triptych, restored in 1950, which has not yet been adequately photographed or fully illustrated anywere. It was donated by Cardinal Stefaneschi, probably for the high-altar of Old St Peter's (according to Grimaldi, around 1320). L. Venturi, 'La data dell'attività romana di Giotto', in *L'Arte* 21, 1918 p. 229; for the history of the work see also W. F. Volbach, in *Orientalia Christiana periodica* XIII, 1947, p. 369*ff.* (disputing the view that the triptych is identical with the high-altar panel). M. Gosebruch (in *Miscellanea Bibliothecae Hertzianae*, Munich 1961, p. 104*ff.*) attempts to prove that also in the artistic sense the altarpiece can be regarded as an authentic work of Giotto's. But we are unable to recognize Giotto's personal style in the type of figures, the style, or the structure of the composition. In our view the very ingenious legendary scenes flanking the Enthroned Christ reveal the conceptions of a younger generation, *i.e.* a Giotto pupil of the type of the Master of the Bardi Chapel (*cf.* p. 110*ff.*). The original rich architectonic frame of the triptych, unfortunatley almost completely lost, can be reconstructed with the help of the model held by the donor in the centre picture on the back (Gosebruch *op. cit.*, *pl. 73*). For the framing and original arrangement of the altarpiece *cf.* M. Cämmerer-George, *Die Rahmung der toskanischen Altarbilder im Trecento*, Strasbourg 1966, p. 121*ff.*, according to which the relatively small size of the triptych is not surprising as it did not stand freely in the choir of St. Peter's but beneath a Gothic tabernacle above the 'Confessio', which itself was enclosed in the so-called *pergula* supported by 12 twisted, marble columns covered with tendrils of a vine. *Cf.* Schüller-Piroli, *2000 Jahre Sankt Peter*, Olten 1950, pp. 228, 229, *pls 76 (pergula), 397, 398, 256* (tabernacle).

26 (p. 98) Brunetti/Sinibaldi No. 111.

27 (p. 98) Brunetti/Sinibaldi No. 100.

28 (p. 98) Gnudi *pls 164/165.*

28 (p. 98) Gnudi *pls 164/165.*

29 (p. 98) St Lawrence and St John the Evangelist in Châalis: R. Longhi, in *Dedalo* XI, 1930/31, p. 285. Gnudi, *pls 166/167.* M. Cämmerer-George, *op. cit.* (*cf.* note 25), p. 71*ff.*, points out certain differences

in scale, which seem to preclude the possibility that all four panels belong together.

30 (p. 98) *Last Supper, Crucifixion with St Francis and Two Donors, Christ in Purgatory.* Alte Pinakothek, Munich (Brunetti/Sinibaldi No. 104). *Adoration of the Kings*: Metropolitan Museum, New York (Brunetti/Sinibaldi No. 105). *Presentation in the Temple*: Isabella Stewart Gardner Museum, Boston. *Entombment*: Villa I Tatti, Settignano (Brunetti/Sinibaldi No. 106). *Pentecost*: National Gallery, London (T. Borenius, in *The Burlington Magazine* 81, 1942, p. 277). Gnudi, *pls 160 to 163c.*

31 (p. 99) Ghiberti p. 36. Good illustration (details) in Brunetti/Sinibaldi No. 102.

32 (p. 99) The 19th C. overpainting has recently been removed, and important, through faint remnants of the original have come to light. A. Graziani, in *Proporzioni* I, 1943, p. 65*ff.* has ascribed the fresco of the *Assumption*, rightly, in our view, to the 'Master of Figline' (= Master of the Fogg Pietà) and dated it *c.* 1320. Offner, *Corpus*, sec. III, vol. VI, *pls* XXXI, XXXII.

33 (p. 99) G. Marchini, 'Gli affreschi perduti di Giotto in una cappella di S. Croce', in *Rivista d'Arte* XX, 1938, p. 215*ff.*

34 (p. 99) As the perspective in the Berlin version of the *Death of the Virgin* is from the left, the fresco must have been on the left wall of the chapel (the viewpoint is the entrance to the chapel).

35 (p. 100) The common source is probably Byzantine, *cf.* also the miniature in the *Berthold-Missale* from Weingarten (New York), in Hanns Swarzenski, *Vorgotische Miniaturen*, 1927, *pl.* 65.

36 (p. 100) Also called the 'Maestro delle Vele' because of the extensive, sailshaped vaults on which his frescoes are painted. Kleinschmidt p. 177*ff.*; Toesca, *Trecento*, p. 612*ff.*

37 (p. 100) The St Nicholas Chapel was already dated by Kleinschmidt (vol. II, pp. 174, 175) to the first decade of the 14th C. (1306 or shortly after). According to M. Meiss, *Giotto und Assisi*, 1960, pp. 3, 4, Giuliano da Rimini copied a figure from the St Nicholas Chapel in his retable, in Boston, dated 1307; and the 'Master of Cesi' used other motifs for his retable of 1308. This must have been so if we exclude the assumption that the models (for the St Nicholas Chapel as well) were in Rimini itself, *i.e.* in the works that Giotto presumably painted there before 1305 (*cf.* pp. 81-2); in this case the Master of the St Nicholas Chapel must have been one of Giotto's collaborators in the Rimini

355

38 (p. 101) The documents are reproduced in O. Morisani, *Pittura del Trecento in Napoli*, Naples 1947, p. 140*ff.*

39 (p. 101) M. Salmi, 'Maso di Banco a Napoli', in *Atti dell'Accademia Fiorentina di Scienze Morali la Colombaria* XI, 1947, p. 415*ff.* Morisani *op. cit.* (*cf.* note 38) p. 63*ff.*, *pls 81–92.*

40 (p. 101) *Cf.* p. 357 note 68.

41 (p. 102) Originally the chapel was not vaulted. With its open rafters it must have approximated the transept of Santa Croce in Florence.

42 (p. 102) Morisani (*cf.* note 38) *pls 93, 94;* the fragments have since been removed.

43 (p. 102) W. Paatz, 'Die Gestalt Giottos im Spiegel einer zeitgenössischen Urkunde', in *Festschrift für C. G. Heise*, Berlin 1950, p. 85*ff.* D. Gioseffi, *Giotto architetto*, Milan 1963.

44 (p. 102) W. Braunfels, 'Giottos Campanile', in *Das Münster* I, 1948, p. 193*ff.* See also p. 186.

45 (p. 102) Salvini Nos 6, 135.

46 (p. 102) Milanesi, in *Vasari* I, p. 419, already realized that the frescoes could not have been done by Giotto. The donor, Fidesmino da Varano, was *Podestà* of Florence in the second half of 1337. F. Rossi, 'Relazione dei lavori eseguiti nella cappella giottesca del Palazzo del Podestà', in *Rivista d'Arte* XIX, 1937, p. 390*ff.*

47 (p. 103) Salvini Nos 19, 25b, 26. Milanesi, in *Vasari* I, pp. 415/16.

48 (p. 103) For the history of the alleged 'rediscovery', *cf.* P. L. Rambaldi, in *Rivista d'Arte* XIX, 1937, p. 286*ff.*

49 (p. 103) Ghiberti p. 36.

50 (p. 104) W. and E. Paatz, *Die Kirchen von Florenz* I, p. 600 and note 597.

51 (p. 104) The Bardi Chapel was restored in 1957/8, and the Peruzzi Chapel in 1958–63. Earlier investigation and protective work were done in 1937 (*cf.* U. Procacci, *Rivista d'Arte* XIX, 1937, p. 377*ff.*), in the course of which the *Stigmatization* scene above the entrance arch was thoroughly cleaned. For restoration of the Peruzzi Chapel, L. Tintori and E. Borsook, *Giotto/La Cappella Peruzzi*, Turin 1965 (detailed documentation, many illustrations).

52 (p. 104) In the Bardi Chapel the restorer, Gaetano Bianchi, completely redesigned the figure of St Louis of France on the window wall; *cf.* C. Guasti, *Gli affreschi di Giotto nella cappella de' Bardi in Santa Croce*, Florence 1853, p. 35 (Salvini Nos 227, 238). This painting was removed in 1957/8 without any traces of an earlier figure being found underneath. Louis of Toulouse, on the other hand, although damaged, is the original figure. The date of his canonization, 1317, is the earliest date the fresco could have been painted.

53 (p. 107) From the holes found in connection with these dividing lines it can be inferred that we are dealing with *pontate*, *i.e.* sections of scaffolding. The holes made for the poles of the scaffolding were sealed up and painted when the work was completed. As the heads of the figures and the critical upper parts of the architectural decoration were on the top level of the plaster, the composition as a whole was determined by this top level. In most of the scenes (with the exception of the lunette picture of *St John on the Island of Patmos*) the composition had only to be continued on the lower levels along the lines of the painting above. No preliminary drawings were found on the wall surfaces beneath the plaster, and we therefore should assume that small-scale preparatory drawings existed. This, however, did not prevent alterations being made during the execution, as an extensive pentiment found in the upper part of the *Assumption of St John* proves (Tintori/Borsook *op. cit.* p. 15, *pls 35, 37*).

54 (p. 107) R. Oertel, 'Die nachpaduanischen Werke Giottos', lecture at the second German congress of art historians in Nymphenburg 1949; report in *Kunstchronik* II, 1949, p. 216*ff.*

55 (p. 111) The bearded Oriental looking to the front and wearing a fiery yellow-ochre cloak; the cloak of the figure beside him looking to the left is preserved only in the underdrawing (reddish-brown, probably the base for blue).

56 (p. 111) O. Sirén *op. cit.* (*cf.* p. 354, note 18), *pls 109, 110.* A. Chiappelli, in *Dedalo* X, 1929/30, p. 199*ff.* R. Oertel, in *Mitt. d. Kunsthistor. Inst. in Florenz* V, 1940, p. 233*ff.*

57 (p. 111) Kleinschmidt p. 128, after Bonaventura. Antonius preaches on the text of the caption on the cross: 'Jesus of Nazareth, King of the Jews', and hence St Francis stands with his arms outstretched, a posture made much more impressive in Assisi by the intersecting door posts. In the Bardi Chapel the stress is on the Benediction and the Stigmata.

58 (p. 112) The similar type of head: narrow with straight high forehead, negligible protrusion of the back of the head, and sullen facial features, and other stylistic elements make it likely that the Baroncelli

Altar was painted by the same artist as the frescoes in the Bardi Chapel.

59 (p. 112) Fully reproduced in Gnudi, *pl. LIII.*

60 (p. 186) Shortly afterwards there followed the commercial setbacks that eventually brought about the bankruptcy of the great Florentine houses, including the Bardi (A. Sapori, 'La crisi delle compagnie mercantili dei Bardi e dei Peruzzi', in *Bibl. Storica Toscana* II, Florence 1926).

61 (p. 186) *Cf.* p. 100*ff.* Only scanty records relating to the Peruzzi Chapel have survived, and they give no clue to the dating of the frescoes; *cf.* E. Borsook, 'Notizie su due cappelle in Santa Croce a Firenze', in *Rivista d'Arte* XXXVI, 1961/62, p. 89*ff.*

62 (p. 186) *Cf.* Ilse Falk, *Studien zu Andrea Pisano,* Hamburg 1940, who says rightly (p. 6) that Andrea can be called 'in the true sense Giotto's pupil.' According to E. Borsook (in Tintori/Borsook *op. cit.* pp. 10, 11), Andrea Pisano drew only from the scenes on the left wall of the Peruzzi Chapel (the life of St John the Baptist); Falk therefore thinks it possible that the pictures on the right wall were painted after 1330. However, in our opinion this is not correct. The figure bending forward in the left group of the *Assumption of St John* was used by Andrea in his relief of the *Visit of the Disciples to the Prison* (Toesca, *Trecento, pl. 274*). Painting from the top downwards could have proceeded simultaneously on both walls, which is technically most probable.

63 (p. 186) We have no direct record, but in 1340 a 'magister Andrea' is named as *'maiore magister dicte opere'*, and he was probably Andrea Pisano. I. Falk, *op. cit. (cf.* note 62) p. 11.

64 (p. 186) According to Ghiberti (p. 37) Giotto designed and executed the first reliefs on the Campanile with his own hand. Ghiberti adds that he had himself seen Giotto's designs *(prouedimenti).* In the biography of Andrea Pisano (p. 43) Ghiberti again mentions the Campanile reliefs and adds: 'It is said that Giotto carved the first two reliefs.' Toesca, *Trecento,* p. 314*ff.*

65 (p. 187) Vasari-Milanesi I, p. 573.

66 (p. 188) Julie Gy.-Wilde, 'Giotto-Studien', in *Wiener Jahrb. f. Kunstgesch.* VII, 1930, p. 45*ff.*, esp. p. 52.

67 (p. 188) *Cf.* also W. Gross, *Die abendländische Architektur um 1300,* Stuttgart 1947, p. 210*ff.*

68 (p.188) According to Cennini (chap. I) Taddeo Gaddi was Giotto's godchild, and his pupil for 24 years, *i.e.* a more or less independent member of the workshop. He was probably born around 1300.

69 (p. 189) According to C. A. Isermeyer (*Rahmen-gliederung und Bildfolge in der Wandmalerei bei Giotto und den Florentiner Malern des 14. Jhs.,* Würzburg 1937, p. 48*ff.*) the payments extending from 1332 till 1338 refer to another chapel of the Baroncelli family, the St Martin Chapel adjoining the monks' choir, which was destroyed by Vasari in 1566. The only clue to the dating of the Gaddi frescoes is in the date 'February 1327' *(stile fiorentino)* on the tomb of the Baroncelli family in the entrance wall of the chapel. See also Paatz, *Die Kirchen von Florenz* I, pp. 556/57. For the destroyed St Martin Chapel adjoining the former monks' choir see Paatz *op. cit.,* p. 594; and E. Borsook, in *Rivista d'Arte* XXXVI, 1961/62, p. 89*ff.*

70 (p. 189) Unfortunately the figure of the twelve-year-old Mary half-way up the stairs is badly damaged *(cf.* our *pl. 73).* Joachim and Anna are standing on the left of the picture, and the High Priest is seen in much smaller scale at the entrance to the temple above.

71 (p. 189) The illusionistic niches in the base zone of the Baroncelli Chapel with painted liturgic vessels are examples of these bold experimental ventures. *Cf.* C. de Tolnay, 'Postilla sulle origini della natura morta moderna, in *Rivista d'Arte* XXXVI, 1961/62, p. 3 ff. (with illustration).

72 (p. 189) The theological virtues are shown twice, on the vault and in the window recesses. In the latter they are augmented by the addition of the monastic virtues to a total of fifteen half-lenght figures, in medallion-shaped frames, strongly foreshortened *(cf.* our *pl. 75a).* Evidently they too were executed for the most part by Taddeo Gaddi himself.

73 (p. 189) Cennini chap. IX.

74 (p. 191) I. Maioni, 'Fra Simone Fidati e Taddeo Gaddi', in *L'Arte* XVII, 1914, p. 107*ff.*

75 (p. 191) *Cf.* the vivid description in the story by Franco Sacchetti *(cf.* p. 240 and p. 364 note 1). Taddeo Gaddi died in 1366 or shortly before.

76 (p. 191) The *Last Supper,* on the rear wall of the refectory (recently restored), is the oldest surviving example of a 'Cenacolo' in the typical thematic and logical arrangement, and is probably derived from a lost model by Giotto himself. For the allegorical representation of the *Tree of St Bonaventure* above the *Last Supper, cf.* p. 311. By the addition of scenes from the Passion in about 1400, the *Crucifixion* in the sacristy became the centre-piece of an impressive 'picture wall' (Niccolò di Pietro Gerini, *cf.* p. 315).

77 (p. 191) Twenty-two quatrefoil pictures and the crowning lunette (with two scenes) are in the Florence

357

Accademia, two quatrefoils in Berlin-Dahlem, and two in Munich. Paatz, *Kirchen von Florenz* I, p. 598 *ff.*; Brunetti/Sinibaldi No. 137. For a reconstruction of the sacristy cupboard, *cf.* L. Marcucci, 'Per gli *armarj* della sacrestia di Santa Croce', in *Mitt. des Kunsthist. Inst. in Florenz* IX, 1960, p. 141 *ff.*

78 (p. 192) The medallions on the vault of the crypt of San Miniato al Monte in Florence (*c.* 1341) are stylistically the closest parallels to the sacristy cupboard pictures. For the work of Taddeo Gaddi, *cf.* also R. Longhi, 'Qualità e industria in Taddeo Gaddi', in *Paragone* X, 1959, No. 109, p. 31 *ff.*, and No. 111, p. 3 *ff.* For his late style *cf.* K. Steinweg, 'Zwei Predellentafeln des T. G.', in *Mitt. des Kunsthist. Inst. in Florenz* XI, 1964, p. 194 *ff.* Further contributions: G. Gandolfo, 'Per Taddeo Gaddi, storia del problema critico', in *Critica d'Arte*, 1956, p. 32 *ff.*; P. P. Donati, *Taddeo Gaddi*, Florence 1966.

79 (p. 192) *Cf.* Offner, *Corpus* sec. III, vols III, IV, V, VIII. Brunetti/Sinibaldi Nos 154–77.

80 (p. 192) Bigallo triptych by Bernardo Daddi: Brunetti/Sinibaldi No. 155. A free copy by Taddeo Gaddi in Berlin-Dahlem, Gemäldegalerie: Brunetti/Sinibaldi No. 138.

81 (p. 193) For Maso di Banco in Naples, *cf.* note 39. For the frescoes in S. Croce: P. Toesca, 'Gli affreschi della cappella di S. Silvestro in S. Croce', in *Artis Monumenta photographice edita* II, Florence 1944. For Maso's panel-paintings: R. Offner, in *The Burlington Magazine* 54, 1929, p. 224 *ff.* (four panels of a polyptych: a half-length Madonna figure, in Berlin-Dahlem, Gemäldegalerie; two saints, formerly also in Berlin, lost since 1945; St Anthony of Padua, formerly in the Griggs collection, now in the Metropolitan Museum, New York, Brunetti/Sinibaldi Nos 151, 152). Another five-panelled polyptych is in Santo Spirito in Florence (Brunetti/Sinibaldi No. 150). For Maso's influence on contemporary Florentine painting *cf.* also R. Longhi, 'Qualità e industria in Taddeo Gaddi' (*cf.* note 78).

8 Duccio

1 (p. 195) See p. 44 *ff.* C. Brandi, *Duccio*, Florence 1951. E. Carli, *Duccio*, Florence/Milan 1952.

2 (p. 195) Ghiberti p. 43: 'tenne la maniera greca'.

3 (p. 196) See p. 57 and 347, notes 22, 23.

4 (p. 196) E. Carli, *Vetrata duccesca*, Florence 1946; C. Brandi, *Duccio*, Florence 1951, pp. 24 *ff.*, 136, 137.

5 (p. 196) Attribution by Toesca in *L'Arte* 33, 1930, p. 5 *ff.*

6 (p. 197) For the contract for the *Maestà* see p. 97; even the bill for the musicians engaged to take part in the procession carrying the picture to the cathedral has been preserved (Brandi, *Duccio*, 1951, p. 87).

7 (p. 197) In 1506 the *Maestà* was removed from the high altar of the cathedral. Isolated parts are now dispersed in London, New York, and Washington. The part of the predella showing the *Nativity and Two Prophets* that was in the Kaiser-Friedrich Museum in Berlin was relinquished after 1933, and is now in the National Gallery in Washington.

8 (p. 197) SS. Ansanus, Savinus, Crescentius, and Victor. The same saints kneel in the same order in Simone Martini's *Maestà* (see p. 202; *pl. 78*).

9 (p. 198) Brandi, *Duccio*, 1951, *pl.* 49.

10 (p. 198) Brandi, *Duccio*, 1951, *pls. 40, 66–68*.

11 (p. 198) R. van Marle, *Recherches sur l'iconographie de Giotto et de Duccio*, Strasbourg 1920. V. Lasareff, 'Duccio and Thirteenth-century Greek Ikons', in *The Burlington Magazine* 59, 1931, p. 154 *ff.* D. Frey, 'Giotto und die Maniera Greca, Bildgesetzlichkeit und psychologische Deutung' in *Wallraf-Richartz-Jahrb.* XIV, 1952, p. 73 *ff.*

12 (p. 199) The *Maestà* was cleaned in 1953–7 with exceptional success, *cf.* C. Brandi (ed.), *Il restauro della 'Maestà' di Duccio*, Ministero Pubblica Istruzione, Istituto Centrale del Restauro, Rome 1959 (with many illustrations).

13 (p. 200) For Ugolino di Nerio, called Ugolino da Siena, *cf.* P. Bacci, *Dipinti inediti e sconosciuti di Pietro Lorenzetti, Bernardo Daddi ecc. in Siena e nel contado*, Siena 1939, chap. IV, p. 121 *ff.*; C. Brandi, *Duccio*, 1951, pp. 152, 153. Ugolino's major work was the high altar for S. Croce in Florence, probably done around 1321–25. Only some parts survive and these are dispersed in Berlin-Dahlem, London, and other places. *Cf.* G. Coor-Achenbach, 'Contributions to the Study of Ugolino di Nerio's Art', in *The Art Bulletin* 37, 1955, p. 153 *ff.*; for the reconstruction of the high altar, *cf.* M. Cämmerer-George, *Die Rahmung der toskanischen Altarbilder im Trecento*, Strasbourg 1966, pp. 149, 150, *pl.* XII. A seven-panelled polyptych (half-length figures of the Madonna and six saints) recently acquired by the Williamstown Museum (Mass.), *cf.* J. Pope-Hennessy, *Sterling and Francine Clark Art Institute, Heptaptych Ugolino da Siena*, Wil-

liamstown 1962. For Segna di Buonaventura, *cf.* C. Brandi, *Duccio,* 1951, p. 150*ff.* Segna's large *Maestà* in Castiglione Fiorentino is probably a repetition of a Maestà (now lost) painted by Duccio in 1302 for the Cappella dei Nove in the Palazzo Pubblico in Siena (*cf.* Brandi *op. cit.,* p. 141, note 23). The tradition of Segna's workshop was carried on by his son Niccolò di Segna, *cf.* P. Bacci, 'Identificazione e restauro della tavola del 1336 di Niccolò di Segna da Siena', in *Bollettino d'Arte* 29, 1935/36, p. 1*ff.*

14 (p. 200) van Marle, II p. 81*ff.* Brandi, *Duccio,* 1951, p. 148*ff.*

15 (p. 200) Brunetti/Sinibaldi No. 35. Brandi, *Duccio,*

1951, p. 142 note 25, *pls 113–115;* G. Coor-Achenbach, 'A Dispersed Polyptych by the Badia a Isola Master', in *The Art Bulletin* 34, 1952, p. 311*ff.;* also addenda *op. cit.* 38, 1956, p. 119. For bibliography see also the exhibition catalogue *Arte in Valdelsa dal sec. XII al sec. XVIII* (Certaldo 1963), Florence 1963, p. 17*ff.* The attempt to include the Madonna of Badia a Isola among Duccio's early works is, in our view, unconvincing (E. Carli, in *Duccio,* Milan/Florence 1952).

16 (p. 201) H. Keller, *Giovanni Pisano,* Vienna 1942, p. 11: 'Between 1270 and 1275 Giovanni Pisano must have been in France'.

9 Simone Martini

1 (p. 202) According to G. Mazzoni ('Influssi danteschi nella *Maestà* di Simone Martini', in *Arch. storico ital.* 94, 1936, p. 145*ff.*), the date mentioned in the inscribed verse means 'end of June 1316'. The working-over of the fresco in 1321 by Simone and his pupils affected only isolated parts. The composition as a whole was done in 1315/16. *Cf.* Toesca, *Trecento,* p. 522. For this and later works of the master *cf.* the monograph by G. Paccagnini, *Simone Martini,* Milan 1955; supplementing this, G. Gnudi, 'Grandezza di Simone', in *Scritti di storia dell'arte in onore di Lionello Venturi* I, Rome 1956, p. 87*ff.*

2 (p. 203) Attempts to detect Simone Martini's early works among those of Duccio's circle have so far been unsuccessful. G. H. Edgell, 'A Crucifixion by Duccio with Wings by Simone Martini', in *The Burlington Magazine* 88, 1946, p. 107*ff.* (triptych in Boston, Garrison No. 350). According to L. Coletti (in *The Art Quarterly* XII, 1949, p. 291*ff.*) the *Maestà* in the cathedral of Massa Marittima is an early work of Simone; *cf.* to the contrary, Brandi, *Duccio,* 1951, p. 151.

3 (p. 203) The exceptionally wide frame of the *Maestà* with medallions containing busts of saints is reminiscent of the frame of the Navicella mosaic in Rome with its angel medallions, *cf.* pl. 55 in Paeseler *op. cit.* (see p. 351, note 35); this is possibly an indication that Simone stayed in Rome before 1315, where he could have met Giotto, who must have worked in Rome around 1310/11. *Cf.* the document of 8 December 1313 (L. Chiappelli, in *L'Arte* 26, 1923, p. 132*ff.*), and Paeseler *op. cit.* p. 62/63.

4 (p. 204) The only surviving document is a payment voucher from the year 1317 'pro Symone Martini milite': Morisani *op. cit.* (*cf.* p. 356, note 38) p. 134. King Robert knighted the painter, the first known case of an artist being so honoured.

5 (p. 205) For the political significance of the portrait *cf.* H. Keller, 'Die Entstehung des Bildnisses am Ende des Hochmittelalters', in *Röm. Jahrb. f. Kunstgesch.* III, 1939, p. 320*ff.*; F. Antal (*cf.* p. 354, note 10) pp. 163 and 216 note 27.

6 (p. 204) A good illustration in M. Meiss, *Painting in Florence and Siena after the Black Death,* Princeton 1951, *pl. 133;* for the origins and development of the Madonna dell'Umiltà type see M. Meiss *op. cit.,* p. 132*ff.*

7 (p. 205) Berlin-Dahlem, Staatl. Gemäldegalerie, No. 1072 (as 'Lippo Memmi').

8 (p. 205) The Pisa polyptych is signed but not dated; the date of its installation, 1320, has been handed down in the records (Milanesi, in *Vasari* I, p. 554 note 2; L. Dami, 'Il polittico pisano di Simone Martini', in *Dedalo* III, 1922/23, p. 5*ff.*). According to Paccagnini *op. cit.* (*cf.* note 1) p. 108, the date is given in accordance with the Pisan custom, *i.e.* in fact 1319. An illustration of the altarpiece as reconstructed in 1949, *op. cit.* p. 106. Fragments of two polyptychs in Orvieto (Opera del Duomo) and of an analogous five-panelled polyptych also from Orvieto (now in Boston), and three panels of unknown provenance in Cambridge, are all of the middle or second half of the 1320s, *cf.* J. Pope-Hennessy, in *The Burlington Magazine* 91, 1949, p. 195*ff.*; the date

359

'MCCCXX...' on the polyptych in Orvieto is probably incomplete (Toesca, *Il Trecento,* p. 528, note 53). *Cf.* also K. Steinweg, 'Beiträge zu Simone Martini und seiner Werkstatt', in *Mitt. d. Kunsthistor. Institutes in Florenz* VII, 1953–56, p. 162 *ff.* (the Madonna illustrated on p. 161 is now in the Wallraf-Richartz-Museum in Cologne).

9 (p. 205) The date of these frescoes is disputed. There is no documentary evidence. The dating between 1322 and 1326 given by us first appears in A. Venturi, *Storia dell'arte italiana* V, p. 604; also van Marle II, p. 202. For the arrangement of the frescoes in the chapel see Borsook, *pls 16, 18, 20.*

10 (p. 206) Illustration in Keller *op. cit.* (*cf.* note 5), p. 333/34 (with detail of the head); Keller rightly stresses the characteristic features in the cardinal's portrait. *Cf.* also Borsook, *pls 18, 19.*

11 (p. 206) Early studies of this problem in A. Péter, 'Quand Simone Martini est-il venu en Avignon?', in *Gazette des Beaux-Arts* 1939 (March), p. 153 *ff.* *Cf.* R. Oertel, in *Zeitschr. f. Kunstgesch.* IX, 1940, p. 123.

12 (p. 209) Painted to commemorate the conquest of the castles of Montemassi and Sassoforte in 1328. The date beneath the fresco is the date of these events. The execution was probably slightly later, *cf.* P. Bacci, *Fonti e commenti per la storia dell'arte senese. Dipinti e sculture in Siena, nel suo contado ed altrove,* Siena 1944, p. 155 *ff.* (Also synopsis of the entire documentary material concerning Simone Martini.)

13 (p. 210) *Cf.* H. Keller *op. cit.* (*cf.* note 5) p. 324.

14 (p. 210) *Cf.* E. Carli, 'Difesa di un capolavoro' in *Domus,* No. 182; Carli, in *I capolavori dell'arte senese,* Florence 1947, pp. 23, 24; *pls 36–48.* Paccagnini *op. cit.* (*cf.* note 1), p. 50, dates the work, unconvincingly in our opinion, before the Assisi frescoes.

15 (p. 210) Painted for Siena Cathedral with the participation of Lippo Memmi, who probably did the two saints on the sides; *cf.* Bacci, *op. cit.* (*cf.* note 12) p. 163 *ff.* According to L. Marcucci, 'I dipinti toscani del secolo XIV' *(Cataloghi dei musei e gallerie d'Italia, Gallerie Nazionali di Firenze),* Rome 1965, p. 149 *ff.,* the part of the frame with the artist's signature is original, but the remaining parts of the frame are of the 19th C.

16 (p. 210) W. Pinder, *Die deutsche Plastik des 14. Jhs.,* Munich 1925, *pls 22, 23.*

17 (p. 211) The size of the panel is 48 × 35 cm. Van Marle II (p. 237) doubts that it represents the *Return from the Temple,* and thinks that the subject is an indefinite scene from the Childhood of Jesus. The inscription in the Virgin's book, however, clearly refers to Luke 2, 48: *Filii quid fecisti* [*nobis sic?*] – 'My son why have you done so to us?'

18 (p. 212) According to A. Péter, *op. cit.* (*cf.* note 11), Simone was still in Siena in October 1340, and thus could have come to Avignon at the earliest at the end of 1340.

19 (p. 212) G. de Nicola, 'L'affresco di Simone Martini ad Avignon', in *L'Arte* IX, 1906, p. 336 (with illustration of a 17th C. copy); illustration of the copy also in *Paragone* X, 1959, No. 119, *pl. 1.* Jacopo Stefaneschi was cardinal deacon of S. Giorgio at Velabro.

20 (p. 212) Published with many illustrations and comprehensive documentation by F. Enaud, 'Les fresques de Simone Martini à Avignon', in *Les Monuments Historiques de la France,* N. S. IX, 1963, p. 115 *ff.* Good illustration of the Madonna tympanum prior to its removal in M. Meiss (*cf.* note 6) *pl. 130.*

21 (p. 212) *Cf.* the illustration of the copy by Denuelle (1859) in F. Enaud *op. cit.,* p. 125.

22 (p. 213) Between the acanthus leaves there were six medallions with heads of angels, with the dove of the Holy Ghost, boldly foreshortened, at the apex of the arch; F. Enaud *op. cit., pls 122, 148, 149.* E. Castelnuovo, 'Avignone rievocata', in *Paragone* X, 1959, No. 119, *pls 3–5.*

23 (p. 213) The bipartite *Annunciation* picture, the *Crucifixion,* and the *Deposition* with a bishop as donor, in the Antwerp Museum; the *Road to Calvary,* in the Louvre in Paris; the *Entombment,* in the Staatl. Gemäldegalerie in Berlin-Dahlem. On the back of the *Road to Calvary* panel are the coats-of-arms of the Orsini family. The attempted early dating of the small altar by A. Péter (*cf.* note 11) and by G. Paccagnini (*cf.* note 1), pp. 40 *ff.,* 110 *ff.,* is not convincing; for a different opinion see C. Gnudi *op. cit.* p. 96 *ff.* F. Enaud *op. cit.* pp. 118, 173, note 11 (and further references) is undecided. For the question of the possible donor, Cardinal Napoleone Orsini, see M. Laclotte and P. Quarré.

24 (p. 213) *Cf.* p. 189. Illustration of the miniature in G. Ring, *A Century of French Painting,* London 1949, *pl. 2;* the *Road of Calvary* in A. Weese, 'Skulptur und Malerei in Frankreich im 15. u. 16. Jh.', in *Handbuch d. Kunstwiss.,* Wildpark-Potsdam 1927, *pl. 73.*

25 (p. 214) *Cf.* p. 337, note 1.

26 (p. 214) M. Dvořák, 'Das Rätsel der Kunst der Brüder van Eyck', in *Jahrb. d. Kunsthistor. Sammlungen d.*

Allerh. Kaiserhauses XXIV, Vienna 1903, pp. 161*ff.*, esp. 206*ff.*

27 (p. 214) Now in the Ambrosiana in Milan; van Marle II, p. 235, *pl. p. 236*; Toesca, *Trecento*, p. 815, *pl.* XIX; Paccagnini *op. cit.*, *pl. 41*. On the back of the sheet there is a distich apostrophizing Virgil and Simone Martini, which, according to Paccagnini (p. 169), was written by Petrarch's hand.

28 (p. 214) Salvini No. 9. Petrarca, *Rime* Nos 77, 78. For the Laura portrait H. Keller *op. cit.* (*cf.* note 5) p. 247.

29 (p. 214) Van Marle II, p. 277*ff.*; van Marle, Italian edition II, p. 292*ff.* (with further illustrations); Toesca, *Trecento*, pp. 546, 816; Marcucci *op. cit.* (*cf.* note 15) pp. 165, 166, with additional bibliography.

30 (p. 215) For Memmo di Filipuccio and the beginnings of Lippo Memmi, *cf.* E. Carli, 'Ancora dei Memmi a San Gimignano', in *Paragone* XIV, 1963, No. 159, p. 27*ff.*, with many illustrations; according to Carli (p. 38*ff.*) the large 'Madonna of Mercy' panel in Orvieto Cathedral, signed 'LIPPUS DE SENA', also belongs to Lippo's early works – soon after 1317.

31 (p. 215) Colour plate in R. Oertel, *Frühe italienische Malerei in Altenburg*, Berlin 1961, pp. 69, 70, *pls 6, 7*.

32 (p. 215) For Barna *cf.* A. M. Gabbrielli, 'Ancora del Barna, pittore delle storie del Nuovo Testamento nella Collegiata di S. Gimignano', in *Bullettino Senese di Storia Patria* N. S. VII, 1936, p. 113*ff.* J. Pope-Hennessy, 'Barna, the Pseudo-Barna and Giovanni d'Asciano' in *The Burlington Magazine* 88, 1946, p. 35*ff.* Further references in Toesca, *Trecento*, pp. 551, 554. Borsook, p. 138; *pls 31–4* (including 3 photographs of the frescoes in the Chapel); *pl. p. 139*.

33 (p. 216) E. Castelnuovo, 'Avignone rievocata', in *Paragone* X, 1959, No. 119, p. 28*ff.*; E. Castelnuovo, *Un pittore italiano alla corte di Avignone/Matteo Giovannetti e la pittura in Provenza nel sec. XIV*, Turin 1962.

34 (p. 216) R. Longhi, in *Arte Veneta* II, 1948, p. 41*ff.*; C. Volpe, 'Un'opera di Matteo Giovannetti', in *Paragone* X, 1959, No. 119, p. 63 *ff.*; E. Castelnuovo, *Un pittore italiano* (*cf.* note 33), *pls 69–75*.

35 (p. 217) E. Castelnuovo, *Un pittore italiano* (*cf.* note 33), *pls 119–121*. These are not *sinopie*, but preliminary brush-drawings that served as a direct base for the painting. The latter was evidently executed *a secco*, and is now largely lost.

10 Pietro and Ambrogio Lorenzetti

1 (p. 218) G. Sinibaldi, *I Lorenzetti*, Siena 1933. E. T. DeWald, *Pietro Lorenzetti*, Cambridge (Mass.) 1930; printed also as an essay, partly in greater detail, in *Art Studies* VII, 1929, p. 131*ff.* E. Cecchi, *Pietro Lorenzetti*, Milan 1930. For further references see following notes.

2 (p. 218) By the bishop of Arezzo, Guido Tarlati; *cf.* Milanesi, in *Vasari* (I), p. 475.

3 (p. 219) P. Bacci, *Dipinti inediti e sconosciuti di Pietro Lorenzetti, Bernardo Daddi ecc. in Siena e nel contado*, Siena 1939, p. 35*ff.*, also (p. 75*ff.*) all available records concerning Pietro, who can be traced from 1306 (?) until 1345. For the Carmelite Altar *cf.* C. Brandi, in *Bollettino d'Arte* 33, 1948, p. 68*ff.* (with 12 plates). For a reconstruction of the polyptych, based on the surviving predella, *cf.* M. Cämmerer-George, *Die Rahmung der toskanischen Altarbilder im Trecento*, Strasbourg 1966, p. 151, sketch 12.

4 (p. 220) Nos 79, 81, 82 (C. Brandi, *La Regia Pinacoteca di Siena*, Rome 1933, p. 144*ff.*).

5 (p. 221) Siena, Pinacoteca, Nos 83, 84 (Catalogue Brandi 1933, p. 147); Bacci *op. cit.* (*cf.* note 3) repro-duced the centre panel of the predella that was discovered beneath later over-painting.

6 (p. 221) Earlier scholars dated the Assisi frescoes mainly in Pietro's late period, and the Passion scenes on the vault were considered by most of them to be workshop products (including Toesca, in *Trecento*, p. 56*ff.*). C. Volpe, on the other hand, proposes a considerably earlier date, which basically agrees with our view (C. Volpe, 'Proposte per il problema di Pietro Lorenzetti', in *Paragone* II, 1951, No. 23, p. 13*ff.*); *cf.* also our note 10. Detailed account and illustrations of all these frescoes, in Kleinschmidt.

7 (p. 222) F. Horb (*Das Innenraumbild des späten Mittelalters*, Zürich and Leipzig, n.d.) p. 63*ff.*, shows that the motif of the hexagonal aedicula was derived from classical painting.

8 (p. 225) The representation of the thieves in the Crucifixion is already found in Early Christian art, and was also common in Duecento painting (frequently as subsidiary figures on the painted crucifixes). In Duccio's *Crucifixion* scene, on the reverse side of the *Maestà*, the thieves are specially emphasized. The

only novelty in Pietro Lorenzetti's representation is their monumental size and deep pathos, possibly inspired by Giovanni Pisano's pulpit-reliefs in Pistoia und Pisa.

9 (p. 226) The 'predella' with the crucifix and donor portrait proves that this fresco served as a retable. Cecchi (*cf.* note 1) *pls 31–35*. The parts done in tempera are now largely lost, *e.g.* the tunic of St John; the cowl of St Francis is probably only the underpainting (Kleinschmidt, *pl. 28*).

10 (p. 226) Compared with the Arezzo polyptych the Passion scenes reveal a diminution of the Giottesque elements. Pietro's personal style emerges more strongly, and the delight in narrative detail and decorative elements suppresses the original economy and severity of forms inspired by Giotto. We do not accept the view of C. Volpe (*cf.* note 6), who dates the frescoes on the vault even before the Arezzo altarpiece and divides Pietro's activity in Assisi into several periods relatively far apart in time.

11 (p. 227) Kleinschmidt II, *pl.* 211.

12 (p. 227) All the known records concerning Pietro Lorenzetti are collected by Bacci *op. cit.* (*cf.* note 3) p. 75*ff.* In 1324 a painter, Pietro, received payment of the painting of flag-poles. It is uncertain whether this refers to Pietro Lorenzetti, and such a minor commission could well have been executed by his workshop.

13 (p. 227) According to Toesca (*Trecento,* p. 612) the allegories were 'certainly painted after 1317, probably in the third decade', and the scenes of the Childhood of Jesus, in the right transept, directly afterwards. At the same time (probably between 1322 and 1326) Simone Martini was working on the frescoes in the St Martin Chapel (*cf.* p. 205*ff.*).

14 (p. 228) Illustrations in Bacci and Brandi (*cf.* note 3).

15 (p. 228) *Cf.* the attempted reconstruction by A. Péter, in 'Szépmüvészeti Múzeum' *(Jahrbücher d. Museums d. bild. Künste in Budapest)* VI, 1929/30, p. 52 (German p. 256*ff.*); discussed by G. Marchini, in *Rivista d'Arte* XX, 1938, p. 304*ff.*

16 (p. 228) According to Bacci *op. cit.* (*cf.* note 3) p. 90*ff.*, it was already begun at the end of 1335.

17 (p. 228) According to Ghiberti (p. 41) the first two frescoes, the *Birth of the Virgin* and her *Presentation in the Temple,* were by Ambrogio, and the last two scenes by Pietro. See also Marchini (*cf.* note 15); Péter thinks that all four scenes were designed by Ambrogio, and that Pietro participated only in the execution.

18 (p. 229) Two scenes of the Santa Umiltà legend in the Gemäldegalerie in Berlin-Dahlem. For dating see following note.

19 (p. 230) Toesca (*Trecento,* p. 556) prefers to place the Umiltà panel as well as the Uffizi Madonna at the beginning of Pietro Lorenzetti's career (between the Cortona Madonna and the Arezzo Altar). E. Carli, *La pittura senese,* Milan 1955, p. 84*ff.*, dates the Santa Umiltà panel 1316, and the Madonna with Angels 1340. In the dates MCCCXL and MCCCXLI the horizontal lines of the 'L's have peculiarly raised tips so that they can easily be confused with the Trecento stylized form of 'V'; hence the mistaken readings, 1315 and 1316. The date of the Madonna is original though damaged and possibly incomplete; according to an earlier tradition it was 1343. The inscription of the Umiltà panel is a mere copy, possibly taken from the original frame. L. Marcucci, in *I dipinti toscani del secolo XIV* (*cf.* p. 360 note 15), pp. 153*ff.*, 157*ff.*, has recently supported the late dating of both pictures. Accordingly, the Santa Umiltà panel might possibly have been commissioned as early as 1330–32, but only completed in 1341. For a history and reconstruction of the Umiltà panel, of which parts of the predella and crowning sections have also been preserved, see L. Marcucci, in *Arte antica e moderna* Nos 13–16 (*Studi di storia dell'arte/Raccolta di saggi dedicati a Roberto Longhi* . . .) 1961, p. 21*ff.*

20 (p. 230) G. Rowley, *Ambrogio Lorenzetti,* 2 vols, Princeton 1958 (a penetrating monograph, though it possibly goes too far in its effort to rid the master's *oeuvre* of untenable attributions). *Cf.* R. Offner, 'Reflexions on Ambrogio Lorenzetti', in *Gazette des Beaux-Arts* 56 (102), 1960, p. 235*ff.*

21 (p. 233) Ghiberti p. 42. Vasari I, p. 523. L. Marcucci *op. cit.* (*cf.* p. 360 note 15) p. 159*ff.* Cinelli (1677) still saw Ambrogio's signature and the date 1332. The Madonna panel was in the B. Berenson collection until 1959. G. Rowley, *op. cit.* (see previous note) doubts that this is the one mentioned by Cinelli, and attributes the three Uffizi panels to an artist he calls the 'Rofeno Master'.

22 (p. 233) A. Grunzweig ('Una nuova prova del soggiorno di Ambrogio Lorenzetti a Firenze intorno al 1320', in *Rivista d'Arte* XV, 1933, p. 249) mentions a record 'Ambruogii pictoris de Senis' – without the father's name! – of the year 1321; G. de Nicola, 'Il soggiorno fiorentino di A. L.', in *Bollettino d'Arte* 1922/ 23, II, p. 49*ff.* G. Rowley *op. cit.* (*cf.* note 20) p. 129. For the Vico l'Abate Madonna, see Brunetti/Sinibaldi No. 194 (with bibliography).

23 (p. 234) A. Péter ('Giotto and Ambrogio Lorenzetti', in *The Burlington Magazine* 76. 1940, p. 3 *ff*.) arrives at a date between 1324 and 1327. C. Volpe ('Ambrogio Lorenzetti e le congiunzioni fiorentine-senesi nel quarto decennio del Trecento', in *Paragone* I, 1951, No. 13, p. 40 *ff*.) on stylistic grounds accepts the traditional yet unsecured date of 1331. It is also uncertain whether these frescoes are connected with the fresco mentioned by Ghiberti on p. 40/41, which filled a whole wall in the cloister of San Francesco and represented scenes from the history of the Franciscan Order, evidently in continuous sequence. The two surviving frescoes were originally in the chapterhouse of S. Francesco, and were transferred from there to one of the choir chapels. G. Sinibaldi (*I Lorenzetti*, Siena 1933, p. 212 *ff*., with a bibliography) does not agree that these are identical with the 'storia' described by Ghiberti and consequently does not accept the connection with the date 1331. G. Rowley *op. cit.* (*cf.* note 20), pp. 85, 86, dates the two frescoes (too early in our opinion) c. 1325; *cf.* note 25 below. Many excellent illustrations in Rowley (vol. II *pls 104–120*).

24 (p. 234) Ambrogio's concept of space is similar to that which we presuppose for Giotto in the second decade of the Trecento (*cf.* for instance the Gothic elements in the subsequent development of this style in the scenes from the Childhood of Jesus in the Lower Church at Assisi).

25 (p. 234) *Cf.* A. Péter *op. cit.* (*cf.* note 23); the chronological inferences that Péter draws from this undisputed connection, which incidentally has long been noted, are by no means conclusive. Even if the frescoes of the Peruzzi Chapel were done shortly before 1328, as we believe (see p. 186), Ambrogio could have seen them. He could have made repeated journeys from Siena to Florence and back between 1328 and 1332.

26 (p. 234) *Cf.* p. 228 and notes 15 and 17.

27 (p. 234) G. Rowley *op. cit.* (*cf.* note 20) pp. 32 *ff*., 57 *ff*., *pls 21–3*, 61–72 (including many details). Rowley dates the *Maestà,* in our opinion a little too early, 'c. 1330'. For a chronology of Ambrogio see Rowley p. 137 *ff*.

28 (p. 235) See also the numerous excellent collotypes in Rowley *op. cit., pls 153–235.* For the restoration of the frescoes in 1950–51, *cf.* C. Brandi, 'Chiarimenti sul *Buon Governo* di Ambrogio Lorenzetti', in *Bollettino d'Arte* XL, 1955, p. 119 *ff*. According to Brandi the section to the right of the figure of *Buon Governo* and the left part of the view of the city of Siena were restored in the later Treceno.

29 (p. 235) For an iconographical interpretation *cf.* G. Rowley *op. cit.,* p. 99 *ff*. and N. Rubinstein, 'Political Ideas in Sienese Art: the Frescoes by Ambrogio Lorenzetti and Taddeo di Bartolo in the Palazzo Pubblico', in *Journal of the Warburg and Courtauld Institutes* XXI, 1958, p. 179 *ff*. According to Rubinstein the figure of *Buon Governo* is also a personification of the *bonum commune* in the Thomistic-Aristotelian sense, *i.e.* public welfare as the guiding principle of the bourgeois republican form of government. Its counterpart on the left wall is *Tyrannia, i.e.* the tyranny of the autocratic rulers that the Italian city-states feared.

30 (p. 235) No. 77, and the *Entombment* No. 77 a, probably the predella belonging to it; from S. Petronilla in Siena. Brandi (catalogue 1933) p. 130 *ff*., dates the altarpiece, in our opinion too early, around 1331/32. According to Toesca (*Trecento,* p. 578) it belongs to the master's late period. Rowley *op. cit., pls 35–37, 39,* attributes it to the 'Petronilla Master'.

31 (p. 236) The *Presentation in the Temple*: Uffizi, Florence; probably painted for Siena Cathedral, *cf.* Sinibaldi (*cf.* note 1) p. 189/90. *Annunciation*: Siena Pinacoteca; originally in the Sala del Consistoro in the Palazzo Pubblico. Brandi (catalogue 1933) p. 135 *ff*.

32 (p. 236) The perspective would be empirical even if Ambrogio had constructed it, for practical reasons, on a uniform converging point; this could not be regarded as a scientifically determined vanishing point, in the later sense. We can take it for granted that Ambrogio had not developed for himself the scientific basis of the perspective system of the Renaissance.

33 (p. 237) R. Nicoli, 'Scoperta di un capolavoro', in E. Carli, *I capolavori dell'arte senese,* Siena 1946 (not in the second edition of this work, Florence 1947). Toesca, *Trecento,* p. 590 and *pl.* XVI. S. M. Setti ('Il "Maestro di S. Agostino" e Ambrogio Lorenzetti', in *Commentari* I, 1950, p. 207) rejects the attribution to Ambrogio, and so does Rowley *op. cit.* (*cf.* note 20) p. 64 *ff*.; his dating of the frescoes in the late Trecento is, in our opinion, not convincing.

34 (p. 237) F. Mason Perkins, in *Rassegna d'arte* IV, 1904, p. 186 *ff*., and in *La Diana* IV, 1929, p. 261 *ff*. G. Rowley, in *Art Studies* VII, 1929, p. 107 *ff*. G. Mazzoni, 'L'Eva di Monte Siepi', in *Bollettino d'Arte* XXX, 1936, p. 149 (an interpretation of the inscription). Sinibaldi (*cf.* note 1) p. 193 *ff*. with further bibliographical references. Rowley (1958) p. 62 *ff*. disputes any personal participation by Ambrogio; good illustrations *op. cit.* vol. II, *pls 72–81*.

35 (p. 287) Rowley (1958) p. 63, *pls 78, 79,* believed that the original representation was not the Annunciation, but rather an Apparition of St Michael. This interpretation has been nullified by the discovery of the sinopia. *Cf.* the exhibition catalogue *Omaggio a Giotto,* Florence 1967, No. 10a, b; *pls* XVI, XVII.

36 (p. 239) M. Meiss, in *Rivista d'Arte* XVIII, 1936, p. 113 *ff.*

37 (p. 239) For Lippo Vanni see B. Berenson, *Studies in Mediaeval Painting,* New Haven 1930, p. 39 *ff.*; E. Borsook, 'The Frescoes at San Leonardo al Lago', in *The Burlington Magazine* 98, 1956, p. 351 *ff.* For Niccolò di

Ser Sozzo Tegliacci and Luca di Tommè, see C. Brandi, 'Niccolò di Ser Sozzo Tegliacci', in *L'Arte* 35, 1932, p. 223 *ff.*; M. Meiss, *Painting in Florence and Siena after the Black Death,* Princeton 1951, pp. 169, 170; F. Zeri, 'Sul problema di Niccolò Tegliacci e Luca di Tomè', in *Paragone* IX, 1958, No. 105, p. 3 *ff.*; M. Bucci, 'Proposte per Niccolò di Ser Sozzo Tegliacci', in *Paragone* XVI, 1965, No. 181, p. 51 *ff.*

38 (p. 239) C. Wolters, 'Ein Selbstbildnis des Taddeo di Bartolo', in *Mitt. d. Kunsthistor. Inst. in Florenz* VII, 1953, p. 70 *ff.*

11 Orcagna and his circle

1 (p. 240) Franco Sacchetti, *Trecento novelle,* No. 136; printed by J. v. Schlosser in *Quellenbuch zur Kunstgesch. d. Abendländ. Mittelalters,* Vienna 1896, p. 349 *ff.*; *cf.* M. Meiss, *Painting in Florence and Siena after the Black Death,* Princeton 1951, p. 3 *ff.*

2 (p. 240) K. Steinweg, *Andrea Orcagna,* Strasbourg 1929. H. D. Gronau, *Andrea Orcagna und Nardo di Cione,* Berlin 1937. Very good stylistic analysis of the Strozzi Altar by R. Salvini, in *L'Arte* VIII, 1937, p. 16 *ff.* M. Meiss (*cf.* note 1) pp. 9 *ff.,* 172 *ff.* Offner, *Corpus,* sec. IV, vol I (1962). Orcagna was admitted between 1343 and 1346 to the doctors' and apothecaries' guild, which in Florence was also the painters' guild; he is entered in the register as '*Andreas Cionis, uocatus Orchagna*'. *Cf.* Offner *op. cit.* p. 7.

3 (p. 241) Like Orcagna, Nardo di Cione was admitted to the doctors' and apothecaries' guild between 1343 and 1346; he died in 1365 or shortly after. The Strozzi Chapel frescoes, for which no date has been recorded, have recently been restored with good results. Offner, *Corpus,* sec. IV, vol. II (1960).

4 (p. 242) Gronau *op. cit.* (*cf.* note 2) p. 43.

5 (p. 243) Toesca, *Giotto,* (Turin 1941) p. 26.

6 (p. 244) Gronau *op. cit.* (*cf.* note 2) *pls 45–54;* Meiss *op. cit.* (*cf.* note 1) p. 14 *ff., pls 11, 51. The Madonna with Four Saints,* now in the possession of the New-York Historical Society, is especially characteristic of Nardo's principles of composition (Offner, *Corpus,* sec. IV, vol. II, *pls* XVI–XVIc).

7 (p. 244) Offner, *Corpus,* IV, vol. I, p. 8.

8 (p. 244) L. Becherucci, 'Ritrovamenti e restauri orcagneschi I', in *Bollettino d'Arte* 33, 1948, p. 24 *ff.* Offner (*Corpus,* IV, vol. I, p. XI, and p. 25, N. 5)

attributes the medallions to 'followers of Maso di Banco'.

9 (p. 244) L. Becherucci, in *Bollettino d'Arte* 33, 1948, p. 143 *ff.* Offner, *Corpus,* IV, vol. I, p. 65 *ff., pls* V to V 28.

10 (p. 245) From the first half of the Trecento, Longinus and the centurion, as converted heathens and witnesses to Christ's sacrifice, came to be treated as the equal of saints, and so was the Good Thief. The latter is already shown in the Magdalen Chapel in S. Francesco at Assisi as an isolated figure with a halo and the inscription 'S(ANCTVS) LATRO'. His counterpart is Longinus, also with halo and holding a lance (Kleinschmidt *pl. 152*); all the other figures are saints and apostles. In the crucifix of the Master of the Fogg Pietà (Master of Figline) in S. Croce in Florence (Brunetti/Sinibaldi No. 180) are half-length figures of Longinus, the centurion, and the Good Thief, together with Franciscans and saints on either side of the crucified Christ. The special veneration for the converted heathens could, therefore, have had its origin in the Franciscan doctrine.

11 (p. 245) Offner, *op. cit.* (*cf.* note 2), attributes the fresco to two of Orcagna's pupils: the 'Master of the Pentecost', so-called after the triptych showing the Pentecost scene, in the Florence Accademia (*op. cit., pl.* VI *ff.*) and the 'Master of the Santo Spirito Refectory'. Offner dates the work 'after 1370', *i.e.* after Orcagna's death.

12 (p. 245) Vasari I, p. 600.

13 (p. 245) See p. 187. Paatz, *Kirchen von Florenz* I, p. 593 *ff.*

14 (p. 245) Offner, *Corpus,* IV, vol. I, p. 43 *ff., pl.* III 1–25; reconstruction *pl.* III.

15 (p. 246) Offner (*op. cit.* pp. IX, 43) dates the frescoes in Santa Croce after 1361 (the end of Orcagna's activity in Orvieto), and probably only shortly before 1368.

16 (p. 246) The fact that the left part of Orcagna's triptych is obviously a simplified version of the pictorial scheme in the Campo Santo suggests that the latter was the earlier work. Orcagna omitted the scene of the *Meeting of the Quick and the Dead,* and changed the shape of the composition of the *Triumph of Death* from a horizontal to a vertical oblong. This seems to have involved some constriction, for in the process the group of beggars, which had already been anticipated in a group of pilgrims in Francesco Traini's altarpiece of 1345, was divided down the middle. The reverse idea, that the wide expansive representation in Pisa, with its impressive group of beggars, was derived from Orcagna's fresco, carries no conviction.

12 The Triumph of Death

1 (p. 247) H. D. Gronau, *Andrea Orcagna,* Berlin 1937, *pl. 22.* Painted around the end of the 14th C.

2 (p. 247) Gronau *op. cit. pl. 21.* Probably datable soon after the middle of the Trecento. The fresco in the Dominican church in Bozen, which is similar in theme, is approximately contemporaneous; *cf.* Coletti III, *pls 70b, 71b;* text pp. XXXVIII *ff.,* and note 84. *Cf.* Offner, *Corpus,* sec. IV, vol. I, pp. 46, 47 (with other examples, some even earlier, of Death riding a horse or an ox).

3 (p. 247) The inspiration for this possibly came from Siena, *cf.* the *Allegory of the Redemption,* by Pietro Lorenzetti (?) in the Siena Pinacoteca, No. 92 (Catalogue Brandi 1933, p. *150ff.*).

4 (p. 248) The skull, which originally meant *Golgotha* (the place of skulls) was taken to be the skull of Adam who, according to the legend, was buried beneath the cross. In the central tympanum of the west façade of Strasbourg Cathedral there is a whole skeleton at the foot of the cross. *Mors* as the vanquished demon is on the left of the crucified Christ in the *Uta-Evangelistar* in Regensburg (1002–25; Goldschmidt, *Deutsche Buchmalerei* II, *pl. 77*).

5 (p. 248) *Cf.* the tomb of Francis of La Sarraz who died 1362 in La Sarraz (Switzerland, Canton Waadt), see H. Reiners, *Burgundisch-alemannische Plastik,* Strasbourg 1943, *pl. 370* and p. 319, note 99 (with bibliography).

6 (p. 248) L. Guerry, *Le thème du 'Triomphe de la Mort' dans la peinture italienne,* Paris 1950, p. *58ff.*

7 (p. 305) L. Guerry (*cf.* note 6) p. *38ff.* For the motif in the north, see E. Male, *L'art religieux de la fin du moyen âge en France,* Paris 1908, p. *388ff.* Offner, *Corpus,* sec. III, vol. V (1947), p. *261ff.* W. Rotzler, *Die drei Lebenden und die drei Toten,* Winterthur 1961.

8 (p. 305) E. Dobbert, in *Repertorium f. Kunstwiss.* IV, 1881, p. *1ff.*

9 (p. 305) From Seneca's *Trojan Women* (Dobbert, *cf.* note 8, p. 29).

10 (p. 305) R. Papini, *Pisa (Catalogo delle cose d'arte e di antichità d'Italia,* Serie I, vol. II, 2, Rome, n. d.). R. Oertel, 'Francesco Traini, Der Triumph des Todes im Campo Santo zu Pisa', in *Der Kunstbrief,* Berlin 1948. E. Carli, *Pittura pisana del Trecento* I, Milan 1958. Further references *cf.* notes 11, 14.

11 (p. 306) P. Sanpaolesi, 'Le sinopie del Camposanto di Pisa', in *Bollettino d'Arte* 33, 1948, p. *34ff. Camposanto monumentale di Pisa, affreschi e sinopie* (Exhibition catalogue, Pisa 1960); large edition with same title (published by Opera della Primaziale Pisana, text by P. Sanpaolesi, M. Bucci and L. Bertolini, Pisa 1960). U. Procacci, *Sinopie e affreschi,* Florence 1960, pp. *50ff., 236ff.;* pls *4–9, 134–7.*

12 (p. 306) To escape the temptation the hermit puts his hands in the fire. The temptress is St Alexandra, who is then shown again after her conversion kneeling beside a sarcophagus. *Cf.* E. Carli (*cf.* note 10) *pl. 70.* G. Kaftal, *Iconography of the Saints in Tuscan Painting,* Florence 1952, No. 10.

13 (p. 307) The figure was damaged long ago by Pisan urchins throwing stones, and was repeatedlay overpainted; it inspired certain features in the last scenes of Goethe's *Faust;* the same applies to the fresco of the *Anchorites of Thebaid. Cf.* G. Dehio, in *Goethe-Jahrbuch* (published by Ludwig Geiger) vol. VII, Frankfurt 1886, p. 251.

14 (p. 308) Francesco Traini is recorded in Pisa as a painter as early as 1321. In addition to the St Dominic retable two panel paintings have survived that can be attributed to him: the St Anna in Princeton, and a half-length figure of the Madonna from San Giusto in Cannicci in Pisa. Pisan manuscript illumination, as M. Meiss has pointed out, was influenced by

Traini's style from about 1330. A number of votive frescoes in the baptistry in Parma reflect the style of the Pisan frescoes. The largest of these, a St George and the Dragon, could have been done by Traini himself; but it is more likely that such a minor commission was executed by an assistant, who had already worked with Traini in Pisa. Even without this clue it may be assumed that Traini was closely connected with artistic circles in Emilia, and especially in Bologna. The frescoes in the Campo Santo contain unmistakably Bolognese stylistic elements. These associations thus go back at least as far as the 1340s; possibly Traini himself was active for a while in Bologna, and perhaps he took assistants from there for the large commission in the Campo Santo. Despite this undeniable connection there is, in our opinion, no reason to attribute the Pisan frescoes as a whole to an otherwise unknown Bolognese master. Their stylistic conformity with Traini's signed St Dominic retable of 1345 remains conclusive. This applies not only to the morphological details and figurative types, but also to the construction of the compositions in graduated layers one above the other, the ornamental motifs, and the architectural elements in the pictures, which recur in the fresco of the *Anchorites of the Thebaid*. In general, Tuscan features are predominant in Traini's style, and are especially apparent in the monumental drawings. The question whether these drawings are all by Traini's own hand or were done partly by assistants must remain open for the time being. Unfortunately there is still no comprehensive study and critical analysis of the *sinopie* found in Pisa.

For the attribution of the frescoes to Traini, *cf.* M. Meiss, 'The Problem of Francesco Traini', in *The Art Bulletin* XV, 1933, p. 97*ff.*; Meiss, *Painting after the Black Death,* p. 171; Meiss, 'A *Madonna* by Francesco Traini', in *Gazette des Beaux-Arts* 56/102, 1960, p. 49*ff.*; Meiss, 'An Illuminated *Inferno* and Trecento Painting in Pisa', in *The Art Bulletin* XLVII, 1965, p. 21*ff.* Also Offner, *Corpus,* sec. IV, vol. I (1962), p. VIII

(with dating soon after 1345) and p. 46 above ('mid-century'). R. Longhi (*Paragone* I, 1950, No. 5, pp. 12, 13) considers the Pisan frescoes to be the work of a Bolognese painter (*c.* 1360), but not Vitale da Bologna, as Longhi had thought for a while. Likewise M. Bucci, in *Camposanto monumentale di Pisa* (*cf.* note 11) p. 46*ff.* ('Maestro del Trionfo della Morte'), with a survey of all research to date. E. Carli, *Pittura pisana* (*cf.* note 10) attributes the *Triumph of Death,* and the *Last Judgment* with the Inferno, to an anonymous Emilian master ('Maestro padano'), and for the *Anchorites of the Thebaid* he assumes a collaboration between this master and Traini.

The documents concerning Traini were published by P. Bacci, in *La Diana* V, 1930, p. 161*ff.*; *cf.* also M. Meiss, in *The Art Bulletin* VX, 1933, pp. 172, 173; G. Paccagnini, 'Il Problema documentario di Francesco Traini', in *Critica d'Arte* XXIX, 1949, p. 19*ff.* (with some diverging conclusions). For further attributions of panel-paintings to Traini and to masters of his circle, see M. Bucci, in *Paragone* XIII, 1962 (No. 147), p. 40*ff.*, and R. Longhi, *op. cit.* p. 43*ff.*

An interesting contribution to the iconography of the *Inferno,* which also has some relevance to the question of dating, is in J. Polzer, 'Aristotle, Mohammed and Nicholas V in Hell', in *The Art Bulletin* 46, 1964, p. 457*ff.* According to this article the anti-Pope Nicholas V (1328–30), appointed by Ludwig of Bavaria, is portrayed among the Damned. The date 1330 would then be the *terminus post quem* for the fresco. During the 1330s Pisa followed a conciliatory policy towards the Curia and the Guelphs of Florence; since such a polemic representation presupposes that the events of 1330 were still fresh in men's minds, Polzer thinks it likely that the frescoes were painted in the second quarter of the Trecento, possibly as early as the 1330s.

15 (p. 308) For the dating see p. 246.

16 (p. 308) S. Morpuro, 'Le epigrafi volgari in rima del *Trionfo della Morte* etc.', in *L'Arte* II, 1899, p. 51*ff.*

13 The end of the Trecento in Florence

1 (p. 311) H. Thode, *Franz von Assisi*, 4th edition, Vienna, 1934, p. 530*ff*. Offner, *Corpus*, sec. III, vol. VI (1956), pp. 122–35.

2 (p. 311) Van Marle III, *pl. 143*. Brunetti/Sinibaldi No. 124. Offner, *Corpus*, sec. III, vol. II/1 (1930), *pl.* II*ff*. L. Marcucci, *Gallerie Nazionali di Firenze, I dipinti toscani del secolo XIV* (1965), No. 4.

3 (p. 311) Van Marle III, *pl. 197*; Borsook *pl. 13*. There is a replica in San Francesco in Pistoia.

4 (p. 311) The room adjoining the 'Chiostro Verde' in S. Maria Novella was converted in 1566/67 by Eleonore of Toledo into the chapel of St James of Compostella for the Spanish colony in Florence. For the frescoes *cf.* J. v. Schlosser, 'Giustos Fresken in Padua und die Vorläufer der Stanza della Segnatura', in *Jahrb. d. Kunsthistor. Sammlungen d. Allerhöchsten Kaiserhauses* XVII, Vienna 1896, p. 13*ff*.; P. I. Taurisano O. P., in *Il Rosario* 36, 1916 (ser. III, vol. III) p. 217*ff*.; M. Meiss, *Painting in Florence and Siena after the Black Death* (1951), p. 94*ff*. Borsook *pls 35–38*.

5 (p. 312) Surrounded by an aureole, Christ hovers above an open sarcophagus on which sit two angels. The light radiating from Christ illuminates the landscape, which extends relatively far in depth. In Padua, Giotto had shown only the empty sarcophagus with the angels, while the resurrected Christ appeared in the same scene facing Mary Magdalen and standing on the ground. Andrea da Firenze also depicted this scene, the *Noli me Tangere,* in the same picture on the right, and the three women are approaching Christ's tomb on the left.

6 (p. 313) Milanesi in *Vasari* I, p. 572. Paatz, *Kirchen von Florenz* I, pp. 564, 655. U. Procacci ('Il primo ricordo di Giovanni da Milano', in *Arte Antica e Moderna,* Nos 13–16, 1961, p. 49*ff*.) ascertained that the painter Giovanni da Milano, who was born in Caversago near Como, was mentioned as early as 1346 as one of the non-native artists living in Florence. Further see A. Marabottini, *Giovanni da Milano,* Florence 1950; M. Boskovits, *Giovanni da Milano,* Florence 1966; Toesca, *Trecento,* p. 762*ff*.; Coletti III, p. LXV, *pls 126–32*; M. Meiss (*cf.* note 4) *pls 27, 36, 37*. For the panel-paintings of the master, *cf.* the exhibition catalogue *Arte Lombarda dai Visconti agli Sforza,* Milan 1958, p. 19*ff*., *pl.* XXII*ff*., and colour plate (frontispiece); L. Marcucci, 'Del Polittico di Ognissanti di Giovanni da Milano', in *Antichità Viva* I,

1962, No. 4, p. 11*ff*.; also *I dipinti toscani del sec. XIV* (*cf.* note 2) Nos 48, 49.

7 (p. 313) According to U. Procacci (*cf.* note 6), during the restoration of 1960 it was discovered that the coat-of-arms of the Rinuccini family was done in tempera, *i.e. a secco,* with the coat-of-arms of the Guidalotti family below in *fresco*. Procacci concludes from this that a change in patronage must have occurred before 1371. The inscription of the Rinuccini family on the gate of the chapel is of that year. This was probably also the reason for the interruption of the work by Giovanni da Milano.
For the Master of the Rinuccini Chapel *cf.* R. Offner, *Studies in Florentine Painting,* New York 1927, pp. 109–126. The fresco of the Rinuccini Master, the *Presentation in the Temple,* is a free copy of Taddeo Gaddi's composition in the Baroncelli Chapel. The drawing in the Louvre in Paris, which is intermediate between these two versions, was possibly done by the Rinuccini Master, *cf.* R. Oertel, in *Mitt. d. Kunsthist. Inst. in Florenz* V, 1940, p. 236*ff*. (with illustrations). M. Meiss (in Tintori/Meiss, *The Painting of the Life of St Francis in Assisi,* New York 1962, pp 21, 22), on the other hand, has given renewed support for the attribution of the Louvre drawing to Taddeo Gaddi. In spite of the arguments advanced by Meiss, the author is inclined to persist in the view that we are dealing with an 'exemplum', *i.e.* a drawing from the original, much retouched in later times.

8 (p. 314) Offner, *Corpus,* sec. IV, vol. III (1965).

9 (p. 314) R. Offner, 'A Ray of Light on Giovanni del Biondo and Niccolò di Tommaso', in *Mitt. d. Kunsthist. Inst. in Florenz* VII, 1956, p. 173*ff*. (with index of works).

10 (p. 314) Ser Lapo Mazzei, *Lettere di un notaro a un mercante del sec. XIV,* edited by C. Guasti, II, Florence 1880, p. 96.

11 (p. 314) Mazzei, *Lettere* (*cf.* note 10), p. 401*ff*. Also R. Oertel, in *Mitt. d. Kunsthistor. Inst. in Florenz* V, 1940, pp. 241, 242.

12 (p. 314) Painted for Orsanmichele, it was in the neighbouring church of San Carlo dei Lombardi from 1526; in 1781, in the Uffizi; in 1841, in the Galleria dell'Accademia; since 1931 it is again the high altarpiece of San Carlo. L. Marcucci, *I dipinti toscani* (*cf.* note 2), No. 66. For Niccolò di Pietro

Gerini, *cf.* R. Offner, *Studies in Florentine Painting*, New York 1927, p. 83*ff.*

13 (p. 315) Paatz, *Kirchen von Florenz* I, pp. 563, 654, 655; Toesca, *Trecento, pl. 558*.

14 (p. 315) Cennino Cennini, *Il libro dell'arte,* chapter I. R. Salvini, *L'arte di Agnolo Gaddi*, Florence 1936.

15 (p. 315) H. D. Gronau, 'The Earliest Works of Lorenzo Monaco', in *The Burlington Magazine* 92, 1950, pp. 183*ff.*, 217*ff.*; also recently L. Bellosi (see note 16).

16 (p. 316) For Niccolò di Tommaso, *cf.* R. Offner, *Studies* (*cf.* note 12), p. 109*ff.*; Offner, in *Mitt. des Kunsthist. Inst. in Florenz* VII, 1956, p. 173*ff.* (with index of works). For Antonio Veneziano, *cf.* R. Offner, *Studies* (*cf.* note 12) p. 67*ff.*; M. Salmi, in *Bollettino d'Arte* VIII, 1928/29, p. 433*ff.*; K. Steinweg, in *Berliner Museen*, N.S. XV, 1965, p. 4*ff.* For Spinello Aretino, *cf.* G. Gombosi, *Spinello Aretino*, Budapest 1926; L. Bellosi, 'Da Spinello Aretino a Lorenzo Monaco', in *Paragone* XVI, 1965, No. 187, p. 18*ff.*; further contributions in the same by A. Gonzalez-Palacios (p. 44*ff.*) and R. Longhi (p. 52*ff.*).

17 (p. 316) U. Procacci, 'Gherardo Starnina', in *Rivista d'Arte* XV, 1933, p. 151*ff.*

18 (p. 316) Cristoforo Landino (1481) says of Masaccio 'Puro sanza ornato'.

14 Trecento painting outside Tuscany

1 (p. 318) See pp. 60, 100*ff.*, 204.

2 (p. 318) Painted *c.* 1370; construction begun 1352 (?), *cf.* O. Morisani, *Pittura del Trecento in Napoli*, Naples 1947, p. 76*ff.*; Toesca, *Trecento,* p. 690.

3 (p. 318) Van Marle V, *pl. 203*.

4 (p. 318) In 1346 he was admitted to the Florentine guild of St Luke; died 1373/74. Van Marle V, p. 130*ff.*; Toesca, *Trecento,* p. 677; A. Marabottini Marabotti, in *Rivista d'Arte* 27, 1951/52, p. 23*ff.*

5 (p. 319) See p. 352, note 49.

6 (p. 319) See Vasari I, p. 392.

7 (p. 319) See p. 82.

8 (p. 319) C. Gnudi, *Giotto* (Milan 1958), p. 193, dates the crucifix between 1312/13 and 1316/17, and thinks it is likely that it was done in Giotto's workshop in Padua, but he does not rule out the possibility that it was done in Rimini itself.

9 (p. 319) D. Gioseffi, 'Lo svolgimento del linguaggio giottesco da Assisi a Padova: il soggiorno riminese e la componente ravennate', in *Arte Veneta* XV, 1961, p. 11*ff.*; Gioseffi, *Giotto architetto*, Milan 1963, pp. 34, 35, 46*ff.*

10 (p. 319) S. Pichon, 'Gli affreschi di Giotto al Santo di Padova', in *Bollettino d'Arte* XVIII, 1924/25, p. 26*ff.*; see also the photographs Anderson Nos 27143–8.

11 (p. 319) A critical synopsis of the literature in M. Bonicatti, *Trecentisti riminesi*, Rome 1963. For other important material on Riminese painting, see *Mostra della pittura riminese del Trecento, Catalogo a cura di C. Brandi*, Rimini 1935 (with illustrations of the frescoes we have mentioned). Toesca, *Trecento,* p. 718*ff.* Coletti III, p. VI*ff.* S. Bottari, 'I grandi cicli di affreschi riminesi', in *Arte Antica e Moderna* I, 1958, p. 130*ff.* C. Volpe, 'Sul trittico riminese del Museo Correr', in *Paragone* XVI, 1965, No. 181, p. 3*ff.* The following work was issued after this book went to press: C. Volpe, *La pittura riminese del Trecento*, Milan 1965.

12 (p. 319) Bonicatti *op. cit.* (*cf.* note 11) *pl. 28;* good details by Gioseffi, *Arte Veneta* XV, 1961, p. 11*ff.*

13 (p. 320) M. Meiss, *Giotto and Assisi*, New York 1960, p. 3, *pls 6, 7*.

14 (p. 320) Further illustrations in the catalogue of Brandi 1935 (*cf.* note 11) *pls 70–76*. Bonicatti *op. cit. pls 19–21*. Gioseffi, *Arte Veneta* XV, 1961, p. 11*ff.*

15 (p. 321) Bonicatti *op. cit.*, *pl. 69*.

16 (p. 321) Coletti III, *pls 18–20*; M. Salmi, *L'abbazia di Pomposa*, Rome 1936, p. 156*ff.*, *pls XXIV–XXIX*.

17 (p. 321) Salmi (*cf.* previous note) p. 163.

18 (p. 321) Another fresco fragment signed by Pietro and dated 1333 has been preserved in Montottone. Catalogue Brandi 1935, Nos 15, 16 and *pls 92–96*. The retable (unfortunately lost) of the high altar of the Eremitani church in Padua, signed by Pietruccio and Giuliano da Rimini, was done in 1324. 'Pietruccio' could possibly be Pietro da Rimini. *Cf.* F. Flores d'Arcais, in *Arte Antica e Moderna* 17, 1962, p. 99*ff.*; following a reference by F. Zeri, the author attributes to Pietro a sequence of eighteen fresco fragments containing scenes with Christ and the Virgin that were originally in the Eremitani, and are now in the Museo Civico in Padua.

19 (p. 322) Bonicatti *op. cit.* (*cf.* note 11), p. 36, note 60. According to A. Martini ('Appunti sulla Ravenna

riminese', in *Arte Antica e Moderna* 5–8, 1959, p. 310*ff.*) the inscription that has been found, with the date 1314, refers to the construction of the Gothic choir. Martini dates the frescoes in the first half of the 1350s.

20 (p. 322) *Cf.* Toesca (*Trecento*, p. 727) and Longhi (in *Proporzioni* II, 1948, p. 53). C. Brandi who in 1935 still listed the Mercatello Crucifix as a work of Baronzio (Rimini catalogue, *cf.* note 11, No. 33), distinguished later between 'Giovanni da Rimini' (the master of the crucifix) and Giovanni Baronzio, to whom he attributes the polyptych in Mercatello in addition to his major work, the retable in Urbino (in *La Critica d'Arte* II, 1937, p. 193).

21 (p. 322) *Cf.* the crucifix by Giunta Pisano (*cf.* p. 344, note 15); also E. B. Garrison, 'A Berlinghieresque Fresco in S. Stefano, Bologna', in *The Art Bulletin* 28, 1946, p. 211*ff.* A Madonna from Cimabue's workshop, in S. Maria dei Servi, Bologna (Brunetti/Sinibaldi No. 84).

22 (p. 323) See p. 93*ff.*; Brunetti/Sinibaldi No. 108.

23 (p. 323) One of them was Francesco da Rimini, who around 1330–40 painted frescoes (at one time bearing his signature) from the lives of Christ and St Francis in the refectory of S. Francesco in Bologna, now in the Pinacoteca, Bologna. Brandi, catalogue 1935 (*cf.* note 11), Nos 27–9; for the dating see also M. Salmi, in *Bollettino d'Arte* XXVI, 1932, p. 249*ff.* ('*c.* 1340').

24 (p. 323) C. Gnudi, *Vitale da Bologna*, Milan 1962 (with numerous illustrations, many of them in colour). Toesca, *Trecento*, p. 734*ff.* For Vitale and the other Trecento painters in Bologna, *cf.* also R. Longhi, 'La Mostra del Trecento Bolognese', in *Paragone* I, 1950, (No. 5), p. 5*ff.*; and the exhibition catalogue *Mostra della Pittura Bolognese del '300*, Bologna 1950.

25 (p. 323) Gnudi *op. cit.* (*cf.* note 24) pp. 28*ff.*, 64*ff.*, *pl.* XXIX*ff.* In its present state the panel is fragmentary; originally there were also two small upright figures of female saints on each side. Two of these are now in the Lanckoronski Collection in Vienna. Whether the two panels depicting full-length figures of saints, now in the Bolognese municipal collections, are part of the same work is uncertain. If they are, they must have been the two left side-panels of a polyptych, the centre panel of which was the Madonna. The Madonna has recently been cleaned of much overpainting, and in the process was discovered that the golden griffins on her cloak are not original, but were probably added during the Renaissance (Gnudi p. 65).

26 (p. 324) All the frescoes have been lifted off the walls, some in 1949 and some in 1958 (Gnudi, *op. cit.* p. 65) and can now be seen in an impressive arrangement, which is very similar to the original, in the Bologna Pinacoteca, together with the surviving monumental drawings that belong to them. Examples of the *sinopie* are in Gnudi *op. cit. pl. 33* and in U. Procacci, *Sinopie e affreschi* Florence 1960, pls *10, 12* (text p. 51).

27 (p. 324) Gnudi *op. cit. pl.* LXXXIX*ff.* The date 1351 (restored) is in the main apse, in the decoration of which Vitale also participated.

28 (p. 324) Gnudi *op. cit.* pp. 48*ff.*, p. 68, *pl.* LXIX*ff.*; according to Gnudi, Vitale could have begun the frescoes at the earliest in 1349.

29 (p. 324) R. Longhi, in *Paragone* I, 1950 (No. 5), p. 13*ff.*, pls *10, 11*. As the name Jacopo recurs frequently in Bolognese painting, the identity of 'Jacopo di Francesco' is not completely authenticated.

30 (p. 324) M. Salmi, *L'abbazia di Pomposa*, Rome 1936, p. 175*ff.*, pls XXXII–LXIII. Gnudi *op. cit.* (*cf.* note 27).

31 (p. 325) Remnants of figurative paintings of the 12th (?) C. have been preserved in the south side-aisle; Salmi (*cf.* note 30) p. 136 and *pl.* XV. The motif of the Enthroned Christ in the mandorla in the main apse is reminiscent of much Romanesque apse decoration north of the Alps (Knechtsteden, Berzé-la-Ville).

32 (p. 325) R. Longhi, in *Paragone* I, 1950 (No. 5), p. 15*ff.*

33 (p. 325) Barnaba da Modena can be traced from 1361 until 1383; he was mainly active in Liguria and Piedmont. In 1362 he had already acquired citizenship in Genoa; in 1380 he was summoned from there to Pisa, where he painted a Madonna with eight angels for the Compagnia dei Mercanti. Toesca, *Trecento*, p. 747*ff.* Coletti III, p. XXXIV*ff.* P. Rotondi, 'Il polittico di Barnaba da Modena a Lavagnola', in *Quaderni della Soprintendenza alle Gallerie ed Opere d'Arte della Liguria*, No. 3, Genoa 1955. E. Carli, *Pittura pisana del Trecento* II, Milan 1961, pp. 21, 22.

34 (p. 325) *Cf.* the monograph by L. Coletti, *Tomaso da Modena*, Venice 1963 (with bibliography). J. v. Schlosser, 'Tomaso da Modena und die ältere Malerei in Treviso', in *Jahrb. d. Kunsthist. Sammlungen des Allerh. Kaiserhauses* XIX, Vienna 1898, p. 240*ff.*

35 (p. 326) Coletti *op. cit.* (*cf.* note 34) pp. 54, 55, does not think Tomaso made a journey to Bohemia; nor does Toesca, *Trecento*, p. 753/54. The panel with the *Ecce Homo* bears Tomaso's signature, but is on the whole badly damaged. The triptych (also signed), the gold of which has been restored, was originally intended for the Chapel of the Relics of St Palmatius in Budnian

369

(near Karlstein); Coletti, *op. cit.* pp. 51, 52, *pls 101 to 103*; dateable between 1356 and 1365.

36 (p. 326) The light ochre tone which now predominates was formerly balanced by the light blue, now mostly faded, and other *a secco* colours. The flesh tone is a warm pink with brownish-black contours. The frescoes, painted *c.* 1360–65, were originally in a chapel in Santa Margherita.

37 (p. 326) Coletti *op. cit.*, *pls 67, 94*, colour *pl. 9*.

38 (p. 327) O. Demus, *Die Mosaiken von San Marco in Venedig 1100–1300*, Baden near Vienna 1935, p. 67.

39 (p. 328) For the most recent information about Paolo Veneziano, see R. Pallucchini, *La pittura veneziana del Trecento*, Venice 1964, p. 17 *ff*. According to Pallucchini, Paolo's activity began as early as 1310 (relief-panel of St Donatus with a kneeling pair of donors, in Murano, *pls 16–18*); altar dossal in Dignano: *pls 27–34*.

40 (p. 328) In the *Nativity* from S. Maria a Mezzaratta (see p. 323); *cf.* R. Longhi (1945/46) and Pallucchini *op. cit.* p. 46. Paolo's large polyptych in S. Giacomo Maggiore in Bologna, with the central panel unfortunately missing (Pallucchini p. 41 *ff.*, *pls 121–127*, V) makes it appear likely that the master undertook a journey to Bologna in about 1350. As a source of inspiration for the Gothic stylistic elements and especially for the kneeling angels Guariento must also be considered (see below).

41 (p. 328) Pallucchini *op. cit.*, *pl. 117*.

42 (p. 328) For Lorenzo Veneziano: Pallucchini *op. cit.* (*cf.* note 39) p. 163 *ff*. The *Enthroned Christ* in the Correr Museum is probably the centre-piece of a polyptych that had four side-panels with full-length figures of saints, formerly in the Kaiser-Friedrich-Museum in Berlin (burned in 1945). The five-panelled predella with scenes from the life of St Peter is now in the Gemäldegalerie in Berlin-Dahlem (Pallucchini *pls 530–538*, XXII).

43 (p. 329) For most recent information about Guariento see Pallucchini (*cf.* note 39), p. 105 *ff.*; Francesca Flores d'Arcais, *Guariento*, Venice 1965; *cf.* also the recension by H.-W. Kruft, in *Kunstchronik* 19, 1966.

44 (p. 329) F. Flores d'Arcais *op. cit.* (*cf.* note 43), pp. 23 *ff.*, 65 *ff.*, *pls 41–68*, IV–VII. The chapel in the 'Reggia Carrarese', the palace of the Carrara family, is now the assembly hall of the Accademia di Scienze, Lettere e Arti. On one wall of the room the original fresco decoration, also painted by Guariento, has been preserved; these representations from the Old Testament were recently restored (F. Flores d'Arcais, pp. 69, 70,

pls 70–84, VIII–X). A possible date for them is the second half of the 1340s.

45 (p. 329) The bombing in 1944 that devastated the adjoining chapel with the Mantegna frescoes also destroyed the right wall of the choir chapel and the larger part of the apse vault. For the surviving frescoes *cf.* Pallucchini *op. cit.* p. 113 *ff.*; F. Flores d'Arcais *op. cit.* p. 28 *ff.*, p. 61 *ff* (with bibliography). They are scenes from the lives of SS. Philip, James and Augustine.

46 (p. 329) The fresco adorned the rear wall of the Sala del Maggior Consiglio in the Palazzo Ducale; it was badly damaged in the 1577 fire, and when the room was redecorated it was covered by Tintoretto's canvas of *Paradise*. The remnants that were removed from the wall in 1903 are on view in one of the adjoining rooms. Good illustrations in Pallucchini and F. Flores d'Arcais.

47 (p. 329) Pallucchini *op. cit.*, *pl. 326*; for the late dating, *cf.* R. Longhi, *Viatico per cinque secoli di pittura veneziana*, Florence 1946, pp. 46, 47.

48 (p. 329) S. Bettini, *Giusto de' Menabuoi e l'arte del Trecento*, Padua 1944; S. Bettini, *Le pitture di Giusto de' Menabuoi nel Battistero del Duomo di Padova*, Venice 1960 (with 48 colour plates). Toesca, *Trecento*, p. 794.

49 (p. 329) Bettini *op. cit.* (1960), ills in text 3–7.

50 (p. 330) Bettini *op. cit.* (1960), *pl. 23*.

51 (p. 330) H.-W. Kruft (*cf.* note 52) pp. 153, 154, points out that Giusto was the first to diverge from the traditional principle of representation, which treated the interior as an 'opened-up exterior'. In many cases, he no longer showed the front limit of the room, but instead allowed the perspective view of the interior to be overlapped by the borders of the picture. This produces the effect of a genuine interior, which we can visualize as a real room. *Cf.* for instance *Jesus among the Doctors,* and the *Wedding at Cana.* Bettini *op. cit.* (1960) *pls 30, 35*.

52 (p. 331) G. L. Mellini, *Altichiero e Jacopo Avanzi*, Milan 1965 (with comprehensive illustrative material). H.-W. Kruft, *Altichiero und Avanzo, Untersuchungen zur oberitalienischen Malerei des ausgehenden Trecento* (thesis, Bonn 1964), Bonn 1966. As regards Avanzo's share in the two fresco cycles in Padua, the two authors reach completely contrary conclusions. Mellini identifies Avanzo with the Bolognese painter of the Crucifixion panel in the Colonna Gallery in Rome, which is signed 'Jacobus de ava(n)ciis de bononia f.', and attributes to him most of the lunette frescoes in the Cappella di San Giacomo. Kruft thinks he recognizes Avanzo's style in several frescoes in the

lower zone of the Cappella di San Giorgio, which are notable for their advanced principles of composition, especially in the representation of architecture and space. The controversy is not yet resolved, and the fact that the name of Avanzo is not mentioned at all in the contenporary records of the Padua works, and that the secondary sources are contradictory,

makes it difficult to arrive at a satisfactory solution. Hence his identity and artistic origin remain obscure. *Cf.* also the discussion of Mellini's book by H.-W. Kruft, in *Kunstchronik,* 19, 1966.

53 (p. 332) For the documents *cf.* A. Sartori, 'Nota su Altichiero', in *Il Santo* III, 1963, p. 291*ff.* Kruft *op. cit.* (*cf.* note 52), p. 8*ff.*

Photographic sources

Colour plates
Hirmer, Munich: VII; P. Gerhard Ruf, Assisi: III, XI; Scala, Florence: I, IV, V, VIII, IX, X; Skira, Geneva: II, VI, XII

Black and white illustrations
Alinari, Florence: 3b, 17, 20a, 21a, 29, 35, 36, 37a, 49, 51, 62a, 66b, 74, 80, 82a, 82d, 85, 91b, 100a, 103, 107, 116, 117, 122, 126, 127, 128; Anderson, Rome: 5, 6a, 6b, 7, 8, 19b, 19c, 20b, 27, 28, 40, 54, 60, 66a, 67, 77, 90a, 94, 97, 98, 99, 101a, 114b, 115; Bencini e Sansoni, Florence: 14a, 14b, 15a, 15b, 47b, 52, 55, 57, 58, 59; Brogi, Florence: 9, 22, 23, 24a, 24b, 25, 30b, 34a, 39, 41, 43, 44, 45, 61, 63, 64, 65, 72, 81, 86, 87, 91a, 101b, 102b, 105a, 108, 113a, 113b; Casa Editrice Francescana, Assisi: 46, 47a; Cooper, London: 83; De Giovanni, Assisi: 48, 50, 82c, 88, 89, 90b

Deutsche Fotothek, Dresden: 84; Fotofast, Bologna: 118; Foto-Marburg: 123; Fototeca Unione, Rome: 10b; Gabinetto Fotografico Nazionale, Rome: 2, 3a, 10a, 11, 12a, 12b, 13, 16a, 16b, 18, 19a, 76, 114a; Dr F. Goldkuhle, Bonn: 1; Grassi, Siena: 95; Istituto Centrale del Restauro, Rome: 53; Istituto Italiano d'-Arti Grafiche, Bergamo: 4; Musée Royal, Antwerp: 82b; Museo Civico, Padua; 125: Museo Civico, Treviso: 124; Reali, Florence: 37b, 93; Sansoni, Rome: 21b; Schwarz, Berlin: 121; Soprintendenza alle Gallerie, Florence: 26, 30a, 31, 33, 34b, 42a, 42b, 62b, 68, 69a, 69b, 70, 71a, 71b, 73, 75a, 75b, 78, 92, 102a, 104, 105b, 106a, 106b, 109, 110, 111, 112; Soprintendenza alle Gallerie, Naples: 79; Soprintendenza Monumenti e Gallerie, Pisa: 100b; Staatliche Gemäldegalerie, Berlin-Dahlem: 91c; University Gallery, Princeton: 38; Villani, Bologna: 119, 120

Index